The New York Review Abroad

Fifty Years of International Reportage

The New York Review Abroad

Fifty Years of International Reportage

EDITED BY
Robert B. Silvers

PROLOGUES BY
Ian Buruma

NEW YORK REVIEW BOOKS

New York

THE NEW YORK REVIEW ABROAD
FIFTY YEARS OF INTERNATIONAL REPORTAGE
Copyright © 2013 by The New York Review of Books
Prologues © 2013 by Ian Buruma
All pieces © by individual authors:

"Left Out in Turkey" © 2005 by Christopher de Bellaigue. Reprinted with permission.
"A Farewell to Haiti" © 2012 by Mischa Berlinski. Reprinted with permission.
"Liverpool: Notes from Underground" © 1979 by Caroline Blackwood. Reprinted with permission.
"Tibet Disenchanted" © 2000 by Ian Buruma. Reprinted with permission.
"Delusions in Baghdad" © 2003 Mark Danner. Reprinted with permission.
"In El Salvador" © 1982 by Joan Didion. Reprinted with permission.
"Going Crazy in India" © 1981 by Rosemary Dinnage. Reprinted with permission.
"The Nowhere City" © 1993 by Amos Elon. Reprinted with permission.
"AIDS: The Lesson of Uganda" © 2001 by Helen Epstein. Reprinted with permission.
"An Exclusive Corner of Hebron" © 2012 by Jonathan Freedland. Reprinted with permission.
"The Revolution of the Magic Lantern" © 1990 by Timothy Garton Ash. Reprinted with permission.
"Letter from South Africa" © 1976 by Nadine Gordimer. Reprinted with permission.
"Love and Misery in Cuba" © 1998 by Alma Guillermoprieto. Reprinted with permission.
"Sad Brazil" © 1974 by Elizabeth Hardwick. Reprinted with permission.
"The Sakharovs in Gorky" © 1984 by Natalya Viktorovna Hesse and Vladimir Tolz. Reprinted with permission.
"With the Northern Alliance" © 2001 by Tim Judah. Reprinted with permission.
"Fire on the Road" © 1986 by Ryszard Kapuściński. Reprinted with permission.
"The Suicide Bombers" © 2003 by Avishai Margalit. Reprinted with permission.
"Report from Vietnam I. The Home Program" © 1967 by Mary McCarthy. Reprinted with permission of
The Mary McCarthy Literary Trust.
"The Corpse at the Iron Gate" © 1972 by V.S. Naipaul. Reprinted with permission.
"Is Libya Cracking Up?" © 2012 by Nicolas Pelham. Reprinted with permission.
"'I Am Prepared for Anything'" © 1984 by Jerzy Popiełuszko. Reprinted with permission.
"The Battle for Egypt's Future" © 2011 by Yasmine El Rashidi. Reprinted with permission.
"The Burial of Cambodia" © 1984 by William Shawcross. Reprinted with permission.
"Godot Comes to Sarajevo" © 1993 by Susan Sontag. Reprinted with permission of The Wylie Agency, Inc.
"Paris in the Spring" © 1968 by Stephen Spender. Reprinted with the kind permission of
the Estate of Stephen Spender.
"Arrested in China" © 2001 by Kang Zhengguo. Reprinted with permission.

All reasonable attempts have been made to contact the proper copyright holders.
If insufficient credit has been shown please contact the Publisher for proper citation in all future editions.

Published by The New York Review of Books, 435 Hudson Street, Suite 300, New York, NY 10014
www.nyrb.com

Library of Congress Cataloging-in-Publication Data

The New York Review Abroad: Fifty Years of International Reportage/ edited and with a preface by
Robert B. Silvers.
p. cm. — (New York Review Books collections)
ISBN 978-1-59017-631-3 (alk. paper)

ISBN 978-1-59017-631-3
Available as an electronic book; ISBN 978-1-59017-632-0

Cover Design: Pentagram
Printed in the United States of America on acid-free paper

1 3 5 7 9 10 8 6 4 2

Contents

A Note from the Editor

OVER THE LAST fifty years, many of the writers of these reports set to clarify some corner of history they thought was misunderstood, particularly the ways people were being treated and mistreated by governments and by their neighbors. In some cases they took considerable risks in order to observe and understand baffling violence. How much we owe them and how grateful we are to all of them.

—Robert B. Silvers

Report from Vietnam I. The Home Program
Mary McCarthy

Mary McCarthy traveled in Vietnam after Operation Rolling Thunder began in 1965, and before the Tet Offensive of 1968. Rolling Thunder (along with Operation Arc Light and Operation Commando Hunt) was a terrifying bombing assault on North Vietnam, Laos, and Cambodia that laid a toxic trail of devastation for several years. The US mission was to stop North Vietnamese support of the Vietcong, Communist guerrillas operating in the South. The mission failed.

In 1968, during the Tet, or Chinese New Year holiday, the Vietcong managed to attack dozens of cities in South Vietnam. Vietcong guerrillas even penetrated the US embassy in Saigon. Their mission was to spark a national uprising in the South. This, too, failed, at least in a military sense. Politically, it was the beginning of the end of the US war in Indochina.

In 1967, General Westmoreland still promised a victory against the Communists by the end of the year. The South was showered not just in weaponry, but fine American cars, refrigerators, rock-and-roll records, ice cream, hot dogs, Coca Cola, TV sets, garden sprinklers, and dollars. Meanwhile, the bombing rolled and thundered on and on and on.

—Ian Buruma

I CONFESS THAT when I went to Vietnam early in February I was looking for material damaging to the American interest and that I found it, though often by accident or in the process of being briefed by an official. Finding it is no job; the Americans do not dissemble what they are up to. They do not seem to feel the need, except through verbiage; e.g., napalm has become "Incinder-jell," which makes it sound like Jello. And defoliants are referred to as weed-killers—something you use in your driveway. The resort to euphemism denotes, no doubt, a guilty conscience or—the same thing nowadays—a twinge in the public-relations nerve. Yet what is most surprising to a new arrival in Saigon is the general unawareness, almost innocence, of how what "we" are doing could look to an outsider.

At the airport in Bangkok, the war greeted the Air France passengers in the form of a strong smell of gasoline, which made us sniff as we breakfasted at a long table, like a delegation, with the Air France flag planted in the middle. Outside, huge Esso tanks were visible behind lattice screens, where US bombers, factory-new, were aligned as if in a salesroom. On the field itself, a few yards from our Caravelle, US cargo planes were warming up for takeoff; US helicopters flitted about among the swallows, while US military trucks made deliveries. The openness of the thing was amazing (the fact that the US was using Thailand as a base for bombing North Vietnam was not officially admitted at the time); you would have thought they would try to camouflage it, I said to a German correspondent, so that the tourists would not see. As the Caravelle flew on toward Saigon, the tourists, bound for Tokyo or Manila, were able to watch a South Vietnamese hillside burning while consuming a "cool drink" served by the hostess. From above, the bright flames looked like a summer forest fire; you could not believe that bombers had just left. At Saigon, the airfield was dense with military aircraft; in the "civil" side, where we landed, a passenger jetliner was loading GI's for Rest and Recreation

4

in Hawaii. The American presence was overpowering, and, although one had read about it and was aware, as they say, that there was a war on, the sight and sound of that massed American might, casually disposed on foreign soil, like a corporal having his shoes shined, took one's breath away. "They don't try to hide it!" I kept saying to myself, as though the display of naked power and muscle ought to have worn some cover of modesty. But within a few hours I had lost this sense of incredulous surprise, and, seeing the word, "hide," on a note-pad in my hotel room the next morning, I no longer knew what I had meant by it (as when a fragment of a dream, written down on waking, becomes indecipherable) or why I should have been pained, as an American, by this high degree of visibility.

* * *

As we drove into downtown Saigon, through a traffic jam, I had the fresh shock of being in what looked like an American city, a very shoddy West Coast one, with a Chinatown and a slant-eyed Asiatic minority. Not only military vehicles of every description, but Chevrolets, Chryslers, Mercedes Benz, Volkswagens, Triumphs, and white men everywhere in sport shirts and drip-dry pants. The civilian takeover is even more astonishing than the military. To an American, Saigon today is less exotic than Florence or the Place de la Concorde. New office buildings of cheap modern design, teeming with teazed, puffed secretaries and their Washington bosses, are surrounded by sandbags and guarded by MP's; new, jerry-built villas in pastel tones, to rent to Americans, are under construction or already beginning to peel and discolor. Even removing the sandbags and the machine guns and restoring the trees that have been chopped down to widen the road to the airport, the mind cannot excavate what Saigon must have been like "before." Now it resembles a gigantic PX. All those white men seem to be carrying brown paper shopping bags, full of whiskey and other goodies; rows of ballpoints gleam in the breast pockets of their checked shirts. In front of his villa, a leathery oldster, in visored cap, unpacks his golf clubs from his station wagon, while his cotton-haired wife, in a flowered print dress, glasses slung round her neck, stands by, watching, her hands on her hips. As in the American vacation-land, dress is strictly informal; nobody but an Asian wears a tie or a white shirt. The Vietnamese old men and boys, in wide, conical hats, pedaling their Cyclos (the modern version of the rickshaw) in and out of the traffic pattern, the Vietnamese women in high heels and filmy ao-dais of pink, lavender, heliotrope, the signs and Welcome banners in Vietnamese actually contribute to the Stateside impression by the addition of "local" color, as though you were back in a Chinese restaurant in San Francisco or in a Japanese suki-yaki place, under swaying paper lanterns, being served by women in kimonos while you sit on mats and play at using chopsticks.

Perhaps most of all Saigon is like a stewing Los Angeles, shading into Hollywood, Venice Beach, and Watts. The native stall markets are still in business, along Le Loi and Nguyen Hue Streets, but the merchandise, is, for Asia, exotic. There is hardly anything native to buy, except flowers and edibles and fire-crackers at Tet time and—oh yes—souvenir dolls. Street vendors and children are offering trays of American cigarettes and racks on racks of Johnnie Walker, Haig & Haig, Black & White (which are either black market, stolen from the PX, or spurious, depending on the price); billboards outside car agencies advertise Triumphs, Thunderbirds, MG's, Corvettes, "For Delivery here or Stateside, Payment on Easy Terms"; non-whites, the less affluent ones, are mounted on Hondas and Lambrettas. There are photo-copying services, film-developing services, Western tailoring and dry-cleaning services, radio and TV repair shops, air-conditioners, Olivetti typewriters, comic books, *Time, Life,* and *Newsweek,* airmail paper—you name it, they have it. Toys for Vietnamese children (there are practically no American kids in Vietnam) include US-

style jackknives, pistols, and simulated-leather belts, with holsters—
I did not see any cowboy suits or Indian war-feathers. Pharmaceuti-
cals are booming, and a huge billboard all along the top of a building
in the central marketplace shows, for some reason, a smiling Negro
with very white teeth advertising a toothpaste called Hynos.

* * *

If Saigon by day is like a PX, at night, with flares overhead, it is like
a World's Fair or Exposition in some hick American city. There are
Chinese restaurants, innumerable French restaurants (not surprising), but also La Dolce Vita, Le Guillaume Tell, the Paprika (a Spanish restaurant on a rooftop, serving paella and sangría). The national
cuisine no American wants to sample is the Vietnamese. In February,
a German circus was in town. "French" wine is made in Cholon, the
local Chinatown. In the nightclubs, if it were not for the bar girls,
you would think you were on a cruise ship: a *chanteuse* from Singapore sings old French, Italian, and American favorites into the microphone; an Italian magician palms the watch of a middleaged
Vietnamese customer; the band strikes up "Happy Birthday to You,"
as a cake is brought in. The "vice" in Saigon—at least what I was able
to observe of it—has a pepless *Playboy* flavor.

As for virtue, I went to church one Sunday in the Cathedral (a
medley of Gothic, Romanesque, and vaguely Moorish) on John F.
Kennedy Square, hoping to hear the mass in Vietnamese. Instead, an
Irish-American priest preached a sermon on the hemline to a large
male white congregation of soldiers, construction-workers, newspaper correspondents; in the pews were also some female secretaries
from the Embassy and other US agencies and a quotient of middle-
class Vietnamese of both sexes. The married men present, he began,
did not have to be told that the yearly rise or fall in skirt lengths
was a "traumatic experience" for a woman, and he likened the contemporary style centers—New York, Chicago, San Francisco—to the

ancient "style centers" of the Church—Rome, Antioch, Jerusalem. His point seemed to be that the various rites of the Church (Latin, Coptic, Armenian, Maronite—he went into it very thoroughly) were only *modes* of worship. What the Sunday-dressed Vietnamese, whose hemline remains undisturbed by changes emanating from the "style centers" and who were hearing the Latin mass in American, were able to make of the sermon, it was impossible to tell. Just as it was impossible to tell what some very small Vietnamese children I saw in a home for war orphans were getting out of an American adult TV program they were watching at bedtime, the littlest ones mother-naked. Maybe TV too is catholic, and the words do not matter.

Saigon has a smog problem, like New York and Los Angeles, a municipal garbage problem, a traffic problem, power failures, inflation, juvenile delinquency. In short, it meets most of the criteria of a modern Western city. The young soldiers do not like Saigon and its clip joints and high prices. Everybody is trying to sell them something or buy something from them. Six-year-old boys, cute as pins, are plucking at them: "You come see my sister. She Number One fuck." To help the GI resist the temptations of merchants—and soak up his buying power—diamonds and minks are offered him in the PX, tax free. (There were no minks the day I went there, but I did see a case of diamond rings, the prices ranging up to 900-odd dollars.) Unfortunately, the PX presents its own temptation—that of resale. The GI is gypped by taxidrivers and warned against Cyclo men, (probably VC) and he may wind up in a Vietnamese jail, like some of his buddies, for doing what everybody else does—illegal currency transactions. If he walks in the center after nightfall, he has to pick his way among whole families who are cooking their unsanitary meal or sleeping, right on the street, in the filth. When he rides in from the airport, he has to cross a bend of the river, bordered by shanties, that he has named, with rich American humor, Cholera Creek.

* * *

To the servicemen, Saigon stinks. They would rather be in base camp, which is clean. And the JUSPAO press officer has a rote speech for arriving correspondents: "Get out of Saigon. That's my advice to you. Go out into the field." As though the air were purer there, where the fighting is.

That is true in a way. The Americanization process smells better out there, to Americans, even when perfumed by napalm. Out there, too, there is an enemy a man can respect. For many of the soldiers in the field and especially the younger officers, the Viet Cong is the only Vietnamese worthy of notice. "If we only had them fighting on our side, instead of the goddamned Arvin [Army of the Vietnamese Republic], we'd *win* this war" is a sentiment the newspapermen like to quote. I never heard it said in those words, but I found that you could judge an American by his attitude toward the Viet Cong. If he called them "Charlie" (cf. John Steinbeck), he was either an infatuated civilian, a low-grade primitive in uniform, or a fatuous military mouthpiece. Decent soldiers and officers called them "the VC." The same code of honor applied in South Vietnamese circles; with the Vietnamese, who are ironic, it was almost a pet name for the enemy. Most of the American military will praise the fighting qualities of the VC, and the more intellectual (who are not necessarily the best) praise them for their "motivation." Americans have become very incurious, but the Viet Cong has awakened the curiosity of the men who are fighting them. From within the perimeter of the camp, behind the barbed wire and the sandbags, they study their habits, half-amused, half-admiring; a gingerly relationship is established with the unseen enemy, who is probably carefully fashioning a booby trap a few hundred yards away. This relation does not seem to extend to the North Vietnamese troops, but in that case contact is rarer. The military are justly nervous of the VC, but unless they have been wounded out on a patrol or have had the next man killed by a mine or a mortar, they do not show hatred or picture the black-pajama saboteur as a "monster," a word heard in Saigon offices.

In the field, moreover, the war is not questioned: it is just a fact. The job has to be finished—that is the attitude. In Saigon, the idea that the war can ever be finished appears fantastic: the Americans will be there forever, one feels; if they go, the economy will collapse. What postwar aid program could be conceived—or passed by Congress—that would keep the air in the balloon? And if the Americans go, the middle-class Saigonese think, the Viet Cong will surely come back, in two years, five years, ten, as they come back to a "pacified" hamlet at Tet time, to leave, as it were, a calling card, a reminder—we are still here. But, at the same time, in Saigon the worth of the American presence, that is, of the war, seems very dubious, since the actual results, in uglification, moral and physical, are evident to all. The American soldier, bumping along in a jeep or a military truck, resents seeing all those Asiatics at the wheels of new Cadillacs. He knows about corruption, often firsthand, having contributed his bit to it, graft, theft of AID and military supplies from the port. He thinks it is disgusting that the local employees steal from the PX and then stage a strike when the manageress makes them line up to be searched on leaving the building. And he has heard that these "apes," as some men call them, are salting away the profits in Switzerland or in France, where De Gaulle, who is pro-VC, has just run the army out.

Of course, all wars have had their profiteers, but it has not usually been so manifest, so inescapable. The absence of the austerity that normally accompanies war, of civilian sacrifices, rationing, shortages, blackouts (compare wartime London or even wartime New York, twenty-five years ago) makes this war seem singularly immoral and unheroic to those who are likely to die in it—for what? So that the Saigonese and other civilians can live high off the hog? The fact that the soldier or officer is living pretty high off the hog himself does not reconcile him to the glut of Saigon; rather the contrary. Furthermore, an atmosphere of sacrifice is heady; that—and danger—is what used to make wartime capitals gay. Saigon is not gay. The peculiar thing is that with all those young soldiers wandering about, all those young journalists news-chasing, Saigon seems so middle-aged—inert, listless, bored. That, I suppose, is because everyone's principal interest there is money, the only currency that is circulating, like the stale air moved by ceiling-fans and air-conditioners in hotels and offices.

* * *

The war, they say, is not going to be won in Saigon, nor on the battlefield, but in the villages and hamlets. This idea, by now trite (it was first discovered in Diem's time and has been rebaptized under a number of names—New Life Hamlets, Rural Construction, Counter Insurgency, Nation-Building, Revolutionary Development, the Hearts and Minds Program), is the main source of inspiration for the various teams of missionaries, military and civilian, who think they are engaged in a crusade. Not just a crusade against Communism, but something *positive*. Back in the Fifties and early Sixties, the war was presented as an investment: the taxpayer was persuaded that if he stopped Communism *now* in Vietnam, he would not have to keep stopping it in Thailand, Burma, etc. That was the domino theory, which our leading statesmen today, quite comically, are busy repudiating before Congressional committees—suddenly nobody will admit to ever having been an advocate of it. The notion of a costly investment that will save money in the end had a natural appeal to a nation of homeowners, but now the assertion of an American "interest" in Vietnam has begun to look too speculative as the stake increases ("When is it going to pay off?") and also too squalid as the war daily becomes more savage and destructive. Hence the "other" war, proclaimed by Johnson in Honolulu, which is simultaneously pictured as a strategy for winning War Number One and as a top priority in itself. Indeed, in Vietnam, there are moments when the "other" war seems to be viewed as the sole reason for the American presence, and it is certainly more congenial to American officials, brimming with public spirit, than the war they are launching from the skies. Americans do not like to be negative, and the "other" war is constructive.

To see it, of course, you have to get out of Saigon, but, before you go, you will have to be briefed, in one of those new office buildings, on what you are going to see. In the field, you will be briefed again, by a military man, in a district or province headquarters, and frequently all you will see of New Life Hamlets, Constructed Hamlets, Consolidated Hamlets, are the charts and graphs and maps and symbols that some ardent colonel or brisk bureaucrat is demonstrating to you with a pointer, and the mimeographed hand-out, full of statistics, that you take away with you, together with a supplement on Viet Cong Terror. On paper and in chart form, it all sounds commendable, especially if you are able to ignore the sounds of bombing from B-52s that are shaking the windows and making the charts rattle. The briefing official is enthusiastic, as he points out the progress that has been made, when, for example, the activities organized under AID were reorganized under OCO (Office of Civilian Operations). You stare at the chart on the office wall in which to you there is no semblance of logic or sequence ("Why," you wonder, "should Youth Affairs be grouped under Urban Development?"), and the official rubs his hands with pleasure: "First we organized it *vertically*. Now we've organized *horizontally!*" Out in the field, you learn from some disgruntled officer that the AID representatives, who are perhaps now OCO representatives without knowing it, have not been paid for six months.

In a Saigon "backgrounder," you are told about public health measures undertaken by Free World Forces. Again a glowing progress report. In 1965, there were 180 medical people from the "Free World" in Vietnam treating patients; in 1966, there were 700—quite a little escalation, almost four times as many. The troop commitment, of course, not mentioned by the briefer, jumped from 60,000 to 400,000—more than six-and-a-half times as many. That the multiplication of troops implied an obvious escalation in the number of civilian patients requiring treatment is not mentioned either. Under questioning, the official, slightly irritated, estimates that the civilian casualties comprise between 7 1/2 and 15 per cent of the surgical patients treated in hospitals. He had "not been interested particularly, until all the furore," in what percentage of the patients were war casualties. And naturally he was not interested in what percentage of civilian casualties never reached a hospital at all.

* * *

But the treatment of war victims, it turned out, was not one of the medical "bull's eyes" aimed at in the "other" war. Rather a peacetime-type program, "beefing up" the medical school, improvement of hospital facilities, donation of drugs and antibiotics (which, as I learned from a field worker, are in turn sold by the local nurses to the patients for whom they have been prescribed), the control of epidemic diseases, such as plague and cholera, education of the population in good health procedures. American and allied workers, you hear, are teaching the Vietnamese in the government villages to boil their water, and the children are learning dental hygiene. Toothbrushes are distributed, and the children are shown how to use them. If the children get the habit, the parents will copy them, a former social worker explains, projecting from experience with first-generation immigrants back home. There is a campaign on to vaccinate and immunize as much of the population as can be got to cooperate; easy subjects are refugees and forced evacuees, who can be lined up for shots while going through the screening process and being issued an identity card—a political health certificate.

All this is not simply on paper. In the field, you are actually able to see medical teams at work, setting up temporary dispensaries under the trees in the hamlets for the weekly or bi-weekly "sick call"—distributing medicines, tapping, listening, sterilizing, bandaging; the most common diagnosis is suspected tuberculosis. In Tay Ninh Province, I watched a Philcag (Filipino) medical team at work in a Buddhist hamlet. One doctor was examining a very thin old man, who was stripped to the waist; probably tubercular, the doctor told me, writing something on a card which he gave to the old man. "What happens next?" I wanted to know. Well, the old man would go to the province hospital for an X-ray (that was the purpose of the card), and if the diagnosis was positive, then treatment should follow. I was impressed. But (as I later learned at a briefing) there are only sixty civilian hospitals in South Vietnam—for nearly 16 million people— so that the old man's total benefit, most likely, from the open-air consultation was to have learned, gratis, that he might be tubercular.

Across the road, some dentist's chairs were set up, and teeth were being pulled, very efficiently, from women and children of all ages. I asked about the toothbrushes I had heard about in Saigon. The Filipino major laughed. "Yes, we have distributed them. They use them as toys." Then he reached into his pocket—he was a kindly young man with children of his own—and took out some money for all the children who had gathered round to buy popsicles (the local equivalent) from the popsicle man. Later I watched the Filipino general, a very handsome tall man with a cropped head, resembling Yul Brynner, distribute Tet gifts and candy to children in a Cao Dai orphanage and be photographed with his arm around a little blind girl. A few hours earlier, he had posed distributing food in a Catholic hamlet—"Free World" surplus items, such as canned cooked beets.

The photography, I was told, would help sell the Philcag operation to the Assembly in Manila, where some leftist elements were trying to block funds for it. Actually, I could not see that the general was doing any harm—unless not doing enough is harm, in which case we are all guilty—and he was more efficient than other Civic Action leaders. His troops had just chopped down a large section of jungle (we proceeded through it in convoy, wearing bullet-proof vests and bristling with rifles and machine-guns, because of the VC), which was going to be turned into a New Life Hamlet for resettling refugees. They had also built a school, which we stopped to inspect, finding, to the general's surprise, that it had been taken over by the local district chief for his office headquarters.

* * *

The Filipino team, possibly because they were Asians, seemed to be on quite good terms with the population. Elsewhere—at Go Cong, in the delta—I saw mistrustful patients and heard stories of rivalry between the Vietnamese doctor, a gynecologist, and the Spanish and American medical teams; my companion and I were told that we were the first "outsiders," including the resident doctors, to be allowed by the Vietnamese into *his* wing—the maternity, which was far the cleanest and most modern in the hospital and contained one patient. Similar jealousies existed of the German medical staff at Hue. In the rather squalid surgical wing of the Go Pong hospital, there were two badly burned children. Were they war casualties, I asked the official who was showing us through. Yes, he conceded, as a matter of fact they were. How many of the patients were war-wounded, I wanted to know. "About four" of the children, he reckoned. And one old man, he added, after reflection.

The Filipinos were fairly dispassionate about their role in pacification; this may have been because they had no troops fighting in the war (those leftist elements in the Assembly!) and therefore did not have to act like saviors of the Vietnamese people. The Americans, on the contrary, are zealots, above all the blueprinters in the Saigon offices, although occasionally in the field, too, you meet a true believer—a sandy, crew-cut, keen-eyed army colonel who talks to you about "the nuts and bolts" of the program, which, he is glad to say, is finally getting the "grass roots" support it needs. It is impossible to find out from such a man what he is doing, concretely; an aide steps forward to state, "We sterilize the area prior to the insertion of the RD teams," whose task, says the colonel, is to find out "the aspirations of the people." He cannot tell you whether there has been any land reform in his area—that is a strictly Vietnamese pigeon—in fact he has no idea of *how* the land in the area is owned. He is strong on coordination: all his Vietnamese counterparts, the colonel who "wears two hats" as province chief, the mayor, a deposed general are all "very fine sound men," and the Marine general in the area is "one of the finest men and officers" he has ever met. For another army zealot every Vietnamese officer he deals with is "an outstanding individual."

These springy, zesty, burning-eyed warriors, military and civilian, engaged in AID or Combined Action (essentially pacification) stir faraway memories of American college presidents of the fund-raising type; their diction is peppery with oxymoron ("When peace breaks out," "Then the commodities started to hit the beach"), like a college president's address to an alumni gathering. They see themselves in fact as educators, spreading the American way of life, a new *propaganda fide*. When I asked an OCO man in Saigon what his groups actually did in a Vietnamese village to prepare—his word—the people for elections, he answered curtly, "We teach them Civics 101."

* * *

The American taxpayer who thinks that aid means help has missed the idea. Aid is, first of all, to achieve economic stability within the present system, i.e., political stability for the present ruling groups. Loans are extended, under the counterpart fund arrangement, to finance Vietnamese imports of American capital equipment (thus aiding, with the other hand, American industry). Second, aid is *education*. Distribution of canned goods (instill new food habits), distribution of seeds, fertilizer, chewing gum and candy (the Vietnamese complain that the GI's fire candy at their children, like a spray of bullets), lessons in sanitation, hog-raising, and crop rotation. The program is designed, not just to make Americans popular but to shake up the Vietnamese, as in some "stimulating" freshman course where the student learns to question the "prejudices" implanted in him by his parents. "We're trying to wean them away from the old barter economy and show them a market economy. Then they'll really *go*."

"We're teaching them free enterprise," explains a breathless JUS-PAO official in the grim town of Phu Cuong. He is speaking of the "refugees" from the Iron Triangle, who were forcibly cleared out of their hamlets, which were then burned and leveled, during Operation Cedar Falls ("Clear and Destroy"). They had just been transferred into a camp, hastily constructed by the ARVN with tin roofs painted red and white, to make the form, as seen from the air, of a giant Red Cross—1,651 women, 3,754 children, 582 men, mostly old, who had been kindly allowed to bring some of their furniture and pots and pans and their pigs and chickens and sacks of their hoarded rice; their cattle had been transported for them, on barges, and were now sickening on a dry, stubbly, sandy plain. "We've got a captive audience!" the official continued excitedly. "This is our big chance!"

To teach them free enterprise and, presumably, when they were "ready" for it, Civics 101; for the present, the government had to consider them "hostile civilians." These wives and children and grandfathers of men thought to be at large with the Viet Cong had been rice farmers only a few weeks before. Now they were going to have to pitch in and learn to be vegetable farmers; the area selected for their eventual resettlement was not suitable for rice-growing, unfortunately. Opportunity was beckoning for these poor peasants, thanks to the uprooting process they had just undergone. They would have the chance to buy and build their own homes on a pattern and of materials already picked out for them; the government was allowing them 1700 piasters toward the purchase price. To get a new house free, even though just in the abstract, would be unfair to them as human beings: investing their own labor and their own money would make them feel that the house was really *theirs*.

In the camp, a schoolroom had been set up for their children. Interviews with the parents revealed that more than anything else they wanted education for their children; they had not had a school for five years. I remarked that this seemed queer, since Communists were usually strong on education. The official insisted. "Not for five years." But in fact another American, a young one, who had actually been working in the camp, told me that strangely enough the small children there knew their multiplication tables and possibly their primer—he could not account for this. And in one of the razed villages, he related, the Americans had found, from captured exercise books, that someone had been teaching the past participle in English, using Latin models—defectors spoke of a high school teacher, a Ph.D. from Hanoi.

Perhaps the parents, in the interviews, told the Americans what they thought they wanted to hear. All over Vietnam, wherever peace has broken out, if only in the form of a respite, Marine and army officers are proud to show the schoolhouses their men are building or rebuilding for the hamlets they are patrolling, rifle on shoulder. At Rach Kien, in the delta (a Pentagon pilot-project of a few months ago), I saw the little schoolhouse Steinbeck wrote about, back in January, and the blue school desks he had seen the soldiers painting. They were still sitting outside, in the sun; the school was not yet rebuilt more than a month later—they were waiting for materials. In this hamlet, everything seemed to have halted, as in "The Sleeping Beauty," the enchanted day Steinbeck left; nothing had advanced. Indeed, the picture he sketched, of a ghost town coming back to civic life, made the officers who had entertained him smile—"He used his imagination." In other hamlets, I saw schoolhouses actually finished and one in operation. "The school is dirty," the colonel in charge barked at the Revolutionary Development director—a case of American tactlessness, though he was right. A young Vietnamese social worker said sadly that he wished the Americans would stop building schools. "They don't realize—we have no teachers for them."

Yet the little cream schoolhouse is essential to the American dream of what we are doing in Vietnam, and it is essential for the soldiers to believe that in *Viet Cong* hamlets no schooling is permitted. In Rach Kien I again expressed doubts, as a captain, with a professionally shocked face, pointed out the evidence that the school had been used as "Charlie's" headquarters. "So you really think that the children here got no lessons, *nothing*, under the VC?" "Oh, indoctrination courses!" he answered with a savvy wave of his pipe. In other words, VC Civics 101.

* * *

If you ask a junior officer what he thinks our war aims are in Vietnam, he usually replies without hesitation: "To punish aggression." It is unkind to try to draw him into a discussion of what constitutes aggression and what is defense (the Bay of Pigs, Santo Domingo, Goa?), for he really has no further ideas on the subject. He has been indoctrinated, just as much as the North Vietnamese POW, who tells the interrogation team he is fighting to "liberate the native soil from the American aggressors"—maybe more. Only the young American does not know it; he probably imagines that he is *thinking* when he produces that formula. And yet he does believe in something profoundly, though he may not be able to find the words for it: free enterprise. A parcel that to the American mind wraps up for delivery hospitals, sanitation, roads, harbors, schools, air travel, Jack Daniels, convertibles, Stim-U-Dents. That is the C-ration that keeps him going. The American troops are not exactly conscious of bombing, shelling, and defoliating to defend free enterprise (which they cannot imagine as being under serious attack), but they plan to come out of the war with their values intact. Which means that they must spread them, until everyone is convinced, by demonstration, that the American way is better, just as American seed-strains are better and American pigs are better. Their conviction is sometimes baldly stated. North of Da Nang, at a Marine base, there is an ice-cream plant on which is printed in large official letters the words: "ICE-CREAM PLANT: ARVN MORALE BUILDER." Or it may wear a humanitarian disguise, e.g., OPERATION CONCERN, in which a proud little town in Kansas airlifted 110 pregnant sows to a humble little town in Vietnam.

Occasionally the profit motive is undisguised. Flying to Hue in a big C-130, I heard the pilot and the co-pilot discussing their personal war aim, which was to make a killing, as soon as the war was over, in Vietnamese real estate. From the air, while they kept an eye out for VC, they had surveyed the possibilities and had decided on Nha Trang—"beautiful sand beaches"—better than Cam Ranh Bay—a "desert." They disagreed as to the kind of development that would make the most money: the pilot wanted to build a high-class hotel and villas, while the co-pilot thought that the future lay with low-cost housing. I found this conversation hallucinating, but the next day, in Hue, I met a Marine colonel who had returned to the service after retirement; having fought the Japanese, he had made his killing as a "developer" in Okinawa and invested the profits in a frozen-shrimp import business (from Japan) supplying restaurants in San Diego. War, a cheap form of mass tourism, opens the mind to business opportunities.

All these developers were Californians. In fact, the majority of the Americans I met in the field in Vietnam were WASPS from Southern California; most of the rest were from the rural South. In nearly a month I met *one* Jewish boy in the services (a nice young naval officer from Pittsburgh), two Boston Irish, and a captain from Connecticut. Given the demographic shift toward the Pacific in the United States, this Californian ascendancy gave me the peculiar feeling that I was seeing the future of our country as if on a movie screen. Nobody has dared make a war movie about Vietnam, but the prevailing unreality, as experienced in base camps and headquarters, is eerily like a movie, a contest between good and evil, which is heading toward a happy ending, when men with names like "Colonel Culpepper," "Colonel Derryberry," "Captain Stanhope," will vanquish Victor Charlie. The state that has a movie actor for governor and a movie actor for US senator seemed to be running the show.

* * *

No doubt the very extensive press and television coverage of the war has made the participants very conscious of "exposure," that is, of roleplaying. Aside from the usual networks, Italian television, Mexican television, the BBC, CBC were all filming the "other" war during the month of February, and the former Italian Chief of Staff, General Liuzzi, was covering it as a commentator for the *Corriere della Sera*. The effect of all this attention on the generals, colonels, and lesser officers was to put a premium on "sincerity."

Nobody likes to be a villain, least of all a WASP officer, who feels he is playing the heavy in Vietnam through some awful mistake in type-casting. He *knows* he is good at heart, because everything in his home environment—his TV set, his paper, his Frigidaire, the President of the United States—has promised him that, whatever shortcomings he may have as an individual, collectively he is good. The "other" war is giving him the chance to clear up the momentary misunderstanding created by those bombs, which, through no fault of his, are happening to hit civilians. He has *warned* them to get away, dropped leaflets saying he was coming and urging "Charlie" to defect, to join the other side; lately, in pacified areas, he has even taken the precaution of having his targets cleared by the village chief before shelling or bombing, so that now the press officer giving the daily briefing is able to reel out: "OPERATION BLOCKHOUSE. 29 civilians reported wounded today. Two are in 'poor' condition. Target had been approved by the district chief." Small thanks he gets, our military hero, for that scrupulous restraint. But in the work of pacification, his real self comes out, clear and true. Digging wells for the natives (too bad if the water comes up brackish), repairing roads ("Just a jungle trail before we came," says the captain, though his colonel, in another part of the forest, has just been saying that the engineers had uncovered a fine stone roadbed built eighty years ago by the French), building a house for the widow of a Viet Cong (so far unreconciled; it takes time).

American officers in the field can become very sentimental when they think of the good they are doing and the hard row they have to hoe with the natives, who have been brainwashed by the Viet Cong. A Marine general in charge of logistics in I-Corps district was deeply moved when he spoke of his Marines: moving in to help rebuild some refugee housing with scrap lumber and sheet tin (the normal materials were cardboard boxes and flattened beer cans); working in their off-hours to build desks for a school; giving their Christmas money for a new high school; planning a new marketplace. The Marine Corps had donated a children's hospital, and in that hospital, up the road, was a little girl who had been wounded during a Marine assault. "We're nursing her back to health," he intoned, with prayerful satisfaction—a phrase he must have become attached to by dint of repetition; his PIO (Information Officer) nodded three times. In the hospital, I asked to see the little girl. "Oh, she's gone home," said the PIO. "Nursed her back to health." In reality the little girl was still there, but it was true, her wounds were nearly healed.

A young Marine doctor, blue-eyed, very good-looking, went from bed to bed, pointing out what was the matter with each child and showing what was being done to cure it. There was only the one war casualty; the rest were suffering from malnutrition (the basic complaint everywhere), skin diseases, worms; one had a serious heart condition; two had been badly burned by a stove, and one, in the contagious section, had the plague. The doctor showed us the tapeworm, in a bottle, he had extracted from one infant. A rickety baby was crying, and a middle-aged corpsman picked it up and gave it its bottle. They were plainly doing a good job, under makeshift conditions and without laboratory facilities. The children who were well enough to sit up appeared content; some even laughed, shyly. No amusements were provided for them, but perhaps it was sufficient amusement to be visited by tiptoeing journalists. And it could not be denied that it was a break for these children to be in a Marine hospital, clean, well-fed, and one to a bed. They were benefiting from the war, at least for the duration of their stay; the doctor was not sanguine, for the malnutrition cases, about what would happen when the patients went home. "We keep them as long as we can," he said, frowning. "But we can't keep them forever. They have to go back to their parents."

* * *

Compared to what they were used to, this short taste of the American way of life must have been delicious for Vietnamese children.

John Morgan in the London *Sunday Times* described another little
Vietnamese girl up near the DMZ—do they have one to a battalion?
—who had been wounded by Marine bullets ("A casualty of war,"
that general repeated solemnly. "A casualty of war") and whom he
saw carried in one night to a drinking party in sick bay, her legs ban-
daged, a spotlight playing on her, while the Marines pressed candy
and dollar bills into her hands and had their pictures taken with her;
she had more dolls than Macy's, they told him—"that girl is real
spoiled." To spoil a child war victim and send her back to her parents,
with her dolls as souvenirs, is patently callous, just as it is callous to
fill a child's stomach and send it home to be hungry again. The young
doctor, being a doctor, was possibly conscious of the fakery—from a
responsible medical point of view—of the "miracle" cures he was
effecting; that was why he frowned. Meanwhile, however, the Marine Corps brass could show the "Before" and "After" to a captive
audience. In fact two. The studio audience of children, smiling and
laughing and clapping, and the broader audience of their parents,
who, when allowed to visit, could not fail to be impressed, if not
awed, by the "other" side of American technology. And beyond that
still a third audience—the journalists and their readers back home,
who would recognize the Man in White and his corpsman, having
brought them up, gone to school with them, seen them on TV, in
soap opera. I felt this myself, a relieved recognition of the familiar
face of America. These are the American boys we know at once, even
in an Asian context, bubbling an Asian baby. We do not recognize
them, helmeted, in a bomber aiming cans of napalm at a thatched
village. We have a credibility gap.

Leaving the hospital, I jolted southward in a jeep, hanging on,
swallowing dust; the roads, like practically everything in Vietnam,
have been battered, gouged, scarred, torn up by the weight of US
materiel. We passed Marines' laundry, yards and yards of it, hanging

outside native huts—the dark green battle cloth spelled money. Down the road was a refugee camp, which did not form part of the itinerary. This, I realized, must be "home" to some of the children we had just seen; the government daily allowance for a camp family was ten piasters (six cents) a day—sometimes twenty if there were two adults in the family. Somebody had put a streamer, in English, over the entrance: "REFUGEES FROM COMMUNISM."

This was a bit too much. The children's hospital had told the story the Americans were anxious to get over. Why put in the commercial? And who was the hard sell aimed at? Not the refugees, who could not read English and who, if they were like all the other refugees, had fled, some from the Viet Cong and some from the Americans and some because their houses had been bombed or shelled. Not the journalists, who knew better. Whoever carefully lettered that streamer, crafty Marine or civilian, had applied all his animal cunning to selling himself.

—April 20, 1967

2

Paris in the Spring
Stephen Spender

In 1950, Hemingway said: "If you are lucky enough to have lived in Paris as a young man, then wherever you go for the rest of your life, it stays with you, for Paris is a moveable feast."

It must have felt a bit like that eighteen years later to the many pilgrims at the fountain of youth that was Paris during its brief student rebellion. The much-hoped-for fusion of students and workers never came about; the gulf was too wide. Many of the slogans and much of the rhetoric now appears naive and vague, though not devoid of wit. The admiration of far away heroes—Mao, Castro—was misguided.

There was no repeat of 1789 in 1968 in Paris.

And yet '68 left its mark. And not just on the generation, now known as the soixante-huitards. *There was an expansion of freedom, a loosening of moral and social restrictions, a gust of fresh air that, however faintly, is still felt, even perhaps among some of the people who abhor the spirit of Paris '68 as the devil's work.*

—I.B.

THE BARRICADES

THE STREET BATTLES which took place near the Sorbonne in mid-May between students and police were very ritualistic. In the late afternoon while it was still daylight, the students started building barricades. On Friday (May 24) these were particularly elaborate. First they tore up paving stones and piled them up as though they were rebuilding memories of 1789, 1848, 1870. Then, in a mood of dedicated desecration, they axed down—so that they fell lengthwise across the street—a few of the sappy plane trees, spring-leafed, just awake from winter. Then they scattered over the paving stones and among the leaves, boxes, wood, trash from the uncollected strikebound garbage on the sidewalks. Lastly, as the night closed in, they tugged, pulled with much rumblings, neighboring parked cars, braked but dragged over the streets just the same, and placed them on their sides, like trophies of smashed automobiles by the sculptor César, on top of the paving stones, among the branches. In an arrangement of this kind on the Boulevard St. Germain, they had extended the contour of a burned-out car by adding to it the quarter section of one of those wrought-iron grills which encircle at the base the trunks of trees on the boulevards to protect their roots. After the night's fighting, this chassis had acquired a wonderful coral tint. On its pediment of bluish paving stones it looked like an enshrined museum object. It was left there for two or three days and much photographed by the tourists who poured into the Latin Quarter during the daytime.

* * *

There is not a sign of a policeman while the barricades are being built. Presumably the rules of what has become a war game are being observed; within a few days the police, after having attempted to occupy, have abandoned the territory of the Sorbonne. The Boulevard

Saint-Michel is student territory, as witness the fact that students control the traffic. However the completion of the barricades is the sign that the territory may be invaded. The police are now to be let out of the long crate-like camions with thick wire netting over the windows behind which they wait like mastiffs. One sees them assembled at the end of the Boulevard near the bridge. Their massed forms in the shadows, solid, stirring, helmeted, some of them carrying shields, seem those of medieval knights. A few of the students also carry shields, the lids of dust-bins, and swords or spear-length sticks. Slowly the massed police advance up the street like a thick wedge of mercury up a glass tube. The students retreat to their barricades and set the trash and wood alight. The police now start firing tear gas shells and detonators which make heavy explosions. When they are within a few feet of the advancing black mass of police the students run away, occasionally picking up and hurling back shells which have not exploded.

The beatnik word "cat" suddenly occurs to me. The wild, quickly running, backward and sideways turning, yowling and scratching students are like cats, the police stolidly massively pursuing them are like dogs.

Terrible things happen to students who are caught and taken to the police cells.

Note that my friend, the painter Jean Hélion, told me of a couple seen weeping over the burned-out cadaver of their car on which they had spent their savings.

THE SORBONNE

The center of the Sorbonne is a courtyard enclosed by cliffs of buff-colored stucco walls. They don't shut out the sky but at the top they make an ugly edge against it. There are two tiers of rather grandiose steps across the whole width of one end of the courtyard leading up to the pillared chapel. Along the sides of the courtyard there are now tables piled with books, magazines, pamphlets, leaflets, etc., all of them "revolutionary." Behind the tables students sit, displaying these wares. Most of the slogans and posters appear to proclaim communism. But on closer inspection one finds that there is no variety of communism here to offer any comfort to Moscow or the French official Communist Party. Even a magazine called *La Nouvelle Humanité* turns out to be Trotskyist, abhorrent to the sellers of the old *Humanité* who have been banished to the outer gates at the entrance of the Sorbonne. The brands of revolution offered by the students are Maoist, Castroite, Trotskyist. Pictures of Mao, Che Guevara, Trotsky, Lenin, Marx are displayed on walls, hoardings, pamphlets, and leaflets. Stalin's portrait put in a brief appearance one day, but quickly disappeared.

One day there was a table for Kurds, Turks, Arabs, and Algerians; posters attacking Zionism were on the wall behind them. The Sorbonne is cosmopolitan French culture. I noticed among the bewildering assortment of advertisements—appeals, bulletins posted everywhere or leaflets thrust into your hand—directives to Greek, Spanish, Portuguese, and German students. And of course there were Americans. Two sat rather innocuously at a table collecting signatures for a petition in support of Mendès-France. A committee of American students hangs out at the sister offices of the Sorbonne in the Rue Censier, where there are also the American draft resisters, a bit left out of all this.

Entrances lead out of the Sorbonne courtyard onto passages and stairways, all of them plastered with notices. Almost every departmental office and classroom has been taken over by committees, organizers, planners, talkers: Committee of Action, Committee of

Coordination, Committee of Occupation, Committee of Cultural Agitation, and the sinisterly named Committee of Rapid Intervention.

There seems a tendency for the movement to proliferate cells, activities, categories, subdivisions. I noticed that the Commando Poétique has its functions subdivided into *"Tracts poétiques—affiches poétiques—création collective—publications à bon marché—liaisons interartistiques—Recherches théoretiques—commandos poétique revolutionnaires—praxis poétique revolutionnaire."*

* * *

The poems I saw (*Le Monde* published a selection from them) seemed unoriginal—a mixture of surrealism with the socially conscious leftist writing of the Thirties, and a return to the political style of Eluard. The real poetry of the revolution is its slogans, politically revolutionary, but imaginative and witty. They are more revealing of the deepest impulses of the movement than most of the pamphlets and pronouncements. They all come together—as do all the finest impulses of the students—in the magnificent summary: "Imagination is Revolution." One understands from the slogans why the students cannot get on with the great trade unions, political parties, official communism:

> *Prenez vos désirs pour des réalités. Monolithiquement bête, le Gaullisme est l'inversion de la vie. Ne changer pas d'employeurs changer l'emploi de la vie. Vive la communication à bas la téle communication. Plus je fais l'amour plus je fais la revolution plus je fais la revolution plus je fais l'amour. Luttez dans la perspective d'une vie passionante. Toute vue des choses qui n'est pas étrange est fausse.*

They equate revolution with spontaneity, participation, communication, imagination, love, youth. Relations between the students and young workers who share—or who are converted to—these values are of the first importance. They dramatize a struggle not between proletarian and capitalist interest so much as between forces of life and the dead oppressive weight of the bourgeoisie. They are against the consumer society, paternalism, bureaucracy, impersonal party programs, and static party hierarchies. Revolution must not become ossified. It is *la revolution permanente*.

One thing—perhaps the only one—which the Paris students have in common with the beatniks and hippies of the psychedelic generation is that they wish to live the life of the revolution even while they are taking action to bring it about. But they are opposed to drugs and other such eccentrically individualistic forms of self-realization: partly because their view of the revolution is of a community rather than of the individual, but still more because they have a sharp political awareness of the counter-revolutionary effects of drug-taking.

This May, for a few weeks at the Sorbonne, the students lived the communal life of sharing conditions, of arriving at all-important decisions by the method of "direct democracy"—that is to say by consulting the action committees of the movement (*les bases*) and not by imposing decisions from the top—of having meetings which are as far as possible spontaneous, with a different chairman for each meeting, resisting the "cult of personality."

However, by the end of May, under pressure from government and police, attacked by the Communists and without support from the *Confédération Générale* of workers, the students had to reconsider their concept of organization. This they could not do without questioning "direct democracy." A press conference at the Sorbonne on the first of June developed into a disagreement between Cohn-Bendit and the other student leaders as to whether organization for action and self-defense should arise spontaneously from discussions at *les bases* or should be imposed by the leaders. Cohn-Bendit thought that the dynamism of the movement should continue to come from the *bases*. His own words:

> The only chance of creating revolutionary forms that will not become ossified (*scelerosé*) lies in waiting until a common purpose has been discovered among all the committees of action from discussing matters at the *base*.

His colleagues agreed on "spontaneity" as a principle but did not think that the circumstances left them much time for discussion in action committees. They pointed out that they had to decide on measures for "*auto-defense*" immediately. One of them, Henri Weber, said that the committees were too disorganized and uncoordinated to be capable of *auto-defense* in the face of the very well organized Gaullist forces. The discussion about organization is crucial, because the danger inherent in too little organization is defeat by the Gaullist and communist forces outside the movement; while the danger of too much organization is defeat by loss of spontaneity from below. The demonstrations and marches, the barricades, were extraordinary examples of spontaneity with a minimum of organization. The undirected discussions at the Odéon Theatre, in which the chairman has to struggle with a tumultuous audience, succeed but do result in disorder and waste of energy. The same must be true, I suspect, of the committee of action. But I sympathize with Cohn-Bendit's view that organization should not be imposed from above.

* * *

During the first half of May a good many Parisian intellectuals, as well as many students, seemed to think of the student revolt as part of a larger revolution which had already happened in France. Of course it is not that, and the realization that the university revolt is threatened has added urgency to the debate about "organization" and "direct democracy." The students are reluctant to discuss the Bolsheviks and the anarchists of the Spanish Republic who also said they wanted direct democracy. Or, reminded of this, they take refuge in the idea that theirs is an unprecedented generation. To recall the failures of previous revolutions is to seem in their eyes patronizing, paternalistic. The London *Times* in an editorial pointed out as a weakness of the students that they did not appear to have read George Orwell's *Animal Farm*. But they would not want to read it and if they did read it would find there nothing which they thought applied to their case.

Perhaps because they are so insulated in the Sorbonne, without their being literary, they yet keep on reminding one of behavior and characters in literature. There is something about their movements which reminds one of *The Lord of the Flies*, with a thuggish Katanga "Committee of Sudden Intervention" ready to emerge from the cellars to produce a final fall. And when one has stepped into the Sorbonne one often seems to be in the world of *Alice Through the Looking Glass* where all the values of the circumambient trafficking world outside are reversed.

THE EXPLOSION OF TALK

In a classroom there is a discussion going on about the nature of work in the consumer society. The room is crowded and contains older as well as young people. The discussion is dominated by two young men, one of whom, in the well of the classroom, is evidently a worker. He has a lean face with jutting features and bristly straw-colored hair emphasizing the line of the back of his head which seems almost continuous with his neck. He talks about work, which, he says, in all circumstances must be hard and boring. The opposite of work, he says, is pleasure, and he describes, quite exhibitionistically, his own holidays which are spent, it seems, in driving about the country on his motorcycle and laying as many girls as he can pick up. Obviously this is the opposite of what is meant by work.

He is confronted by a student standing a few feet above him. He is small and dark and vigorous and has in his eyes and on his lips an expression like that of the blind made miraculously to see in a cartoon of Raphael. He says that work is joy if you are one of a group, a collective (any backward echoes of that remark are suppressed by his smile). Joy is participation, it is release from the self. He describes holidays that he and his companions have made together where they have done a great deal of work. The individual must not be like the bourgeois intellectual, alienated and separate, existing in no "social context," but that of other intellectuals like himself; nor must he be a cog in a machine. He must be in society like a fish in the water.

The worker interrupts and says, You are not talking about work, you are talking about sport. Sport is not work, it is the free development of the individual. Work means taking orders from someone set above you. The student says that in the revolution, automation will replace the kind of work which is slavery. Work will then consist of participation. There will be no oppression of power because there will be a constant toing and froing between those at the base of society and those at the top, a vital current. Machines will function but the goods and services they produce will be a means for leading a life of better value, and not ends which prove that the individual owns things or acquires status. He says the students and the workers combining together could achieve this kind of society: not the intellectuals who are void because they reflect problems peculiar to them, outside the context of society. To be truly revolutionary, you have to experience reality.

This discussion was naïve. Often at the Sorbonne and the Odéon one heard things worse than naïve, chaotic and stupid and dull, and one longed to hear a professor talk for half an hour about Racine. There was wisdom though perhaps in the relief of talking simply as an act, like action painting. Talk, uninhibited, crude, theoretical, confessional, has overtaken Paris, Lyons, Bordeaux, and other cities. It is the breaking out of forces long suppressed. Not just the Sorbonne and the Censier, the Beaux Arts, the Odéon, were filled with talk but also the streets themselves. Another part of the French revolutionary tradition had emerged—the idea of joining forces with others in the streets—*dans la rue!* In the Rue de Rennes I find myself standing in a group of shoppers and shop assistants outside a closed Monoprix. A frustrated shopper is saying indignantly, "Where will all this end? In communism, universal poverty." "Not at all," says a natty black-coated worker, "Communism means *more* refrigerators, *more* television sets, *more* automobiles. *Le communisme, c'est le luxe pour tous.*"

* * *

This definition shows how difficult it is for the students—conscious, many of them, of themselves as bourgeois, and seeking for a world in which material things are subservient to other human values—to get on with the workers, most of whom, of course, want consumer goods. The relation of the French students to *"les ouvriers"* is not unlike that of the American students to the Negroes. It cannot be seen just politically, but as a love affair in which the guilt-conscious whites and bourgeois are trying to win the members of what they regard as a wronged class to their own ideas of what are real values.

Not that the students want altogether to dispense with washing machines and refrigerators. Their attitude is shown in a document of thirty theses drafted at the Censier by a group called *Les Yeux Crévés.* It begins by defining the students as a privileged class, not so much economically as because "we alone have the time and possibility to become aware of our own conditions and the condition of society. Abolish this privilege and act so that everyone may become privileged." It goes on to say that students are workers like everyone else. They are not parasites, economic minors. They do not condemn "*en bloc*" the consumer society. "One has to consume, but let us consume what we have decided to produce.... We wish to control not only the means of production but also those of consumption—to have a real choice and not a theoretic one."

It is significant that the movement of the students at the Sorbonne —called the movement of the 22 *Mars*—started among sociologists at the newly built extension of the University in the desolate industrial suburb of Nanterre. A long declaration by Cohn-Bendit and some of his colleagues, in *Esprit* (the May number), depicts the sociology students as seeing sociology as a statistical account of existing society, the result of American influence. The very few sociology students who would get jobs after they left the university would be engaged in such activities as making consumer reports. They realized that sociology instead of being an instrument of bourgeois society, could be turned against it to make a revolution and construct a new society. Here the beginnings of an ideology of the students are implicit.

* * *

Inevitably perhaps, the students are unself-critical. They do not notice inconsistencies in their own attitudes, even when, to an outsider, it must seem that these could be disastrous. This struck me when I heard a student who had organized the revolt at Strasbourg University describe his experiences to a great gathering in the Amphitheatre of the Sorbonne. He spoke about the professors with whom the students had to deal with that kind of contempt which is current among some students. He told how he had been asked by someone why he had not explained things adequately to the authorities at his university, and how he had answered: "because one does not enter into discussions with people who are non-existent." People you do not talk to because they are non-existent! Whatever justification there might be for adopting this attitude when confronted with the stuffed geese of Strasbourg, I could not help wondering as I listened how it would work out in the "direct democracy." Supposing—I thought— our student from Strasbourg goes to a factory or to a village where there are peasants, is it not likely that he will meet a few people with attitudes not altogether dissimilar from those he encountered at Strasbourg—people "who understand nothing," (*qui n'ont rien compris*): that was another of his phrases for describing those who did not agree with him? And had not one heard all this before? Did not the Soviets start off very willing to talk to anyone and everyone who agreed with them, and then make the horrible discovery that there were still bourgeois elements floating around, and that there were very recalcitrant peasants, people who understand nothing, people finally whom one stops talking to—or just stops talking? At this point the phrase "*On ne parle pas avec des gens qui n'existent pas*" begins to acquire a sinister ring.

The students are, I emphasize, conscious of these dangers and do not wish to repeat them. I wonder what might happen if someone wrote on the walls of the Sorbonne: "The streets of Hell are paved with good intentions." If it were written there, I wonder how long it would last. I noticed that they are very good at deleting.

CRABBED AGE AND YOUTH CANNOT LIVE TOGETHER

As I left the Odéon Theatre one evening two youths looking more like Dickensian street urchins perhaps than students called to each other: "Why doesn't he cut his hair?" "Perhaps he should tear it out with his nails!" "Perhaps it's a wig!" Respect for white hairs is certainly not one of the dues paid in Paris this May.

Usually, though, the old just feel invisible as the blacks were supposed to do in America. "The young make love, the old obscene gestures," a slogan in the anarchist magazine *L'Enragé* runs. They have read *Romeo and Juliet* it seems, but not *Antony and Cleopatra*.

I observed to a contemporary that I enjoyed, on the whole, my invisibility. He said: "I thought that too until I went one day with my twenty-year-old son to the Sorbonne. I sat there quietly, and as I had to slip out early was specially grateful to be a ghost. But directly I had gone another student came up and said to my son: '*Qui était ce vieux con avec toi?*'"

One night I am at the Odéon, Jean-Louis Barrault's old-style *avant garde* theater which the students have "liberated" and made open for completely unplanned marathon discussions which go on almost till daybreak. The scene is like the sixth act of some play in the Theater of Cruelty in which the audience have rung down the curtain and taken over the house for their own performance. And they find themselves much more entertaining than Ionesco and Beckett, I am afraid. The performance itself—the debates for which there are no subjects set—can be chaotic, and I am often sorry for the student chairmen who stand in the aisle yelling "*Silence! N'interrompez pas! Un peu de l'ordre! Discipline!*"

* * *

Everyone calls everyone "comrade" and most of us here are in the world where the revolution has already happened, although there are also intruding misbelievers, generously admitted, howled at, but nevertheless, despite many interruptions, intermittently, fragmentarily, listened to, because whatever might happen later (and I have these fears), the students are most noble in their attempt to be open to all points of view—even that of Gaullists and of the Fascist members of the "*Occident.*"

On a particular occasion I was suddenly struck with a thought—or a hysterical seizure—that I ought to communicate to the Sorbonne students the fact that when I spoke with the students at Columbia some of them had asked me whether the students at the Sorbonne had any thoughts about them. I was no emissary, I had not been told to say anything, and yet I felt I should transmit this. So comforting myself that with my white hair I would not be listened to anyway, I touched the arm of the particularly vigorous young man who was conducting the audience and, gradually acquiring some of the mannerism of Leonard Bernstein, I mentioned, humbly, that I would like to say a word. There was only one disapprobating yell (which was silenced by the young chairman with a severe "*On a écouté même Jean-Louis Barrault*") and I started to speak my poor French to what seemed an electric silence. To my amazement they listened and then started asking questions. Could I compare the situation of students in American Universities with that in France? One student even offered the opinion that the American students were far more advanced than "ours." Then someone asked whether it was true that all American students were always under the influence of drugs. I struggled to answer these questions and then, at the first opportunity, left the theater and walked to a bar. I was followed there by three students. Then one of them came up to me very shyly and said: "*Monsieur... Monsieur... Est ce que c'est vrai que vous êtes M. Marcuse?*"

When the discussions at the Odéon happened to light on a "subject" they could be serious and very sympathetic. One night a young man got up in the gallery (people spoke from whatever part of the theater they happened to be sitting in) and (with his head, seen by me from below, seeming to butt against André Masson's multi-colored ceiling) he stated very simply that he had taken into his care some adolescent delinquents and that he felt he was having little success in helping them, and he would like to hear the views of the audience about delinquency. At this person after person got up and discussed the problem, seriously, sensibly, though without saying anything new.

It was surprising how many people there turned out to be social workers. The conditions in prisons and slums that they reported were deplorable. The discussion continued on a level of concern and without silliness for over an hour. After which I got up to leave, but was stopped at the exit by a Tunisian student who said to me: "They all talk about the harm prison does people—but to me it did good. I was sent to prison in Tunis, I cried, I cursed, I kicked them and I was beaten, and I prayed all day, but at the end of two years I started writing poems and stories, and for that reason here I am—thanks to prison—at the Sorbonne." "Go and tell them that," I said and followed him back into the theater where, a few minutes later, he made his speech, which, in the telling, turned out to be mostly an attack on President Bourguiba. Still he made his point and ended dramatically: "From prison, I learned that in order to achieve anything in this life you have to suffer...." A remark which offered none of those present any handle to catch on to.

* * *

At this meeting there was a very distinguished German lady philosopher, with whom I went out afterward for a coffee. She punctured euphoria. What she noticed, she said, in all these discussions, was that they consisted of people saying things as though for the first time, and as though they had no continuity with anything said before or to be said after. Moreover what was said came out of ideas we had all read in books anyway, or were ideas snatched from the intellectual atmosphere. She said she thought the real problem was not that the young wanted to have no contact with the old but that, precisely, they lacked contact with truly adult minds. The teachers and older people with whom they had to deal were in fact mentally adolescent. She attributed a good many of the student's attitudes to a shallow nihilism which had been the fashion for a long while. She wondered whether the university had not already been destroyed, and whether it would recover. A university was to her mind not a place where there were only the best teachers but where there were values so pervasive that even an inferior teacher could fit in without letting the standard down.

ANTI-CLIMAX

Journalism inevitably falsifies by concentrating on the scene and the subject, in a situation where what is most significant may be not the scene and not the subject. More important probably than the happenings which I have been describing in Paris in the spring were the non-happenings. Walk a few hundred yards away from one area of the *Quartier Latin* and despite the strikes and the students there was a remarkably normal atmosphere. One way of describing it would be to say that it was like an over-long rather restrained holiday, with welldressed people strolling on the sidewalks, the cafés crowded, the food in restaurants up to its usual standard, and many small shops open. Most foreign tourists, it is true, had gone away, but then Parisians, having nothing else to do, were touring their own city, including the Sorbonne in which the actors were inextricably mixed up with the spectators. The only people who seemed to be notably suffering from shortages (of their clientèle) were the male tarts. I asked one of them what he thought of "*les étudiants*" and he shrieked, with an extraordinary gesture—"*Scandaleux!*"

Dust and dirt from ungathered rubbish exhaled a vague smog, a halo over the streets like old varnish over a new green painting, but the presence of these odors was largely compensated for by the absence of petrol. One had to walk long distances but this was good for health and not much slower than going by car when there is traffic.

The spring itself reasserted what was so much more apparent than the revolutionary situation—the non-revolutionary one. In fact, if there were going to be a revolution, it would be—everyone I think agreed—against the evidence of one's senses which lay down certain external rules for revolutions. The weather, of course, can be contradictory, but it is difficult to think of a revolution taking place when— in daylight at all events—everyone looks particularly good humored. For the result of the explosion of talk in Paris this May was that most people looked more self-complacent—even friendly—than they have done in Paris for years.

* * *

Yet there was that ugly evening which happened after De Gaulle's second speech in which he adroitly substituted for the referendum he had so mistakenly offered in his first speech a referendum under a more resounding name—a General Election. He accompanied this gesture with the release of a flood of gasoline upon which came floating in their automobiles a flood of *Gaullistes*. They came joyously claxoning up the boulevards, hooting at one another, hooting to urge others to hoot, stopping their cars suddenly, getting out to embrace some fellow driver or passenger, in their chic clothes and their make-up, their tawdry elegance, the triumphant bacchanal of the Social World of Conspicuous Consumption, shameless, crowing, and vulgarer than any crowd I have seen on Broadway or in Chicago. It would have been agonizing at the best of times, but it was more so when one thought of the students, the self-condemned secular monastics of the Sorbonne.

The next day the students had a great parade on the Boulevard Montparnasse and it seemed like a farewell. I walked away from it down the Rue de Rennes and saw an extraordinary sight. In the hot sun, the whole road seemed covered with snow. Actually it was torn-up newspapers. I asked a bystander what had happened. "Nothing," she said, "except that France is mad." The students had seen announcements in *France Soir* of the end of the strikes, the end of their movement, and they had scattered hundreds of copies of the newspaper, in fury, all over the road. Oddly enough, with all the fighting and the barricades, it was the first sign I had seen of real anger.

If it were possible to speak to them, I would like to say two things. The first is that however much the university needs a revolution, and the society needs a revolution, it would be disastrous for them not to keep the two revolutions apart in their minds and their acts. For the university, even if it does not conform to their wishes, is an arsenal from which they can draw the arms which can change society. To say, "I won't have a university until society has a revolution," is as though Karl Marx were to say "I won't go the reading room of the British Museum until it has a revolution."

The second thing is that although the young today do have reasons for distrusting the older generation, anything that is worth doing involves their having to get old. What they are now is not so important as what they will be ten years from now. And if ten years from now they have become their own idea of what it is to be old, then what they are fighting for now will have come to nothing.

—July 11, 1968

3

The Corpse at the Iron Gate
V. S. Naipaul

The worst was yet to come when V.S. Naipaul cast his acid eye on Argentina. The "dirty war," the "disappearances," the strutting butchers in uniform, the unmarked Ford Falcons prowling the streets for kidnap and torture victims, all this would be described by Naipaul in a later essay.

The year 1972 was the time of General Alejandro Agustín Lanusse Gelly, the thirty-eighth president of the Argentine Republic. A military junta, to be sure, that tortured its opponents. But the general was also prepared to talk to the revolutionary guerrillas in the hills, who were just as ready to torture or kill in their armed struggle. Meanwhile, the waiting was for the return of Eva Perón, the corpse of the holy redeemer.

Argentina, then, was a country that had lost its way, or perhaps had never even known which way it wished to go, perfect territory for a specialist in lost places, given to violent fantasies, half in love with death.

—*I.B.*

Buenos Aires, April–June 1972

OUTLINE IT LIKE a story by Borges.

The dictator is overthrown and more than half the people rejoice. The dictator had filled the jails and emptied the treasury. Like many dictators, he hadn't begun badly. He had wanted to make his country great. But he wasn't himself a great man; and perhaps the country couldn't be made great. Seventeen years pass. The country is still without great men; the treasury is still empty; and the people are on the verge of despair. They begin to remember that the dictator had a vision of the country's greatness, and that he was a strong man; they begin to remember that he had given much to the poor. The dictator is in exile. The people begin to agitate for his return. The dictator is now very old. But the people also remember the dictator's wife. She loved the poor and hated the rich, and she was young and beautiful. So she has remained, because she died young, in the middle of the dictatorship. And, miraculously, her body has not decomposed.

"That," Borges said, "is a story I could *never* write."

But at seventy-six, and after seventeen years of proscription and exile, Juan Perón, from the Madrid suburb known as the Iron Gate, dictates peace terms to the military regime of Argentina. In 1943, as an army colonel preaching a fierce nationalism, Perón became a power in Argentina; and from 1946 to 1955, through two election victories, he ruled as dictator. His wife Eva held no official position, but she ruled with Perón until 1952. In that year she died. She was expensively embalmed, and now her corpse is with Perón at the Iron Gate.

* * *

In 1956, just one year after his overthrow by the army, Perón wrote from Panama, "My anxiety was that some clever man would have taken over." Now, after eight presidents, six of them military men,

Argentina is in a state of crisis that no Argentine can fully explain. The mighty country, as big as India and with a population of 23 million, rich in cattle and grain, Patagonian oil, and all the mineral wealth of the Andes, inexplicably drifts. Everyone is disaffected. And suddenly nearly everyone is Peronist. Not only the workers, on whom in the early days Perón showered largesse, but Marxists and even the middle-class young whose parents remember Perón as a tyrant, torturer, and thief.

The peso has gone to hell: from 5 to the dollar in 1947, to 16 in 1949, 250 in 1966, 400 in 1970, 420 in June last year, 960 in April this year, 1,100 in May. Inflation, which has been running at a steady 25 percent since the Perón days, has now jumped to 60 percent. Even the banks are offering 24 percent interest. Inflation, when it reaches this stage of take-off, is good only for the fire insurance business. Premiums rise and claims fall. When prices gallop away week by week fires somehow do not often get started.

For everyone else it is a nightmare. It is almost impossible to put together capital; and even then, if you are thinking of buying a flat, a delay of a week can cost you two or three hundred US dollars (many business people prefer to deal in dollars). Salaries, prices, the exchange rate: everyone talks money, everyone who can afford it buys dollars on the black market. And soon even the visitor is touched by the hysteria. In two months a hotel room rises from 7,000 pesos to 9,000, a tin of tobacco from 630 to 820. Money has to be changed in small amounts; the market has to be watched. The peso drops one day to 1,250 to the dollar. Is this a freak, or the beginning of a new decline? To hesitate that day was to lose: the peso bounced back to 1,100. "You begin to feel," says Norman Thomas di Giovanni, the translator of Borges, who has come to the end of his three-year stint in Buenos Aires, "that you are spending the best years of your life at the money-changer's. I go there some afternoons the way other people go shopping. Just to see what's being offered."

The blanket wage rises that the government decrees from time to time—15 percent in May, and another 15 percent promised soon—cannot keep pace with prices. "We've got to the stage," the ambassador's wife says, "when we can calculate the time between the increase in wages and the increase in prices." People take a second job and sometimes a third. Everyone is obsessed with the need to make more money and at the same time to spend quickly. People gamble. Even in the conservative Andean town of Mendoza the casino is full; the patrons are mainly work-people, whose average monthly wage is the equivalent of $50. The queues that form all over Buenos Aires on a Thursday are of people waiting to hand in their foot-ball-pool coupons. The announcement of the pool results is a weekly national event.

* * *

A spectacular win of some 330 million pesos by a Paraguayan laborer dissipated a political crisis in mid-April. There had been riots in Mendoza, and the army had been put to flight. Then, in the following week, a guerrilla group in Buenos Aires killed the Fiat manager whom they had kidnapped ten days earlier. On the same day, in the nearby industrial town of Rosario, guerrillas ambushed and killed General Sánchez, commander of the Second Army Corps, who had some reputation as a torturer. Blood called for blood: there were elements in the armed forces that wanted then to break off the negotiations with Perón and scotch the elections promised next year. But the Paraguayan's fortune lightened all conversation, revived optimism, and calmed nerves. The little crisis passed.

The guerrillas still raid and rob and blow up; they still occasionally kidnap and occasionally kill. The guerrillas are young and middle class. Some are Peronist, some are communist. After all the bank raids the various organizations are rich. In Córdoba last year, according to my information, a student who joined the Peronist *Montoneros* was paid the equivalent of $70 a month; lawyers were retained at $350. "You could detect the young *Montoneros* by their motocars, their aggressiveness, their flashiness. James Dean types. Very glamorous." Another independent witness says of the guerrillas he has met in Buenos Aires: "They're anti-American. But one of them held a high job in an American company. They have split personalities; some of them really don't know who they are. They see themselves as a kind of comic-book hero. Clark Kent in the office by day, Superman at night, with a gun."

> Once you take a decision [the thirty-year-old woman says] you feel better. Most of my friends are for the revolution and they feel much better. But sometimes they are like children who can't see too much of the future. The other day I went with my friend to the cinema. He is about thirty-three. We went to see *Sacco and Vanzetti.* At the end he said, "I feel ashamed not being a *guerrillero.* I feel I am an accomplice of this government, this way of life." I said, "But you lack the violence. A *guerrillero* must be *despejado*—he mustn't have too much imagination or sensibility. You have to do as you are told. If not, nothing comes out well. It is like a religion, a dogma." And again he said, "Don't you feel *ashamed*?"

The filmmaker says,

> I think that after Marx people are very conscious of history. The decay of colonialism, the emergence of the Third World— they see themselves acting out some role in this process. This is as dangerous as having no view of history at all. It makes people very vain. They live in a kind of intellectual cocoon. Take away the jargon and the idea of revolution, and most of them would have nothing.

The guerrillas look for their inspiration to the north. From Paris of 1968 there is the dream of students and workers uniting to defeat the enemies of "the people." The guerrillas have simplified the problems of Argentina. Like the campus and salon revolutionaries of the north, they have identified the enemy: the police. And so the social-intellectual diversions of the north are transformed, in the less intellectually stable south, into horrible reality. Dozens of policemen have been killed. And the police reply to terror with terror. They too kidnap and kill; they torture, concentrating on the genitals. A prisoner of the police jumps out of a window: *La Prensa* gives it a couple of inches. People are arrested and then, officially, "released"; sometimes they reappear, sometimes they don't. A burned-out van is discovered in a street one morning. Inside there are two charred corpses: men who had been hustled out of their homes two days before. "In what kind of country are we living?" one of the widows asks. But the next day she is calmer; she retracts the accusation against the police. Someone has "visited" her.

* * *

"Friends of friends bring me these stories of atrocities," Norman di Giovanni says, "and it makes you sick. Yet no one here seems to be amazed by what's going on." "My wife's cousin was a *guerrillero*," the provincial businessman says at lunch. "He killed a policeman in Rosario. Then, eight months ago, he disappeared. *Está muerto*. He's dead." He has no more to say about it; and we talk of other matters.

On some evenings the jack-booted soldiers in black leather jackets patrol the pedestrian shopping street called Florida with their Alsatians: the dogs' tails close to their legs, their shoulders hunched, their ears thrown back. The police Chevrolets prowl the neon-lit streets unceasingly. There are policemen with machine-guns everywhere. And there are the mounted police in slate-gray; and the blue-helmeted antiguerrilla motorcycle brigade; and those young men in well-cut suits who appear suddenly, plainclothesmen, jumping out of unmarked cars. Add the army's AMX tanks and Alouette helicopters. It is an impressive apparatus, and it works.

It is as if all the energy of the state now goes into holding the state together. Law and order has become an end in itself: it is part of the Argentine sterility and waste. People are brave; they torture and are tortured; they die. But these are private events, scattered, muffled by the size of the city (Greater Buenos Aires has a population of eight million) and the size of the country, muffled by a free but inadequate press that seems incapable of detecting a pattern in the events it reports. And perhaps the press is right. Perhaps very little of what happens in Argentina is really news, because there is no movement forward; nothing is being resolved. The nation appears to be playing a game with itself; and Argentine political life is like the life of an ant community or an African forest tribe: full of events, full of crises and deaths, but life is only cyclical, and the year always ends as it begins. Even General Sánchez didn't, by his death, provoke a crisis. He tortured in vain, he died in vain. He simply lived for fifty-three years and, high as he was, has left no trace. Events are bigger than the men. Only one man seems able to impose himself, to alter history now as he altered it in the past. And he waits at the Iron Gate.

Passion blinded our enemies [Perón wrote in 1956] and destroyed them....The revolution [that overthrew me] is without a cause, because it is only a reaction....The military people rule, but no one really obeys. Political chaos draws near. The economy, left to the management of clerks, gets worse day by day and...anarchy threatens the social order....These dictators who don't know too much and don't even know where they are going, who move from crisis to crisis, will end by losing their way on a road that leads nowhere.

* * *

The return of Perón, or the triumph of Peronism, is anticipated. It has been estimated that already between six and eight thousand million dollars have been shipped out of the country by Argentines. "People are not involved," the ambassador's wife says. "And you must remember that anybody who has money is not an Argentine. Only people who don't have money are Argentines."

But even at the level of wealth and security, even when escape plans have been drawn up, even, for instance, at this elegant dinner party in the Barrio Norte, passion breaks in. "I'm *dying*," the lady says abruptly, clenching her fists. "I'm dying—I'm dying—I'm dying. It isn't a life any longer. Everybody clinging on by their fingertips. This place is *dead*. Sometimes I just go to bed after lunch and stay there." The elderly butler wears white gloves; all the paneling in the room was imported from France at the turn of the century. (How easy and quick this Argentine aristocracy, how brief its settled life.) "The streets are dug up, the lights are dim, the telephones don't answer." The marijuana ($45 for the last half-kilo) passes; the mood does not alter. "This used to be a great city and a great port. Twenty years ago. Now it's fucked up, baby."

For intellectuals and artists as well, the better ones, who are not afraid of the outside world, there is this great anxiety of being imprisoned in Argentina and not being able to get out, of having one's creative years wasted by a revolution in which one can have no stake, or by a bloody-minded dictatorship, or just by chaos. Inflation and the crash of the peso have already trapped many. Menchi Sábat, the country's most brilliant cartoonist, says, "It is easier for us to be on the moon by TV. But we don't know Bolivia or Chile or even Uruguay. The reason? Money. What we are seeing now is a kind of collective frenzy. Because before it was always easy here to get money.

Now we are isolated. It isn't easy for people outside to understand what this means."

The winter season still begins in May with the opera at the Colón Theater; and orchestra seats at $21 are quickly sold out. But the land has been despoiled of its most precious myth, the myth of wealth, wealth once so great, Argentines tell you, that you killed a cow and ate only the tongue, and the traveler on the pampa was free to kill and eat any cow, providing only that he left the skin for the land-owner. Is it eight feet of topsoil that the humid pampa has? Or it it twelve? So rich, Argentina; such luck, with the land.

In 1850 there were fewer than a million Argentines; and Indian territory began 100 miles west and south of Buenos Aires. Then, less than a hundred years ago, in a six-year carnage, the Indians were sought out and destroyed; and the pampa began to yield its treasure. Vast *estancias* on the stolen, bloody land: a sudden and jealous colonial aristocracy. Add immigrants, a labor force: in 1914 there were eight million Argentines. The immigrants, mainly from Northern Spain and Southern Italy, came not to be smallholders or pioneers but to service the *estancias* and the port, Buenos Aires, that served the *estancias*. A vast and flourishing colonial economy, based on cattle and wheat, and attached to the British Empire; an urban pro-letariat as sudden as the *estancia* aristocracy; a whole and sudden artificial society imposed on the flat, desolate land.

* * *

Borges, in his 1929 poem, "The Mythical Founding of Buenos Ai-res," remembers the proletarian spread of the city:

Una cigarrería sahumó como una rosa el desierto. La tarde se había ahondado en ayeres, los hombres compartieron un pa-sado ilusorio. Sólo faltó una cosa: la vereda de enfrente.

Which in Alastair Reid's translation becomes:

> A cigar store perfumed the desert like a rose. The afternoon had
> established its yesterdays, And men took on together an illusory
> past. Only one thing was missing—the street had no other
> side. *A mí se me hace cuento que empezó Buenos Aires: La juzgo*
> *tan eterna como el agua y el aire.* Hard to believe Buenos Aires
> had any beginning. I feel it to be as eternal as air and water.

The half-made city is within Borges's memory. Now, already, there is
decay. The British Empire has withdrawn *ordenadamente*, in good
order; and the colonial agricultural economy, attempting haphazardly
to industrialize, to become balanced and autonomous, is in ruins.
The artificiality of the society shows: that absence of links between
men and men, between immigrant and immigrant, aristocrat and
artisan, city dweller and *cabecita negra*, the "blackhead," the man
from the interior; that absence of a link between men and the meaningless flat land. And the poor, who are Argentines, the sons and
grandsons of those recent immigrants, will now have to stay.

They have always had their *curanderos* and *brujas*, thaumaturges
and witches; they know how to protect themselves against the ghosts
and poltergeists with which they have peopled the alien land. But
now a larger faith is needed, some knowledge of a sheltering divinity.
Without faith these abandoned Spaniards and Italians will go mad.

At the end of May a Buenos Aires church advertised a special mass
against the evil eye, *el mal de ojo*. "If you've been damaged, or if you
think you are being damaged, don't fail to come." Five thousand city
people turned up, many in motorcars. There were half a dozen stalls
selling holy or beneficent objects; there were cubicles for religious-
medical consultations, from thirty cents to a dollar a time. It was a
little like a Saturday morning market. The officiating priest said,

"Every individual is an individual source of power and is subject to imperceptible mental waves which can bring about ill-health or distress. This is the visible sign of the evil spirit."

"I can never believe we are in 1972," the publisher-bookseller says. "It seems to me we are still in the year zero." He isn't complaining; he himself trades in the occult and mystical, and his business is booming. Argentine middle-class mimicry of Europe and the United States, perhaps. But at a lower level the country is being swept by the new enthusiastic cult of *espiritismo*, a purely native affair of mediums and mass trances and miraculous cures, which claims the patronage of Jesus Christ and Mahatma Gandhi. The *espiritistas* don't talk of mental waves; their mediums heal by passing on intangible beneficent "fluids." The *espiritistas* say they have given up politics; and they revere Gandhi for his nonviolence. They believe in reincarnation and the perfectibility of the spirit. They say that purgatory and hell exist now, on earth, and that man's only hope is to be born on a more evolved planet. Their goal is that life, in a "definitive" disembodied world, where only superior spirits congregate.

* * *

Despair: a rejection of the land, a dream of nullity. But someone holds out hope; someone seeks to resanctify the land. With Perón at the Iron Gate is José López Rega, who has been his companion and private secretary for the last thirty years. Rega is known to have mystical leanings and to be interested in astrology and *espiritismo*; and he is said to be a man of great power now. An interview with him fills ten pages of a recent issue of *Las Bases*, the new Peronist fortnightly. Argentines are of many races, Rega says; but they all have native ancestors. The Argentine racial mixture has been "enriched by Indian blood" and "Mother Earth has purified it all.... I fight for liberty," Rega goes on, "because that's how I am made and because I feel stirring within me the blood of the Indian, whose land this is."

Now, for all its vagueness and unconscious irony, this is an astonishing statement, because, until this crisis, it was the Argentine's pride that his country was not "niggered-up" like Brazil or mestizo like Bolivia, but European; and it was his special anxiety that outsiders might think of Argentines as Indians. Now the Indian ghost is invoked, and a mystical, purifying claim is made on the blighted land.

Other people offer, as they have always offered, political and economic programs. Perón and Peronism offer faith.

* * *

And they have a saint: Eva Perón. "I remember I was very sad for many days," she wrote in 1952 in *La Razón de mi Vida* ("My Life's Cause"), "when I discovered that in the world there were poor people and rich people; and the strange thing is that the existence of the poor didn't cause me as much pain as the knowledge that at the same time there were people who were rich." It was the basis of her political action. She preached a simple hate and a simple love. Hate for the rich: "Shall we burn down the Barrio Norte?" she would say to the crowds. "Shall I give you fire?" And love for "the common people," *el pueblo*: she used that word again and again and made it part of the Peronist vocabulary. She levied tribute from everyone for her Eva Perón Foundation; and she sat until three or four or five in the morning in the Ministry of Labor, giving away Foundation money to suppliants, dispensing a personal justice. This was her "work": a child's vision of power, justice, and revenge.

She died in 1952, when she was thirty-three. And now in Argentina, after the proscribed years, the attempt to extirpate her name, she is a presence again. Her pictures are everywhere, touched up, seldom sharp, and often they seem deliberately garish, like religious pictures meant for the poor: a young woman of great beauty, with blonde hair, a very white skin, and the very red lips of the 1940s.

She was of the people and of the land. She was born in 1919 in Los

Toldos, the dreariest of pampa small towns, built on the site of an Indian encampment, 150 flat miles west of Buenos Aires. The town gives an impression of flatness, of total exposure below the high sky. The dusty brick houses, red or white, are low, flat-fronted, and flat-roofed, with an occasional balustrade; the *paraíso* trees have white-washed trunks and are severely pollarded; the wide streets, away from the center, are still of dirt.

She was illegitimate; she was poor; and she lived for the first ten years of her life in a one-room house, which still stands. When she was fifteen she went to Buenos Aires to become an actress. Her speech was bad; she had a country girl's taste in clothes; her breasts were very small, her calves were heavy, and her ankles thickish. But within three months she had got her first job. And thereafter she charmed her way up. When she was twenty-five she met Perón; the following year they married.

Her commonness, her beauty, her success: they contribute to her sainthood. And her sexiness. "*Todos me acosan sexualmente,*" she once said with irritation, in her actress days. "Everybody makes a pass at me." She was the *macho*'s ideal victim-woman—don't those red lips still speak to the Argentine *macho* of her reputed skill in fel-latio? But very soon she was beyond sex, and pure again. At twenty-nine she was dying from cancer of the uterus, and hemorrhaging through the vagina; and her plumpish body began to waste away. Toward the end she weighed 80 pounds. One day she looked at some old official photographs of herself and began to cry. Another day she saw herself in a long mirror and said, "When I think of the trouble I went to to keep my legs slim! *Ahora que me veo estas piernitas me asusto.* Now it frightens me to look at these matchsticks."

* * *

But politically she never weakened. The Peronist revolution was go-ing bad. Argentina's accumulated wartime wealth was running low;

the colonial economy, unregenerated, plundered, mismanaged, was beginning to founder; the peso was falling; the workers, to whom so much had been given, were not always loyal. But she still cherished her especial pain that "there were people who were rich." Close to death, she told a gathering of provincial governors, "We mustn't pay too much attention to people who talk to us of prudence. We must be fanatical." The army was growing restive. She was willing to take them on. She wanted to arm the trade unions; and she did buy, through Prince Bernhard of the Netherlands, 5,000 automatic pistols and 1,500 machine-guns, which, when they arrived, Perón, more prudent, gave to the police.

And all the time her private tragedy was being turned into the public passion play of the dictatorship. For her, who had turned Peronism into a religion, sainthood had long been decreed; and there is a story that for fifteen days before her death the man who was to embalm her was with her, to ensure that nothing was done that might damage the body. As soon as she died the embalming contract was signed. Was it for $100,000 or $300,000? The reports are confused. Dr. Ara, the Spanish embalmer—"a master," Perón called him—had first to make the body ready for a fifteen-day lying-in-state. The actual embalming took six months. The process remains secret. Dr. Ara, according to a Buenos Aires newspaper, has devoted two chapters of his memoirs (which are to be published only after his death) to the embalming of Eva Perón; color pictures of the corpse are also promised. Reports suggest that the blood was first replaced by alcohol, and then by heated glycerine (Perón himself says "paraffin and other special matter"), which was pumped in through the heel and an ear.

"I went three times to look at Evita," Perón wrote in 1956, after his overthrow, and when the embalmed body had disappeared. "The doors...were like the gates of eternity." He had the impression that she was only sleeping. The first time he went he wanted to touch her, but he feared that at the touch of his warm hand the body would turn to dust. Ara said, "Don't worry. She's as whole (*intacta*) now as when she was alive."

And now, twenty years later, her embalmed wasted body, once lost, now found, and no bigger, they say, than that of a twelve-year-old girl, only the blonde hair as rich as in the time of health, waits with Perón at the Iron Gate.

* * *

It came as a surprise, this *villa miseria* or shantytown just beside the brown river in the Palermo district, not far from the great park, Buenos Aires's equivalent of the Bois de Boulogne, where people go riding. A shantytown, with unpaved streets and black runnels of filth, but the buildings were of brick, with sometimes an upper story: a settled place, more than fifteen years old, with shops and signs. Seventy thousand people lived there, nearly all Indians, blank and slightly imbecilic in appearance, from the north and from Bolivia and Paraguay; so that suddenly you were reminded that you were not in Paris or Europe but South America. The priest in charge was one of the "Priests for the Third World." He wore a black leather jacket and his little concrete shed of a church, oversimple, rocked with some amplified Argentine song. It had been whispered to me that the priest came of a very good family; and perhaps the change of company had made him vain. He was of course a Peronist, and he said that all his Indians were Peronist. "Only an Argentine can understand Peronism. I can talk to you for five years about Peronism, but you will never understand."

But couldn't we try? He said Peronism wasn't concerned with economic growth; they rejected the consumer society. But hadn't he just been complaining about the unemployment in the interior, the result of government folly, that was sending two Indians into his shantytown for every one that left? He said he wasn't going to waste his time talking to a *norteamericano*; some people were concerned only with GNP. And, leaving us, he bore down, all smiles, on some approaching Indians. The river wind was damp, the concrete shed unheated, and I wanted to leave. But the man with me was uneasy. He said we should at least wait and tell the father I wasn't an American. We did so. And the father, abashed, explained that Peronism was really concerned with the development of the human spirit. Such a development had taken place in Cuba and China; in those countries they had turned their backs on the industrial society.

* * *

These lawyers had been represented to me as a group working for "civil rights." They were young, stylishly dressed, and they were meeting that morning to draft a petition against torture. The top-floor flat was scruffy and bare; visitors were scrutinized through the peep-hole; everybody whispered; and there was a lot of cigarette smoke. Intrigue, danger. But one of the lawyers was diverted by my invitation to lunch, and at lunch—he was a hearty and expensive eater—he made it clear that the torture they were protesting against wasn't to be confused with the torture in Perón's time.

He said: "When justice is the justice of the people men sometimes commit excesses. But in the final analysis the important thing is that justice should be done in the name of the people." Who were the enemies of the people? His response was tabulated and swift. "American imperialism. And its native allies. The oligarchy, the dependent bourgeoisie, Zionism, and the 'sepoy' left. By sepoys we mean the Communist Party and socialism in general." It seemed a comprehensive list. Who were the Peronists? "Peronism is a revolutionary national movement. There is a great difference between a movement and a party. We are not Stalinists, and a Peronist is anyone who calls himself a Peronist and acts like a Peronist."

The lawyer, for all his anti-Jewish feeling, was a Jew; and he came of an anti-Peronist middle-class family. In 1970 he had met Perón in Madrid, and he had been dazzled; his voice shook when he quoted Perón's words. He had said to Perón, "General, why don't you declare war on the regime and then put yourself at the head of all the true Peronists?" Perón replied: "I am the conductor of a national movement. I have to conduct the whole movement, in its totality."

"There are no internal enemies," the trade union leader said, with a smile. But at the same time he thought that torture would continue in Argentina. "A world without torture is an ideal world." And there was torture and torture. "*Depende de quién sea torturado*. It depends on who is tortured. An evildoer, that's all right. But a man who's trying to save the country—that's something else. Torture isn't only the electric prod, you know. Poverty is torture, frustration is torture." He was urbane; I had been told he was the most intellectual of the Peronist trade union leaders. He had been punctual; his office was uncluttered and neat; on his desk, below glass, there was a large photograph of the young Perón.

The first Peronist revolution was based on the myth of wealth, of a land waiting to be plundered. Now the wealth has gone. And Peronism is like part of the poverty. It is protest, despair, faith, machismo, magic, *espiritismo*, revenge. It is everything and nothing. Remove Perón, and hysteria will be uncontrollable. Remove the armed forces, sterile guardians of law and order, and Peronism, triumphant, will disintegrate into a hundred scattered fights, every man identifying his own enemy.

"Violence, in the hands of the people, isn't violence: it is justice." This statement of Perón's was printed on the front page of a recent issue of *Fe*, a Peronist paper. So, in sinister mimicry, the south twists the revolutionary jargon of the north. Where jargon turns living issues into abstractions ("Torture will disappear in Argentina," the Trotskyite said, "only with a workers' government and the downfall of the bourgeoisie"), and where jargon ends by competing with jargon, people don't have causes. They only have enemies; only the enemies are real. It has been the South American nightmare since the break-up of the Spanish Empire.

* * *

Was Eva Perón blonde or brunette? Was she born in 1919 or 1922? Was she born in the little town of Los Toldos, or in Junín, 40 kilometers away? Well, she was a brunette who dyed her hair blonde; she was born in 1919 but said 1922 (and had her birth record destroyed in 1945); she spent the first ten years of her life in Los Toldos but ever afterward disclaimed the town. No one will know why. Don't go to her autobiography, *La Razón de mi Vida*, which used to be prescribed reading in Argentine schools. That doesn't contain a fact or a date; and it was written by a Spaniard, who later complained that the book he wrote had been much altered by the Peronist authorities.

So the truth begins to disappear; it is not relevant to the legend. Masses are held in Eva Perón's memory, and students now turn up in numbers; but her life is not the subject of inquiry. Unmarked, seldom visited (though a woman remembers that once some television people came), the one-room house in brown brick in Los Toldos crumbles. The elderly garage-owner next door (two vehicles in his garage, one an engineless Model T), to whom the house now belongs, uses it as a storeroom. Grass sprouts from the flat roof, and the corrugated-iron roof collapses over the patio at the back.

Only one biography of Eva Perón has been attempted in Argentina. It was to be in two volumes, but the publisher went bankrupt and the second volume hasn't appeared. Had she lived, Eva Perón would now be only fifty-three. There are hundreds of people alive who knew her. But in two months I found it hard to get beyond what was well known. Memories have been edited; people deal in panegyric or hate, and the people who hate refuse to talk about her. The anguish of those early years at Los Toldos has been successfully suppressed. The Eva Perón story has been lost; there is now only the legend.

One evening, after his classes at the Catholic University, and while the police sirens screamed outside, Borges told me,

> We had a sense that the whole thing should have been forgotten. Had the newspapers been silent there would have been no Peronism today—the *Peronistas* were at first ashamed of themselves. If I were facing a public audience I would never use his name. I would say *el prófugo*, the fugitive, *el dictador*. The way in poetry one avoids certain words—if I used his name in a poem the whole thing would fall to pieces.

It is the Argentine attitude: suppress, ignore. Many of the records of the Peronist era have been destroyed. If today the middle-class young are Peronists, and students sing the old song of the dictatorship—

> *Perón, Perón, qué grande sos! Mi general, cuánto valés!*
> (Perón, Perón, how great you are! How good and strong, my general!)

—if the dictatorship, even in its excesses, is respectable again, it isn't because the past has been investigated and the record modified. It is only that many people have revised their attitudes toward the established legend. They have changed their minds.

* * *

There is no history in Argentina. There are no archives, there are only graffiti and polemics and school lessons. Schoolchildren in white dustcoats are regularly taken round the Cabildo building in the Plaza de Mayo in Buenos Aires to see the relics of the War of Independence. The event is glorious; it stands in isolation; it is not related, in the textbooks or in the popular mind, to what immediately followed: the loss of law, the seeking out of the enemy, endless civil wars, gangster rule.

Borges said on another evening, "The history of Argentina is the history of its separateness from Spain." How did Perón fit into that? "Perón represented the scum of the earth." But he surely also stood for something that was Argentine? "Unfortunately, I have to admit that he's an Argentine—an Argentine of today." Borges is a *criollo*, someone whose ancestors came to Argentina before the great immigrant rush, before the country became what it is; and for the contemplation of his country's history Borges substitutes ancestor worship. Like many Argentines, he has an idea of Argentina; anything that doesn't fit into this is to be rejected. And Borges is Argentina's greatest man.

An attitude to history, an attitude to the land. Magic is important in Argentina; the country is full of witches and magicians and thaumaturges and mediums. But the visitor must ignore this side of Argentine life because, he is told, it isn't real. The country is full of *estancias*; but the visitor musn't go to that *estancia* because it isn't typical. But it exists, it works. Yes, but it isn't real. Nor is that real, nor that, nor that. So the whole country is talked away; and the visitor finds himself directed to the equivalent of a Gaucho curio shop. It isn't the Argentina that anyone inhabits, least of all one's guides; but *that* is real, *that* is Argentina. "Basically we all love the country," an Anglo-Argentine said. "But we would like it to be in our own image. And many of us are now suffering for our fantasies." A collective refusal to see, an absence of inquiry, an inability to come to terms with the land: an artificial, fragmented colonial society, made deficient and bogus by its myths.

* * *

To be Argentine was not to be South American. It was to be European; and many Argentines became European, of Europe. The land that was the source of their wealth became no more than their base. For these Argentine-Europeans Buenos Aires and Mar del Plata became resort towns, with a seasonal life. Between the wars there was a stable Argentine community of 100,000 in Paris; the peso was the peso then.

"Many people think," Borges said, "that quite the best thing that could have happened here would have been an English victory [in 1806–7, when the British twice raided Buenos Aires]. At the same time I wonder whether being a colony does any good—so provincial and dull."

But to be European in Argentina was to be colonial in the most damaging way. It was to be parasitic. It was to claim—as the white communities of the Caribbean colonies claimed—the achievements and authority of Europe as one's own. It was to ask less of oneself (in Trinidad, when I was a child, it was thought that the white and the rich needed no education). It was to accept, out of a false security, a second-rateness for one's own society.

And there was the wealth of Argentina: the British railways taking the wheat and the meat from all the corners of the pampa to the port of Buenos Aires, for shipment to England. There was no pioneer or nationmaking myth of hard work and reward. The land was empty and very flat and very rich; it was inexhaustible; and it was infinitely forgiving. *Dios arregla de noche la macana que los Argentinos hacen de día*: God puts right at night the mess the Argentines make by day.

To be Argentine was to inhabit a magical, debilitating world. Wealth and Europeanness concealed the colonial realities of an agricultural society which had needed little talent and had produced little, which had needed no great men and had produced none. "Nothing *happened* here," Norman di Giovanni said with irritation one day. And everyone, from Borges down, says, "Buenos Aires is a small town." Eight million people: a monstrous plebeian sprawl, mean, repetitive, and meaningless: but only a small town, eaten up by colonial doubt and malice. When the real world is felt to be outside, everyone at home is inadequate and fraudulent. A waiter in Mendoza said, "Argentines don't work. We can't do anything big. Everything we do is small and petty." An artist said, "There are very few *professionals* here. By that I mean people who know what to do with themselves. No one knows why he is doing any particular job. For that reason if you are doing what I do, then you are my enemy."

Camelero, chanta: These are everyday Argentine words. A *camelero* is a line-shooter, a man who really has nothing to sell. The man who promised to take me to an *estancia*, and in his private airplane, was only doing *camelo*. The *chanta* is the man who will sell everything, the man without principles, the hollow man. Almost everybody, from the president down, is dismissed by somebody as a *chanta*.

The other word that recurs is *mediocre*. Argentines detest the mediocre and fear to be thought mediocre. It was one of Eva Perón's words of abuse. For her the Argentine aristocracy was always mediocre. And she was right. In a few years she shattered the myth of Argentina as an aristocratic colonial land. And no other myth, no other idea of the land, has been found to take its place.

—August 10, 1972

4

Sad Brazil
Elizabeth Hardwick

Ernesto Geisel was by no means the worst military strongman in the history of Brazil. The son of German Lutherans, Geisel— white hair, big glasses, benign smile—looked more like a bank manager in a provincial German town. He promised to restore Brazil to democratic rule and to stop torturing political opponents. Although a staunch enemy of communism, Geisel established relations with China.

Geisel came to power in 1974, the year that Elizabeth Hardwick visited. It was not an especially good time. For the oil crisis, sparked by US support of Israel in the Yom Kippur War, put a severe damper on Brazil's remarkable economic growth, from more than 10 percent a year to half that. This made for a melancholy mood.

Not that Hardwick found the combination of stern paternalism and economic boosterism—ever bigger, ever richer, ever more—any less melancholic. The gulf between aspiration and reality, between super-rich and dirt-poor, was too glaring. And so she turned for solace to that masterpiece about the biggest country in Latin America: Tristes Tropiques.

—I.B.

LARGENESS, MAGNITUDE, QUANTITY: it is commonplace to speak of Brazil as a "giant," a phenomenon spectacular, propitiously born, outrageously favored, and yet marked by the sluggishness of the greatly outsized. And so the giant is not quite on his toes, but always thought of as rising from the thicket of sleep, the jungle of rest, coming forth from the slumbering dawn of undisturbed nature. This signaling, promissory vastness is the curse of the Brazilian imagination. Prophecies are like the fall of great trees in a distant forest. They tell of a fabulous presence still invisible, scarcely audible, and yet surely moving amid the waving silence of real possibility.

Brazil—remember the opening of *Tess of the D'Urbervilles*? The D'Urberville father with his rickety legs, his empty egg basket, his patched hat brim, is addressed on the road as "Sir John" because the parson has discovered that he is a lineal representative of the ancient, noble family of the D'Urbervilles. Brazil is a lineal representative of Paradise, the great, beckoning garden of delicious surfeit—a sweet place, always *to be* blessed. In Brazil the person stands surrounded by a mysterious ineffable plenitude. He lives in a grand immensity and he partakes of it as one partakes of thereness, of a magical placement in the scheme of nature. Small he may be, but the immensity is true. His own emptiness is close to the bone and yet the earth is filled with the precious and semi-precious in prodigious quantity, with unknown glitters and granites, with sleeping minerals—silvery-white, ductile. These confer from their deep and gorgeous burial a special destiny. This is the land of dreams.

Think of the words and their resonance—*grande, grosso, Amazonia*. Numbers enhance, glorify, impress: larger than the continental United States, excluding Alaska, and slightly larger than the great bulk of Europe lying east of France. Its borders flow and curve and scallop to the Guineas, Uruguay, Paraguay, Bolivia, Argentina, Peru, Colombia, Venezuela. Out of this expanding, encroaching, bordering, nudging sovereignty, life reaches for a peculiar consolation and hope. Where there is isolation, loneliness, and backwardness, where the tangle of life chokes with the complexity of blood and region, where torpor, negligence, and a strange historical lassitude simply and finally confuse—there even the worst is thought of as an unredeemed promise, not an implacable lack. Delay, not unalterable natural deprivation, is the worm in the heart of the rose.

* * *

Growth is mystical. The ignominious military rulers carry it as a banner. They kill, torture, repress in the name of the great, floating, swelling, primordial dream. The jungle, the historic, romantic coffee and sugar plantations, the crazy rubber Babylon of Manaus falling into ruin way up the Amazon, the marble shards of its opera house: all of that, the military seems to say, is folly, a siesta slump of some nodding mestizo, the old tropical slack.

A beggar, bereft, a leprous bundle of ancient Brazilian backwardness, a tatter of the rags, an eruption of the sores of underdevelopment: there he sits against an "old" 1920 wall of Sao Paulo. Without a doubt, he, shrunken as he is, salutes the punctured skyline, salutes the new buildings that from the air have the strange look of some vibrating necropolis of megalomaniac tombs and memorial shafts—all, like our own, enshrouded in a thick, inhuman vapor. Around the somnolent beggar the cars whir in a thick, migrating stream. And there it is, magic visible, vastness palpable, quantity realized, things delivered.

Yes, all will be filled, all will be new, tall, thrusting, collective, dominating, rapid, exhausting, outsized like the large, stalky watercress, the big, round tasteless tomatoes grown by the inward, enduring will of the Japanese farmers. It is an emanation, sacred; and yet, of course, a mean, mocking paradox, for this "growth" now seems an anachronistic mode—embracing late what has elsewhere been created early and has turned into a puzzle and challenge and menace.

Poor Brazil: the beginning and the end meet in a tragic collusion and collision. Still it must be as it is. There is indeed no other way. No one will consent to turn back.

In Brazil the presence of a great, green density makes the soul long to create a gray, smooth highway. Thus Corbusier in 1929 saw Rio, radiant, and said, "I have a strong desire, a bit mad perhaps, to attempt here a human adventure—the desire to set up a duality, to create 'the affirmation of man' against or with 'the presence of nature.' " The affirmation was to be a huge motor freeway. Underdevelopment, rest, nature turn the inspiration to engineering. Glory in Brazil is glory elsewhere, a vast junk heap of Volkswagens, their horns stuck for eternity. The new world rises from the hole in the ground where once stood a mustard-colored, decorated stucco with its little garden. Buildings, offices, hotels: in the swimming pools beautiful butterflies float in their blue-tiled graves. The mellifluousness of the tropics—birds, hammers, the high hum of traffic.

* * *

The endless, aching shore lines. Life under the Great Southern Cross. Cruzero du Sul: under the blazing sky or the hanging humidity a resurrection of steel, stones; the transfiguration of metals, of dollars and yen. And death to students, to culture, to the young, the teacher, the writer, the priest, the radical, the democrat, the guerrilla, the humorous, the theatrical, the mocking, the generous, the reporter, the political past. The pastoral, romantic world of Gilberto Freyre, with the masters and slaves in a humid comingling, the old stately prints of the family and servants trailing, single file, in dramatic dresses and hairbands, to the plantation chapel. The land and its murky history are buried under the devastation of death squads with their motorized units, their electric prods, their "methods," their Nordic interrogations, DOPS (Department of Public Order and Safety), decompression. Words fill a vacancy, the hole in the heart of the Brazilian government. No desire to heal, to warm, only to rule without pity.

I had been here for some months in 1962 and now in 1974 I returned—to see what? It was a time of celebration for the military regime. *They* had ruled for ten years and yes his time had come. Geisel, the new president, stands in the pictures; he is colorless, as ice is colorless, a white, still representative of the Will. No need to seduce, attract, or solicit; this Will has been chosen by the previous Will. He moves into his spot, as a large block of ice shifts in the floe. Glacial emptiness, oppressive, his wife and daughter, impenetrable, large, no claim to please. There only the arctic will, its white face shielded by dark glasses, as if to filter, darken, shadow the tropical light and the color of its multitudinous, chaotic, brazen hoard of persons, insects, slums, its alive sufferings. This country with its marvelous people, its mad cars, its noise, its insane building, its amorous languors, its sinuously rich chic, its longings, its poverty: before the dark glasses of Geisel all seems to pass as before the blind. Prosperity flows to the chosen and to those who have more shall be given.

For the rest, the huge remainder, their time has not yet come. History still will not consent to touch so many ignorant, hungry, dying-early persons of this land. Those who are moved to concern and pity glow in the white military coldness with menacing fire—they must be destroyed. But then it is not uncommon to hear that torture has become "boring." One brave old lady predicted that it would be replaced by murder, disappearance, gun shots in the streets. So it has proved to be. The idea of human sacrifice—a profane and secular purification rite, practiced in the name of progress, investment, and the holy "Growth"—has left the country a ruin. The land is rich in heroes created by the military Will.

A small card sent out by the family of a young student killed by the police:

Consummatus in brevi, explecit tempora multa
Tendo vivido pouco, cumpriu a tarefa de una longa existen-
cia. Profundamente sensibilizada, a familia de JOSE CARLOS
NOVAIS DA MATA-MACHADO agradece a solidariedade
recebida por ocasian da sua morta.
(Having lived little [1946–1973] he accomplished the task of
a long existence.)

* * *

The beautiful Rio landscape: thick, jutting rocks, which Lévi-Strauss
thought of as "stumps left at random in the four corners of a tooth-
less mouth." *Tristes Tropiques* is to me the second most interesting
book about Brazil.[*] Like the first, *Os Sertoes* (*Rebellion in the Back-
lands*) by Euclides da Cunha, it is scientific, philosophical, personal,
a quest for the past, the country, for oneself, for Brazil, a quest carried out with an intense and almost painful concentration. The late
(Lévi-Strauss) surely learned from the early (da Cunha).

The pictorial in Brazil consumes the imagination; leaf and scrub,
seaside and backlands long for their apotheosis as word. Otherwise it
is as if a great part of the earth lay silent, unrealized. Your own sense
of yourself is threatened here and, thus, speculative description seizes
the mind and by surrender to it a sort of tranquility comes. Strange
that the landscape should be so drenched in philosophical questions.

Speaking of the towns in the state of Paraná, Lévi-Strauss writes:

And then there was that strange element in the evolution of so
many towns: the drive to the west which so often leaves the

---

*My quotations are from the 1961 (Atheneum) translation of *Tristes Tropiques* done by
John Russell. A new edition based on the 1969 revised French edition and translated by
John and Doreen Weightman was published by Atheneum in February 1974.

eastern part of the towns in poverty and dereliction. It may be merely the expression of that cosmic rhythm which has possessed mankind from the earliest times and springs from the unconscious realization that to move with the sun is positive, and to move against it is negative; the one stands for order, the other for disorder. It's a long time since we ceased to worship the sun; and with our Euclidean turn of mind we jib at the notion of space as qualitative.

Naturally, the military government has laid waste to the freedom and distinction of the University of Sao Paulo and the University of Brasilia, places scarcely venerable in terms of age and yet the best the country had to offer. At a freer time, Lévi-Strauss left France in 1934 and went to teach in Sao Paulo and from there to travel into the interior of Brazil, to follow his anthropological studies of various Indian groups. A French mind, ambitious, abstract, learned and yet almost violently open, as one may speak of violence at the moment when a mind and spirit assault and engulf their subject—this mind met the obstinate, dazed fact of Brazil. And immediately Lévi-Strauss conveys to us that sense of things standing in an almost amorous stillness, so piercing and stirring is the way Brazil seduces the imagination. Standing still—or when moving somehow arduously turning in a circle that sets the foreign mind on edge, agitates thought of possibility, of meaning, of past and future.

* * *

And always Brazil lies before you, even now, demanding to be named, to have its prophecy explicated, its dream and memory honored. *Tristes Tropiques* is literally a memory, written fifteen years after Lévi-Strauss left Brazil for the last time. It is a work of Brazilian anthropology, with its strangely and grandly speculative intensity about the Caduveo, the Bororo, the Nambikwara. But it is anthropology that lives like a kernel in the shell of Brazil. The trembling search for metaphor and the pull, always downward, to despair, to a weight of doleful contradiction: these tell you exactly where you are.

The body painting, leather and pottery designs of the Caduveo seem to Lévi-Strauss to represent a profound and striking sophistication. This elaboration is a part of his quest, his spectacular journey of self-definition:

> The dualism, to begin with, which recurs over and over again, like a hall of mirrors, men and women, painting and sculpture, abstraction and representation, angle and curve, border and centerpiece, figure and ground. But these antitheses are glimpsed *after* the creative process, and they have a static character.

The Caduveo and their style of representation—hierarchical, still, symbolic in the manner of playing cards—will inevitably call forth in Lévi-Strauss's mind a sense of "structural" kinship with things far away in time and place. But in the beautiful and bitter isolation of Brazil, the configurations are not only united by longing or innate design in man's mind to the plains of Asia or North Dakota, they are united and standing in their setting. Here it is the town of Nalike, on the grassy plateau of the Mato Grosso. And we feel, so unlike a merely investigative work are these remarkable chapters, everywhere among the Indians an absorbed, special French investigator, creating in a hut next to a witch doctor his youth, his exemplary personal history and intellectual voyage.

Great indeed is the fascination of this culture, whose dream-life was pictured on the faces and bodies of its queens, as if, in making themselves up, they figured a Golden Age they would never know in reality. And yet as they stand naked before us, it is as much the mysteries of that Golden Age as their own bodies that are unveiled.

* * *

The mysteries of the Golden Age. When Lévi-Strauss traveled to Brazil in 1934 and later, fleeing the Nazi occupation in 1941, he found, one might say, in Brazil this great autobiographical moment, found it as if it were an object hidden there, perhaps a rock with its ornate inscriptions and elaborate declamations waiting to be translated into personal style. The book is a deciphering, one of many kinds. In one way it is a magical and profound answering of the descriptive and explicatory demand this odd country has at certain times made upon complex talents like Lévi-Strauss and da Cunha.

What is created is a work of science, history, and a rational prose poetry, springing out of the multifariousness of the landscape, its mysterious adaption or maladaption to the human beings crowding along the coast or surviving in small clusters elsewhere. Lévi-Strauss was only twenty-six when he first went to Brazil. He is far from home but the conditions are brilliantly right. He is in the new world and it is ready to be his as Europe, Africa, or Asia could not be. This newness, freshness, the exhilaration of the blank pages are like the map of Brazil waiting to be filled—this brings with it an intense literary inspiration. He is deep, also, in his professional studies; everything is right, everything can be used. When the passage grates it is still *material*. The two French exiles in their decaying, sloppy *fazienda* on the edge of the Caduveo region, a glass of maté, the old European avenues of Rio, the town of Goiânia: he speculates, observes, places, re-creates with a sort of waterfall of beautiful images.

It is the brilliance of his writing at this period that is Lévi-Strauss's greatest, deepest preparation for his journey through the Amazon basin and the upland jungles. He is pursuing his studies, but he is also creating literature. The pause before the actual writing was begun, when he was forty-seven, is a puzzle; somehow he had to become forty-seven before the real need for the inspiration of his youth presented itself once more. It was all stored away, clear, shining, utterly immediate. Often he quotes from the notes he made on the first trip and always, seem to have brought back the mode, the mood also, and to have carried the parts written later along on the same pure, uncluttered flow.

A luminous moment recorded by pocket-lamp as he sat near the fire with the dirty, diseased, miserable men and women of the Nambikwara tribe. He sees these people, lying naked on the bare earth, trying to still their hostility and fearfulness at the end of the day. They are a people "totally unprovided for" and a wave of sympathy flows through him as he sees them cling together in the only support they have against misery and against "their meditative melancholy." The Nambikwara are suddenly transfigured by a pure, benign light:

> In one and all there may be glimpsed a great sweetness of nature, a profound nonchalance, an animal satisfaction as ingenuous as it is charming, and beneath all this, something that came to be recognized as one of the most moving and authentic manifestations of human tenderness.

* * *

In one way *Tristes Tropiques* is a record, not a life. There is nothing of love, of family, of personal memory in it, and little of his roots in France. At the same time, the work is soaked in passionate remembrance and it does tell of a kind of love—the great projects of a great man's youth. It is the classical journey, taken at the happy moment. Every step has its trembling drama; all has meaning, beauty, and the mornings and evenings, the passage from one place to another, are fixed in a shimmering, vibrating present.

And it is no wonder that *Tristes Tropiques* begins: "Travel and travelers are two things I loathe..." and ends, "Farewell to savages, then, farewell to journeying!" The mood of the journey has been one of youth and yet, because it is Brazil, the composition is a nostalgic one. At the end there is a great sadness. The tropics are *triste*. "Why did he come to such a place? And to what end? What, in point of fact, *is* an anthropological investigation?" How poignant it is to remember that often in places "few had set eyes upon" and living among unknown people, how often he would feel his own past stab him with thoughts of the French countryside or of Chopin. This is the pain of the journey, the hurting knock of one place against another.

Lévi-Strauss was in his youth, moving swiftly in his first great exploration, and yet what looms up out of the dark savannahs is the suffocating knowledge that so much has already been lost. Even among the unrecorded, the irrecoverable and the lost are numbing. The wilderness, the swamps, the little encampments on the borders, the overgrown roads that once led to a mining camp: even this, primitive still and quiet, gives off its air of decline, deterioration, displacement. The traveler never gets there soon enough. The New World is rotting at its birth. In the remotest part, there, too, a human bond with the past has been shattered. *Tristes Tropiques* tells of the anguish the breakage may bring to a single heart.

* * *

Breakage—you think of it when the plane lets you down into the bitter fantasy called Brasilia. This is the saddest city in the world and the main interest of it lies in its being completely unnecessary. It testifies to the Brazilian wish to live without memory, to the fatigue every citizen of Rio and Sao Paulo must feel at having always to carry with him those implacable Brazilian others: the unknowable, accusing kin of the northeast, the back-lands, the *favelas*. If you send across, the miles and miles the stones and glass and steel, carry most of it by plane, and build a completely new place to stand naked, blind and blank for your country (*Brasilia*, diminutive of the whole place, sharing its designation), you are speaking of the unbearable burden of the past. Brazilians are always fleeing their past and those capitals that stand for the collective history; they move from Bahia to Rio and now to Brasilia. This new passage the crossing, is one of the starkest in history. It is a sloughing off, thinning out, abandoning, moving on like some restless settler in the veld seeking himself. At last, in Brasilia there is the void.

It is colder, drearier in 1974 than in 1962. Building, building everywhere, so that one feels new structures are as simply produced as Kleenex, In every direction, on the horizon, in the sky, the buildings stand, high, neat, blank. Each great place leads to a highway. There are strictly speaking no streets and thus no village or corner life. Utter boredom, something like a resort which has no real season. A soulless place, a prison, a barracks. Rigidity, boredom, nothing. Try to take a walk around the main hotel. Even if there were a place you wanted for pleasure to get to, you must drive. *There are no streets*, you tell yourself again, as if perhaps it was something in Portuguese you misunderstood. Around you are roadways, wide, smooth, full of cars.

The military likes Brasilia. It is their Brazil. Nothing to do with the sad tropics, with the heart of history. So here in the deadness, in the agitating quiet of this city without memory, you remind yourself that this is the dead center. Everything indeed comes from this clean, silent tomb. There is nothing without its consent: no killing, no deaths in the street of young people brought back from Chile, no maiming, no interrogation and torture in the nude of Catholic lay women, seized in their night classes for adult workers.

* * *

There is no place to go. You came to see if it had changed and it had not, except downward. So back to the hotel room, on a red-dirt, desert plain. Relief comes in reading once more the great prose work,

Rebellion in the Backlands, by da Cunha. It is a peculiar epic, military, mournful, seized with the old idea that there is a Brazil somewhere; it must be described. Its flowers, leaves, scrub, its thirsting cows and its drinking tapirs. And a tragic battle between 1896 and 1898, when an ill-prepared military expedition went out from the capital of Bahia to subdue a band of ragged religious fanatics.

—June 27, 1974

5

Letter from South Africa
Nadine Gordimer

June 16 is now a public holiday in South Africa, known as Youth Day. That day in 1976 is when children, most of them from schools in Soweto, the sprawling black township of Johannesburg, gave their elders a lesson in courage.

The moment oppressive regimes begin to show cracks is the moment when people stop being intimidated by the violence. That moment came in South Africa when the schoolkids of Soweto marched in protest against being forced to learn Afrikaans, "the language of the oppressor" in Bishop Tutu's words.

The cause was almost incidental, one out of many grievances worthy of protest. What mattered was that the protesters kept protesting even when the police, aided by helicopters and armored cars, killed the children with guns and attack dogs. They refused to be cowed. It was the government of Apartheid that showed its fear by shooting unarmed children. And that was the beginning of its end.

—I.B.

I FLEW OUT of Johannesburg on a visit abroad two and a half months after the first black school child was killed by a police bullet in Soweto. Since June 16, when the issue of protest against the use of the Afrikaans language as a teaching medium in black schools, long ignored by the white authorities, finally received from them this brutal answer, concern had been the prevailing emotion in South Africa.

Concern is an over-all bundle of like feelings in unlike people: horror, distress, anguish, anger—at its slackest manifestation, pity.

There was no white so condemnatory of black aspirations, so sure of a communist plot as their sole source, that he or (more likely) she didn't feel "sorry" children had died in the streets. Black children traditionally have been the object of white sentimentality; it is only after the girls grow breasts and the boys have to carry the passbook that chocolate suddenly turns black.

There was no black so militant, or so weary of waiting to seize the day, that he or she did not feel anguish of regret at the sacrifice of children to the cause. Not even a mighty rage at the loathed police could block that out.

* * *

I was away for the month of September. Henry Kissinger came to South Africa to discuss the Rhodesia settlement with Mr. Vorster; six children were killed while demonstrating against his presence. A day or two after I arrived home in October, a girl of fifteen was shot by police at the Cape. The six were already merely a unit of the (disputed) official figures of the dead (now 358), some adult but in the main overwhelmingly the young, in unrest that has spread from blacks to those of mixed blood, and all over the country by means of arson, homemade bomb attacks, boycotts, and strikes. The fifteen-year-old girl was added to the list of fatalities; no one, I found, was shocked afresh at the specific nature of this casualty: the killing of a child by a police bullet.

Like the passing of a season, there was something no longer in the air. People had become accustomed, along with so much else unthinkable, to the death of children in revolt.

* * *

I try to recognize and set out the reasons for this acclimation before daily life here, however bizarre, makes me part of it.

When striking children met the police that Wednesday morning in June in the dirt streets of Soweto and threw stones that promptly drew bullets in return, who would have believed that the terrible lesson of white power would not be learned? The lesson for these children wasn't free, any more than their school-books are (white children get theirs for nothing); they paid with the short lives of some of their number. No one could conceive they would ever present themselves again, adolescent girls bobbing in gym frocks, youths in jeans, little barefoot boys with shirts hanging out as in a wild game of cops and robbers—to police who had shown they would shoot real bullets. But the children did. Again and again. They had taken an entirely different lesson: they had learned fearlessness.

Of course, white attitudes toward them began to change, even then. It was immediately assumed by the government and the majority of white people that since the issue of the Afrikaans language had been quickly conceded, and the children now demanded the abolition of the entire separate educational system for blacks, and then bluntly "everything whites get," such intransigence must be the work of agitators. Among black people—among the outlawed liberation organizations inside and outside the country, and those perforce confined to balancing cultural liberation on a hair's breadth of legality within it—all began to claim credit for the first popular uprising since the early Sixties. No one will know, for years perhaps, how to apportion the influence of the banned African National Congress and Pan-Africanist Congress—their leadership in prison and exile—

in the development of schoolchildren's defiance into the classic manifestations of a general uprising.

Neither can one measure how much of the children's determined strategy was planned by older students of the black university-based South African Students' Organization. There surely were—there are—agitators; if agitators are individuals able and articulate enough to transform the sufferings and grievances of their people into tactics for their liberation. There surely was—there is, has never ceased to be—the spirit of the banned political movements in the conceptual political attitudes and sense of self, passing unnamed and without attribution to their children from the tens of thousands who once belonged to the mass movements.

* * *

What neither the accusations of the white government nor the claims of black adult leadership will ever explain is how those children learned, in a morning, to free themselves of the fear of death.

Revolutionaries of all times, who know this is the freedom that brings with it the possibility of attaining all others, have despaired of finding a way of teaching it to more than a handful among their trained cadres. To ordinary people it is a state beyond understanding. We knew how to feel outrage or pity when we saw newspaper photographs of the first corpses of children caught by the horrible surprise of a death nobody believed, even in South Africa, would be meted out by the police. Blacks still burn with an anger whose depth has not yet been fathomed—it continues to show itself as it did at the Soweto funeral of Dumisani Mbatha, sixteen, who died in detention. Seven hundred mourners swelled to a crowd of 10,000 youths that burned 100,000 rands worth of the Johannesburg municipality's vehicles and buildings. Yet—not without bewilderment, not without shame—black people have accepted that the weakest among them are the strongest, and thus by grim extension also accept the inconceivable: the death of children and adolescents has become a part of the struggle.

We whites do not know how to deal with the fact of this death when children, in full knowledge of what can happen to them, continue to go out to meet it at the hands of the law for which we are solely responsible, whether we support white supremacy or, opposing, have failed to unseat it.[1]

> When you make men slaves you deprive them of half their virtue, you set them in your own conduct an example of fraud, rapine and cruelty, and compel them to live with you in a state of war....
> —Olaudah Equiano, eighteenth-century black writer

White people have turned away from concern to a matter-of-fact preoccupation with self-protection. A Johannesburg parents' committee has a meeting to discuss whether or not teachers at a suburban school should be armed, as they might once have planned a school fête. I bump into a friend who tells me, as if he were mentioning arrangements for a cattle show, that he and fellow farmers from a district on the outskirts of Johannesburg are gathering next day to set up an early warning system among themselves—one of them uses a two-way radio for cattle control, the gadget may come in handy.

---

1. The South African Institute of Race Relations in Johannesburg released on November 8 the following analysis gleaned from cases reported in the national press between June 16 and October 31: 1,200 people have already stood trial. Three thousand are facing trials not yet completed. Of the 926 juveniles tried and convicted, 528 have been given corporal punishment, 397 have received suspended sentences or fines, and one has been jailed. The minister of justice's figure of 697 people detained for "security reasons" is broken down thus: 123 held under the Internal Security Act without charges pending against them; 217 held under the Terrorism Act who will either be brought to trial or released; 34 detained as witnesses; 323 held in cases "relating to security."

Now it is not only the pistol-club matrons of Pretoria who regard guns as necessary domestic appliances. At the house of a liberal white couple an ancient rifle was produced the other evening, the gentle wife in dismay and confusion at having got her husband to buy it. Gunsmiths have long waiting lists for revolvers; 50 percent of small arms come illegally from Iron Curtain countries who call for a total arms embargo against South Africa at the UN.

Certainly, in that house a gun was an astonishing sight. Pamphlets appear with threats to whites and their children; although the black movements repudiate such threats, this woman feels she cannot allow her anti-apartheid convictions to license failure to protect her children from physical harm. She needn't have felt so ashamed. We are all afraid. How will the rest of us end up? Hers is the conflict of whites who hate apartheid and have worked in "constitutional" ways to get rid of it. The quotes are there because there's not much law-abiding virtue in sticking to a constitution like the South African one, in which only the rights of a white minority are guaranteed. Gandhi had our country in mind when he wrote, "The convenience of the powers that be is the law in the final analysis."

* * *

My friend Professor John Dugard, Dean of the Faculty of Law at the Witwatersrand University, says that if whites do not show solidarity with blacks against apartheid, their choice is to "join the white *laager* or emigrate." Few, belonging to a country that is neither in the Commonwealth nor the Common Market, have the chance to emigrate. Of the *laager*—armed encampment—my friend David Goldblatt, the photographer, says to me: "How can we live in the position where, because we are white, there's no place for us but thrust among whites whose racism we have rejected with disgust all our lives?"

There is not much sign that whites who want to commit themselves to solidarity with blacks will be received by the young anonymous blacks who daily prove the hand that holds the stone is the whip hand. They refuse to meet members of the Progressive-Reform Party, who, while assuming any new society will be a capitalist one, go farther than any other white constitutional group in genuine willingness to share power with blacks. They will not even talk to white persons (there are still no white parties that recognize the basic principle of Western democracy although they would all call themselves upholders of the Western democratic system) who accept one man one vote and the rule by a black majority government as the aim of any solidarity, and understand, as John Dugard puts it, that "the free enterprise system is not the only system" to be discussed.

The black moderate Chief Gatsha Buthelezi, whose position as a Bantustan leader fiercely attacking the government that appointed him has made him exactly the figure—legal but courageous—to whom whites have talked and through whom they hope to reach blacks, lately is reported to have made a remark about "white ultra-liberals who behave as though they are making friends with the crocodile so they will be the last to be eaten." He also said, "Nobody will begrudge the Afrikaner his heritage if it is no threat to the heritage and freedom of other people." It seems old white adversaries might be accepted but white liberals will never be forgiven their inability to come to power and free blacks.

Nevertheless, I don't think the whites he referred to would be those with the outstanding fighting record of Helen Suzman, let alone radical activists like Beyers Naude of the Christian Institute, and others, of the earlier generation of Bram Fischer, who have endured imprisonment and exile alongside blacks in the struggle.

* * *

If fear has taken over from concern among whites, it has rushed in to fill a vacuum. In nearly six months, nothing has been done to meet the desperate need of blacks that seems finally to have overcome every threat of punishment and repression: the need, once and for all and no less, to take their lives out of the hands of whites. The first week of the riots, Gatsha Buthelezi called for a national convention and the release of black leaders in prison to attend it. As the weeks go by in the smell of burning, the call for a national convention has been taken up by other Bantustan leaders, black urban spokesmen, the press, the white political opposition. After five months, the prime minister, Mr. Vorster, answered: "There will be no national convention so far as this government is concerned." Most of the time he leaves comment to his minister of justice, police, and prisons, Mr. Jimmy Kruger. The only attempt to deal with a national crisis is punitive. It is Mr. Kruger's affair. He continues to project an equation that is no more than a turn of phrase: "South Africa will fight violence with violence."

Three hundred and sixty people have died, of whom two were white. The police, who carry guns and still do not wear riot-protective clothing but army camouflage dress and floppy little-boy hats that could be penetrated by a slingshot, have not lost a single man.

Neither the prime minister nor his minister in charge of black lives, M.C. Botha (Bantu Administration, Development and Education), has yet talked to urban black leaders more representative than members of the collapsed Urban Bantu Councils. (They do not have normal municipal powers.) On their own doleful admittance, these are dubbed "Useless Boys' Clubs" by the youths who run the black townships now.

* * *

Of the black leaders whom the vast majority of urban blacks would give a mandate to speak for them, Nelson Mandela and his lieutenants Walter Sisulu and Govan Mbeki, of the banned African National Congress, are still imprisoned for life on Robben Island. Robert Sobukwe of the Pan-Africanist Congress is banished to and silenced in a country town.

Black intellectuals who might stand in for these have been detained one by one, even while whites of unlikely political shades continue to affirm a fervent desire to talk to blacks, just *talk* to them—as if 300 years of oppression were a family misunderstanding that could be explained away, and as if everyone did not know, in the small dark room where he meets himself, exactly what is wrong with South African "race relations."

The government leaders refuse to meet the Black People's Convention, perhaps in the belief that by not recognizing Black Consciousness organizations the power of blacks to disrupt their own despised conditions of life and (at the very least) the economy that sustains the white one will cease to exist. Fanonist theory of the black man as an image projected upon him by the white man takes a new twist; the white man goes to the door of his shop in central Johannesburg one September morning this year and fails to recognize the black man marching down the street shouting, in his own image, "This is our country."

The government won't speak to the Black Parents' Association, formed originally to finance the burial of Soweto children in June. In this ghastly bond, the association moved on under the leadership of Nelson Mandela's wife and Dr. Manas Buthelezi, an important Black Consciousness leader about to be consecrated Lutheran Bishop of Johannesburg. It became a united front combining youthful black consciousness inspiration with the convictions of older people who followed the African National Congress and Pan-Africanist Congress.

Finally, the government does not consider speaking to the militant students themselves who are still effectively in leadership, sometimes preventing their parents from going to work (two successful strikes in Johannesburg). Daily and determinedly, they pour into the gutters the shebeen liquor they consider their elders have long allowed themselves to be unmanned by.

Meanwhile, since June 926 black schoolchildren have received punishments ranging from fines or suspended sentences to jail (five years for a seventeen-year-old boy) and caning (five cuts with a light cane for an eleven-year-old who gave the black power salute, shouted at the police, and stoned a bus). They are some of the 4,200 people charged with offenses arising out of the riots, including incitement, arson, public violence, and sabotage. Many students are also among the 697 people, including Mrs. Winnie Mandela, detained in jail for "security reasons"; the other week one hanged himself by his shirt in the Johannesburg prison, an old fort two kilometers from the white suburban house where I write this.[2] Several students, not twenty years old, have just begun that reliable apprenticeship for African presidents, exile and education in Britain. When, in September, Mr. Vorster met blacks with whom he *will* talk—his appointed Bantustan leaders—he would not discuss urban unrest or agree to a national conference of blacks and whites to decide what ought to be done about it.

There is a one-man commission of inquiry into the riots, sitting now. Mr. Justice Cillie, the white judge who constitutes it, complains that few people actually present at these events have volunteered evidence. In fact, the schoolchildren and students themselves boycott it, and for the rest, South Africans' faith in the efficacy of commissions to lead to positive action has long gone into the trash basket along with the recommendations the government steadily rejects. The Cil-

---

2. The South African Institute of Race Relations in Johannesburg released on November 8 the following analysis gleaned from cases reported in the national press between June 16 and October 31: 1,200 people have already stood trial. Three thousand are facing trials not yet completed. Of the 926 juveniles tried and convicted, 528 have been given corporal punishment, 397 have received suspended sentences or fines, and one has been jailed.

The minister of justice's figure of 697 people detained for "security reasons" is broken down thus: 123 held under the Internal Security Act without charges pending against them; 217 held under the Terrorism Act who will either be brought to trial or released; 34 detained as witnesses; 323 held in cases "relating to security."

lie Commission keeps extending the period in which it will sit, as the riots continue to be part of the present and not a matter of calm recollection. January 27 next year is the latest limit announced. Historical analogies are easily ominous. But a commission of inquiry was Czar Nicholas II's way of dealing with the implications of the "unrest" of Bloody Sunday, the beginning of the 1905 revolution.

* * *

A chain-store owner whose business has been disrupted by strikes and the gutting of a store has burst out of the conventions of his annual report to shareholders to say, "Decades of selfishness and smugness by South African whites is the principal reason for widespread unrest among blacks."

Yet most changes suggested by whites do not approach a call for a national convention, with its implication of a new constitution and the end of white supremacy. Black certainty that *nothing* will bring equality without power is dismantled by whites into component injustices they can admit and could redress without touching the power structure. The Federated Chamber of Industries calls for job "reservations" discriminating against blacks in industry to be ended, and has the support of the most powerful trade union group and the opposition parties. The National Development and Management Foundation goes farther and calls for the ending of business and residential apartheid as well. Afrikaner big business, government supporters all, in their *Afrikaanse Handelsinstituut* ask for blacks to be given "greater" rights in their own urban areas and training to increase their skills.

Although the Progressive-Reform Party has demanded a national convention and the release of all people from detention, it was still necessary, before its 1976 congress agreed to change its education policy to enforced desegregation, for Helen Suzman to remind rank-and-file members that the separate-but-equal dictum for education had been "thrown out by the United States twenty years ago."

With unprecedentedly strong criticism of the government coming from its own newspapers and prominent Afrikaners as well as the opposition, it is baffling to read that at the same time 60 percent of whites—an increase of 5 percent over the majority gained by the government in the 1974 election—support Mr. Vorster's National Party. The reliability of this particular poll is in some doubt; but perhaps the contradiction is not so unlikely after all. It is possible to see a dire necessity for change and fear it so greatly that one runs to give oneself to the father figure who will forbid one to act.

* * *

For months the white political opposition parties—Progressive-Reform, United Party, and Democratic Party—have been trying to agree to some sort of realignment. If a liberal front comes about, it will trample the old sand castle fort of the United Party, the conservative official parliamentary opposition, already eroded by the departure of most of its politically vigorous members to the Progressive-Reform Party.

The numerical strength of such a front cannot be measured until it is known whether a major part of the United Party, which still polled 31.49 percent in the 1974 elections, will enter it alongside the Progressive-Reform Party, in the last few years grown from a pressure group to a real presence in parliament, with twelve seats and 6.25 percent of the vote. (The crankish Democratic Party has a minute following.) Only when the extent of United Party commitment is revealed will it be possible to estimate roughly what percentage of the 40 percent who voted against the government in the last election are liberals. There are rumors that some disaffected *verlaigte* ("enlightened") National Party MPs may defect to the front too.

The declared aim of the front is to protect the rights of whites while giving Blacks, Coloreds, and Indians a direct say in government—which careful phrasing suggests its policy will be to the right of the present Progressive-Reform Party. The spectral raison d'être of such a realignment is surely not the chance of ousting Vorster's government but of getting ready a white "negotiating party" to treat with blacks on a shared power basis when he finds he can no longer govern. The viewpoint of enlightened white politics now includes urgently the wide angle of acceptability to blacks, although they have no vote to be wooed. When Mr. Vorster can no longer govern, it is not likely any other white government will be able to.

No one knows whether the Bantustan leaders are, in their different circumstances, preparing themselves for a particular role on that day. They meet at a Holiday Inn at Johannesburg's airport, exactly like Holiday Inns all over the world, down to its orgy-sized beds and cozy smell of French fried potatoes piped along with muzak, but deriving its peculiar status as neutral country outside apartheid from the time when it was the first hotel here to be declared "international": not segregated—for foreign blacks, anyway.

From there the Bantustan leaders demand "full human rights for blacks and not concessions." With the exception of the Transkei and Bophutha Tswana—the former having celebrated the homeland brand of independence on October 26, the latter soon to do so—they reject ethnic partitions of South Africa. Which means they walk out on the many-mansions theory of apartheid, abandoning the white government which set them up inside; and they identify themselves as part of the liberation movement for an undivided South Africa. They present themselves to the black population in general as *black* leaders, not tribal leaders. Is this a bid for power? If Nelson Mandela were to come back from the prison island, would they step aside for him? Has the most imposing of them, Gatsha Buthelezi, a following cutting across his Zulu tribal lines?

Whites believe so. He attracts large audiences when he speaks in cosmopolitan black townships. Many blacks say no; and the African

National Congress in exile continues to deride the Bantustan leaders as collaborators, making no exceptions. Other blacks imply that the best of the Bantustan men are keeping warm the seats of leaders in prison. Among politically articulate blacks, this year's is their (Southern hemisphere) hot summer of brotherhood. Tsietsi Mashinini, the student leader who fled the police to exile in Britain, suggests that the tremendous force his movement shows itself to represent is loyal to Mandela. It does not seem to matter to blacks whether it is a Gatsha Buthelezi or anyone else who is the one to say to whites, as he has, "The future is a Black future and we Blacks want our future now."

* * *

From the Market Theatre, newly opened in what was the Covent Garden of Johannesburg, comes a strange echo—Cucurucu, Kokol, Polpoch, and Rossignol, asylum clowns in Peter Weiss's *Marat/Sade*, singing: "*Give us our rights...and we don't care how—We want—our re-vo-lu-tion—NOW.*" The author granted performances on condition everyone could see the work and has donated his royalties to a Soweto riot victims fund. His play has never been performed before in a city atmosphere such as ours, it has never been heard as we hear it.

During the "quiet" years of successful police repression, before the young emptied the Dutch courage of shebeens down the drain and sent through people's veins the firewater of a new spirit, there have been political trials in progress continually in South Africa. Not only those of blacks who have left the country for military training and re-entered illegally, but also those reflecting aspects of the struggle against apartheid carried on by an intellectual elite.

While the riots have been taking place, two young white university lecturers in Cape Town have given the black power clench and, avowing "no regrets," have accepted long sentences under the Terrorism and Internal Security acts; their uncompromising personal suffering serves as proof of solidarity with blacks that must be granted even by those whites who abhor the white far left. In Johannesburg I have been to hear the trial of four white university students and a lecturer accused of trying "to change South Africa" by organizing black workers, who have no recognized trade unions. The five were charged under the Suppression of Communism Act, and the state's principal evidence consisted of papers read at a seminar.

The backs of these young men in blue jean outfits suggested a pop group; but when they turned in the witness stand it was not to greet fans but to smile at the wife of one of them, whose hands, while she followed the proceedings, were working at a complicated length of knitting—the danger of active dissent does make risk of imprisonment part of the daily life of courageous people. Yet I felt events had overtaken them. The segregated public gallery was almost empty of white and black spectators. The struggle was a few miles away in the streets of Soweto.

But it is another trial, which has gone on almost two years, that seems to have the opposite relation to present events. Four years ago, the nine black members of the South African Students' Organization accused under the Terrorism Act seemed to the ordinary public, black and white, to represent a radical fringe movement on the far side of the generation gap. The state's evidence against them was literary and clumsily esoteric—it consisted of black plays in the idiom of New York black theater of seven years ago, mimeographed Black Consciousness doggerel that couldn't compete with comic books, poetry readings that surely could appeal only to the educated young.

The paper flowers of literary rhetoric have come alive in the atmosphere of tragic exaltation and discipline that can't be explained.

* * *

In the city streets of Johannesburg black people go about their white-town working lives as they always did: the neat clerks, waiters in their baggy parody of mess dress, dashing messengers in bright helmets on motor scooters, shop-cleaners, smart girls who make tea in offices or shampoo the clients' hair in white hairdressing salons. Polished shoes, clean clothes; and most of the time, when the youngsters don't stop them from boarding township trains, people get to work every day.

How do they do it? Daily life in Soweto is in hellish disruption. One-third of the country's school-leavers may not be able to write the final exams of the school year that ends in December; not all schools in the Johannesburg area have reopened. Those that have function irregularly, either because militant pupils stop classes, or teachers suspected of sympathetic alignment with them are detained. Buses and trains don't run when stoning and burning start; commuters crush into the big old American cars that serve as taxis or walk to stations outside the area. No one knows when his neighbor's house may cave in, set alight because he is a policeman. If he himself owns a precious car, it too may burn, should he be suspected of being, or even be mistaken for, some less obvious form of collaborator.

While we white people picnic, Sundays are the most dreadful days of all in Soweto: funerals, the only category of public gathering not banned, have become huge mass meetings where the obsequies of the riot victim being buried are marked by new deaths and fresh wounds as the police attack mourners singing freedom songs and shaking black power salutes. A black intellectual whose commitment to liberation no one would question, although he risks the violent disapproval of blacks by still having contact with whites, tells me, "When I go home tonight, I don't know which to be more afraid of—the police getting me when they shoot at anything that moves, or my own people getting me when I walk across the yard to the lavatory."

* * *

White Johannesburg appears as it always was. Across the veld to the southwest Soweto has been severed from the city, to drift in its fury and misery. Refuse, carted away in municipal vehicles that are vulnerable symbols of white rule, is collected when it can be. The Johannesburg medical officer of health has warned of possible outbreaks of measles and diptheria in Soweto, and the reappearance of poliomyelitis; the white doctors and nurses who staffed most clinics have had to be withdrawn. It is no longer safe for any white to enter there. Only the white police go in; stand guard, their chrome whiplash aerials giving away the presence of riot squad cars and men in leaf-spattered jumpsuits at the crossroads where Soweto leads to Johannesburg. And the black workers come out every morning and go back every night, presenting faces that won't distress the white city.

What may the clean, ironed clothes and calm faces carry concealed, of disease and violence, to a city that has cut such things loose from itself?

Postscript

A Johannesburg newspaper asks if I will accept nomination for the "Woman of the Year." I decline. Someone else will have that honor, perhaps even a black woman from the small black professional elite. But this year the only candidates are surely Winnie Mandela, who came out of house arrest to stand between the police and the schoolchildren and be imprisoned, or any one of the black township women who have walked beside their marching children, carrying water to wash the tear gas from their eyes.

—December 9, 1976

6

Liverpool: Notes from Underground
Caroline Blackwood

It was called, after Shakespeare's Richard III, *"the Winter of Discontent," the winter of 1978–1979, when constant strikes almost brought Britain to a standstill.*

Labour was still in power, under James Callaghan. Inflation had run as high as 26.9 percent in 1975. To bring inflation down, the trade unions were asked—no, almost begged—to limit the demand for higher wages to about 5 percent.

First it was the workers at Ford Motors, who wanted 25 percent. Then came the transport workers, who wanted the same; then the truck drivers; then workers in the public sector. Airports closed, schools closed, houses went unheated. Even hospital nurses went on strike. And finally, the gravediggers joined in too.

They had some success. Wages did go up above 5 percent. But one day after the dateline of Caroline Blackwood's piece, Margaret Thatcher became the new prime minister of Britain.

—I.B.

AS AN EXCELLENT example of a topic with which he would choose to open any committee meeting, Harold Macmillan once suggested "a debate on the implications of a possible gravediggers' strike." This would dissipate the emotional energies of the committee members, allowing Macmillan to get his way on any subsequent matters he cared more about.

An English gravediggers' strike is no longer a possibility. It is a fact. In Liverpool, Manchester, Newcastle, and numerous northern provincial towns no one was buried in the public cemeteries for nearly three weeks. The gravediggers went on strike for higher pay against the elected "council" that runs each of these towns. Liverpool was "most gravely affected," the BBC news reporter said—an unintended pun. When I left Liverpool in early March the city had hundreds of bodies decomposing. The mortuaries, the hospitals, the funeral homes, or "Chapels of Rest," were full to overflowing. There were pickets at the gates of the cemeteries, more pickets at the gates of the crematoriums. The overflow of corpses was being put in storage in unrefrigerated, disused warehouses. The city had run out of embalming oils and it was apparently impossible for it to obtain any more. No one explained to me why. Doubtless because of some other British strike.

* * *

Spokesmen for the Liverpool council and the local Health Authority were reluctant to reveal how many bodies had accumulated since the strike began. They gave out varying figures, two hundred, three hundred and fifty. Liverpool's chief undertaker told me that they were deliberately underplaying the real numbers because they felt that the public, if they knew the truth, might start to panic. This strike stirred up particularly unpleasant historical memories—cholera in Liverpool, the great pits, the mass graves into which the victims of the Great Plague of London were thrown. The council kept denying there was any health hazard, fearing for the safety of the pickets at the gates of the cemeteries. Under pressure from the national press the Liverpool Health Authority eventually admitted they had sixty "critical coffins." These apparently contained the bodies of Liverpool ladies who had lived decrepitly in solitude and whose deaths had not been discovered for several days, by which time their embalmment became an impossibility.

To a nation that has become accustomed to being crippled by a succession of disastrous major strikes, the gravediggers' strike was traumatic in its melancholy symbolism. It seemed the inevitable outcome of the way the country has been going. It was generally seen as some horrific last straw.

"England has now become a country where it is no longer possible even to get buried!" When Mrs. Thatcher made her shrill complaint in February, her accusation was not entirely rhetorical. This strike has had a different impact from all the recent and current English strikes, the trains, the truck drivers, the ambulance men, the garbage collectors, the buses, the subway, the milk, the bread, the gas, the diesel oil, the school canteen staff, the teachers, and the printers.... The current hospital and blood donors' strikes though potentially much more serious still did not have such a demoralizing effect as the strike of the gravediggers. This eerie and unexpected strike aroused feelings of outrage, a sense of violation. There is a general feeling that if one's society owes one nothing else at least it owes one the right to be decently buried. In a pub I heard a woman saying, "The bereaved can't bear the idea that the people that they've just lost are floating around rotting in warehouses."

* * *

In the eighteenth century Liverpool was an important seaport, international, glamorous, and gay. It thrived on the slave trade. Now it is intensely depressing, provincial, and poor. Only a few Georgian terraces remain as a reminder of the city's vanished beauty. Most of its eighteenth-century buildings have been razed and replaced by tower blocks and unsightly concrete high-rises. Architecturally it is a mess. The center of Liverpool was bombed by the Germans and gutted in the war and now at its very heart all that has been reconstructed is an ill-planned and tawdry shopping complex. The whole city gives one the feeling that it died long ago and no one chose to bury it. It is therefore ironic that of all English towns it should have been the most seriously affected by the gravediggers' strike.

When I arrived there during the second week of the strike it was freezing weather and the garbage-strewn streets were shrouded in an unhealthy gray mixture of sea mist and industrial fog. My journey by train from London had taken twice the time it should have done because the train workers were staging a go-slow strike. No refreshments were served on the train because the railway canteen staff were also striking. The hall porter of my hotel told me that Liverpool recently had been even more plagued by strikes than London. It had no bread, milk, ambulance service, social security workers, rubbish collection, or working hospitals. The water-workers were just about to strike, so were the sewage men, the firemen, and the police.

He found the gravediggers' strike particularly upsetting. "Can you imagine the distress it's causing to the people who've just lost someone? They are making the bereaved remove all the jewelry from their relatives' bodies. The council are frightened there may be looting in the warehouses. It's barbaric. It's like something in science fiction!" The porter told me that the council was trying its best to keep the bodies of dead children on ice in the hospitals. "No mother can bear the idea of her dead kid being put in storage with lots of cancerous old people in some bloody warehouse. The trouble is the hospital morgues are very small and they are running out of space...."

Like many other people that I spoke to in Liverpool he felt the government ought to bring in the army. About the gravediggers as a group his feelings were ambivalent. He felt that they were ill-paid (they earn an average of £45 a week) and that their working conditions were undesirable. On the other hand he thought it was ludicrous that such a small group of men should have the power to create such distress. Liverpool has only fifty-six gravediggers. Manchester has fourteen. He saw no reason in this modern age why there should be any gravediggers at all. He found it ridiculous that three men should still be spending up to six hours hacking away at frozen earth with a pick in order to dig one solitary grave when machinery could do the same job with much more speed and efficiency.

* * *

One of the chief complaints of the diggers themselves is that whenever they dig a grave, they almost always find another coffin in the ground. Their feet go through it and they find themselves wading around in foul water which is floating with rotting human remains. They often also see grinning skulls staring them in the face. Their opponents remain skeptical about the validity of this particular grievance and take the attitude that unless the council is allowing people to be buried one on top of another with no time lapse at all, the bones that the diggers come across must be ancient and therefore clean—this leads to the argument that if the gravediggers are so fastidious that they can't bear to come upon a few clean bones, they have clearly chosen the wrong trade.

The ancient operatic image of the gravedigger as a diabolic scavenging creature with spade and dark cloak apparently still lingers in the psyche of this modern community. In Liverpool I often heard the gravediggers charged with hypocrisy. They were accused of claiming to be underpaid while all the time they were holding down a job which brings them in inestimable untaxed wealth in the form of buried treasure. I also heard them denounced as fraudulent because while they bemoan their £45 a week wage, they refuse to admit either to the general public or to the tax officials that for every grave they dig they receive automatic and handsome tips—in Liverpool, which has a predominantly Irish-Catholic population, it is a custom that the bereaved must "give something to the gravediggers."

Never, so I was told, has there been a more unpopular union strike. The striking gravediggers were frightened to go into any pub or bar in case they encountered the relations or the friends of someone who had ended up stored in a warehouse.

I asked a doctor working for the city Health Authority what he felt about the strike. He said that its effects obviously were not very pretty—that it was being suggested that the council put the bodies in the ice-rink, submerge them in water, and simply freeze them in so that the kids could figure skate above them. He still felt that the public's hostile attitude toward the diggers was unfair. "Have you any idea what the morbidity rate of the average gravedigger is?" he asked me angrily. "No," I said. "No...No...I'm afraid I have no idea." "Did you know that any gravedigger has *three* times the morbidity rate of the average British working-class man!"

* * *

Later I asked a taxi driver to take me to the nearest cemetery. He looked at me with alarm and horror. It occurred to me that it is not customary to ask to be taken to the *nearest* graveyard. In general people tend to be specific about which particular one they wish to visit. I explained that I was writing about the strike, that I hoped to be able to talk to the pickets. He said I wouldn't find any pickets, that they'd locked the cemetery gates and gone home. "I'll take you up to see one of the factories where they are putting the bodies," he said. "The bodies are just as much to do with the strike as the gravediggers." "Yes, I suppose they are," I said. I had a vivid and ghastly image of the "critical coffins" and I felt nauseated by the idea of having to inspect them.

We drove out of the center of Liverpool into a terrible suburb called Speke. A sprawling industrial complex, it covers a vast area. We kept driving and driving through a hellish landscape where cheap prefabricated factories lie so close together they roll on like fields. Barbed-wire fences provide the only hedges, and the menacing silhouettes of pylons are the nearest things to trees. Driving through this fearful industrialized wasteland the taxi seemed like a tumbrel and the factory with the unburied buried dead about as appealing as the guillotine. We turned off the highway into a hinterland of factories separated by ribbon lanes of concrete. We stopped outside a huge, modern, vomit-colored building, beside which there was an ambulance and a policeman.

"That's where they've put the bodies," the driver said. "Can you wait?" I asked him nervously. "I really don't want to stay here very long." "Sorry, I have to go to the airport," he said. "Don't look so frightened, luv.... The bodies aren't going to eat you."

I got out and the taxi drove off. I went up to the policeman and explained I was writing about the strike. I asked him if this was the factory where they were storing the bodies. "Oh, we have hundreds of bodies in here." His tone was jovial and complacent. "What do you want to know about them?"

"Exactly how many hundreds of bodies are being stored here?" I asked him. He looked at me with suspicion. His voice became gruff and accusatory. "Why do you care how many bodies we've got in this factory? What makes you so very interested?" "Well...." I couldn't understand why he didn't see that the precise numbers had a certain interest.

"Are they in coffins?" I asked. I had heard unpleasant rumors that they were being stored in plastic bags. "Coffins?" He looked astounded. I then saw that the taxi driver had dropped me off at the wrong place. I was at a Leyland factory, one of Britain's largest car manufacturers. When the policeman had spoken of having hundreds of bodies he had been speaking all the time of car bodies. Since Leyland workers were planning a major strike the following day this coincidence had added to our misunderstanding.

"You want the place where they've put the deceased," the policeman said.

Apparently they were just down the road in a disused electronics factory. I wondered if it had closed down as a result of some other strike. As I walked down the road I noticed the most vile and overpowering smell. I tried to pretend it was the stench of industrial waste. But I knew quite well I was getting very near to the deceased.

The factory that held them was a pretentious red brick building with a neo-Georgian façade. It looked as if it had been built around 1930. It had a white flagpole on its roof, but no flag. The pole looked too upright, jaunty and festive. Perhaps it was respect for the unburied that had prompted the council to choose this untypical warehouse with its imposing neoclassical design, this terrible mockery of a stately home. The stateliness of its façade was fatally marred by the fact that where there should have been ivy or Virginia creeper there was an impenetrable entanglement of barbed wire, put there to ward off possible looters.

There was no one on the premises. The bodies had been locked up—sealed off with barbed wire and totally deserted. Who could be expected to sit day and night in this lonely neo-Georgian factory with the dead? Yet I felt the unburied should have been given the symbolic honor of at least being guarded by a policeman. It seemed disturbing that the cars in the Leyland factory were being given preferential treatment. But then what exactly would a policeman guard the dead from? The possibility of looters was minimal. Time was the enemy of these unlucky corpses, not marauders.

* * *

The following day I went to the General Municipal Workers center where the gravediggers were holding a mass meeting in order to decide if they would return to work. There was a feeling of excitement and tension, and suspense. The building was surrounded by reporters, including television crews. On top of their demand for a "substantial pay increase" the gravediggers are asking for better facilities in the cemeteries. They want to have showers and changing rooms. They complain they have nowhere to wash after work, and they have to go home in filthy clothes.

The cemeteries have a machine that flattens the graves. This machine is housed in a shed, with spades and other tools. The diggers are bitter because they are not provided with a shed of any kind and they feel that the graveyard equipment is given a care and respect which they are denied. They receive almost unanimous public sympathy for this complaint. The diggers, however, are also asking to have tea machines in the cemeteries. This demand is being much less sympathetically received. Most urban British graveyards are vast and they cover countless square acres. For this reason a single tea machine per graveyard would be impractical. If the diggers are to have hot tea made conveniently available to them a plethora of machines will have to be installed. This creates a genuine dilemma for the local council; to any religious person who sees the cemetery as a hallowed and sacred spot, the thought of it being dotted with multicolored machines is blasphemy. People visualize the graves of their loved ones littered with paper cups. They see this particular union demand as the thin end of the wedge. Once there are tea machines in the graveyards—why not cigarette machines, candy machines, pinball and fruit machines? "The gravediggers are going a bit too far with their tea machines," Liverpool's leading undertaker said to me. "You'd think they'd never heard of such a thing as the thermos."

The mass meeting in the Municipal Workers building dragged on.

The press were not allowed to attend it. The television crews and the camera men and the host of national reporters waited impatiently outside for the gravediggers' verdict. Suddenly a spokesman for the National Union of Public Employees which represents the diggers came out of the door of the building. The reporters surged toward him. The union official was Irish and he looked very pleased with himself. As all the TV cameras focused on him, he announced that the gravediggers had decided to go back to work "but only with a skeleton staff." Having made his joke he quickly disappeared back into the building.

After another hour and a half the meeting broke up in earnest. The gravediggers filed out of the committee room. They were stared at with a curiosity far more intense than that accorded to other union strikers. Their faces were closely scrutinized to see if their daily dealings with death had imprinted special traces of woe upon their features. In fact the diggers looked no more woeful than any other group of working men. They were mostly rather small, with the stunted look of the badly nourished. None of them had the huge arm muscles one expects from those whose life has been spent digging. Quite a few of them were extremely old, some were very young with the John the Baptist hair of hippies.

* * *

One gravedigger was black and I was puzzled how he had been allowed to join this selective white union. The gravediggers have a family tradition—their fathers, their grandfathers, their great grandfathers, etc., were usually all gravediggers before them. Some of these gravedigging dynasties can be traced back to the eighteenth century. They have a pride in their craft which they pass on from father to son. There was evidence of this during their strike in Manchester, a town where you are allowed to bury your own dead, unlike Liverpool, where there is a local law that declares amateur burial illegal. Two brothers carrying their father's coffin staggered into a graveyard and passed the Manchester pickets. They then proceeded to try to bury it. The pickets watched them with horror. The brothers made such a hideous mess of their grave that the gravediggers could stand it no longer. They left their posts, took the spades from the brothers' hands, dug a perfect grave—finished it off—then returned to be on strike and keep vigil at the gates of the cemetery.

The gravediggers are a closed shop. They allow no one to join their union unless he is a son, a nephew, a brother-in-law of one of the present diggers. When I later asked the undertaker how the black gravedigger had been accepted he said that a lot of the Liverpool girls "slip up" with the foreign seamen and therefore the black gravedigger must be a relation too.

As the gravediggers filed past the press and the television cameras after their meeting they looked sheepish and bashful. They had been given orders by the union officials that they were not to speak to the press. Their spokesman however gave a press conference. He said that for humanitarian reasons the diggers had agreed to go back to work, but only for four weeks. If the council had not met their demands by that time they were going on strike indefinitely.

What were the gravediggers going to do about the "backlog"? He said they were not going to knock themselves out dealing with the "backlog" unless they were paid overtime for the work involved. He said the gravediggers feel that their services are appreciated only once they are withdrawn. At the same time they regretted and sympathized with the distress the strike caused the bereaved.

After the meeting I went in a taxi to Liverpool's Jewish cemetery to see if it had been affected by the strike. My driver was a tough Church of England man. It soon emerged he was also anti-Semitic. He said that he bet that Jews were getting away with it. "Trust them to get themselves buried when no one else can manage it." When we got to the cemetery he got out of his taxi and came in with me. "Look at all the expensive marble they've got in here," he said. He then became wildly excited because he found a freshly dug grave. "Didn't I tell you! Trust the Jews!"

Usually newly dug graves are a depressing sight but in the curious atmosphere of the Liverpool strike I found myself staring at a dismal strip of wet mud in the Jewish cemetery with a kind of wonder. It looked rather beautiful and miraculous—just because it existed. When a tiny elf-like Jewish gravedigger came out of a lodge, I asked him if he was affected by the strike. He told me he did all his own digging and he was not paid by the council. But he looked terrified, as if he felt it was dangerous to admit this. He obviously was afraid that a peculiar new phenomenon of "grave envy" might stir up ancient racial and religious prejudices, that he might suffer retaliation, and Protestant and Catholic vandals would arrive to despoil and desecrate his graves.

* * *

Liverpool's leading undertaker is brisk and dapper—a businessman. He and his three younger brothers own four Chapels of Rest and also a trucking firm. Undertaking, he said, was a profession that was handed down in families, like that of the gravediggers. The strike had made his life a nightmare. In the Chapel of Rest where we were talking he usually had two occupied coffins, but he now had one hundred and fifty. None of the corpses had been properly embalmed. It was no good pretending they had. He was an embalmer himself. As a small child his father had taught him the trade. There was not much to it. Embalming was similar to what any woman does when she stuffs and prepares a chicken for the oven, he said. It was a question of plugging up the appropriate orifices.

Unfortunately he simply hadn't had the time to work on the bodies since the strike. He was much too frantic trying to arrange for his hearses to do all the "pick ups" and the "drop offs." He was using a "freelance" embalmer. The poor man was at the end of his tether and the work was "snowing him under." The freelance embalmer had done his best, but it was a makeshift job as he hadn't got the proper oils and salts. The undertaker waved his hand toward the back of the Chapel of Rest on the door of which was written "Enter with joy— all you who enter here." "None of the bodies in here at present are satisfactory...," he said. "Not what I'd call satisfactory at all...." In normal times he apparently got few requests for embalmment. The process was not required by the health laws and was too expensive for most families. It costs £50 and the results last only seven weeks. Now in the emergency the relatives were insisting on it. "Fortunately they can't see what a bad job we are doing here. We don't dare to let the relatives in."

* * *

During the strike bereaved Liverpool families still insisted on hiring a hearse and three black cars to take them to a funeral at the church. After the service the mourners would go back to their homes while the hearse with the coffin went off in a different direction, to one of the suburban warehouses. "That's not what most families want from a funeral," the undertaker said. "People want their dead to have some little patch of ground that belongs to them—a definite place where the mourners can come in order to shed a tear—or plant a rose." One thing he would say in favor of the strike, though—there was equality in the warehouses at the moment. People who would normally be given a pauper's grave were getting exactly the same treatment as the well-to-do. He was worried that once the strike stopped, the coffins would get muddled up.

The undertaker said that some of the bereaved families were being extremely unreasonable. They seemed unable to sympathize with the problems of logistics that would face him in the next weeks. They refused to have their coffin taken from the warehouses directly to the cemetery. They insisted it be first taken to a church for a service before it went on to the graveyard. They wouldn't acknowledge they had already been given a church service—that he'd already once provided them with a hearse and three black cars. They wanted to start from scratch. He warned them he would have to charge them the price of two funerals.

I asked him how he would cope if the gravediggers went on strike indefinitely. He clasped his head in a gesture of agony. "Don't ask me," he said. "As I've told you, I can't cope with the backlog we have got at the moment. I have new bodies coming in every day and I have to put them at the back of the queue. A funeral is a slow thing—that's the trouble. You can't hurry up the funeral procedures in order to fit more people in...." I could see his point, that it would be startling to see solemn black hearses whizzing like racing cars through the streets of Liverpool as they did their "pick ups" and their "drop offs."

As I sat in the Chapel of Rest and listened to the problems of the undertaker, they seemed like those of the nation, almost insuperable. Once the backlog of this particular strike eventually had been cleared up the gravediggers seemed likely to go back on strike—as have so many other strikers who cleared up other backlogs. The general prospects, like the condition of the badly embalmed bodies, appeared "unsatisfactory."

—May 3, 1979

7

Going Crazy in India
Rosemary Dinnage

*One good way to get a fix on a place is to visit its mental insti-
tutions; margins explain the mainstream; pathologies reveal
what people regard as normal.*

*But patterns of neurosis, like so much else, change with
time. Rosemary Dinnage investigated psychiatric problems in
India before the stockmarket booms created a global elite of
New Indians, overcompetitive, overachieving, overrich—the
very opposite of the self-effacing, family-minded, insular creatures kneeling at the feet of mental health gurus in 1981.*

*Are the New Indians in a happier mental state than the Old
Indians? Perhaps not. But their troubles are probably less revealing of the state of India than of the state of the world.*

—I.B.

HALFWAY BETWEEN THE southern cities of Madras and Bangalore, Vellore is a small town with a thirteenth-century fort, a long, busy bazaar, and Christian Medical College. Founded in 1900 as a one-bed dispensary, CMC has grown to employ 2,500 staff, train graduates in thirty different specialties, and treat patients from many countries outside India. It is a reminder of the benevolent aspects of the Raj; supported by Protestant churches abroad as well as missions and diocesan councils from all over India, it still adjusts its charges to the patients' purses and prides itself on dispensing two or three hundred thousand dollars' worth of free care in a year.

* * *

To the Psychiatry Department's Mental Health Centre it is a three-mile drive into the dry countryside. The Centre is a collection of low buildings spread out around a compound. (Even the "snakepit" mental hospitals of India's big cities tend to be less oppressive than their Western counterparts because they are built outward rather than up: space is something India is not short of.) Inside, doctors' offices open off shady corridors; half-doors allow what air there is to circulate.

Dr. Abraham Verghese—his name shows him to be a Christian and probably from Portuguese Goa—is holding a teaching session for his juniors with the day's new patients. Mr. Krishnan Reddy is called first: quiet and docile, fifty years old and head of a joint family that includes four married sons and their wives. He has been lucky, until recently, in having a secure job: he is a government forester earning Rs. 300 a month (in 1978, about $38). Reddy is an alcoholic. He gazes with submissive intensity at Dr. Verghese and ignores the circle of other people in the room; he needs no interpreter because he speaks English (of a sort), the *lingua franca* of southern India.

He has been drinking arak heavily for the past ten years, he says. In the past two years his drinking has got worse, and for six months now he hasn't worked. This morning he had a fight with his wife and she brought him to the main hospital, which referred him to the Centre. His father was an alcoholic. He can't work or concentrate; when he is drunk he cries. He drinks to forget financial and family worries, he says. He has no sexual intercourse now; he is "too weak." He has tried a cure for his drinking before, was given medicines but didn't take them; but "from today I won't drink." He leaves as gently as he arrived, and it is decided he will be admitted to the Centre, if he really wants to be cured.

Govind Ramathayan, twenty-two years old, a teacher, is equally self-effacing in manner. Since he speaks neither Tamil nor English, one of the junior doctors interprets to the group. He has come alone to the Centre (which is unusual), sent by his doctor. He can't sleep or eat properly; he has fits of dizziness and he aches all over; he too suffers from "weakness." Before his marriage he was chaste; his illness began soon after his marriage, and is getting worse. The interpreter conveys the message that he must come back with his wife before any therapy can be started. After he has gone one of the junior doctors reads his notes on a similar case: a twenty-year-old man, married six months ago, suffering from pains, sleeplessness; he had a sexual relationship before marriage, but has been impotent with his wife. (These marriages, of course, would almost certainly have been arranged ones.)

The third patient, a pretty woman in her twenties in a peasant sari, enters with an air of drama. In the few steps from the door to the chair her walk succeeds in suggesting that she is suffering greatly and that it is somebody's fault—perhaps the fault of all of us in the room. This time a Tamil doctor interprets. She wants to die, she says. She has a pain in the shoulder—she jerks her left shoulder continually—and terrible headaches every day. She can't sleep; she doesn't care about anything. She went to her local hospital (she has come 200 miles) and they gave her electric shocks and antidepressant medicine; she was better for four days and then worse than ever, so she was sent to CMC. She can hear sounds coming from all over her body. She suspects her husband of being interested in their neighbor's wife, but when she accuses him he shouts at her that she is a jealous woman, and she can't bear that.

Dr. Verghese has a hunch and asks if her husband has had a vasectomy; yes, returns the interpreter. "We quite often hear this story," says Verghese. And she has only two children—both girls. There is a rustle of surprise in the room. The financial award for vasectomy might be tempting, but scarcely enough to take the place of a son. Perhaps her husband is a farmer who was refused fertilizer supplies until he had the operation; perhaps he wanted a driving license, or rehousing from a slum. Or perhaps his village was offered a new well in return for thirty vasectomies.

* * *

Going to India from the West is like stepping onto another planet; but is having a mental illness in India any different from having it in Manhattan? Is treatment similar—if it is available? Do you get ill as often there, or less, or more? Do poverty and overwork leave any time for mental illness, is it a side effect of affluence—or do the hardships of a poor country provide all the more cause for disintegration? Are there differences in the Indian character structure itself that make mental illness and its treatment take different forms from those in the West? And does a third world country, obviously so much less well equipped with psychiatric and psychotherapeutic services than affluent societies, need more mental health care—or does greater provision for illness conjure up the illness to meet it, as new roads bring out more traffic?

Dr. Verghese does not believe that poverty provides a miraculous immunity to mental afflictions. Suicides, for instance, happen fairly often, even though attempted suicide is a punishable offense. He quotes a survey of his district that found psychological disturbance in 66 per 1,000 people, of which about a third were psychotic. Psychotic illness, schizophrenia in particular, occurs in a relatively constant pattern from culture to culture; the interesting question regards the other two-thirds, the nature of the less severe mental illnesses of a third world country. Their incidence may vary between the less and the more sophisticated sections of society, for one thing: a study carried out in Bengal found Brahmins to have about four times as many symptoms as non-Hindu tribesmen.[1]

It is at any rate safe to say that rural India does not run to the shrink with a problem as Manhattan does; nor indeed could it in view of the scarcity of psychiatric resources. When India gained independence, there were about fifty psychiatrists in the country, many of them army doctors; now the number is estimated at only about 500 for India's 640 million people; others—perhaps too many—leave India to practice abroad. Medical and psychiatric facilities range from the basic care given free in clinics and large hospitals, through part-payment, to expensive private treatment.

Only the severest cases from the 66 per 1,000 seek official medical help, Verghese considers, the criterion being inability to go out to work or to housekeep. Most—about 80 percent, he estimates—have been to at least one local healer before coming to the hospital. With hysterical and neurotic symptoms he believes the healers can have great success; patients, particularly those from rural areas, are likely to attribute their symptoms to witchcraft or the violation of a taboo, which provides a rationale for the healer.

Erna Hoch, a Swiss psychiatrist who has lived in rural Kashmir, has studied the work of "pirs" and "faquirs" there. She argues that

---

1. D. N. Nandi, *Psychoanalysis in Urban and Rural India*. National Seminar on Psychotherapeutic Processes (National Institute of Mental Health and Neuro Sciences, Bangalore, 1978).

they use processes that—covertly, anyway—also have a place in Western psychotherapy. The healer may act as a catalyst to the illness; he may "transfer" some of his own health or energy to the patient; he may offer a symbolic rebirth; he may operate a kind of temporary "dialysis" whereby he absorbs the patient's sickness ("every psychotherapist at some time or other has felt like blotting paper that has to absorb the patient's anger and other negative emotions," she adds). She observed frequent instant "cures," not always lasting ones—though where illness is attributed to wrong actions there is a strong incentive to stay cured. The prescribing of rituals and penances seemed to be among the most effective therapies.[2]

* * *

In their study of mental illness in a south Indian community, the British psychologists G. M. Carstairs and R. L. Kapur describe the work of a local healer, the Mantarwadi, or expert in horoscopes and mantras:

There were about 20 clients who, it seemed, had been waiting patiently since the early hours of the morning. Without even looking at them the Mantarwadi sat down on the only chair in the room (a bench was soon brought in for us) and started drawing with a chalk the zodiac chart for the day on the desk in front of him.

Having completed this chart he casually summoned the client sitting nearest and from the clock checked the exact time the client came face to face with him. With a wave of the hand he forbade the man from talking—as he evidently wanted to—about his present misery. The next few minutes were spent in some further calculations while the client waited patiently. Having finished the calculations the Mantarwadi spoke out with a clear commanding voice: "You are 60, you come from a place where the fish abound and you want relief from

---

2. Erna Hoch, *Process in Instant Cure*. National Seminar on Psychotherapeutic Processes (National Institute of Mental Health and Neuro Sciences, Bangalore, 1978).

the pains and aches which have been haunting you for a long time."
"And fever," said the client. "And fever," agreed the Mantarwadi....
"Is it true or is it not that your father is dead?" "Yes," agreed the client. "Then is it true or is it not that during the last three years at least once you did not complete the ritual of Shradda?" The client hung his head down and acquiesced meekly. "Well this is what comes of not attending to your dead ancestors. You will need to arrange a ritual feast to which at least five Brahmins must be invited. You will have to go to Dharmasthala and bathe in the holy water. And here is a thread which you must wear on your aching knees." Saying this he held out a piece of string, whispered a mantra over it and gave it to the man.

The man folded his hands, touched his forehead to the ground in front of the healer, and left after putting a rupee note on the desk.[3]

In the community of 9,000 people studied by Carstairs and Kapur there were twenty-three healers, two doctors, and a government health center. It was common for patients to consult both doctor and healer. "There are many ways to truth," says Indian tradition and philosophy.

* * *

Conventional psychiatric techniques, however, in Vellore and elsewhere, are borrowed from the Western repertoire: electro-convulsive therapy, drugs, occupational therapy, simple psychotherapy, behavior therapy; and psychiatric training follows the Western pattern. ECT is cheaper than drugs and so is freely prescribed. Dr. Verghese's department gives twenty-five to thirty a day—without anaesthetic because an anaesthetist would be an expensive luxury. His psychotherapeutic sessions are not, of course, modeled on psychoanalysis (though Freudian concepts are familiar here, as everywhere else); Indian patients, he says, expect support and advice from their doctors.

---

3. G. M. Carstairs and R. L. Kapur, *The Great Universe of Kota* (University of California Press, 1976).

One aspect of his work he is justifiably proud of: his "family participation" scheme, which is either as old as the hills, or very new, or both. The Centre has facilities for forty-two patients to be accommodated with one or two family members. (There is far less institutionalization in India than in the West; patients who are really "put away" are either from the dispossessed of the big cities, or else have no relatives.) Each family has a simple suite in the huts that surround the compound. The scheme has several advantages: cheapness is one, for relatives cook for the patient and look after him. Another is that they can be taught to understand the illness and care for the patient on discharge. And it agrees well with the Indian tradition of expecting relatives to provide much of the food and care for hospital patients; the Centre's patients, with their strong family ties, find it comforting. "They are frightened of coming here," says Dr. Verghese, "but when it is time to leave they don't want to go."

* * *

What does Vellore's pattern of mental health care have to say about ordinary neurotic illness in an undeveloped area? One striking difference between West and East is that most of the patients coming to the Centre complain of physical rather than mental symptoms. This might seem to be a result of CMC's special position: because it is well known for its neurological department, many patients have been sent there for physical investigations before being referred as psychiatric cases. But the observation is supported by the very careful research done by Carstairs and Kapur. They studied psychiatric symptoms in a community rather than a hospital; and they too found pains, headaches, and hysterical symptoms to be the commonest complaints, present in about 18 percent of their population, after they had established that malnutrition and anemia were not the causes. Sleeplessness, forgetfulness, anxiety, and depression followed with diminishing frequency.

Medard Boss, a Swiss psychiatrist who visited and lectured in India, has suggested that Indian patients may actually be more like the patients from whom Freud drew his theories than are modern Westerners.[4] Greater self-consciousness, an intellectual acquaintance, however vague, with the concept of repression, has, for instance, in some mysterious way caused "conversion hysteria" almost to disappear from the sophisticated patient's repertoire of symptoms. Patients in the West now generally present themselves plainly as sad or anxious rather than hampered by the pains, paralyses, ties, and fugues that once took their way more or less dissociated from their owners' awareness.

Another fact plainly different from Western expectations is that more men than women are admitted to Vellore's Mental Health Centre. This does not necessarily mean that the women have fewer psychological problems—Dr. Verghese believes that they suffer from neurotic symptoms more than men, and this has some support from research—but that men seem more likely to become psychotic. Carstairs and Kapur found the same, and it would be interesting to know whether there is other corroboration. Verghese's explanation is that, while Indian communities can tolerate schizophrenic members who in the West would be hospitalized, women are more easily carried by the family and community in this way than the breadwinners, for whom a cure is urgent.

South to Pondicherry, ceded to India by the French in 1954, home of the Aurobindo ashram. It was here that the distinguished psychiatrist N.C. Surya came when he threw up his job as director of the National Institute of Mental Health at Bangalore. Trained in Europe and the US, formerly a Marxist, he was following an Indian tradition of abandoning the world for spiritual concerns when the moment is right; Aurobindo, founder of the ashram, did the same when he gave

---

4. Medard Boss, *A Psychiatrist Discovers India* (Dufour Editions, 1965).

up his fight for Indian independence and retreated to Pondicherry. While outside Pondicherry steams in the sun, the ashram library is all greenery, coolness, and hush. Dr. Surya comes out of the library carrying the rolled umbrella (against the sun) that, like an Englishman, he seldom opens.

"You must understand first that I am leading a perfectly selfish life. I am doing what I know is right for *me*; about other people I don't know. I only know that I must get this machine"—he slaps his chest—"into better harmony, gradually and bit by bit. First I am learning to drive my own chariot; after that I can think of outside affairs. All illness is caused here, in ourselves. We treat machines well, we treat animals well, but we wreck the body. Yet people don't want to change; man is in love with suffering, Aurobindo said. If only we don't perceive things as harmful then they won't make us ill. This suffering is the same anywhere: yes, the rich have the leisure to be neurotic, but the poor man out on the street has his illnesses too. There is just as much strife and anger in the villages as anywhere else.

"The doctor, the psychiatrist, can only heal by being in alignment with himself and *absorbing* the patient's illness. Yes, just like a sponge. For this he must have experience in the management of at least one total human being, and that can only be himself. And he must never start to believe he can take on the burdens of the whole world; he must limit himself and be humble.

"I mistrust explanations. A man can come to you with one headache and you can end up sending him away with ten more. More and more people are making money by writing books, thinking up more and more psychological explanations. The simplest, quickest method is best. I don't necessarily consider myself the agent of cure. The patient is that himself; or someone else may come along, a kind uncle....

"Do you know the books of Ivan Illich? I have much sympathy with him. We are teaching people to be helpless with our explanations. Everyone has a natural problem-solving ability and psychiatry is eroding it. A man came to me saying that he had suffered so much through his parents. I said, 'How old are you?' 'Twenty-one.' 'Where are your parents?' 'Three hundred miles away.' 'Then why do you still tell me about your mother and father—are they in the next room? Are they sitting on your head?' When a man is grown-up he must decide to liberate himself and he can do so."

* * *

Pondicherry, in its steamy south-eastern corner, could hardly be more different from Ahmedabad in the northern state of Gujerat. This is a large and relatively prosperous industrial city which has been dominated for centuries by its textile industry. Gandhi, returning to live in India in 1915, set up his first ashram on the bank of the Sabarmati River there; and in 1918 he led a mill-workers' strike against the powerful mill owner Ambalal Sarabhai.

Gandhi's helper in organizing the strike was Sarabhai's sister Anasuya, a suffragette and trade union leader who became known as the Mother of the Labour Union. Even though Sarabhai fought the strike, he was an admirer of Gandhi and an enlightened man who was unconventional enough to keep his wife out of purdah.

The Sarabhais clearly are an unusual family and so it is no surprise that Kamalini Sarabhai, wife of Ambalal's son Gautam, is one of the rare Indian psychoanalysts who trained abroad but works in India. (There is an autonomous Indian Psychoanalytic Society in Calcutta, established in 1922 by Girindrasekhar Bose, a distant admirer of Freud; it has about thirty-five members of whom a number have emigrated or retired.) "My father-in-law made it quite clear to me that I had to go out and do something for myself," Mrs. Sarabhai says; she responded by taking her two daughters with her to England—her husband joining her whenever he could—and undertaking six years of psychoanalytic training at London's Psychoanalytical Society. Perhaps she was influenced by the fact that Ambalal Sarabhai once visited Vienna—anonymously—to consult Freud.[5]

Mrs. Sarabhai is also a director of the Bakubhai Mansukhai (BM for short) Institute of Ahmedabad. Here perhaps Indian mental health care at its most Western is to be found—though there is nothing slavish about its attitudes and it is entirely staffed by Indians. The American psychologists Lois and Gardner Murphy advised on its founding in 1951, and it has strong links with English centers such as the Tavistock. The BM Institute has a school and workshop for the retarded, an infant assessment clinic, an audiology clinic, a family therapy center, and a day-care unit, as well as its psychotherapy program, school for normal children, and training and research schemes.

At a case conference the previous day's cases are discussed. A depressed, backward boy of twelve: he has lived in the city with his grandparents since he was four so that he could attend school, and his grandmother beats him; his aunt wants the Institute's intervention. The baby daughter of a well-to-do family doesn't speak or respond to speech; her hearing is to be tested. An adolescent has failed his exams, won't read, has few employment prospects; he also has fits, and is referred by the school for neurological tests. A nine-year-old Tamil boy who had tuberculous meningitis at two years old did not walk or talk until he was six; the Institute's help is asked in giving him special education.

* * *

Though the Institute's prime concern is children, it takes more adults than children for psychotherapy. The clientele for therapy is probably

---

5. Erik H. Erikson, *Gandhi's Truth* (Norton, 1969).

rather more sophisticated and well-to-do than that of the CMC Mental Health Centre. The therapy given is not only classical psychoanalysis but a mixture of counseling, family therapy, and group work. What sort of patient explicitly seeks psychotherapy, I ask. Mrs. Sarabhai gives the example of a severely depressed Muslim foreman from one of the mills who complained that the hospital's pills had done him no good; he wanted "talking treatment" instead. Did she encounter any specially typical psychiatric problems? Two that came to mind were the young male who is anxious, afraid of a strict father, unable to make independent decisions; and the "first-generation learner" who comes from an illiterate family and breaks down under the pressure of social change.

The surprise, at first, is that mental illness and its treatment in India are *not* more strikingly different from Western patterns. Even a profoundly different religious outlook, social organization, and standard of living clearly do not affect basic vulnerability to anxiety, depression, or breakdown. Freud may have been partly right, though, in assuming that neurosis is the price we pay for civilization, for even in India urbanization and increased sophistication are apparently accompanied by a higher incidence of symptoms. A recent collection of papers[6] from a seminar led in India by Erik Erikson presents a picture of increasingly prevalent anomie, Eastern-style. In it the associate director of the BM Institute argues that there is an "identity vacuum" for Indians at the present time: values that are appropriate in an uncompetitive agrarian society break down under modern pressures; traditions and established roles are threatened by the mass media.

But after similarities between East and West are noted, the dissimilarities become more evident. One of the most distinct is the

---

6. *Identity and Adulthood*, edited by Sudhir Kakar, with an introductory lecture by Erik H. Erikson (Oxford University Press, 1979).

greater tendency among Indian psychiatric patients to convert mental pain into physical; perhaps convert is the wrong word—the Indian patient may not feel the strict body/mind distinction that we take for granted. Erna Hoch has written that "if one tries to differentiate whether a person who says 'my heart does not feel like it' or 'my liver is not doing its work' actually means the physical organ or some emotional disturbance, one often evokes puzzlement, as a separation of the two has never been made in the patient's way of thinking."[7]

An Indian psychoanalyst now practicing in England describes another way in which she found Indian patients different from Western ones. "They seemed to have no resistances! They accepted everything I said, just swallowed it up. This was very hard for me. I found myself making too many interpretations. And they would arrive so early and so eagerly!" Many—superficially at any rate—had an almost religious faith in the therapist's mystique. Medard Boss, however, noted that although his Indian patients had boundless faith in him, their dependency and immaturities close to the surface and causing them no conflict, they were relatively lacking in motivation to mature and become more independent.

J. S. Neki of the All-India Institute of Medical Sciences in New Delhi has suggested a different model for the therapeutic relationship in India, that of guru and disciple. Though there are obvious differences between the roles of guru and therapist—the guru teaches the control of negative emotions rather than their exploration, and he does not withhold himself emotionally from the disciple—Neki sees many similarities: both are dispassionate and persevering, preferring to help the pupil formulate questions rather than give the answer

---

7. Erna Hoch, "A Pattern of Neurosis in India," *American Journal of Psychoanalysis*, 1966.

themselves, and both teach him to look inward rather than outward.[8]

Neki has also examined the great difference between India and the West in attitudes toward dependency. In psychotherapy it becomes a key issue: the Western patient fights against dependence, the Western therapist treats it as a problem that has to be managed and kept under control. Neki sees both partners as caught in an anxiety specific to Western culture: "both of them engage in a struggle to defend their own personal independence in a climate that inevitably becomes charged with anxiety and sometimes even with hostility."[9] In India, he argues, dependency of one person on another is taken for granted, and "where letting others take charge of you is not considered ignoble or undignified, no outrage of personal dignity occurs by depending on them." The Western therapist's formality is taken for unfriendliness; the Indian's natural behavior is to

> strive to establish a friendly relationship, and look for signs of reciprocity in the therapist's behaviour and utterance. [Indians] offer gifts, extend invitations to visit their residences or to marriages and other social functions.... A distrust of formal contacts and a cosy feeling of security and reassurance in informal contacts is the common characteristic of our people. Even if we are buying some goods from a shopkeeper, we either try to transact business with a known person or attempt to develop familiarity during the business.[10]

8. J.S. Neki, "Guru-Chela Relationship: The Possibility of a Therapeutic Paradigm," *American Journal of Orthopsychiatry*, 1973, pp. 755–766.

9. J.S. Neki, "An Examination of the Cultural Relativism of Dependence as a Dynamic of Social and Therapeutic Relationships," I and II, *British Journal of Medical Psychology*, No. 49 (1976), pp. 1–22.

10. A.S. Mahal, "Problems of Psychotherapy with Indian Patients," in *Personality Development and Personal Illness*, edited by J.S. Neki and G.G. Prabhu (Mental Health Mono-

Psychotherapeutic work in India may be developing a pattern of its own that incorporates these attitudes.

* * *

In a study of the inner world of the Indian, Sudhir Kakar, trained on the Continent, a former lecturer at Harvard who practices in New Delhi, discusses the pervasive and seldom examined world-picture of a culture, the "heart of a community identity": the Indian, he believes, is deeply molded by his background of belief in a progression of incarnations, of an inescapable karma, of the *samskaras* (innate dispositions) with which he is born. He is consequently—by our standards—more passive as well as more dependent and gregarious.

With the cultural acceptance of the notion of *samskara*, there is little social pressure to foster the belief that if only the caretakers were good enough, and constantly on their toes, the child's potentialities would be boundlessly fulfilled. With the Hindu emphasis on man's inner limits, there is not that sense of urgency and struggle against the outside world, with prospects of sudden metamorphoses and great achievements just around the corner, that often seem to propel Western lives.[11]

Yet the Indian, he continues, always knows above all that he is part of a network of his fellows, always functions as part of a close group.

Perhaps they have always been the norm, and the Western sense of separateness and lonely achievement an aberration of the past hundred years or so. Through the eyes of Indians we can catch a glimpse of our own cultural peculiarities. The Western therapist's anxiety about dependency is understandable, Neki says, because "most Western patients are lonely in life and have unsatisfied dependency crav-

graph No. 2, New Delhi: All-India Institute of Medical Sciences, 1974).

11. Sudhir Kakar, *The Inner World: A Psychoanalytic Study of Childhood and Society in India* (Oxford University Press, 1978).

ings, and therapists are afraid that resolution of dependency will be resisted by the patient. In India, patients nearly always have a variety of 'significant others' around them to whom dependency-leanings can always be transferred by a deft therapist." And the Westerner "has become cut off from introspection and meditation. Psychotherapy perhaps serves to provide him with a substitute for it." He quotes a colleague who puts it even more strongly:

> The institution of psychotherapy, indeed the movement for mental health itself, may be viewed as both a symbolic and substantive cultural undertaking to meet the deficits in the Western way of life and to cope with the negative psychological implications of its premises.[12]

Whether India, with its close and comforting network of family and community ties, should ever aim at psychiatric provision on the Western scale is doubtful. If it needs to, it will perhaps be a sign of social disintegration. Nor should we assume that therapeutic methods and attitudes adapted to Westerners are the only ones for the less isolated, less striving, less intellectualized Indian patient. Indian psychiatry will surely begin to reject what feels inappropriate and foreign. Surya has written that the present-day Indian psychiatrist "has learnt his medical and psychiatric lessons in a language and in conceptual frameworks which are wholly foreign to the milieu of his birth and habitation"; that unless this is changed "we will end up as ineffectual caricatures of Western psychiatric theory and practice, or reduce our living patients into a set of prestige-loaded foreign

---

12. S. K. Pande: "The Mystique of 'Western' Psychotherapy and Eastern Interpretation," *Journal of Nervous and Mental Disease*, No. 146 (1968), pp. 425–432.

jargon."[13] Perhaps India has acquired all it needs from Western concepts of mental health and Western methods of trying to restore it, and will draw more confidently now on its own.

—November 19, 1981

---

13. N.C. Surya and S.S. Jayaram, "Some Basic Considerations of Psychotherapy in the Indian Setting," *Indian Journal of Psychiatry*, No. 6 (1964), pp. 153–156.

8

In El Salvador
Joan Didion

This was the heyday of Roberto D'Aubuisson, also known as "Blowtorch Bob" after his favorite torture methods, a man who learned his grisly trade in the US from American military instructors. He was just one of many killers able to run around shooting, maiming, and terrorizing their own people in the name of anti-communism.

You had them in Asia, you had them in Latin America, you had them anywhere in the world where the red tide of revolution threatened an assortment of strongmen, Big Men, and Caudillos, who were on the right side of communism.

In El Salvador, "Blowtorch Bob" could have an archbishop murdered, or Maryknoll sisters, or anyone he goddamn liked, for he was "our boy."

The heyday did not last. The national murder spree ended in the 1990s. Roberto D'Aubuisson died in 1992, in his bed, of cancer. In 1984 he received a prize in Washington DC for being "an inspiration to freedom-loving people everywhere."

—I.B.

I.

THE THREE-YEAR-OLD El Salvador International Airport is glassy and white and splendidly isolated, conceived during the waning of the Molina "National Transformation" as convenient less to the capital (San Salvador is forty miles away, until recently a drive of several hours) than to a central hallucination of the Molina and Romero regimes, the projected beach resorts, the Hyatt, the Pacific Paradise, tennis, golf, waterskiing, condos, Costa del Sol; the visionary invention of a tourist industry in yet another republic where the leading natural cause of death is gastrointestinal infection. In the general absence of tourists these hotels have since been abandoned, ghost resorts on the empty Pacific beaches, and to land at this airport built to service them is to plunge directly into a state in which no ground is solid, no depth of field reliable, no perception so definite that it might not dissolve into its reverse.

The only logic is that of acquiescence. Immigration is negotiated in a thicket of automatic weapons, but by whose authority the weapons are brandished (army or national guard or national police or customs police or treasury police or one of a continuing proliferation of other shadowy and overlapping forces) is a blurred point. Eye contact is avoided. Documents are scrutinized upside-down. Once clear of the airport, on the new highway that slices through green hills rendered phosphorescent by the cloud cover of the tropical rainy season, one sees mainly underfed cattle and mongrel dogs and armored vehicles, vans, and trucks and Cherokee Chiefs fitted with reinforced steel and bullet-proof Plexiglas an inch thick.

Such vehicles are a fixed feature of local life, and are popularly associated with disappearance and death. There was the Cherokee Chief seen following the Dutch television crew killed in Chalatenango province in March. There was the red Toyota three-quarter-ton pickup sighted near the van driven by the four American

Maryknoll workers on the night they were killed in December 1980. There are the three Toyota panel trucks, one yellow, one blue, and one green, none bearing plates, reported present at each of the summer mass detentions (a "detention" is another fixed feature of local life, and often precedes a "disappearance") in the Amatepec district of San Salvador. These are the details—the models and colors of armored vehicles, the makes and calibers of weapons, the particular methods of dismemberment and decapitation used in particular instances—on which the visitor to Salvador learns immediately to concentrate, to the exclusion of past or future concerns, as in a prolonged amnesiac fugue.

* * *

Terror is the given of the place. Black-and-white police cars cruise in pairs, each with the barrel of a rifle extruding from an open window. Roadblocks materialize at random, soldiers fanning out from trucks and taking positions, fingers always on triggers, safetys clicking on and off. Aim is taken as if to pass the time. Every morning *El Diario de Hoy* and *La Prensa Gráfica* carry cautionary stories. "*Una madre y sus dos hijos fueron asesinados con arma cortante (corvo) por ocho sujetos desconocidos el lunes en la noche*": a mother and her two sons hacked to death in their beds by eight *desconocidos*, unknown men. The same morning's paper: the unidentified body of a young man, strangled, found on the shoulder of a road. Same morning, different story: the unidentified bodies of three young men, found on another road, their faces partially destroyed by bayonets, one face carved to represent a cross.

It is largely from these reports in the newspapers that the United States embassy compiles its body counts, which are transmitted to Washington in a weekly dispatch referred to by embassy people as "the grim-gram." These counts are presented in a kind of tortured code that fails to obscure what is taken for granted in El Salvador, that government forces do most of the killing. In a January 15 memo to Washington, for example, the embassy issued a "guarded" breakdown on its count of 6,909 "reported" political murders between September 16, 1980, and September 15, 1981. Of these 6,909, 922 were "believed committed by security forces," 952 "believed committed by leftist terrorists," 136 "believed committed by rightist terrorists," and 4,889 "committed by unknown assailants," the famous *desconocidos* favored by those San Salvador newspapers still publishing. (By whom the remaining ten were committed is unclear.) The memo continued:

> The uncertainty involved here can be seen in the fact that responsibility cannot be fixed in the majority of cases. We note, however, that it is generally believed in El Salvador that a large number of the unexplained killings are carried out by the security forces, officially or unofficially. The Embassy is aware of dramatic claims that have been made by one interest group or another in which the security forces figure as the primary agents of murder here. El Salvador's tangled web of attack and vengeance, traditional criminal violence and political mayhem make this an impossible charge to sustain. In saying this, however, we make no attempt to lighten the responsibility for the deaths of many hundreds, and perhaps thousands, which can be attributed to the security forces....

* * *

The body count kept by what is generally referred to in San Salvador as "the Human Rights Commission" is higher than the embassy's, and documented periodically by a photographer who goes out looking for bodies. The bodies he photographs are often broken into unnatural positions, and the faces to which the bodies are attached (when they are attached) are equally unnatural, sometimes unrecognizable as human faces, obliterated by acid or beaten to a mash of misplaced ears and teeth or slashed ear to ear and invaded by insects. "*Encontrado en Antiguo Cuscatlán el día 25 de marzo 1982: camison de dormir celeste,*" the typed caption reads on one photograph: found in Antiguo Cuscatlán March 25, 1982, wearing a sky-blue night shirt. The captions are laconic. Found in Soyapango May 21, 1982. Found in Mejicanos June 11, 1982. Found at El Playón May 30, 1982, white shirt, purple pants, black shoes.

The photograph accompanying that last caption shows a body with no eyes, because the vultures got to it before the photographer did. There is a special kind of practical information that the visitor to El Salvador acquires immediately, the way visitors to other places acquire information about the currency rates, the hours for the museums. In El Salvador one learns that vultures go first for the soft tissue, for the eyes, the exposed genitalia, the open mouth. One learns that an open mouth can be used to make a specific point, can be stuffed with something emblematic; stuffed, say, with a penis, or, if the point has to do with land title, stuffed with some of the dirt in question. One learns that hair deteriorates less rapidly than flesh, and that a skull surrounded by a perfect corona of hair is not an uncommon sight in the body dumps.

All forensic photographs induce in the viewer a certain protective numbness, but dissociation is more difficult here. The disfigurement is too routine. The locations are too near, the dates too recent. There is the presence of the relatives of the disappeared: the women who sit every day in this cramped office on the grounds of the archdiocese, waiting to look at the spiral-bound photo albums in which the photographs are kept. These albums have plastic covers bearing soft-focus color photographs of young Americans in dating situations (strolling through autumn foliage on one album, recumbent in a field of daisies on another), and the women, looking for the bodies of their husbands and brothers and sisters and children, pass them from hand to hand without comment or expression.

One of the more shadowy elements of the violent scene here [is] the death squad. Existence of these groups has long been disputed, but not by many Salvadorans....Who constitutes the death squads is yet another difficult question. We do not believe that these squads exist as permanent formations but rather as ad hoc vigilante groups that coalesce according to perceived need. Membership is also uncertain, but in addition to civilians we believe that both on- and off-duty members of the security forces are participants. This was unofficially confirmed by right-wing spokesman Maj. Roberto D'Aubuisson who stated in an interview in early 1981 that security force members utilize the guise of the death squad when a potentially embarrassing or odious task needs to be performed.

—from the confidential but later declassified January 15, 1982, memo previously cited, drafted for the State Department by the political section at the embassy in San Salvador

The dead and pieces of the dead turn up in El Salvador everywhere, everyday, as taken for granted as in a nightmare, or a horror movie. Vultures of course suggest the presence of a body. A knot of children on the street suggests the presence of a body. Bodies turn up in the brush of vacant lots, in the garbage thrown down ravines in the richest districts, in public rest rooms, in bus stations. Some are dropped in Lake Ilopango, a few miles east of the city, and wash up near the lakeside cottages and clubs frequented by what remains in San Salvador of the sporting bourgeoisie. Some still turn up at El Playón, the lunar lava field of rotting human flesh visible at one time or another on every television screen in America but characterized as recently as June in the *El Salvador News Gazette*, an English-language weekly edited by an American named Mario Rosenthal, as an "uncorroborated story...dredged up from the files of leftist propaganda." Others turn up at Puerta del Diablo, above Parque Balboa, a national *Turicentro* still described, in the April-July 1982 issue of *Aboard TACA*, the magazine provided passengers on the national airline of El Salvador, as "offering excellent subjects for color photography."

* * *

I drove up to Puerta del Diablo one morning last summer, past the Casa Presidencial and the camouflaged watchtowers and heavy concentrations of troops and arms south of town, on up a narrow road narrowed further by landslides and deep crevices in the roadbed, a drive so insistently premonitory that after a while I began to hope that I would pass Puerta del Diablo without knowing it, just miss it, write it off, turn around and go back. There was however no way of missing it. Puerta del Diablo is a "view site" in an older and distinctly literary tradition, nature as lesson, an immense cleft rock through which half of El Salvador seems framed, a site so romantic and "mystical," so theatrically sacrificial in aspect, that it might be a cosmic parody of nineteenth-century landscape painting. The place presents itself as pathetic fallacy: the sky "broods," the stones "weep," a constant seepage of water weighting the ferns and moss. The foliage is thick and slick with moisture. The only sound is a steady buzz, I believe of cicadas.

Body dumps are seen in El Salvador as a kind of visitors' must-do, difficult but worth the detour. "Of course you have seen El Playón," an aide to President Alvaro Magaña said to me one day, and proceeded to discuss the site geologically, as evidence of the country's geothermal resources. He made no mention of the bodies. I was unsure if he was sounding me out or simply found the geothermal aspect of over-riding interest. One difference between El Playón and Puerta del Diablo is that most bodies at El Playón appear to have been killed somewhere else, and then dumped; at Puerta del Diablo the executions are believed to occur in place, at the top, and the bodies thrown over. Sometimes reporters will speak of wanting to spend the night at Puerta del Diablo, in order to document an actual execution, but at the time I was in Salvador no one had.

The aftermath, the daylight aspect, is well documented. "Nothing fresh today, I hear," an embassy officer said when I mentioned that I had visited Puerta del Diablo. "Were there any on top?" someone else asked. "There were supposed to have been three on top yesterday." The point about whether or not there had been any on top was that usually it was necessary to go down to see bodies. The way down is hard. Slabs of stone, slippery with moss, are set into the vertiginous cliff, and it is down this cliff that one begins the descent to the bodies, or what is left of the bodies, pecked and maggoty masses of flesh, bone, hair. On some days there have been helicopters circling, tracking those making the descent. Other days there have been militia at the top, in the clearing where the road seems to run out, but on the morning I was there the only people on top were a man and a woman and three small children, who played in the wet grass while the woman started and stopped a Toyota pickup. She appeared to be learning how to drive. She drove forward and then back toward the edge, apparently following the man's signals over and over again.

We did not speak, and it was only later, down the mountain and back in the land of the provisionally living, that it occurred to me that there was a definite question about why a man and a woman might choose a well-known body dump for a driving lesson. This was one of a number of occasions, during the two weeks my husband

and I spent in El Salvador, on which I came to understand, in a way I had not understood before, the exact mechanism of terror.

* * *

Whenever I had nothing better to do in San Salvador I would walk up in the leafy stillness of the San Benito and Escalón districts, where the hush at midday is broken only by the occasional crackle of a walkie-talkie, the click of metal moving on a weapon. I recall a day in San Benito when I opened my bag to check an address, and heard the clicking of metal on metal all up and down the street. On the whole no one walks up here, and pools of blossoms lie undisturbed on the sidewalks. Most of the houses in San Benito are more recent than those in Escalón, less idiosyncratic and probably smarter, but the most striking architectural features in both districts are not the houses but their walls, walls built upon walls, walls stripped of the usual copa de oro and bougainvillea, walls that reflect successive generations of violence: the original stone, the additional five or six or ten feet of brick, and finally the barbed wire, sometimes concertina, sometimes electrified; walls with watchtowers, gun ports, closed-circuit television cameras, walls now reaching twenty and thirty feet.

San Benito and Escalón appear on the embassy security maps as districts of relatively few "incidents," but they remain districts in which a certain oppressive uneasiness prevails. In the first place there are always "incidents"—detentions and deaths and disappearances—in the barrancas, the ravines lined with shanties that fall down behind the houses with the walls and the guards and the walkie-talkies; one day in Escalón I was introduced to a woman who kept the lean-to that served as a grocery store in a barranca just above the Hotel Sheraton. She was sticking prices on bars of Camay and Johnson's baby soap, stopping occasionally to sell a plastic bag or two filled with crushed ice and Coca-Cola, and all the while she talked in a low voice about her fear, about her eighteen-year-old son, about the boys who had been taken out and shot on successive nights recently in a neighboring barranca.

* * *

In the second place there is, in Escalón, the presence of the Sheraton itself, a hotel that has figured rather too prominently in certain local stories involving the disappearance and death of Americans. The Sheraton always seems brighter and more mildly festive than either the Camino Real or the Presidente, with children in the pool and flowers and pretty women in pastel dresses, but there are usually several bulletproofed Cherokee Chiefs in the parking area, and the men drinking in the lobby often carry the little zippered purses that in San Salvador suggest not passports or credit cards but Browning 9-mm. pistols.

It was at the Sheraton that one of the few American *desaparacidos*, a young free-lance writer named John Sullivan, was last seen, in December of 1980. It was also at the Sheraton, after eleven on the evening of January 3, 1981, that the two American advisers on agrarian reform, Michael Hammer and Mark Pearlman, were killed, along with the Salvadoran director of the Institute for Agrarian Transformation, José Rodolfo Viera. The three were drinking coffee in a dining room off the lobby, and whoever killed them used an Ingram MAC-10, without sound suppressor, and then walked out through the lobby, unapprehended. The Sheraton has even turned up in the investigation into the December 1980 deaths of the four American Maryknoll workers. In *Justice in El Salvador: A Case Study*, prepared and released this summer in New York by the Lawyers Committee for International Human Rights, there appears this note:

> On December 19, 1980, the [Duarte government's] Special Investigative Commission reported that "a red Toyota 3/4-ton pick-up was seen leaving (the crime scene) at about 11:00 PM

on December 2" and that "a red splotch on the burned van" of
the churchwomen was being checked to determine whether the
paint splotch "could be the result of a collision between that
van and the red Toyota pick-up." By February 1981, the Maryknoll Sisters' Office of Social Concerns, which has been actively
monitoring the investigation, received word from a source
which it considered reliable that the FBI had matched the red
splotch on the burned van with a red Toyota pick-up belonging
to the Sheraton hotel in San Salvador....

Subsequent to the FBI's alleged matching of the paint splotch
and a Sheraton truck, the State Department has claimed, in a
communication with the families of the church-women, that
"the FBI could not determine the source of the paint scraping."

There is also mention in this study of a young Salvadoran businessman named Hans Christ (his father was a German who arrived in El
Salvador at the end of World War II), a part-owner of the Sheraton.
Hans Christ lives now in Miami, and that his name should have even
come up in the Maryknoll investigation made many people uneasy,
because it was Hans Christ, along with his brother-in-law, Ricardo
Sol Meza, who, in April of 1981, were first charged with the murders
of Michael Hammer and Mark Pearlman and José Rodolfo Viera at
the Sheraton. These charges were later dropped, and were followed
by a series of other charges, arrests, releases, expressions of "dismay" and "incredulity" from the US Embassy, and even, recently,
confessions to the killings from two former National Guard corpo-
rals, who testified that Hans Christ had led them through the lobby
and pointed out the victims. Christ and Ricardo Sol Meza have said
that the dropped case against them was a government frame-up, and
that they were only having drinks at the Sheraton the night of the
killings, with a National Guard intelligence officer. It was logical for

Hans Christ and Ricardo Sol Meza to have drinks at the Sheraton because they both had interests in the hotel, and Ricardo Sol Meza had just opened a roller disco, since closed, off the lobby into which the killers walked that night. The killers were described by witnesses as well dressed, their faces covered. The room from which they walked is no longer a restaurant, but the marks left by the bullets are still visible, on the wall facing the door.

Whenever I had occasion to visit the Sheraton I was apprehensive, and this apprehension came to color the entire Escalon district for me, even its lower reaches, where there were people and movies and restaurants. I recall being struck by it on the canopied porch of a restaurant near the Mexican embassy, on an evening when rain or sabotage or habit had blacked out the city and I became abruptly aware, in the light cast by a passing car, of two human shadows, silhouettes illuminated by the headlights and then invisible again. One shadow sat behind the smoked-glass windows of a Cherokee Chief parked at the curb in front of the restaurant; the other crouched between the pumps at the Esso station next door, carrying a rifle. It seemed to me unencouraging that my husband and I were the only people seated on the porch. In the absence of the headlights the candle on our table provided the only light, and I fought the impulse to blow it out. We continued talking, carefully. Nothing came of this, but I did not forget the sensation of having been in a single instant demoralized, undone, humiliated by fear, which is what I meant when I said that I came to understand in El Salvador the mechanism of terror.

2.

3/3/81: Roberto D'Aubuisson, a former Salvadoran army intelligence officer, holds a press conference and says that before the US presidential election he had been in touch with a number of

Reagan advisers and those contacts have continued. The armed forces should ask the junta to resign, D'Aubuisson says. He refuses to name a date for the action, but says "March is, I think, a very interesting month." He also calls for the abandonment of the economic reforms. D'Aubuisson had been accused of plotting to overthrow the government on two previous occasions. Observers speculate that since D'Aubuisson is able to hold the news conference and pass freely between Salvador and Guatemala, he must enjoy considerable support among some sections of the army.... 3/4/81: In San Salvador, the US Embassy is fired upon; no one is injured. Charge d'Affaires Frederic Chapin says, "This incident has all the hallmarks of a D'Aubuisson operation. Let me state to you that we oppose coups and we have no intention of being intimidated."

—from the "Chronology of Events Related to Salvadoran Situation" prepared periodically by the United States embassy in San Salvador

Since the Exodus from Egypt, historians have written of those who sacrificed and struggled for freedom: the stand at Thermopylae, the revolt of Spartacus, the storming of the Bastille, the Warsaw uprising in World War II. More recently we have seen evidence of this same human impulse in one of the developing nations in Central America. For months and months the world news media covered the fighting in El Salvador. Day after day, we were treated to stories and film slanted toward the brave freedom fighters battling oppressive government forces in behalf of the silent, suffering people of that tortured country. Then one day those silent suffering people were offered a chance to vote to choose the kind of government they wanted. Suddenly the freedom fighters in the hills were exposed for what they really are: Cuban-backed guerrillas.... On election day the people of El Salvador, an unprecedented [1.5 million] of them, braved ambush and gunfire, trudging miles to vote for freedom.

—*President Reagan, in his June 8, 1982, speech before both houses of the British Parliament, referring to the March 28 election which resulted in the ascension of Roberto D'Aubuisson to the presidency of the Constituent Assembly*

From whence he shall come to judge the quick and the dead. I happened to read President Reagan's speech one evening in San Salvador when President Reagan was in fact on television, with Doris Day, in *The Winning Team*, a 1952 Warner Brothers picture about the baseball pitcher Grover Cleveland Alexander. I reached the stand at Thermopylae about the time that *el salvador del Salvador* began stringing cranberries and singing "Old St. Nicholas" with Miss Day. "*Muy bonita*," he said when she tried out a rocking chair in her wedding dress. "*Feliz Navidad*," they cried, and, in accented English, "*Play ball!*"

As it happened, "play ball" was a phrase I had come to associate in El Salvador with Roberto D'Aubuisson and his followers in the Nationalist Republican Alliance, or ARENA. "It's a process of letting certain people know they're going to have to play ball," embassy people would say, and: "You take a guy who's young, and everything 'young' implies, you send him signals, he plays ball, then we play ball." American diction in this situation tends toward the studied casual, the can-do, as if sheer cool and Bailey bridges could shape the place up. Elliott Abrams told *The New York Times* in July that punishment within the Salvadoran military could be "a very important sign that you can't do this stuff any more," meaning kill the citizens. "If you clean up your act, all things are possible," is the way Jeremiah O'Leary, a special assistant to US national security adviser William Clark, described the American diplomatic effort in an interview given the *Los Angeles Times* just after the March 28 election. He was speculating on how Ambassador Deane Hinton might be dealing with D'Aubuisson. "I kind of picture him saying, 'Goddamnit Bobbie, you've got a problem and . . . if you're what everyone said you are, you're going to make it hard for everybody.'"

* * *

Roberto D'Aubuisson is a chain smoker, as were many of the people I met in El Salvador, perhaps because it is a country in which the possibility of achieving a death related to smoking remains remote. I never met Major D'Aubuisson, but I was always interested in the adjectives used to describe him. "Pathological" was the adjective, modifying "killer," used by former Ambassador Robert E. White (it was White who refused D'Aubuisson a visa, after which, according to the embassy's "Chronology of Events" for June 30, 1980, "D'Aubuisson manages to enter the US illegally and spends two days in Washington holding press conferences and attending luncheons before turning himself in to immigration authorities"), but "pathological" is not a word one hears in-country, where meaning tends to be transmitted in code.

In-country one hears "young" (the "and everything 'young' implies" part is usually left tacit), even "immature"; "impetuous," "impulsive," "impatient," "nervous," "volatile," "high-strung," "kind of coiled-up," and, most frequently, "intense," or just "tense." Offhand it struck me that Roberto D'Aubuisson had some reason to be tense, in that General José Guillermo García, who has remained a main player through several changes of government, might logically perceive him as the wild card who could queer everybody's ability to refer to his election as a vote for freedom. As I write this I realize that I have fallen into the Salvadoran mind-set, which turns on plot, and, since half the players at any given point in the game are in exile, on the phrase "in touch with."

"I've known D'Aubuisson a long time," I was told by Alvaro

Magaña, the banker the Army made, over D'Aubuisson's rather fren-
zied objections ("We stopped that one on the one-yard line," Deane
Hinton told me about D'Aubuisson's play to block Magaña), provisional president of El Salvador. We were sitting in his office upstairs
at the Casa Presidencial, an airy and spacious building in the tropical
colonial style, and he was drinking cup after Limoges cup of black
coffee, smoking one cigarette with each, carefully, an unwilling actor
who intended to survive the accident of being cast in this production.
"Since Molina was president. I used to come here to see Molina,
D'Aubuisson would be here, he was a young man in military intelligence, I'd see him here." He gazed toward the corridor that opened
onto the interior courtyard, with cannas, oleander, a fountain not in
operation. "When we're alone now I try to talk to him. I do talk to
him, he's coming for lunch today. He never calls me Alvaro, it's always *usted, Señor, Doctor.* I call him Roberto. I say, 'Roberto, don't
do this, don't do that,' you know."

Magaña studied in the United States, at Chicago, and his four oldest
children are now in the United States, one son at Vanderbilt, a son and
a daughter at Santa Clara, and another daughter near Santa Clara, at
Notre Dame in Belmont. He is connected by money, education, and
temperament to oligarchal families. All the players here are densely
connected: Magaña's sister, who lives in California, is the best friend of
Nora Ungo, the wife of Guillermo Ungo, and Ungo spoke to Magaña's
sister in August when he was in California raising money for the
FMLN-FDR, which is what the opposition to the Salvadoran government was called this year. The membership and even the initials of this
opposition tend to be fluid, but the broad strokes are these: the FMLN-
FDR is the coalition of the Revolutionary Democratic Front (FDR)
and the five guerrilla groups in the Farabundo Martí National Liberation Front (FMLN). These five groups are the Salvadoran Communist
Party (PCS), the Popular Forces of Liberation (FPL), the Revolution-

ary Party of Central American Workers (PRTC), the Peoples' Revolutionary Army (ERP), and the Armed Forces of National Resistance (FARN). Within each of these groups, there are further factions and sometimes even further initials, as in the PRS and LP-28 of the ERP.

During the time that D'Aubuisson was trying to stop Magaña's appointment as provisional president, members of ARENA, which is supported heavily by other oligarchal elements, passed out leaflets referring to Magaña, predictably, as a communist, and, more interestingly, as "the little Jew." The manipulation of anti-Semitism is an undercurrent in Salvadoran life that is not much discussed and probably worth some study, since it refers to a tension within the oligarchy itself, the tension between those families who solidified their holdings in the mid-nineteenth century and those later families, some of them Jewish, who arrived in El Salvador and entrenched themselves around 1900. I recall asking a well-off Salvadoran about the numbers of his acquaintances within the oligarchy who have removed themselves and their money to Miami. "Mostly the Jews," he said.

In San Salvador
in the year 1965
the best sellers
of the three most important
book stores
were:
The Protocols of the Elders of Zion;
a few books by
diarrhetic Somerset Maugham;
a book of disagreeably
obvious poems
by a lady with a European name
who nonetheless writes in Spanish about our

country
and a collection of
Reader's Digest condensed novels.
—"San Salvador" by Roque Dalton Garcia,
Translated by Edward Baker[*]

The late Roque Dalton García was born into the Salvadoran bourgeoisie in 1935, spent some years in Havana, came home in 1973 to join the ERP, and, in 1975, was executed, on charges that he was a CIA agent, by his own comrades. The actual executioner was said to be Joaquín Villalobos, who is now about thirty years old, commander of the ERP, and a key figure in the FMLN, which, as the Mexican writer Gabriel Zaid pointed out last winter in *Dissent*, has as one of its support groups the Roque Dalton Cultural Brigade. The Dalton execution is frequently cited by people who want to stress that "the other side kills people too, you know," an argument common mainly among those like the State Department with a stake in whatever government is current in El Salvador, since, if it is taken for granted in Salvador that the government kills, it is also taken for granted that the other side kills; that everyone has killed, everyone kills now, and, if the history of the place suggests any pattern, everyone will continue to kill.

"Don't say I said this, but there are no issues here," I was told this summer by a high-placed Salvadoran. "There are only ambitions." He meant of course not that there were no ideas in conflict, but that the conflicting ideas were held exclusively by people he knew; that, whatever the outcome of any fighting or negotiation or coup or countercoup, the Casa Presidencial would ultimately be occupied not by

---

[*]*El Salvador: The Face of Revolution*, by Robert Armstrong and Janet Shenk (South End Press, 1982), p. 11.

campesinos and Maryknolls but by the already entitled, by Guillermo Ungo or Joaquín Villalobos or even by Roque Dalton's son, Juan José Dalton, or by Juan José Dalton's comrade in the FPL, José Antonio Morales Carbonell, the guerrilla son of José Antonio Morales Ehrlich, a former member of the Duarte junta, who had himself been in exile during the Romero regime. In an open letter written shortly before his arrest in San Salvador in June of 1980, José Antonio Morales Carbonell had charged his father with an insufficient appreciation of "Yankee imperialism." José Antonio Morales Carbonell and Juan José Dalton tried together to enter the United States last summer, for a speaking engagement in San Francisco, but were refused visas by the embassy in Mexico City.

Whatever the issues were that had divided Morales Carbonell and his father and Roque Dalton and Joaquín Villalobos, the prominent Salvadoran to whom I was talking seemed to be saying, they were issues that fell somewhere outside the lines normally drawn to indicate "left" and "right." That this man saw *la situación* as only one more realignment of power among "the entitled", a conflict of "ambitions" rather than "issues," was, I recognized, what many people would call a conventional bourgeois view of civil conflict, and offered no solutions, but the people with solutions to offer were mainly somewhere else, in Mexico or Panama or Washington.

* * *

The place brings everything into question. One afternoon when I had run out of the Halazone tablets I dropped every night in a pitcher of tap water (a demented *gringa* gesture, I knew even then, in a country where anyone who had not been born there was at least mildly ill, including the nurse at the American embassy), I walked across the street from the Camino Real to the Metrocenter, which is referred to locally as "Central America's Largest Shopping Mall." I found no Halazone at the Metrocenter but became absorbed in making notes about the mall itself, about the Muzak playing "I Left My Heart in San Francisco" and "American Pie" ("...*singing, This will be the day that I die...*") although the record store featured a cassette called *Classics of Paraguay*, about the pâté de foie gras for sale in the supermarket, about the guard who did the weapons-check on everyone who entered the supermarket, about the young matrons in tight Sergio Valente jeans, trailing maids and babies behind them and buying towels, big beach towels printed with maps of Manhattan that featured Bloomingdale's; about the number of things for sale that seemed to suggest a fashion for "smart drinking," to evoke modish cocktail hours. There were bottles of Stolichnaya vodka packaged with glasses and mixer, there were ice buckets, there were bar carts of every conceivable design, displayed with sample bottles.

This was a shopping center that embodied the future for which El Salvador was presumably being saved, and I wrote it down dutifully, this being the kind of "color" I knew how to interpret, the kind of inductive irony, the detail that was supposed to illuminate the story. As I wrote it down I realized that I was no longer much interested in this kind of irony, that this was a story that would not be illuminated by such details, that this was a story that would perhaps not be illuminated at all, that this was perhaps even less a "story" than a true *noche obscura*. As I waited to cross back over the Boulevard de los Heroes to the Camino Real I noticed soldiers herding a young civilian into a van, their guns at the boy's back, and I walked straight ahead, not wanting to see anything at all.

—November 4, 1982

(This was the first part of a three-part article.)

9

The Sakharovs in Gorky

Natalya Viktorovna Hesse and Vladimir Tolz

Yuri Andropov, the longest-serving chief of the KGB and Party leader since 1982, the destroyer of the Prague Spring and planner of the Afghan invasion, the man who sent Andrei Sakharov into exile, was said to enjoy listening to jazz records. The jazz-lover died in February 1984.

But life in Gorky remained a torment for Sakharov. Things would get still worse: hunger strikes, followed by force-feeding and months in solitary confinement. Both Sakharov and his wife and fellow human rights activist, Elena Bonner, were badly in need of medical treatment, but doctors turned them away. They were abused, robbed, publicly vilified, kept in isolation, and bullied in a thousand little ways that added up to a torture session that never stopped.

And all this for behaving like civilized human beings who insist on thinking for themselves and expressing their views. Sakharov and Bonner were not violent revolutionaries or radicals. They were humane, and they wished to live in a society that was humane. And that was enough to merit punishment from a state that felt threatened by one man and one women who refused to conform to the cynicism of dictatorship.

—I.B.

Note: Natalya Viktorovna Hesse, an old and trusted friend of Nobel prize winner Andrei Sakharov and his family, arrived in Vienna from the Soviet Union on February 5, 1984. Hesse, who is now seventy, has known Elena Georgievna Bonner, Sakharov's wife, for more than thirty years and Sakharov himself since 1970. This friendship, as well as her own views, was not approved of by the Soviet regime. Of her decision to emigrate to the United States to join her son and his family Hesse said:

The pressure against me was intensified. My apartment was searched, I was interrogated, I was called to the KGB many times for all kinds of talks.... But this was not the reason for my leaving the country. I was never afraid of them [the Soviet authorities], and I would have been able to resist them further.... But there was a change in my personal circumstances, and I decided to leave. And the KGB provided all kinds of "assistance."

The purpose of this "assistance" is quite clear. According to Hesse, the KGB is determined to isolate the Sakharovs completely and to deprive them of any help from their friends.

Before her departure from the Soviet Union, Natalya Hesse met privately with Sakharov in Gorky and visited Elena Bonner in Moscow. She has brought alarming news of the deterioration of Sakharov's health and of a new heart seizure suffered in January by Elena Bonner, who had still not completely recovered from the previous one. Upon her arrival in Vienna, Hesse was interviewed by Vladimir Tolz, a former dissident who is now a research analyst for Radio Liberty in Munich. The following is a translation of parts of the interview, which was recorded in Russian by Radio Liberty.

TOLZ: Please tell us about your meeting with Andrei Dmitrievich Sakharov.

HESSE: This was our seventh meeting over the past few years since his forced exile to Gorky. In this case, as also in the case of the six other meetings (I will talk about the first one separately), the meeting took place on the street, at a prearranged place and a prearranged hour. We didn't have much time. I already knew that I would be going away and I came to say goodbye to him. He has aged much, he is full of worries concerning the health of his wife, Elena Georgievna.... But he is not broken, he is not bending; he is full of worry and he is physically weak, but he is strong in spirit as always....

Between incoherent and hurried exchanges—because we had only a few hours at our disposal—between trivia and important topics—which we touched upon sometimes in more detail, sometimes with laughter or with sorrow—between questions about the life of our dear ones—who has been arrested, whose homes have been searched—we recalled Orwell, and I think this was not incidental. We have lived to see the year predicted by Orwell—1984. And it may seem strange to a Western person, it may seem that Orwell has nothing to do with real life, that his terrible utopia still remains a utopia or maybe an anti-utopia. However, the Soviet authorities—our dear KGB—have overtaken Orwell by four whole years. In 1980, Andrei Dmitrievich Sakharov and Elena Georgievna Bonner were plunged into a world that surpassed Orwell's nightmarish fantasies.

* * *

I will try to explain concretely what I mean. In 1980, I had some luck. I arrived in Gorky on January 25, immediately after the seizure and forced transportation of Andrei Dmitrievich to Gorky. His routine at that time had not yet been set; the authorities didn't know how to organize it, and I was able to stay with them for a month. Their entire apartment is bugged, there isn't a corner where each sigh, each cough, each footstep, not to speak of conversations, can't be overheard. Only thoughts can remain secret, if they haven't been put down on paper, because if the Sakharovs go to the bakery or to the post office to mail a letter, the KGB agents will search the place. They will either photograph or steal the written thought.

Andrei Dmitrievich, with his weak heart, his inability to walk up even five or seven steps without pausing for breath and trying to quiet his heartbeat, is forced to carry a bag that I, for example, can't lift. When once we went into a shop, he asked me to watch over this bag, but I wanted to see what was on a shelf, and I had to drag the bag after me. I just could not lift it. In this bag Andrei Dmitrievich carries a radio receiver, because it would be damaged if left at home, all his manuscripts—both scientific and public ones—diaries, photos, personal notes. He has to carry all this around with him. I think all this must weigh no less than thirty pounds. And this man with a bad heart—suffering from acute hypertension—is forced to carry this bag every time he leaves home, even if it is only for ten minutes.

There is in the apartment a special generator that creates additional interference over and above the interferences caused by conventional jammers in all cities of the Soviet Union. This produces a terrible growl that drowns even the jammer's noise. In order to hear at least some free world voice, one has to go away from the house. It would be better to go out of town, but Andrei Dmitrievich cannot take even one step beyond the city limit, cannot go past the sign with the word "Gorky" on it. He is immediately turned back, he is denied such a possibility, although there is no published verdict condemning him to such isolation.

This is complete lawlessness on the part of the so-called competent bodies. It is very interesting that the recent law on citizenship uses this term, "competent bodies," without any explanation. This is one example of the extent of illegality in our state. There cannot exist a judicial term that is not and cannot be explained. However, the law states that some cases must be reviewed by the MVD, while in some other instances, as prescribed by other articles, the same cases are supposed to be dealt with by "competent bodies." It is not clear who these "competent bodies" are. When the term is used in the press, one can only guess who and what they are. But when this is not explained in the text of the law, one may only make a helpless gesture and just wonder.

TOLZ: Natalya Viktorovna, you were going to tell us about your first visit to Gorky in greater detail.

HESSE: Yes. At that time I managed to stay there for a month, together with Sakharov and Elena Georgievna, who, however, often traveled to Moscow in an effort to do something there to make Andrei Dmitrievich's life easier. A lot of interesting things were going on. There was a stream of letters, vast numbers of them, ten and occasionally a hundred a day. After a few days I began to sort them out—having decided to take a look—because there were all kinds of letters: some greeting and supporting him, some bewildered, some neutral ones in which people asked him to explain his position—asking whether what the Soviet papers wrote about him was true.

* * *

But some of the letters were abusive—there were curses, there were threats. Some letters were, I would say, of an extreme nature. One letter was, in my view, very funny. We all laughed terribly hard when it arrived: "We, second-grade pupils, sternly condemn the position of Academician Sakharov, who wants to unleash an atomic war between the Soviet Union's peaceful democracy and the rotten Western world. Shame on Academician Sakharov! Second-grade pupils." Such a letter was obviously dictated by an illiterate teacher.

Another extreme letter was also very interesting and somehow simply touched one's heartstrings. It began with some swear words, but not obscene, no. Then it said: "I am seventy-four years old. I am a construction engineer. I live well and have a separate room in a hostel. The water pump is about three hundred yards from where I live, and I have to carry firewood from the woods, but still I am a patriot. And your studies were paid for by Soviet money, but you have now betrayed your homeland." This letter was from a woman who represents one of the most terrible types of Soviet patriot. When a person exists at the bottom level of human life and does not realize it—imagining that he lives well—this is very frightening.

After about a week I said: "Listen, these letters must be sorted out, so that we can see the result. There are already many hundreds of them. I'll review them and make an assessment, and then we'll see what they add up to." When all this was done, I loudly announced: "Well, this is terribly interesting: 70 percent are messages of greeting, 17 percent are neutral or expressing bewilderment, and only 13 percent are abusive ones." The result of this careless remark—made aloud—was very unexpected. Letters with greetings and voicing approval simply ceased to arrive. From the very next day we began to receive only abusive letters. This was evidence of very attentive and well-organized monitoring and careful analysis of all conversations within the apartment.

The second incident happened after I had left. I heard about it from Elena Georgievna. She had walked to the window and, looking at the joyless, empty lot covered with trash and at the highway beyond with roaring trucks passing by, said: "From the window in Moscow one can see Red Square, but from this window, only a bit of the street, trash, and all kinds of shit. It is better not to look out the window." And then turning to Andrei Dmitrievich, who was standing beside her, she said: "You know, Andrei, I think I'll photograph this, take a picture and send it to the West. Let them look at this wonderful landscape." The next day three trucks arrived and soldiers collected all the trash on the empty lot in front of the windows. Commenting on this, Elena Georgievna used to say jokingly: "Thus I'll bring order to Gorky."

* * *

I have said that Sakharov was not allowed to leave Gorky's city limits, to step beyond the sign that read "Gorky." But the house itself, although within the city limits, is located near the borderline. Then there is a ravine—also still within the city limits; it is a sort of empty lot with a thick aspen grove. Andrei Dmitrievich and Elena Georgievna once decided to take a walk along a narrow path and—in accordance with the rules—two persons in civilian clothes tagged after them. The Sakharovs exchanged some glances and, having gone separately in different directions away from the path, hid in the thick bushes. Having lost sight of them, the agents began running to and fro. Within three minutes a helicopter arrived on the spot, descended to about five meters above the ground, and KGB agents with scared, fierce faces stared out of all the windows, trying to locate the Sakharovs. Thus it is impossible to hide from the KGB's "almighty eye" anywhere—even in thick aspen bushes.

TOLZ: Natalya Viktorovna, a defamation campaign against Sakharov has become especially intense recently in the Soviet press, as well as in some books—one by Nikolai Yakovlev in particular. Please, tell us in greater detail about this stage of Sakharov's persecution, which began, I think, about a year ago.

HESSE: First of all, I will tell you about the Yakovlev episode. Yakovlev has expressed himself in the most shocking manner. His writing cannot be called anything but slop. His book *CIA Against the USSR* [which included attacks on both Sakharov and his wife] was published, I think, in a first edition of 200,000 copies and was later reprinted several times with some changes (one should remember that with changes amounting to 20 percent of the original text, one can collect new royalties).[1] He published this in the magazine

---

1. *CIA-Target–The USSR* was published in English by Progress Publishers (Moscow, 1982).

Smena, which has a circulation of more than a million copies, and, finally, having reworked it and having added a good dose of anti-Semitism, he published it in *Chelovek i Zakon* ["Man and the Law"]. This sounds even more paradoxical, since this periodical has a circulation of more than eight million. So, altogether his ideas have a circulation of about ten million.

* * *

Well, during our last meeting, Andrei Dmitrievich told me in detail about his encounter with Yakovlev, who, strangely enough, was allowed to come to Gorky. Sakharov was very elaborate in his narration, laughing and at the same time expressing horror at the extent to which a man can debase himself.

His doorbell rang. Elena Georgievna was in Moscow at the time. Sakharov was alone and was very much surprised. He decided that it must be a telegram. He opened the door. There was an unfamiliar man standing there with a woman—a man advanced in years ("Of my own age," Andrei Dmitrievich said). Andrei Dmitrievich let them in, and the woman immediately asked whether she could smoke in the apartment. Being an extremely well-brought-up person, Andrei Dmitrievich showed them to the largest room, right across from the entrance, said, "Please go in," and hurried into the kitchen to get an ashtray, since he himself does not smoke.

When he returned, his guests were already seated. He only had time to think: "Maybe some physicians have finally come from the Academy of Sciences in order to have me hospitalized." He thought so because a few months earlier some physicians had come and had concluded that he was urgently in need of hospitalization. But these two were no medical doctors. The visitor by this time had already managed to display a pile of books, and said: "I am Nikolai Nikolaievich Yakovlev. As you know, I am a writer. Or maybe you don't know this. But I brought you my books as a present and, if you agree, I will autograph them for you."

Andrei Dmitrievich was somewhat taken aback by this extreme impudence and said: "I don't need your presents." He waved his hand, and one of the books fell to the floor. Nobody picked it up—neither Yakovlev nor Andrei Dmitrievich. But Yakovlev continued: "Well, I have published, you know, some articles. And so we have received many inquiries, and I am unable to answer them all. Therefore, I came here to ask you some questions and to get answers that we could relate to our readers."

Andrei Dmitrievich replied that he refused to talk to Yakovlev until the latter apologized in writing for slandering Sakharov's wife—Elena Georgievna Bonner—and her and his own—Andrei Dmitrievich's—family, as well as Andrei Dmitrievich himself. After this he grabbed the book, *CIA Against the USSR*, which was lying nearby and feverishly began turning the pages. "How could you write such slander, such horrible slander? How could you have called our children 'dropouts' when they all have a university education...?" To which Yakovlev replied, unperturbed, "Yes, I know."

To most of Andrei Dmitrievich's angry questions, Yakovlev replied that he was aware of this or that. And only when asked, "How did you dare to write that my wife beats me?" Yakovlev said, "Well, so I was told in the prosecutor's office."[2] This man [Yakovlev] is so cynical and so morally degraded that he has no idea of either conscience or shame.

---

2. *Interviewer's note:* At another point Hesse said she had been told that the editor who had allegedly been working on Yakovlev's books asked him once, "Nikolai Nikolaievich, where do you get material for your abominable articles?" And Yakovlev said, "Does one need any sources for this?"

They talked for a few more minutes. Yakovlev said: "I am not going to write an apology. If you think this is slander, you can refer the matter to court. And, generally speaking, try to understand that we are defending you." Andrei Dmitrievich said: "I don't need your defense, and I am not going to go to court—I will just slap your face now." (It was at this point in the narration that I shuddered. I told Andrei Dmitrievich that this was terrible—that it was a frightful moment. And he said he felt the same way.)

Upon hearing this, Yakovlev, who was sitting at the table, covered his cheek with his hand. This is the utmost level of degradation, when a person cannot even face up to a slap honorably, openly, like a man. He covered part of his face with one hand, but Andrei Dmitrievich, who is ambidextrous and so has equal command of both hands, slapped him on the unprotected cheek. At that point Yakovlev and his companion ran away from the apartment—in the exact sense of the term: they jumped up, overturning their chairs, and escaped.

Having finished the story about slapping Yakovlev's face, Andrei Dmitrievich said to me: "You know, I have seen many different people in my life, including many bad ones. But this is something out of Dostoevsky, this is Smerdyakov. One cannot sink any further."

* * *

Yakovlev is an expert on America, and they say that his books on historical topics are not bad at all. But those who know him also say that he is cynical in the extreme, that his motto is that the Soviet regime is so abominable that one can and must be a scoundrel, that everybody must become a scoundrel. Such is Yakovlev's position, and he practices it in real life perfectly well.

TOLZ: Natalya Viktorovna, could you say something concerning the reaction of Soviet citizens—in Gorky, in particular—to the defamation campaign against Sakharov and his wife, which has now been intensified?

HESSE: Yes. The letter written by four Academy members against Andrei Dmitrievich has played a certain role, although not a very big one, within the context of the campaign of defamation and slander that has been unleashed against him and particularly against Elena Georgievna. I think that the West is of the opinion that it was the letter from these four academicians that played the principal part. (However, even among Academy members one can find people who would burden their conscience with heavy sins for the sake of their careers. And these four academicians, in particular, are known for being go-getters ready to do anything.)

But in Gorky itself the campaign—it was unleashed mainly in Gorky—was provoked not by the letter, which was published somewhere in the corner of a newspaper, but by the fact that the Gorky papers reprinted all of Yakovlev's insinuations concerning Elena Georgievna and, furthermore, added their own commentaries. Since then, at somebody's command, an extremely vicious campaign has been organized. The Sakharovs were even afraid to go to the bakery because they would be insulted. People would holler at them: "Your Yid-wife must be killed."

* * *

A neighbor in the Sakharovs' house had been helped by Elena Georgievna, who is a pediatrician (a very good pediatrician, an excellent physician), when the neighbor's child was suffering from an allergy which physicians in Gorky were unable to cure. Elena Georgievna did help the child with her advice, and the child was cured. And this same neighbor used to cry: "It would have been better for my child to rot than to be touched by your dirty hands."

The Sakharovs' car would be covered with graffiti: "Warmonger, get away from here, away from our town!" This seemed to them (and I have discussed this at length with both of them) to be a spontaneous wave of wrath on the part of the people. But whenever I asked Elena

Georgievna to describe each incident in detail, her story would always expose some "stage director" who was behind each particular horrible act.

It is very easy to arouse indignation in our country. Indignation is fostered by the hardships of everyday life, by the lines in front of the stores, by the whole drabness and oppressiveness of Soviet reality, which is very hard. Therefore it is sufficient to make just a little hole, to open up the valve just a bit, and one can direct the stream of hate and bitterness any way one wants to. When people are standing in a line, it is enough for someone to shout: "It's not his turn!" or "Don't give him two kilos instead of one!" and the crowd will release its anger upon the unfortunate victim. Thus it is a very simple task to orchestrate something like that.

TOLZ: Natalya Viktorovna, it is known that Elena Georgievna Bonner does not stay in Gorky with her husband all the time and that she is obliged to come regularly to Moscow. What is her situation there? What is her general situation now?

HESSE: The conditions at their apartment in Moscow became quite terrible after Andropov took over all the positions and jobs that he assumed. Now, in addition to two policemen posted at the entrance to the apartment itself (and it must be noted that whereas in Gorky they are ordinary policemen, in Moscow either senior lieutenants or captains are on duty at the entrance to the apartment upstairs), there is also a police car with flashing lights guarding the downstairs entrance, and the man in charge has the rank of major at least.

It is amusing that these policemen in turn are watched over by KGB agents in civilian clothes who make sure that the policemen dutifully carry out their mission. They all have portable radio sets on their shoulders, and they communicate with each other. All visitors are checked against a special list. If a stranger tries to pass through and his name is not on the list, he must show his documents, and if he does not have any, he is simply not allowed in. No foreigners and no journalists are allowed to visit the apartment.

The telephone at the Moscow apartment has been disconnected ever since Andrei Dmitrievich's illegal exile to Gorky, and whenever Elena Georgievna comes to Moscow they disconnect even the public telephone in the booth downstairs so that in order to call someone she has to walk almost a kilometer up a very steep hill, which is practically impossible because of her heart condition. All in all, Elena Georgievna's health is in a terrible state. She has not yet recovered from her first heart seizure; she takes up to forty nitroglycerine pills; her lips and fingernails are of a dark blue color. It is upsetting to look at her.

* * *

When she came to Moscow the last time, she wanted to come to Leningrad to see me off, but I went to Moscow myself instead because I learned from friends about the state of her health, and it was clear that no farewell parties were possible. It was at this time that she suffered her second heart seizure, not having been completely cured after the first one.

In general, both of them are denied medical help. Andrei Dmitrievich himself also has been in need of a medical checkup and treatment for a long time, and this was admitted by the physicians from the Academy of Sciences who visited Sakharov in Gorky that one and only time. We had some hope then that things would improve; but, like all our hopes, this one was also destroyed. Neither she nor he has been admitted to a hospital, although both are seriously ill and in desperate need of medical treatment.

And they cannot allow themselves to be treated by physicians in

Gorky. These physicians displayed their true nature sufficiently during the Sakharovs' hunger strike. Other physicians at the Arsenal Hospital in Leningrad—it's a prison hospital—once proudly said that they are first and foremost "Chekists"[3] and physicians only afterward. Well, those Gorky doctors, not being professional Chekists, nevertheless behaved as if they were, and it is therefore impossible to trust them and to be treated by them.

Once Andrei Dmitrievich was forced to go to a dentist because he had a toothache (and in such a case a person is willing to go anywhere), and the head of the dental clinic deceived him. She ordered him to leave his briefcase with his precious documents and manuscripts, and then personally turned the briefcase over to KGB agents. I think this incident is known in the West, but it may not be known that she then denied him medical treatment, claiming that he had insulted her—both as a woman and as a citizen. It was naturally very strange to hear such words coming from this particular physician.

As I have already mentioned, Elena Georgievna is being denied proper medical assistance in Moscow. A young woman who recently graduated from a medical institute visits her at home. I've been present during many of her visits. She respectfully and, I would even say, piously listens to advice from Elena Georgievna, who is a physician herself. Elena Georgievna writes her own prescriptions and decides her own treatment. Nevertheless, she urgently needs hospitalization because her condition is becoming ever more serious and her strength is leaving her—the strength that seemed to be inexhaustible. "Constant dripping of water wears away the stone," as we say in Russia. But in this case there were not drops but heavy blows on the stone and it has begun to break. During our last meeting Andrei Dmitrie-

---

3. Members of the Cheka, as the secret police was formerly called.

vich said: "The first thing to be done, the most important thing, is to force the authorities to allow Elena Georgievna to travel abroad for medical treatment. Tell the people you'll meet in the West that her death would be the end of me also. And being an eyewitness to all that has been happening, I can state that she is on the verge of dying, this is the truth."

* * *

We must do everything possible. I don't know, maybe the general public in the West must appeal to their elected deputies so that they, in turn, would raise the question in their respective parliaments. This is very important, especially now that we have a new ruler. He might show his good will and prove to the world that the Soviet Union is really ready to do good and not evil.

TOLZ: Natalya Georgievna, the campaign against Sakharov has been continuing for a long time, but it was especially intensified during the period that has now come to an end—the "Andropov era." Tell me, in your opinion, in the opinion of a person who left the Soviet Union only days ago—did the situation in the country change during the Andropov period?

HESSE: The regime became extremely harsh. It began with mass roundups of people in the streets, and in every city indignant people were told by agitators at meetings that these were only excesses on the local level. But the same thing was going on all over the Soviet Union, just as it was during collectivization. And, in general, the whole moral and spiritual climate in the country became much harsher. It seems that it is difficult to breathe—just as it was in Stalin's time. This is a frightening feeling and it affects a person's whole being. The food situation in large cities has improved but the provinces remain hungry. In the large cities—in Leningrad, in particular—one can get meat, not always the kind one wants, of course, but we became accustomed to this long ago. Sometimes one can get butter without standing in line.... So, it is somewhat better in this sense. But, on the other hand, there is complete suppression of everything, and not a gleam of democracy.

—April 12, 1984

10

The Burial of Cambodia
William Shawcross

Mao Zedong wanted tracking to be more radical than Stalin, and Pol Pot wanted to be more extreme than Mao. In relative numbers, the Khmer Rouge leader, who picked up his version of Marxist-Leninist ideology as a student in Paris, succeeded. Up to two million Cambodians died in his four years of misrule, by being shot or hacked or worked or starved to death. That was almost 20 percent of the population.

In the 1980s, few people wanted to know. The truth was unwelcome to the new rulers, Vietnamese and their Cambodian stooges, many of them with fresh blood on their hands, to Thais and other Southeast Asians who continued to support what remained of the Khmer Rouge to thwart the Vietnamese, to the Chinese who had always backed the Khmer Rouge, to the Western nations who didn't wish to upset their Asian allies, and to the US which had just fought a nasty Asian war of its own.

Genocide followed by silence and lies; not a unique phenomenon, alas, but yet another illustration of what humans at their worst are capable of.

—I.B.

WHEN I WAS in Cambodia in 1980, I told my guide that I wanted to see Tuol Sleng. This was the former Phnom Penh high school that the Khmer Rouge had converted into a prison and interrogation center and the Vietnamese had now made into a museum. He told me I needed the permission of both the Foreign Ministry, which had approved my visa, and the Information Ministry, which ran the museum.

The Foreign Ministry was housed in what was formerly the Buddhist Institute. I waited in a bare reception room until I was joined by a young man named Chum Bun Rong, the head of the press department. Mr. Bun Rong was charming and helpful. Of course I could visit Tuol Sleng, he said. We drove to the Ministry of Information, where my guide disappeared and came back with written permission.

We set off down Monivong Boulevard, the broad central avenue designed by Sihanouk and named after one of Cambodia's kings. People here appeared to have installed themselves only temporarily in the houses and old shops. It was as if after all the forced movement and mayhem of the last ten years no one was now willing to trust any arrangement, any home, to be permanent. In the side roads there were immense piles of rubbish. Cars were rusting where they had been dumped when the Khmer Rouge emptied the city and smashed machinery in April 1975.

We turned right, off the main road, and then right again, down a pretty, leafy lane. We stopped in front of a complex of three plain buildings, built in the early Sixties by the Sihanouk government as one of the city's principal high schools. Now over the gate was a sign, TUOL SLENG EXTERMINATION CENTER. We were met by a young student called Dara, who spoke good English and worked as a guide. About sixteen thousand people were brought to Tuol Sleng, and only about a half-dozen escaped alive in the confusion as the Vietnamese army stormed the city in early 1979; one of them, Ung Pech, was now the museum's curator.

* * *

Most of the people brought to the prison had been Khmer Rouge cadres on whom the party had turned, as communist parties so often do on their own. Whereas straightforward "class enemies" tended to be executed in the fields without ceremony, the party leadership was determined to extract confessions from its own members accused, for whatever cause, of treason—which almost always meant collaboration with Vietnam, with the CIA, or with both.

The classrooms on the ground floor of the first building had all apparently been used as torture rooms. In each was a metal bed frame to which victims had been strapped, a school desk and chair for the interrogator. In each there was also an old US Army ammunition box, into which prisoners were supposed to defecate, and petrol cans, into which they were to urinate. Each cell also had a large photograph of the room as the Vietnamese had apparently found it after their invasion. The Khmer Rouge had departed with such speed that decaying corpses were found bound to the bed in several cells. These bodies were buried in graves in front of the building.

In one of the classrooms was a blackboard on which, the guide said, were written instructions to the prisoners on their behavior under interrogation. Underneath it was a translation into English:

1. You must answer in conformity with the questions I ask you. Don't try to turn away my questions.
2. Don't try to escape by making pretexts according to your hypocritical ideas.
3. Don't be a fool for you are a chap who dares to thwart the revolution.
4. You must immediately answer my questions without wasting time to reflect.
5. Don't tell me about your little incidents committed against

the propriety. Don't tell me either about the essence of the revolution.

6. During the bastinado or the electrisisation you must not cry loudly.

7. Do sit down quietly. Wait for the orders. If there are no orders do nothing. If I ask you to do something you must immediately do it without protesting.

8. Don't make any pretexts about Kampuchea Krom in order to hide your jaw of traitor.[1]

9. If you disobey every point of my regulations you will get either ten strokes of the whip or five shocks of electric discharge.

In the next block the classrooms had been subdivided by crude brick partitions about eight feet high into tiny cells for individual prisoners. Each was shackled by the ankle onto a piece of iron large enough to make a ship's anchor set in the floor. Each lived here awaiting his interrogation, torture, confession, and death.

In another room a huge pile of black clothing lay displayed along one wall in direct imitation of the museum at Auschwitz. I was told these were the dead prisoners' clothes. Also in this room was a heap of typewriters, plates, cooking utensils, and a broken photocopier, which the guide said had been found there.

The most terrible of the exhibits was the photographs. The Khmer Rouge had abolished much of what we think of as modern bureaucracy—except, it seemed, for the function of government with which

---

1. Kampuchea Krom is the Cambodian name for the Mekong Delta, which used to be part of Cambodia and is now in Vietnam, and which the Pol Pot leadership coveted. Presumably, anyone accused of having a Kampuchea Krom accent would be declared a Vietnamese spy.

they are most closely identified, repression. The prisoners at Tuol Sleng had almost all been photographed—either on arrival at the school, or after their grisly deaths. The Vietnamese had found the negatives and taken them away for enlargement, and the pictures were now displayed around the walls.

There were photographs of bodies lying strapped to the metal beds, of others cast on the floor with their throats cut. But the studies of the arrivals were the most poignant. They had been stood or seated before a draped sheet, as in a photographer's studio. For the most part their faces were blank, but some attempted a tentative, slightly hopeful smile, as if they wished to believe that by wooing the cameraman they might, somehow, obtain mercy. There were men, there were women, and there were a lot of children. They had apparently been brought here when their parents were arrested. Some had been photographed with their mothers, some were alone. They were of all ages. Sometimes their faces showed a merciful incomprehension, but often they were as rigid with terror as their elders. All had been murdered.

* * *

Upstairs in the school the files were kept. These were almost the only Khmer Rouge documents to which the Vietnamese had allowed foreigners access; nothing from the party leadership was available. At Tuol Sleng there was a translation, written in pencil, of Lenin's *On the State* and another of an East German book called *Who's Who in the CIA*, which is merely a list of American names and addresses. The other files were filled with confessions. All were laboriously taken down in longhand, and some were then retyped as, one after another, these prisoners of the party had been forced to admit to monstrous and absurd crimes. There were pages and pages of confessions in folders signed by those who admitted to having secretly betrayed the revolution for years by working for the CIA or the Vietnamese. There were elaborate charts and card indexes crossreferencing different "traitors" and groups of "traitors."

The fantastic nature of the confessions is illustrated by the one extracted from John Dewhirst, a young Englishman who was captured along with two friends on their yacht in the Gulf of Thailand. The confession began, "My name is John Dawson Dewhirst, a British citizen. I am a CIA agent who officially works as a teacher in Japan. I was born at Newcastle-upon-Tyne, England, on 2 October 1952. My father was a CIA agent whose cover was headmaster of Benton Road Secondary School."

Dewhirst declared that he himself was recruited to the CIA at the age of twelve by a friend of his father named Edward Fraser. "He was a colonel in the CIA and as a cover was an executive on the Shell BP oil company." According to Dewhirst, his father was a CIA captain whose duty was to report on communist teachers in the Newcastle district. He had been paid $1,000 for his son's induction into the agency.

After being tortured, Dewhirst and his friends, like almost everyone else at Tuol Sleng, were murdered. One of the most prominent Khmer Rouge officials murdered in Tuol Sleng was Hu Nim, who, like many of his peers, had become a communist in Paris in the late Fifties and early Sixties. He had then spent eight years in the Khmer Rouge maquis, and he was minister of information in the Khmer Rouge government until his arrest in 1977.

In his "confession," Hu Nim was compelled to declare that he too had been "an officer of the CIA" since 1957, working toward

the construction of capitalism in Kampuchea ... completely toeing the line of the American imperialists.... On the surface it seemed that I was a "total revolutionary," as if I was "standing on the people's side." ... But, in fact, deep in my mind, the essence was service of the American imperialists.... I wrote a thesis for my law doctorate which even took a progressive stand.... These were the cheapest acts which hid my reactionary, traitorous, corrupted elements, representing the feudalist, capitalist, imperialist establishment and the CIA.... I'm not a human being, I'm an animal.

Hu Nim was "crushed to bits" in July 1977.

* * *

Just as the Khmer Rouge had attempted to impose a fanatical and brutal perspective upon the country, so the Vietnamese have since devised another order of unreality. In one room at Tuol Sleng the new sanitized history of the Cambodian revolution was displayed in texts and old photographs. There were pictures of Mao Tse-tung with Pol Pot to emphasize the evil of that connection and the complicity of Vietnam's own great en the Khmer Rouge. There were many blurred photographs of hitherto obscure Cambodian communist cadres, whose roles were now being exaggerated so as to demonstrate that the party had had a tradition of true Marxism-Leninism and of international solidarity with Vietnam, which the Pol Pot group had sought to extinguish by murder. There was nothing to suggest the extent of Vietnam's own past support for the Khmer Rouge revolution.

In the account of the end of French colonial rule in the 1950s and the growth of the country in the 1960s there was not a single reference to Prince Norodom Sihanouk, who had in fact led his country for twenty-five years. The Prince not only had negotiated independence from France but also had managed, until the end of the Sixties, to keep Cambodia largely out of the growing war in Vietnam. During the 1970–1975 war in Cambodia he had been titular leader of the revolutionary forces, living in exile in Peking without real power, but officially recognized by Hanoi and many other governments as the true head of state of Cambodia. After the Khmer Rouge victory in 1975 he returned to Phnom Penh; his usefulness over, the Khmer Rouge stripped him of office and pt him under close house arrest in the almost empty city. As the Vietnamese tanks drew close to Phnom Penh he was flown out in a Chinese airliner and was dispatched to New York at once by the Chinese to denounce the Vietnamese attack at the United Nations. He had excoriated both the Vietnamese and the Khmer Rouge. Now he was yawing around in uncertain limbo between Peking, Paris, and Pyongyang, while at home he had been removed from history.

"Why is there no mention of Sihanouk?" I asked my guide.

"On the advice of the experts," he replied.

"What experts?" I asked.

"Vietnamese experts," he said.

One entire wall of this room had been made into a map of Cambodia—perhaps fourteen feet high and as many wide. On glass eight inches in front of the wall the rivers and lakes of the country were painted blood red. Behind the glass, arranged in the shape of the country, were hundreds of skulls collected from a nearby mass grave. This was another contribution by the Vietnamese experts.

* * *

The same Vietnamese experts have assiduously tried to associate Pol Pot with Hitler, and they have had considerable success. Thus Tuol Sleng prison has been called "an Asian Auschwitz." The museum was indeed derived in part from Nazi history, but the prison was not. This distinction seems to me to be important. In the spring of 1979, the Vietnamese, with the help of East German advisers, organized Tuol Sleng, according to officials of the Heng Samrin regime, so as to recall images of the Nazi concentration camps. Moreover, in 1983, in preparation for the fifth anniversary of the Vietnamese takeover, the museum was remodeled. The task was carried out in good part by its efficient curator, Ung Pech. He was sent to East Germany to visit Buchenwald and Sachsenhausen for new ideas on how to make Tuol Sleng more closely resemble the Nazi "original."

In fact, it is hard to think of two prisons more different than Auschwitz and Tuol Sleng. Auschwitz was a work camp and an extermination camp in which millions of people—perhaps as many as four million—died or were murdered. About half of them were Jews, and they died precisely because of that. In Tuol Sleng, by contrast, about sixteen thousand people had been killed, most of them because they were members of the Khmer Rouge apparat, or families of such members, on whom the organization had turned in its revolutionary and chauvinistic ferocity. In Auschwitz there was no such thing as a "confession," no "party" to whom disloyalty was alleged and which controlled events. In Tuol Sleng, confessions were meticulously extracted from the tortured victims before they were done to death in the name of the party they were supposed to have betrayed. Forcing such confessions was vile and paranoid. But it was not unprecedented.

The constant invocations of Nazism helped to obscure the fact that the Khmer Rouge was a Marxist-Leninist organization and that Tuol Sleng resembled much more a Stalinist prison than a Nazi concentration camp. ("I have nothing to depend on, I have only the Communist Party of Kampuchea," wrote Hu Nim, in his "confession." "Would the party please show clemency towards me. My life is completely dependent upon the party.") Yet I recall no one describing Tuol Sleng as an "Asian Lubyanka." Stalinist crimes have not been registered upon modern memory to anything like the extent of those of the Nazis.

The Nazi death camps are preserved by both the communist and the social-democratic societies that took over the wreckage of the Reich, as monuments and as warnings. Indeed, the horror of Nazism is one of the few issues on which communist and capitalist propaganda is agreed and which each seeks constantly to reiterate.[2] That is a powerful combination. By contrast there are no similar shrines to the victims of Stalin; on the contrary, the vast apparatus of the Soviet state and its allies, including Vietnam, are geared to obscuring rather than broadcasting the reality of the crimes that were committed.

* * *

Since 1979, Vietnam has refused to compromise over its occupation of Cambodia. It has controlled most of the country; the rest of the world has not allowed it to control Cambodia's seat in the UN. That is still held by the Khmer Rouge, the Government of Democratic Kampuchea. Since 1982, they have been in alliance with an anticommunist resistance group, the Khmer People's National Liberation Front, and with Prince Sihanouk. Indeed, the Prince is the titular head of the government of "Democratic Kampuchea." These three are not happy partners, and inside Cambodia itself the Khmer Rouge is much the strongest militarily.

During the past five years, as a result of Vietnam's intransigence, the Khmer Rouge forces have been rebuilt by Vietnam's enemies.

---

2. In this cold-warring world each side also tends, at least *in extremis*, to try to associate the other with fascism. Such attempts almost always owe more to rhetoric than to reality and, as such, they almost always devalue that reality. When the Soviets shot down the Korean 747 in 1983 not only did they refuse to apologize (this was perhaps the most terrifying element in the whole disaster), but they also tried to shift the blame to the United States. In alleging that the plane was spying, one Soviet spokesman declared that the White House was "worse than the Nazis. The passengers were sacrificed by the White House just as innocent people had been destroyed by the Nazis." A few weeks later Mrs. Thatcher, in a burst of anti-Soviet rhetoric, likened the Soviet system to that of Hitler. Such comparisons inhibit understanding.

They have been supplied with Chinese weapons through Thailand. Their camps along the Thai border have been supplied with food provided by the United Nations. Many hundreds of thousands of genuine refugees have been fed there—but so have Khmer Rouge troops. Without the arms and the food, the Khmer Rouge would not have been able to restore themselves into what now is thought to be a fighting force of some 25,000. In recent months they seem to have been attacking more and more widely across the country.

The strategy of helping the Khmer Rouge, devised by China and implemented with various degrees of enthusiasm by the ASEAN countries of Southeast Asia as well as by China, has the support of the Western nations. Each government involved—though China has been ambiguous—has stated that it never wishes to see the Khmer Rouge back in power and that the strategy being followed is intended merely to force Vietnam to the bargaining table. And many of the countries that have voted for the Khmer Rouge to continue holding the Cambodian seat in the UN have done so because they fear the precedent of legitimizing Vietnam's invasion. Yugoslavia is an obvious and telling example. Nonetheless, the fact remains that the Khmer Rouge have been revitalized. They will not go away.

And while this has happened, there has been a tendency to forget or at least to play down the Khmer Rouge's appalling human rights record when it was in power. There is still no certain calculation of the numbers who were murdered by the Khmer Rouge, or died as a result of its policies, between 1975 and the end of 1978. Most of the estimates that have been made conclude that between one and two million people died or were killed out of a population of roughly seven million. There has been little investigation of the Khmer Rouge regime; a former head of American Amnesty, David Hawk, has found it hard to arouse much interest in the United States, let alone any funds, for a serious commission to study the Khmer Rouge phenomenon. The world has moved on and looked away. The group that Jimmy Carter called "the world's worst violators of human rights" is now used as a convenient strategic chip in international politics.

* * *

The continuation of the Khmer Rouge undoubtedly represents a dreadful failure of political imagination and a denial of memory. But it is hard to attach sole responsibility for it to Vietnam's opponents. Vietnam itself bears considerable responsibility. Leaving aside the support that Hanoi gave to the Khmer Rouge before 1978 (and the extent to which its spokesmen undercut the refugee stories about Khmer Rouge conduct, thus adding to disbelief in them, particularly on the Western left), Vietnam's conduct since its invasion of Cambodia has rarely suggested that it wished to see a compromise in which the Khmer Rouge was removed as a significant force in Cambodia— which was what the ASEAN countries and their Western partners insisted was their aim.

After its occupation of Phnom Penh in January 1979, Hanoi might have signaled a serious desire to reach a compromise satisfactory to its neighbors. It is impossible to say whether any such suggestion would have been accepted by the Chinese or by the ASEAN countries, but the point is that it was never made. Time and again in the months after their invasion, the Vietnamese reiterated that their involvement in Cambodia was "irreversible" despite the fact that so many other nations found it intolerable. In this setting it was inevitable that those other nations would seek to apply all possible forms of pressure upon Hanoi to change its mind. The Vietnamese could have predicted that such pressures would include support for the Khmer Rouge.

When I traveled around Cambodia, it seemed that this was remarkably convenient for the Vietnamese. They could hope to have their occupation given legitimacy by a people who traditionally mistrusted them only if it was seen as the lesser of two evils, preventing the return of the Khmer Rouge. While Thailand and the Chinese were rebuilding Khmer Rouge strength along the Thai border, few if any Cambodians would have wanted the Vietnamese to leave. Within Cambodia, Vietnam's constant propaganda was designed both to instill fear about what would happen were Vietnamese protection against the Khmer Rouge withdrawn and to concentrate responsibility for Khmer Rouge crimes on "the Pol Pot-Ieng Sary clique" alone.

In this way Hanoi avoided any "de-Nazification" or "de-Stalinization" campaign and was able, on the contrary, to fill the Heng Samrin administration with cadres who had previously worked, with varying degrees of diligence, for "Pol Pot." Heng Samrin himself, Hun Sen, the foreign minister, even the minister of justice, Ouk Boun Chheoun, were all Khmer Rouge officials during most of the three years of Khmer Rouge rule. They are only three of thousands of former Khmer Rouge whom the Vietnamese "turned."

* * *

Pol Pot and Ieng Sary were indeed condemned to death in a show-trial that the Vietnamese staged in Phnom Penh in August 1979. But over the next four years hardly any other Khmer Rouge officials were charged with any offense. After 1975, Vietnam imprisoned some 200,000 of its own people without trial and for indefinite periods in harsh "reeducation" camps. But former Khmer Rouge officers were often deemed to be more reliable than former officials or soldiers of the Thieu or Lon Nol regimes. For the Khmer Rouge, "reeducation" might consist of a short course in Hanoi's interpretation of Marxism-Leninism. For noncommunists it could mean indefinite incarceration.[3]

Many of the fruits of "liberation" by Vietnam had been sweet in 1979; but it must have been bitter for many hundreds of thousands of ordinary noncommunist Cambodians to realize that their liberators placed more confidence in the torturers than in their victims, that many of those people were actually being promoted by the new order into positions of new authority over them. In one fishing village on a tributary of the Mekong I met an old woman who described with great passion how the Khmer Rouge murderer of her son was living, unpunished, in the neighboring village. I did not know whether any of the officials with me on that day had also previously worked for Pol Pot, but Elizabeth Becker noted in *The Washington Post* the awful discrepancy between the legacy of the Khmer Rouge rule and the propaganda purposes to which it was put:

---

3. Amnesty International stated in its 1983 annual report that it was "concerned about reports of detention without trial of people suspected of antigovernment activities" in Cambodia. "More than 200 prisoners suspected of supporting the KPNLF [an anticommunist resistance group] were reportedly held in the former *Prison centrale* in Phnom Penh. Other prisons in Phnom Penh believed to hold political prisoners were those of the municipal police, the Ministry of the Interior and the army. Political prisoners were reportedly also held in provincial and district prisons. People arrested near the border with Thailand and suspected of connections with the anti-communist resistance were said to be sent to a labor camp at Trapeaing Phlong in the eastern part of Kompong Cham province. [By contrast] Khmer Rouge deserters were reportedly sent to separate prisons and most released after three to six months' re-education. Most political detainees were held without trial. Amnesty International investigated the arrest in late 1982 in Kompon Thom of two people accused of stealing rice for armed opposition groups; Amnesty International received reports that the reason for their detention may have been their participation in unauthorized Christian gatherings. Amnesty International was also concerned about reports that they were tortured to force them to confess. Amnesty International also received details of several cases of people detained without trial for up to two years on suspicion of antigovernment activities; some were released after admitting the charges and pledging loyalty to the government."

Few official gatherings are complete without a speaker who details how he or she saw children, parents, and friends murdered by Pol Pot's henchmen, and other atrocities. It is not unusual for some of the people who carried out such orders to be seated in the audience or even on the podium with the victim recounting the story.

In a sense Vietnamese leniency toward former Khmer Rouge cadres was rendered the more disagreeable by the fact that Hanoi's propaganda was not content with the actual crimes the Khmer Rouge committed but was determined to exaggerate them sometimes to the point of absurdity. Thus they made the claim that Pol Pot was a madman who, on orders from China, was depopulating Cambodia so that it could be restocked with Chinese. Such extravagant demonology enabled Khmer Rouge spokesmen to claim more plausibly that Vietnamese assertions could not be believed.[4]

There is a comparison to be made here with Nuremberg. At that trial defendants attempted, at various stages, to absolve themselves by directing all guilt toward the demonic Hitler. The strategy did not work, if only because of the vast body of evidence that the trial gathered and published. In Cambodia, by contrast, the Vietnamese deliberately fostered the demon theory and allowed no such exhaustive examination of the records of the Khmer Rouge. No documents from

4. The propaganda declared that the Seventh of January Hospital in Phnom Penh, like almost all other hospitals, had been closed under the Khmer Rouge. But the three Western writers whom the Khmer Rouge had invited at the end of 1978—Elizabeth Becker, Richard Dudman, and Malcolm Caldwell (a British academic who was murdered there)—visited the hospital and found it filled with Cambodian soldiers wounded in fighting along the border with Vietnam. According to the propaganda, there was virtually no industry under the Khmer Rouge. Yet the three foreign journalists were taken to several working factories in 1978; when Becker returned in 1983, she found that they were now closed and it seemed to her that there was even less industrial life than under the Khmer Rouge.

the Central Committee or from the party leadership were released by Hanoi, perhaps because they would not reflect the new version of recent history which the Vietnamese sought to teach. Indeed, the only documents that the Vietnamese allowed to see the light of day were the confessions at Tuol Sleng. While these are a revealing testament to the fanatical brutality of the Khmer Rouge, they hardly constitute an adequate record of its years in power.

* * *

Moreover, even access to the Tuol Sleng records was increasingly restricted. While David Hawk found it difficult to arouse much Western interest in a detailed study of the Khmer Rouge, his problems were not just in the West. Last year I was told by rueful officials of the Heng Samrin regime in Phnom Penh that while they had wanted to grant his request to return to Phnom Penh to make microfiches of the records at Tuol Sleng, their Vietnamese "experts" had vetoed the proposal. They thought that now the Vietnamese did not want even that part of the real history to be fully and independently documented—though in previous years some foreign researchers had been allowed to examine the files.

Thus it seems that no one was really interested in establishing or remembering what happened. Along the border the feeding of the Khmer Rouge continued. The new propaganda that Khmer Rouge spokesmen in Thailand or in the West assiduously distributed was distasteful or absurd, boasting of their progressive outlook. But inside Cambodia, under the Vietnamese, former Khmer Rouge cadres were being fed and promoted, with no questions asked. And inside Cambodia, the propaganda of the Vietnamese was often equally absurd and was usually more pervasive.

The Czechoslovak historian Milan Hubl once remarked, after Soviet orthodoxy was forced again onto his country, "The first step in liquidating a people is to erase its memory. Destroy its books, its culture, its history. Then have somebody write new books, manufacture a new culture, invent a new history. Before long the nation will begin to forget what it is and what it was." Hubl's friend Milan Kundera wondered whether this was hyperbole dictated by despair. If one thinks of applying it to Cambodia, one must remember that Vietnamese rule has been much more benign than that of the Khmer Rouge. Nonetheless, in significant ways it seems now that propaganda threatens to bury the real and dreadful history of the recent past so deeply under new lies, new exaggerations, new ideological contraptions, that it is in danger of being obliterated and thus forgotten.

—May 10, 1984

11

'I Am Prepared for Anything'
Jerzy Popiełuszko

When it comes to oppressive governments, the Catholic Church, like most conservative institutions, religious or secular, has a patchy record. But Father Popiełuszko was the best kind of priest. His faith, for him, was not just a matter of tradition, ritual, sacred texts, the smells and the bells, and all the other paraphernalia of his calling. To him, it was a matter of standing by people in distress, strikers being beaten by brutal militiamen, dissidents being locked up for speaking their minds, workers who demanded the dignity of forming independent unions.

Jerzy Popiełuszko's Church was not a symbol of stern authority, hierarchy, or dogma; it was the center of moral opposition to a dictatorship that had long ago lost all its moral bearings. His Church was both humble and the grandest place of all, for it was there that people could feel free, even as the most powerful forces of the state were still stacked against them.

—I.B.

Note: Jerzy Popiełuszko, a priest at the St. Stanislaw Kostka church in Warsaw, was abducted by the Polish security forces on October 19 on a road outside the city of Torun and killed. He sent this statement abroad last year.

THE STATE OF the Church will always be the same as the state of the people. The Church is not just the Church hierarchy: it is all the people of God, a nation of millions, who constitute the Church in the greater sense, and when they suffer, when they are persecuted, the Church suffers.

The Church's mission is to be with its people day in and day out, partaking in their joys, pains, and sorrows. The primate and the bishops of course have in their care the well-being of all, and diplomacy is therefore at times necessary in the Church's higher ranks, to protect people from suffering and mistreatment whenever it is possible to do so. There are those who sometimes misunderstand and criticize this, for they want the Church to take a more decisive stand against the authorities. But such is not the Church's task.

The Church has repeatedly insisted and continues to insist that the authorities respect human dignity—which is not being respected; that they free the imprisoned. Through the efforts of the Church and of its affiliated Prisoners' Relief Committee, aid has reached those most severely persecuted. There is no better proof than this that the Church has indeed carried out its mission during martial law.

* * *

Has the lifting of martial law changed anything?

I've spoken out several times about this from the pulpit—unequivocally. As recently as the end of July, quoting official Church pronouncements in my argument, I concluded that in lifting martial law, something the bishops had called for so often, the authorities failed to take advantage of yet another opportunity for reconciliation with the nation. The amnesty was a subterfuge, calculated for one-sided gain—whereas the country had every right to expect that the amnesty would right the wrongs, especially the moral wrongs, committed during martial law. To this day our democratically elected brothers, behind whom stand millions of their countrymen, languish in prisons. And even those who have benefited from the amnesty must feel at times like hostages, for this is a conditional amnesty. They must sign statements that go against their own conscience.

The Holy Father has spoken on this subject of the freedom of conscience: conscience is something so holy that even God himself does not put limits on it. To do so through such forced statements is to offend against divine law. The lifting of martial law, a move buttressed by so many new regulations, must give each Pole the distinct impression that the shackles, partially loosened from around the hands, are tightening around the soul and conscience. There are many more restrictions now than before; freedom is curtailed even further. And that's why there is bitterness: here was one more chance to join hands, one more chance to try to get out of a difficult situation. This chance, unfortunately, was not seized.

How do I see the future?

I said this at the beginning. The Church's future will be the same as society's future. The Church's mission is to be with the people here through thick and thin, and this mission I believe the Church will never renounce. What is crucial is that people raise their national, religious, and social awareness. We need courses of public education, lectures in ethics, something along the lines of the interwar workers' universities. It is a fundamental matter, and the Church should participate in it. Its end? So that the next time there is a similar popular rising, a push for freedom, time will not be wasted on the unessential; people must learn to distinguish what is important, on what issues there can be no compromise, and on which, for the time being, there can be.

What is the mood of the country?

It is very difficult to define. One thing is certain: it is not against strong opposition; most people find themselves taking part in it.

It has always been this way: there were leaders who sacrificed themselves for a cause and paid dearly; and then, at the crucial moment, those millions who didn't seem to be on any side supported the just one.

What am I doing?

On August 30, 1980, a Sunday, Cardinal Wyszynski sent a message through a priest asking me to go to the Warsaw Steel Mill, where a strike was in progress in solidarity with the striking shipyard workers. I said mass. I lived through the disorders with the steel workers. I heard confessions from people who, exhausted beyond the limits of endurance, kneeled on the pavement. These people understood that they were strong in unity with God, with the Church.

I suddenly felt the need to remain with them. Whenever I'm about to undertake something, I either decide not to do so at all, or I take it very seriously, and put my heart into it. I stayed with these people. I was with them at the time of triumph, and for this they are grateful to me. I was with them during the black December night. During the trials, I went with their families to the courtroom. I sat in the front rows, and the accused saw that their families were being taken care of. They wrote me letters saying that they knew about my prayers for them, and that these prayers gave them strength.

Many people have since passed through this house, the church. My monthly mass for the country and for those who suffer for it has become one such meeting place. The masses have become very popular. In my sermons I speak about what people think and what they tell me in private, for often they lack the courage or the means to speak publicly. I speak out whenever I discern in their words a truth I think others should share. This truth-saying in church makes people trust me. I express what they feel and think. The numerous renewals of faith bear witness to how important this is. After many years, decades sometimes, people suddenly have the courage to come to me and ask to be reconciled with God, for confession, for holy communion. It is a wonderful experience for me as a priest, and for those people also. They didn't dare go to anyone else. Very often the process of conversion, the return to God, to the Church, or simply the discovery of God, begins when someone takes a patriotic stand. Many paths lead to God.

I receive many letters from people saying that these monthly masses for Poland help them live in hope, help them cleanse themselves of the hatred which, despite all, grows in them. This is a great reward for a priest, who really has no life of his own.

The authorities, trying to suppress me, have often attempted to exert pressure on the curia, on the bishops. They have sent letters charging me with various trespasses, often fabricated. I remember a letter in May—signed, incidentally, by a general of the militia—stating that on May 13 I conducted mass in the Church of the Holy Cross and used certain formulations ill becoming the dignity of the temple. But on the evening of May 13 I was sitting in my own church, in the confessional; I have never in my entire life said mass in the Church of the Holy Cross. If the bishop doesn't yet have the facts, why not burden the priest with more charges, to finally get him?

Recently the prosecutor's office published an item in its own internal paper saying that it had begun an investigation of me on the grounds that I abuse my freedom of conscience and of belief.

How can one abuse freedom of conscience? One can limit freedom of conscience, but one cannot abuse it. That is why these accusations are nonsense, but of course I realize that for the truth one must suffer. If people who have families, children, responsibilities, were in prisons, and still suffer—why should not I, a priest, add my suffering to theirs? Because of this they bully me. There have been certain attempts, very crude ones, and no doubt they will continue. For example: At two o'clock in the morning of December 14, after I had already gone to bed, dead tired, the doorbell rang. I didn't get up. Moments later, an explosion. A brick with explosives had been hurled into the apartment, breaking two windows. I've had two sham burglaries. I am under constant surveillance. On my way to Gdansk I was stopped and detained eight hours in a police station outside Warsaw. The driver was detained fifty hours. These are all very gross tactics, but there are larger matters at stake, and I am convinced that what I am doing is right. And that is why I am prepared for anything.

Translated from the Polish by Klara Glowczewska
—December 6, 1984

12

Fire on the Road
Ryszard Kapuściński

The "first Nigerian civil war" in 1966 was not yet the main event, which began the following year, when mostly Igbo people founded the breakaway Republic of Biafra. Between 1967 and 1970, when Biafra was reabsorbed into Nigeria, a million civilians died, many of starvation.

The war described by Kapuściński was part of a muddled period of coups and counter-coups, whipped up tribal passions, fraudulent elections, and above all of fear; fear of being dominated by other tribes, fear of being marginalized or plotted against, fear of sudden eruptions of extreme violence.

The politics are murky, the rights and wrongs elusive, and the sources of trouble varied: not just differences between the tribes, but also the messy birth of a nation whose boundary lines were sometimes randomly drawn up by British colonial officers.

Kapuściński was not the man to turn to for a precise and dispassionate analysis of the politics in the tropical dystopias he described so well. What he gets is the atmosphere, the taste of fear, the cold sweat, the sickening feeling of total anarchy, when death is ever-present and almost always brutal.

—I.B.

Note: Speaking in April at a rally in Soweto, Winnie Mandela was reported as saying, "Together, hand in hand, with our matches and our necklaces, we shall liberate this country."* In South Africa "necklaces" is the word used for tires filled with gasoline that are placed around the necks of collaborators and traitors to the cause of liberation, who are then doused with more gasoline and set on fire. Mrs. Mandela later said the press had distorted her speech and she repudiated the statement. But this kind of punishment and this kind of death have been practiced in South Africa for some time, to the horror of some and as a warning to others. Black policemen in flames in South Africa, like witches burning at the stake in Europe, and later, during World War II, Jews set on fire by Nazis in Warsaw and Bialystok, are victims of the same cruel myth, a belief deeply rooted among all fanatics, that fire is not only punishment but the only true purification—that all evil, if one wants to be really rid of it, has to be burned out in an absolutely literal sense.

The vision of fire as the highest agent of punishment and condemnation appears in many faiths and religions. It is one of the most suggestive images of the Apocalypse, a horrible sight, which from childhood admonishes us against temptation and sin—or else we will be hurled into the eternal flames of hell. But there is yet another, "educational," side of this phenomenon, well known to those who, by putting their opponents to the torch, treat suffering as a spectacle: by passively observing a man being burned alive we indirectly become participants in the crime, take part in it, have implicated ourselves.

What it feels like during the moments before one is set on fire I experienced myself when I was reporting on the first civil war in Nigeria in 1966 (the second war, which erupted soon thereafter, was over Biafra). The conflict I describe here touched off a series of inter-

---

*Quoted in the Sunday *Observer* (April 20, 1986), p. 10.

nal clashes, coups, and upheavals in this most heavily populated of the African countries. They continue to this day and in two decades have claimed more than one million victims and caused enormous destruction. During the past twenty years only one Nigerian government came to power through elections (in 1979, the government of Shehu Shagari, now deposed). At all the other times, those who gained power gained it through coups (1966—Major General Johnson Aguiyi-Ironsi; 1966—Colonel [later General] Yakubu Gowon; 1975—Brigadier Murtala Muhammad; 1976—Lieutenant General Olusegun Obasanjo; 1983—Major General Muhammadu Buhari; 1985—Major General Ibrahim Babangida).

Most often these takeovers of power are bloody, and those who stage them either perish themselves soon thereafter at the hands of rivals (as did Aguiyi-Ironsi and Murtala Muhammad), or end up in exile (as has General Gowon). Over the last quarter-century the Nigerian officer corps, rent by tribal and political conflicts, obsessed by an implacable struggle for power, has been decimating itself at such a rate that few of those officers who were in the army when Nigeria gained independence in 1960 are alive today. Whoever wants to understand the history of those battles and the tensions and passions behind them should read Shakespeare's plays, and keep in his mind's eye the royal throne constantly dripping with blood.

Translated by Klara Glowczewska

JANUARY 1966. IN Nigeria a civil war is going on. I am a correspondent in that war. On a cloudy day I leave Lagos. In the outskirts police are stopping all cars. They are searching the trunks, looking for weapons. They rip open sacks of corn: Could there be ammunition in that corn?

Authority ends at the city limits.

Now the road leads through a green countryside of low hills covered with close, thick bush. This is a laterite road, rust colored, with a treacherous uneven surface.

These hills, this road, and these villages along the road are the country of the Yorubas, who inhabit southwestern Nigeria. They constitute one fourth of Nigeria's population. The heaven of the Yorubas is full of gods and their earth full of kings. The greatest god is called Oduduwa and he lives on high, higher than the stars, even higher than the sun. The kings, on the other hand, live close to the people. In every city and every village there is a king. The Yorubas are proud of this—they look down on the rest of the world, because no other nation has so many kings.

In 1962 the Yorubas split into two camps. The overwhelming majority belongs to the UPGA party; an insignificant minority belongs to the NNDP party. Thanks to the trickery of the Nigerian central government, the minority party rules the Yorubas' province. The central government, which is dominated by the NPC (National People's Congress) from the north, prefers a minority government in the province as a means of more easily controlling the Yorubas and curbing their separatist ambitions. In this situation the party of the majority—the UPGA—found itself in opposition. The deceived and embittered majority went on the warpath. In the fall of 1965 there were elections in the Yorubas' province. It was obvious that the majority party, UPGA won. Nevertheless, the central government ignored the results and the mood of the Yorubas and announced the victory of the puppet NNDP, which went on to form a government. In protests against the official election results, the majority created a government of its own. For a time there were two governments. The members of the majority government were imprisoned in the end. At that point the UPGA launched an open war against the minority government.

And so we have misfortune, we have a war. It is an unjust, dirty, hooliganish war in which all methods are allowed—whatever it takes to knock out the opponent and gain control. This war needs a lot of fire so houses are burning, plantations are burning, and charred bodies lie in the streets and along the roads.

The whole land of the Yorubas is in flames.

* * *

I am driving along a road where they say no white man can come back alive. I am driving to see if a white man can, because I have to experience everything for myself. I know that a man shudders in the forest when he passes close to a lion. I got close to a lion so that I would know how it feels. I had to do it myself because I knew no one could describe it to me. And I cannot describe it myself. Nor can I describe a night in the Sahara. The stars over the Sahara are enormous. They sway above the sand like great chandeliers. The light of those stars is green. Night in the Sahara is as green as a Mazowsze meadow in Poland.

I might see the Sahara again and I might see the road that carried me through Yoruba country again. I drove that road up a hill and when I got to the crest I could see the first flaming roadblock down below.

It was too late to turn back.

Burning logs blocked the road. There was a big bonfire in the middle of the road. I slowed down, and then stopped, because it was impossible to keep going. I could see fifteen or twenty young people. Some of them had shotguns, some were holding knives, and the rest were armed with machetes. They were all dressed alike, in blue shirts with white sleeves. Those were the colors of the opposition, of the UPGA. On their heads they wore black and white caps with the letters UPGA. They had pictures of Chief Awolowo pinned to their shirts. Chief Awolowo was the leader of the opposition, the idol of the party.

I was in the hands of UPGA activists. They must have been smoking hashish because their eyes were unconscious, mad. They were soaked in sweat, possessed, berserk.

Now they descended on me and pulled me out of the car. I could hear them shouting, "UPGA! UPGA!" On this road, UPGA ruled. Now UPGA held me in its sway. I could feel three knife points against my back and I saw several machetes aimed at my head. Two activists stood a few steps away, pointing their guns at me in case I tried to get away. I was surrounded. Around me I could see sweaty faces, jumpy glances, I could see knives and gun barrels.

My African experience had taught me that the worst thing to do in such situations is to betray the moment of despair, the worst thing is to make some movement of self-defense, because that emboldens the people you face and unleashes a new wave of aggression in them.

In the Congo they poked machine guns in our bellies. We couldn't flinch. The most important thing was keeping still—to learn that keeping still takes practice and willpower, because everything inside screams to run for it or jump the other guy. But they are always in groups and that means certain death. This is a moment when he, the black, is testing me, looking for a weak point in me. He fears attacking my strong point, because he has too much fear of the white in him—that is why he looks for my weakness. So I have to cover all my weakness, hide it somewhere very deep within myself. This is Africa, I am in Africa. They do not know that I am not their enemy. They know that I am white, and the only white they have ever known is the colonizer who abased them, and now they want to make me pay for it.

The paradox of the situation is that I am to die out of responsibility for colonialism, I am to die in expiation of the slave merchants, I am to die to atone for the white planter's whip, I am to die because

Lady Lugard ordered them to carry her in a litter.

* * *

The ones standing in the road wanted money. They wanted me to join the party, to become a member of UPGA, and to pay for it. I gave them five shillings. That was too little, because somebody hit me on the back of the head. I felt pain in my skull. In a moment another bomb went off in my head. After the third blow I felt enormous fatigue. Tired and sleepy, I asked how much they wanted.

They wanted five pounds.

Everything in Africa is getting more expensive. In the Congo soldiers were accepting people into the party for one pack of cigarettes and one blow with a rifle butt. But here I've already got it a couple of times and I'm still supposed to pay five pounds. I must have hesitated because the boss, who was supervising things, shouted to the activists, "Burn the car!" and that car, the Peugeot that was carrying me around Africa, was not mine. It belonged to the Polish state. One of them splashed gasoline onto the Peugeot.

I understood that the discussion had ended and I had no way out. I gave them the five pounds. They started fighting over it.

But they allowed me to drive on. Two boys moved the burning logs aside. I looked around. On both sides of the road there was a village and the village crowd was watching the action on the road. The people were silent; somebody in the crowd was holding up an UPGA banner. Most had photographs of Chief Awolowo pinned onto their shirts. I liked the girls best of all. Naked to the waist, they had the name of the party written on their full breasts: UP on the right breast, and GA on the left one.

I started off.

I could not turn back—they allowed me only to go forward. So I kept driving through a country at war, with a rooster tail of dust behind me. The landscape is beautiful there, all vivid colors, Africa the way I like it. Quiet, empty, with a bird taking flight in the path of the car every now and then. The roaring of a factory was only in my head. But an empty road and a car gradually restore calm.

Now I knew the price: UPGA had demanded five pounds of me. I only had four and a half pounds left, and fifty kilometers to go. I passed a burning village and an empty village where people were fleeing into the bush. Two goats were grazing by the roadside and smoke hung above the road.

Beyond the village was another flaming roadblock.

Activists in UPGA uniforms, knives in their hands, were kicking a driver who did not want to pay his membership fee. Nearby stood a bloody, beaten man—he hadn't been able to come up with the dues, either. Everything looked just as it had at the first roadblock. At this second roadblock I didn't even manage to announce my desire to join UPGA before I took a pair of hooks to the midsection and had my shirt torn. They turned my pockets inside out and took all my money.

I was waiting for them to set me on fire, because UPGA was burning a lot of people alive. I had seen many burned corpses. The boss at this roadblock popped me one in the face and I felt a warm sweetness in my mouth. Then he poured benzene on me, because here they burn people in benzene—it assures complete incineration.

I felt an animal fear, a fear that struck me like paralysis; I stood rooted to the ground, as if I were buried up to the neck. I could feel the sweat flowing over me, but under my skin I was as cold as if I were standing naked in subzero frost.

I wanted to live, but life was abandoning me. I wanted to live, but I did not know how to defend my life. My life was going to end in inhuman torment. I was going to go out in flames.

* * *

What did they want from me? They waved a knife before my eyes. They pointed the knife at my heart. The boss of the operation stuffed my money into his pocket and shouted at me, blasting me with his beery breath: "Power! UPGA must get power! We want power! UPGA is power!" He was shaking, swept up in the passion of power, he was mad about power, the very word "power" sent him into ecstasy, into the highest rapture. His face was covered with sweat, the veins on his forehead were bulging, and his eyes were shot with blood and madness. He was happy and he began to laugh in joy. They all started laughing. That laughter saved me.

They ordered me to drive on.

The little crowd around the roadblock shouted "UPGA!" and held up their hands with two fingers stretched out in the V sign: victory for UPGA on all fronts.

Some four kilometers down the road a third roadblock was burning. The road was straight here and I could see the smoke a long way off, and then the fire and the activists. I could not turn back. There were two barriers behind me. I could only go forward. I was trapped, falling out of one ambush and into another. But now I was out of money for ransom, and I knew that if I didn't pay up they would burn the car. Above all, I didn't want another beating. I was whipped, my shirt was in tatters, and I reeked of benzene.

There was only one way out: to run the roadblock. It was risky, because I might wreck the car or it might catch fire. But I had no choice.

I pressed the accelerator to the floor. The roadblock was a kilometer ahead. The speedometer needle jumped—110, 120, 140. The car shimmied and I gripped the wheel more tightly. I leaned on the horn. When I was right on top of it I could see that the bonfire stretched all the way across the road. The activists were waving their knives for me to stop. I saw that two of them were winding up to throw bottles of gasoline at the car and for a second I thought, *so this is the end, this is the end*, but there was no turning back. There was no turning....

I smashed into the fire, the car jumped; there was a hammering against the belly pan, sparks showered over the windshield. And suddenly—the roadblock, the fire, and the shouting were behind me. The bottles had missed. The knives had missed. Hounded by terror, I drove another kilometer and then stopped to make sure the car wasn't on fire. It wasn't on fire. I was all wet. All my strength had left me, I was incapable of fighting, I was wide open, defenseless. I sat down on the sand and felt sick to my stomach. Everything around me was alien. An alien sky and alien trees. Alien hills and manioc fields. I couldn't stay there, so I got back in and drove until I came to a town called Idiroko. On the way in, there was a police station and I stopped there. The policemen were sitting on a bench. They let me wash and straighten myself up.

I wanted to return to Lagos, but I couldn't go back alone. The commandant started organizing an escort. But the policemen were afraid to travel alone. They needed to borrow a car, so the commandant went into town. I sat on a bench reading the *Nigerian Tribune*, the UPGA paper. The whole paper was dedicated to party activities and the way the party was fighting for power. "Our furious battle," I read, "is continuing. For instance, our activists burned the eight-year-old pupil Janet Bosede Ojo of Ikere alive. The girl's father had voted for the NNDP." I read on: "In Ilesha the farmer Alek Aleke was burned alive. A group of activists used the 'Spray-and-Lite' method [also known as 'UPGA candles'] on him. The farmer was returning from his fields when the activists grabbed him and commanded him to strip naked. The farmer undressed, fell to his knees, and begged for mercy. In this position he was sprayed with benzene and set afire." The paper was full of similar reports. UPGA was fighting for power, and the flames of that struggle were devouring people.

The commandant returned, but without a car. He designated three policemen to ride in my car. They were afraid to go. In the end they got in, pointed their rifles out the windows, and we drove off that way, like an armored car. At the first roadblock the fire was still burning but there was nobody in sight. The next two roadblocks were in full swing, but when they saw the police they let us through. The policemen weren't going to let anything stop the car; they didn't want to get into a fight with the activists. I understood them—they live here, and they want to survive. Today they had their rifles, but usually the police go unarmed here. Many policemen had been killed in the region.

At dusk we were in Lagos.

Translated by William Brand and Katarzyna Mroczkowska-Brand
—June 12, 1986

13

The Revolution of the Magic Lantern
Timothy Garton Ash

The year 1989, two hundred years after the French Revolution, was the best of times, in Europe. At last, to the surprise of almost everyone, the Soviet Empire crumbled; the rot had set in, rising expectations, encouraged by Gorbachov's reforms, corroded the foundations of authoritarian rule. And when the Empire cracked, so did its satellites, run by corrupt satraps. One by one, they fell: Poland, Hungary, Czechoslovakia, East Germany, Romania, Bulgaria.

Only the Communist Chinese, never a dependency of the Soviet sphere, held out, by turning tanks on their own people.

For once, in Europe, the good guys won. If there was at least one moral to this tale, it was this: men and women, brave enough to dissent from the rancid orthodoxies of dictatorship, always a tiny minority, often dismissed, even ridiculed, as naive and pointless troublemakers, can suddenly change from being marginal figures to becoming the leading actors of change. Havel, Dienstbier, Michnik, Kisch will still be celebrated long after their gray oppressors are forgotten.

—I.B.

MY MODEST CONTRIBUTION to the revolution was a quip. Arriving in Prague on Day Seven (November 23), when the pace of change was already breathtaking, I met Václav Havel in the back room of his favored basement pub. I said: "In Poland it took ten years, in Hungary ten months, in East Germany ten weeks: perhaps in Czechoslovakia it will take ten days!" Grasping my hands, and fixing me with his winning smile, he immediately summoned over a video-camera team from the samizdat *Video-journál*, who just happened to be waiting in the corner. I was politely compelled to repeat my quip to camera, over a glass of beer, and then Havel gave his reaction: "It would be fabulous if it could be so...." Revolution, he said, is too exhausting. The camera team dashed off to copy the tape, so that it could be shown on television sets in public places. Havel subsequently used the conceit in several interviews. And because he used it, it had a fantastic career. It was repeated in the Czechoslovak papers. An opposition spokesman recalled it in a television broadcast just before the general strike—on Day Eleven. It was on the front page of the Polish opposition daily, *Gazeta Wyborcza*. It popped up in the Western press. And when I finally had to leave Prague on Day Nineteen, with the revolution by no means over, people were still saying, "You see, with us—ten days!" Such is the magic of round numbers.

* * *

I tell this story not just from author's vanity, but also because it illustrates several qualities of the most delightful of all this year's Central European revolutions: the speed, the improvisation, the merriness, and the absolutely central role of Václav Havel, who was at once director, playwright, stage manager, and leading actor in this, his greatest play. I was only one of many—indeed of millions—to feed him some lines.

Next morning I got a complimentary theater ticket. A ticket to the Magic Lantern theater, whose subterannean stage, auditorium, foyers, and dressing rooms had become the headquarters of the main opposition coalition in the Czech lands, the Civic Forum, and thus, in effect, the headquarters of the revolution. The ticket changed. At first it was just a small note with the words "Please let in and out" written in purple ink, signed by Václav Havel's brother, Ivan, and authenticated by the play-wright's rubber stamp. This shows a beaming pussycat with the word "Smile!" across his chest. Then it was a green card worn around the neck, with my name typed as "Timothy Gordon Ash," and the smiling cat again. Then it was a xeroxed and initialed paper slip saying "Civic Forum Building," this time with two smiling cats (one red, one black) and a beaming green frog. I have it before me as I write. Beneath the frog it says "*très bien.*"

In any case, the tickets worked wonders. For nearly two weeks I, as an historian, was privileged to watch history being made inside the Magic Lantern. For most of that time, I was the only foreigner to sit in on the hectic deliberations of what most people called simply "the Forum." But before I describe what I saw, we must briefly recall—or reconstruct—the beginning of the revolution.

1.

Students started it. Small groups of them had been active for at least a year before. They edited faculty magazines. They organized discussion clubs. They worked on the borderline between official and unofficial life. Many had contacts with the opposition, all read samizdat. Some say they had a conspiratorial group called "The Ribbon"—the Czech "White Rose," as it were. But they also worked through the official youth organization, the SSM. It was through the SSM that they got permission to hold a demonstration in Prague on November 17, to mark the fiftieth anniversary of the martyrdom of Jan Opletal, a Czech student murdered by the Nazis. This began as officially scheduled in Prague's second district, with speeches and tributes at the cemetery.

But the numbers grew, and the chants turned increasingly against the present dictators in the castle. The demonstrators decided—perhaps some had planned all along—to march to Wenceslas Square, the stage for all the historic moments of Czech history, whether in 1918, 1948, or 1968. Down the hill they wound, along the embankment of the River Vltava, and then, turning right at the National Theater, up Národní Street into Wenceslas Square. Here they were met by riot police, with white helmets, shields, and truncheons, and by special antiterrorist squads, in red berets. Large numbers of demonstrators were cut off and surrounded, both along Národní and in the square. They went on chanting "freedom" and singing the Czech version of "We Shall Overcome." Those in the front line tried to hand flowers to the police. They placed lighted candles on the ground and raised their arms, chanting, "We have bare hands." But the police, and especially the red berets, beat men, women, and children with their truncheons.

* * *

This was the spark that set Czechoslovakia alight. During the night from Friday to Saturday—with reports of one dead and many certainly in hospital—some students determined to go on strike. On Saturday morning they managed to spread the word to most of the Charles University, and to several other institutions of higher learning, which immediately entered the occupation strike. (Patient research will be needed to reconstruct the precise details of this crucial moment.) On Saturday afternoon they were joined by actors, already politicized by earlier petitions in defense of Václav Havel, and drawn in directly by the very active students from the drama and film academies. They met in the Realistic Theater. Students described the "massacre," as it was now called. The theater people responded with a declaration of support. This not only brought the theaters out on strike—that is, turned their auditoriums into political debating cham-

bers—but also, and, as far as I could establish, for the first time, made
the proposal for a general strike on Monday, November 27, between
noon and 2 PM. The audience responded with a standing ovation.

On Sunday morning the students of the film and drama academies
came out with an appropriately dramatic declaration. Entitled "Don't
Wait—Act!" it began by saying that 1989 in Czechoslovakia might
sadly be proclaimed the "year of the truncheon." "That truncheon,"
it continued, "on Friday, November 17 spilled the blood of students."
And then, after appealing "especially to European states in the year
of the two hundredth anniversary of the French Revolution," they
went on to list demands which ranged from the legal registration of
the underground monthly *Lidové Noviny* to removing the leading
role of the Communist party from the constitution, but also crucially
repeated the call for a general strike. (Incidentally, within a few days
the students had all their proclamations neatly stored in personal
computers, and many of the flysheets on the streets were actually
computer printouts.)

*   *   *

It was only at ten o'clock on Sunday evening (Day Three), after the
students and actors had taken the lead, proclaiming both their own
and the general strike, that the previously existing opposition groups,
led by Charter 77, met in another Prague theater. The effective con-
vener of this meeting was Václav Havel, who had hurried back from
his farmhouse in Northern Bohemia when he heard the news of the
"massacre." The meeting included not only the very diverse opposition groups, such as the Committee for the Defense of the Unjustly
Prosecuted (VONS), the Movement for Civic Freedoms, and *Obroda*
(Rebirth), the club of excommunicated Communists, but also individual members of the previously puppet People's and Socialist parties. The latter was represented by its general secretary, one Jan
Skoda, who was once a schoolmate and close friend of Havel's, but

who had carefully avoided him throughout the long, dark years of so-called normalization.

This miscellaneous late-night gathering agreed to establish an *Obcanské Forum*, a Civic Forum, "as a spokesman on behalf of that part of the Czechoslovak public which is increasingly critical of the existing Czechoslovak leadership and which in recent days has been profoundly shaken by the brutal massacre of peacefully demonstrating students." It made four demands: the immediate resignation of the Communist leaders responsible for preparing the Warsaw Pact intervention in 1968 and the subsequent devastation of the country's life, starting with the President Gustav Husák and the Party leader Miloš Jakeš; the immediate resignation of the Federal interior minister, František Kincl, and the Prague first secretary, Miroslav Stepán, held responsible for violent repression of peaceful demonstrations; the establishment of a special commission to investigate these police actions; and the immediate release of all prisoners of conscience. The Civic Forum, it added, supports "with all its authority" the call for a general strike. From this time forward, the Forum assumed the leadership of the revolution in the Czech lands.

* * *

Over the weekend there had been tens of thousands of people, mainly young people, milling around Wenceslas Square, waving flags and chanting slogans. Students had taken over the equestrian statue of the good king, at the top of his square, covering its base with improvised posters, photographs, and candles. But the popular breakthrough came on Monday afternoon. For now the square was not merely teeming; it was packed. Dense masses chanted "freedom," "resignation," and, most strikingly, a phrase that might be translated as "now's the time" or "this is it." And neither the white helmets nor the red berets moved in.

As in East Germany, when the authorities woke up to what was happening, it was already too late. In East Central Europe today, with Gorbachev in the Kremlin, the kind of violence that would be needed to crush such masses of people just does not appear to be an available option. (But the then prime minister, Ladislav Adamec, went out of his way to emphasize that martial law would not be declared, thus implying that the option had been considered.)

On Tuesday, Day Five, the demonstration—at 4 PM, after working hours—was still bigger. And the publishing house of the Socialist party, under Jan Skoda, made available its balcony, perfectly located halfway down the square. From here the veteran Catholic opposition activist, Radim Palouš, a dynamic banned priest, Václav Malý, and then Havel addressed the vast crowd, repeating the Forum's demands. Next morning the first edition of the Communist party daily, *Rudé Právo*, had a headline referring to a demonstration of "200,000" in the square. The second edition said "100,000." Someone made a collage of the two editions, xeroxed it, and stuck it up on shop windows next to the photographs of Thomas Garrigue Masaryk, the mimeographed or computer-printed flysheets, and the carefully typed declarations that this or that shop would join in the general strike, declarations signed by all the employees and often authenticated with a seal or rubber stamp.

On Wednesday and Thursday, Days Six and Seven, there were yet larger demonstrations, while first talks were held between Prime Minister Adamec and a Forum delegation, which, however, at the prime minister's earnest request, was not led by Václav Havel. The prime minister, Havel told me, sent word through an aide that he did not yet want to "play his trump card." At the same time, however, Havel had direct communication with Adamec through a self-constituted group of mediators, calling itself "the bridge." "The bridge" had two struts: Michal Horácek, a journalist on a youth paper, and Michael Kocáb, a rock singer.

The revolution was thus well under way, indeed rocking around the clock. And its headquarters was just a hundred yards from the bottom of Wenceslas Square, in the theater called the Magic Lantern.

2.

Through the heavy metal-and-glass doors, past the second line of volunteer guards, you plunge down a broad flight of stairs into a curving, 1950s-style, mirror-lined foyer. People dart around importantly, or sit in little groups on benches, eating improvised canapés and discussing the future of the nation. Down another flight of stairs there is the actual theater. The set—for Dürrenmatt's *Minotaurus*—is like a funnel, with a hole at the back of the stage just big enough for a small monster to come through. Here, instead of the Magic Lantern's special combination of drama, music, pantomime, and audiovisuals, they hold the daily press conference: the speakers emerging from the hole instead of Dürrenmatt's monster. Journalists instead of tourists are let in for the performance.

At one end of the foyer there is a room with a glass wall on which it says, in several languages, "smoking room." There is another guard at the door. Some are allowed in. Others are not. Flash your magic ticket. In. Familiar bearded faces, old friends from the underground, sit around on rickety chairs, in a crisis meeting. At one end, a television mounted high on the wall shows an operetta, without the sound. The room smells of cigarette smoke, sweat, damp coats, and revolution. I remember the same smell, precisely, in Poland in the autumn of 1980.

This, you think, is the real headquarters. But after a few hours you discover a black door at the other end of the foyer. Through the door you plunge down a metal stairway into a narrow, desperately overheated corridor, as if in the bowels of an ocean liner. Here, in dressing rooms ten and eleven, is the very heart, the epicenter, of the revolution. For here sits Václav Havel, with his "private secretary" and the few key activists from the Forum who are thrashing out the texts of the latest communiqué, programmatic statement, or negotiating position.

In front of the dressing room door stands a wiry, bearded man in a combat jacket, with his thinning hair knotted at the back, hippie fashion. This is John Bok, a friend of Havel's now in charge of the personal bodyguard, composed mainly of students. During the war, John Bok's father was a Czech pilot in the Royal Air Force, and the spirit lives. Don't try to mix it with John Bok. He and Havel's other personal security chief, Stanislav Milota, a former cameraman married to a famous actress, are highly visible characters throughout the performance, surrounding Havel as he dashes around in clouds of nervous flurry, John Bok barking into his walkie-talkie, Milota forever saying "SHUSH, SHUSH!" in a stage whisper somewhat louder than the original interruption. In every hectic move, they confirm the playwright's unique status.

* * *

A political scientist would be hard pressed to find terms to describe the Forum's structure of decision making, let alone the hierarchy of authority within it. Yet the structure and hierarchy certainly exist, like a chemist's instant crystals. The "four-day-old baby," as Havel calls it, is, at first glance, rather like a club. Individual membership is acquired by personal recommendation. You could draw a tree diagram starting from the founding meeting in the appropriately named Players' Club theater: X introduced Y, who introduced Z. Most of those present have been active in opposition before, the biggest single group being signatories of Charter 77. Twenty years ago they were journalists, academics, politicians, lawyers, but now they come here from their jobs as stokers, window cleaners, clerks, or, at best, banned writers. Sometimes they have to leave a meeting to go and stoke up their boilers. A few of them come straight from prison, from which they have been released under the pressure of popular protest. Politically, they range from the neo-Trotskyist Petr Uhl to the deeply conservative Catholic Václav Benda.

In addition, there are representatives of significant groups. There are The Students, brightly dressed, radical, and politely deferred to by their elders. For, after all, they started it. Occasionally there are The Actors—although we are all actors now. Then there are The Workers, mainly represented by Petr Miller, an athletic and decisive technician from Prague's huge CKD heavy machinery conglomerate. All intellectual voices are stilled when The Worker rises to speak. Sometimes there are The Slovaks—demonstratively honored guests. And then there are those whom I christened The Prognostics, that is, members of the Institute for Forecasting (*Prognostický Ustav*) of the Czechoslovak Academy of Sciences, one of the very few genuinely independent institutes in the whole country's official academic life.

The Prognostics are, in fact, economists. Their particular mystique comes from knowing, or believing they know, or, at least, being believed to know, what to do about the economy—a subject clearly high in the minds of the people on the streets, and one on which most of the philosophers, poets, actors, historians, assembled here have slightly less expertise than the ordinary worker on the Vysocany tram. The Prognostics are not, of course, unanimous. Dr. Václav Klaus, a silver-gray-haired man with glinting metal spectacles, as arrogant as he is clever, favors the solutions of Milton Friedman. His more modest colleague, Dr. Tomáš Jezek, by contrast, is a disciple (and translator) of Friedrich von Hayek. But you get the general drift.

* * *

All these tendencies and groups are represented in the full meetings of the Forum, which move, as the numbers grow from tens to hundreds, out of the smoking room into the main auditorium. This "plenum"—like Solidarity in Poland, the Forum finds itself inadvertently adopting the Communist terminology of the last forty years—then appoints a series of "commissions." By the time I arrive there are, so far as I can gather, four: Organizational, Technical, Informational, and Conceptional—the last "to handle the political science aspect," as one Forum spokesperson-interpreter rather quaintly puts it. By the time I leave there seem to be about ten, each with its "in tray"—a white cardboard box lying on the foyer floor. For example, in addition to "Conceptional" there is also "Programmatic" and "Strategic."

As well as voting people onto these commissions, the plenum also sometimes selects ad hoc "crisis staffs," and the groups or individuals to speak on television, negotiate with the government, or whatever. I say "voting," but what actually happens is that the chairman chooses some names, and then others propose other names—or themselves. There is no vote. The lists are, so to speak, open, and therefore long. Thus "for the Conceptional commission I propose Ivan Klíma," says Havel, adding: "Ivan, you don't want to write any more novels, do you?" Generally the principle of selection is crudely representative: there must be The Student, The Worker, The Prognostic, etc. Sometimes this produces marvelous comments to a Western ear.

"Shouldn't we have a liberal?" says someone, in discussing the Conceptional. "But we've already got two Catholics!" comes the reply. Thus Catholic means liberal—which here actually means conservative.

To watch all this was to watch politics in a primary, spontaneous, I almost said "pure" form. All men (and women) may be political animals, but some are more political than others. It was fascinating to see people responding instantly to the scent that wafted down into the Magic Lantern as the days went by. The scent of power. Some who had never before been politically active suddenly sat up, edged their way on stage, proposed themselves for a television slot; and you could already see them in a government minister's chair. Others, long active in the democratic opposition, remain seated in the audience. Not for them the real politics of power.

Like Solidarity, the Forum was racked from the very outset by a conflict between the political imperative of rapid, decisive, united action, and the moral imperative of internal democracy. Should they start as they intended to go on, that is, democratically? Or did the conditions of struggle with a still totalitarian power demand that they should say, to adapt Brecht, We who fight for democracy cannot ourselves be democratic?

* * *

On the face of it, the Forum was, after all, hardly democratic. Who chose them? They themselves did. Yet already on the second day of their existence they wrote, in a letter addressed to Presidents Bush and Gorbachev, that the Civic Forum "feels capable of acting as a spokesman for the Czechoslovak public." By what right? Why, by right of acclamation. For the people were going on the streets every day and chanting, "Long live the Forum!" In Prague at least, the people—the *demos*—were obviously, unmistakably behind them. In this original sense, the Forum was profoundly, elementally democratic. The *demos* spoke, in demos, and declared the Forum to be its mouthpiece.

If one had to describe Havel's leadership, Max Weber's often misused term "charismatic" would for once be apt. It was extraordinary the degree to which everything ultimately revolved around this one man. In almost all the Forum's major decisions and statements he was the final arbiter, the one person who could somehow balance the very different tendencies and interests in the movement. In this sense, as in Solidarity, many decisions were not made democratically. Yet a less authoritarian personality than Havel it would be hard to imagine. (The contrast with Lech Walesa is striking.) And the meetings of the plenum were almost absurdly democratic. The avuncular Radim

Palouš was an exemplary chairman. Everyone had his or her say. Important issues were decided by vote. At one point, an assembly of perhaps two hundred people was editing the latest Forum communiqué, line by line.

So all this—the plenums, the commissions, the ad hoc groups, Havel, John Bok, the *Minotaurus* set, the smoking room, the dressing rooms, the hasty conversations in the corridors, the heat, the smoke, the laughter, and the exhaustion—made up that unique political thing, "the Magic Lantern." The story of the revolution, in the days I witnessed it, is that of the interaction of "the Magic Lantern" with three other compound forces, or theaters. These may be called, with similar poetic license, "the people," "the powers that be," and "the world."

3.

For those in the Magic Lantern, "the people" meant first of all Prague. In a sense, all of Prague became a Magic Lantern. It was not just the great crowds on Wenceslas Square. It was the improvised posters all over the city, the strike committees in the factories, the Civic Forum committees that were founded in hospitals, schools, and offices. It was the packed theaters every evening, debating with the guest speakers on stage: a Forum spokesman, or perhaps an exiled writer, back for the first time in years. It was the crowds standing in front of the television sets in shop or office windows at all hours of the day and night, watching the *Videojournál* tape of the events of November 17 played over and over again. It was ordinary people on the streets. As you walked down to the Old Town you overheard snippets of excited conversation: "free elections!" "human face!" and (darkly) "demagogic tendencies!" At six o'clock in the morning on Wenceslas Square you saw a queue of hundreds of people waiting patiently in the freezing mist. They were waiting to buy a copy of the Socialist party newspaper, *Svobodné Slovo* (*The Free Word*), which was the first to carry accurate reports of the demonstrations and Forum statements. Lining up for the free word.

Outside Prague, the situation was very different from place to place, with much more fear and nastiness in, for example, the industrial district around Ostrava. And then of course there was Slovakia, a different nation. To reach out to this wider audience the crucial medium was television and, to a lesser extent, radio. As in all this year's Central European revolutions/transformations the battle for access to television and radio was one of the two or three most important political issues. Here, the battle was comically visible on screen, with direct transmission of a demonstration suddenly interrupted by some inane light music, and then the picture wrenched back again—as if by some invisible hand—to the demonstration. "Live transmission!" they chanted on Wenceslas Square, "live transmission!" Once it had access to television and radio, a good deal of the Forum's energy was devoted to discussing what to say there.

* * *

The second compound force was "the powers that be." This term from the King James Bible was repeatedly used by Rita Klimová, a former professor of economics (sacked for political reasons), who translated into English for the speakers at the Forum press conferences with magnificent aplomb. At first hearing it may sound quaint, but it is actually a very good term, for one of the recurrent problems in describing Communist systems (or should I say, former Communist systems) is precisely to find an appropriate collective noun for the people and institutions who actually wielded power. To say "the government," for example, would be wrong, since in such systems the government did not really govern: the Party did, or some mixture of the Party, the police, the army, and the Soviet Union. All these elements were in play here, and well embraced by the biblical term "the powers that be."

At the beginning, the Forum negotiated with the federal prime minister, who was also, of course, a Politburo member. They did this, in the first place, because he was the only senior power holder who would talk to them. But, making a virtue of necessity, they said: we are talking to the government of our country because we want a proper government, responsible to a proper parliament, not the rule of one party. As well as the federal prime minister they also negotiated with the Czech prime minister, for in Czechoslovakia's elaborate federal structure, the Czech lands and Slovakia each have their own governments. Only then did they start talking to Party leaders as such.

Behind everything there was the benign presence of Gorbachev's Soviet Union: the Soviet embassy in Prague receiving a Forum delegation with demonstrative courtesy. Gorbachev himself making it clear during the Warsaw Pact post-Malta briefing in Moscow that Party leader Urbánek and Prime Minister Adamec should implement fundamental reforms, the demonstrative renunciation of the invasion in 1968. Others will have to assess how far (and how) Gorbachev deliberately pushed the changes in Czechoslovakia, and to what extent this was affected by his personal timetable of East-West relations, leading up to the Malta summit. Just as in 1980 the very worst place from which to assess the Soviet intention to invade was the Solidarity headquarters in Warsaw (a point never entirely grasped by television and radio interviewers), so in 1989 the worst place from which to assess the Soviet intention to do the opposite of invading was the Forum headquarters in Prague. Yet, of course, in a larger historical frame, the Soviet attitude was fundamental.

* * *

At this point the "powers that be" shade into the third force, or theater, called "the world." As I recounted in these pages just a year ago,* the first protesters in Prague on the national anniversaries last year chanted at the riot police, "The world sees you." Yet in the autumn of 1988 it was, in fact, very doubtful if the world did see them. On the whole, the world considered that life was elsewhere. But now there was absolutely no doubt that the world saw them. It saw them through the eyes of the television cameras and the thousands of foreign journalists who flocked into the Magic Lantern for the daily performance. They were a sight in themselves: television crews and photographers behaving like minotaurs, journalists shouting each other down and demanding to know why the revolution could not keep to their deadlines.

Yet a few of the questions were good, and the journalists served two useful functions. First, they concentrated minds. When there was a Forum plenum at, say, 5 PM, the knowledge that their spokesmen would have to field the hardest questions at 7:30 PM made for a much sharper discussion. Even so, Forum policy on crucial issues— the future of the Warsaw Pact, for example, or that of socialism itself—was sometimes made up on the wing, in impromptu answers to Western journalists' questions. Secondly, the "eyes of the world" offered protection. Particularly in the days before the Malta summit, the Czechoslovak authorities must have been left in little doubt that there were certain things that they could no longer do, or could only do at an immense price in both Western and *Soviet* disapproval. Beating children, for example. Both externally and internally, the crucial medium was television. In Europe at the end of the twentieth century all revolutions are telerevolutions.

4.

Day Eight (Friday, November 24). In the morning, a plenum in the smoking room. Appointing people to the commissions. The agenda for this afternoon's demonstration. The proposed slogans, someone says, are "objectivity, truth, productivity, freedom." It is no surprise that two out of four have to do with truth. But "productivity" is interesting. From several conversations outside I gather that the "Polish example" is widely seen here as a negative one. If economic misery were to be the price for political emancipation, many people might not want to pay it. So the Forum places a premium on economic credibility. Demos only after working hours. The lunchtime general strike on Monday as a one-time necessity.

* * *

In the early afternoon comes Dubcek. He looks as if he has stepped straight out of a black-and-white photograph from 1968. The face is older, more lined, of course, but he has the same gray coat and paisley scarf, the same tentative, touching smile, the same functionary's hat. Everything contributes to the feeling that we have just stepped out of a time warp, the clocks that stopped in 1969 starting again in 1989. Protected by Havel's bodyguards—lead on, John Bok—we emerge from the belly of the Lantern, Dubcek and Havel side by side, and scuttle through covered shopping arcades and tortuous back passages to reach the balcony of the Socialist Party publishing house and *Svobodné Slovo*: the balcony of the free word. Along the arcades people simply gape. They can't believe it. Dubcek! It is as if the ghost of Winston Churchill were to be seen striding down the Burlington Arcade.

But when he steps out onto the balcony in the frosty evening air, illuminated by television spotlights, the crowds give such a roar as I have never heard. "DUBCEK! DUBCEK!" echoes off the tall houses up and down the long, narrow square. Many people mourn his ambiguous role after the Soviet invasion, and his failure to use the magic of his name to support the democratic opposition. He has changed little with the times. His speech still contains those wooden, prefabricated newspeak phrases, the *langue de bois*. (At one point he refers to "confrontationist extremist tendencies.") He still believes in socialism—that is, reformed communism—with a human face. The true leader of this movement, in Prague at least, is Havel, not Dubcek. But for the moment none of this matters.

For the moment all that matters is that the legendary hero is really standing here, addressing a huge crowd on Wenceslas Square, while the emergency session of the Central Committee has, we are told, been removed to a distant suburb. "Dubcek to the castle!" roars the crowd—that is, Dubcek for president. The old man must believe he will wake up in a moment and find he is dreaming. For the man who supplanted him and now sits in the castle, Gustav Husák, it is the nightmare come true.

After Dubcek comes Havel. "Dubcek-Havel" they chant, the name of '68 and the name of '89. (People point out with delight that 89 is 68 turned upside down.) Then Václav Malý, the banned padre, reads a message from the man he calls "the third great symbol" of this movement, the ninety-year-old František Cardinal Tomášek. "The Catholic Church stands entirely on the side of the people in their present struggle," says the message. "I thank all those who are fighting for the good of us all and I trust completely the Civic Forum which has become a spokesman for the nation." "Long live Tomášek," they cry, but I notice that when Malý later strikes up the old Czech Wenceslas hymn, much of the crowd either do not know the words or are reluctant to sing them. A striking contrast with Poland.

At the end of the demonstration, after more speakers, including a football player, a theater director, and the obligatory Student and Worker, the people down in the square make the most extraordinary spontaneous gesture. They all take their keys out of their pockets and shake them, three hundred thousand key rings, producing a sound like massed Chinese bells.

7:30 PM. The press conference. Havel and Dubcek together on

stage. They are just starting to field questions about their different ideas of socialism when someone brings the news—from television—that the whole politburo and Central Committee secretariat has resigned. The theater erupts in applause. Havel leaps to his feet, makes the V for Victory sign, and embraces Dubcek. Someone brings them champagne. Havel raises his glass and says "to a free Czechoslovakia!"

* * *

Then, rather absurdly, we settle down again to discuss "What is socialism?" Havel says the word has lost all meaning in "the Czech linguistic context" over the last fifteen years, but he is certainly in favor of social justice and a plural economy, with different forms of ownership. The models for a rational social policy are to be found rather in social-democratic than in Communist-ruled countries. The shortest and best answer comes from Václav Malý. I'm also for social justice, he says, but the only way to secure it is through parliamentary democracy.

10 PM. Plenum in the smoking room. Arrangements for the weekend. The need for finance: establish a Treasury commission! An interesting but inconclusive discussion about the way in which Dubcek should or should not be associated with the Forum. Of course his name is magic, domestically and internationally. But he is, you know, still sort of, well...a Communist. On every face you see elation fighting a battle against exhaustion. Everyone is very, very tired. At one point, reading a draft declaration about the general strike, the writer Eva Kanturková says "Democratic Forum" instead of "Civic Forum." "Oh, sorry, I was thinking of Hungary."

Civic Forum, Democratic Forum, New Forum—Czechoslovakia, Hungary, East Germany—you can easily lose track; it's that kind of year. Someone suggests the general strike should be described as an "informal referendum" on the leading role of the Party. Someone else says "symbolic," not "informal." Writers debate a fine point of style. Agreement by mutual exhaustion. Meeting over.

* * *

After midnight. Back in Havel's basement pub, with a wall painting of a ship in stormy seas. Beer and *becherovka*. What do you talk about on the night of such a tremendous victory, when, in just over a week, you have removed the gibbering thugs who have ruined the country for twenty years? In the first instant, on the stage of the Magic Lantern, you may cry, "To a free Czechoslovakia!" But you can't go on talking like characters in a nineteenth-century play. So you suddenly find yourself talking about cats. Yes, cats. Two cats called "Yin" and "Yang," whom their owner has not seen for more than a week. Poor things. Victims of the revolution.

So what will happen after the revolution? I ask a beaming Jiří Dienstbier, the star journalist reduced to working as a stoker after signing Charter 77. Quick as ever, he says: Either the counterrevolution or...a Western consumer society. (Just over two weeks later he is appointed Czechoslovakia's foreign minister. Kindly delete that remark from the record. No, of course you never said that, Mr. Minister. Someone else did. I imagined it. It was a voice from the wall.)

* * *

Day Nine (Saturday, November 25). Two Forum statements. One issued after the plenum last night at 11:30 PM (events move so fast they have not only to date but to time the communiqués) describes the general strike as a "symbolic referendum" on the "leading role." A second, issued at 4:30 AM, expresses dismay at some of the people elected to the new politburo (formally: Presidium) and Central Committee secretariat. The general strike is here described as "an informal, nationwide referendum on whether or not they should go on humiliating us, and whether this country should continue to be ruined by the leaders of one political party, permanently abrogating to itself the leading role."

The waiter in my hotel sees me reading *Svobodné Slovo*. "Ah, victoria!" he says, pointing to the blue, white, and red ribbon which he, like so many others, is now wearing in his lapel. Then he leans over and whispers in my ear: "finished communism." Straightening up, he rubs his shoe across the carpet, as if crushing a beetle. Then he takes my *Svobodné Slovo*, but not my breakfast order, and disappears into the kitchen.

* * *

This morning there is, by happy chance, a festive mass in the cathedral on the castle hill, to celebrate the canonization of Agnes of Bohemia. The actual canonization took place in Rome on November 12, just five days before the revolution started. (An old legend has it, so a Catholic friend informs me, that wonders will occur in Bohemia when Agnes is canonized.) In the freezing cold, a large crowd gathers inside and all around the cathedral, and in front of the Archbishop's Palace. "Frantši Tomášek! Frantši Tomášek!" they chant, a wonderfully chummy way to greet a venerable cardinal. An old woman quaveringly sings patriotic hymns, pausing only to take a swig of vodka between verses.

The Church here is nothing like the force that it is in Poland, for Czechoslovakia has historically been bitterly divided between Catholics (associated with the Habsburg counterreformation) and Protestants (from Jan Hus to Masaryk), while both churches were ruthlessly suppressed in the Stalinist period, and again after 1969. Yet Catholic intellectuals and banned priests like Václav Malý play a crucial part in the opposition leadership. Tomášek himself has become ever bolder as he gets ever older. A petition for religious freedom last year got more than half a million signatures, and was a major factor in breaking the political ice. And anyway, who could resist the glorious coincidence of this ceremony and the revolution? So there is a goodly crowd here too, some from the countryside and even from Slovakia. And the mass for the patron saint of Bohemia, the king's daughter who came down to live among the poor, is a further celebration of national renewal. Angels at work. Oh yes, and the whole service is broadcast live on television: so far as I can establish, the first time that has ever happened here.

* * *

At 2 PM, in freezing snow, there is the biggest demonstration of all: over half a million people, in the park before the Letná football stadium, just behind the place where the giant statue of Stalin once stood. With the banners and flags and upturned faces vivid against the white snow, it looks like a painting by L. S. Lowry. Whole sections of the crowd jump up and down together, to keep warm. The essential fact is that they are there, at the Forum's invitation. In a sense, that is all that matters. But of course there is a program.

Havel reiterates the Forum's dissatisfaction with some of the new leaders, and especially with the survival in office of the deeply unpopular Prague Party secretary, Miroslav Stepán. "Shame, shame!" cry the crowd. And then he says that the only person in power who had responded to the wishes of the people is the prime minister, Ladislav Adamec. "Adamec! Adamec!" roar the crowd, and one trembles for a moment at the ease with which they can be swayed. This is of course a quite deliberate (but high-risk) tactic, worked out in the dressing rooms of the Magic Lantern: to build up the prime minister's position as a negotiating partner by showing the authorities that he can enjoy popular support. In fact, this is precisely what Adamec asked Havel to do for him a few days ago. Dubcek, who, rather to some people's surprise, has not yet returned to Bratislava, repeats the same support for Adamec. He also says, rather nicely, that he is pleased about the canonization of Agnes of Bohemia—Anezka—and that, although he will speak in Slovak, what matters is not how you speak but what you say.

Petr Miller, The Worker, repeats the strike call, stressing once again that it must not damage the national economy. Ballads are sung, including President Masaryk's favorite song; and students and actors talk. "I speak in the name of Jesus Christ," says one actor, modestly, "and call upon you to stamp out the devil." Roars of applause. Then, in the extraordinary way these crowds have of talking back, they given an almost instant response: "The devil is in the castle, the devil is in the castle!" (If you stand in the crowd you see how one man can start a chant which, being taken up by those around him, becomes the voice of half a million.)

7:30 PM. The press conference. Repeating the Forum positions about the compromised leaders, the general strike and so forth. Tomorrow a delegation will meet with Prime Minister Adamec. The agenda is to include the legalization of independent groups, the release of political prisoners, arrangements for further talks, oh yes, and an end to the leading role of the Party. Foreign journalists keep asking about things they cannot possibly know, such as the power balance inside the Party or the relations between the Soviet and Czechoslovak leadership. Jirí Dienstbier gives a good answer to the last question. Of course we feel the Soviet leadership should have some sense of responsibility for the 1968 invasion, he says, but we are certainly not asking for any more international "assistance."

Television is now clearly opening up to report the revolution. Beside the live broadcast of the mass it shows an interview with Havel: down with the leading role, he says, up with free elections. And the crowds outside grasp that as the essential point: "Free elections," they chant. As in Poland, in Hungary, in East Germany....

* * *

Day Ten (Sunday, November 26). 11 AM. A delegation led by Prime Minister Adamec, and formally described as representing the government and National Front (uniting the Communist with the formerly puppet parties), meets with a Forum delegation led by Havel. "We don't know each other," says the prime minister, extending his hand across the table. "I'm Havel," says Havel. Just in case you didn't guess. It's a short getting-to-know-you session, but they agree to meet again on Tuesday. The prime minister promises the release of political prisoners (several of whom do indeed appear in the Magic Lantern in the course of the day), and also to come to this afternoon's rally.

2 PM at the Letná stadium again. Adamec arrives before the Forum leaders, and stands around stamping his feet in the cold. How do you feel? someone asks him. "Very nice," he says, "I think this was necessary," as the crowd roars, "Dubcek! Dubcek!" I notice his aide trying to suppress a broad grin. Havel delivers a brief speech, describing the Forum as a bridge from totalitarianism to democracy, and saying that it must exist until free elections. Then they give Adamec his chance. But he blows it, talking about the need for discipline, for no more strikes, for economic rather than political change. You feel he is talking as much to the emergency Central Committee meeting that will take place this evening as to the people in front of him. And they feel it too. They boo and jeer.

The crowd again displays an extraordinary capacity to converse with the speakers in rhythmic chant. "Make way for the ambulance," they cry, or "Turn up the volume." When a long list of political prisoners is read out they chant, "Stepán to prison." "Perhaps we should give him a spade," says Václav Malý from the platform. "He'd steal it!" comes the almost instantaneous response, half a million speaking as one. And then "Here it comes!" Sure enough, there is a spade held aloft at the front of the crowd. "Stepán. Stepán," they cry as in a funeral chant, and once again they ring their keys, as for the last rites. (Next morning we have the news that Stepán, along with other discredited members of the leadership, has resigned at the emergency meeting of the Central Committee.)

6 PM. An important plenum at the Magic Lantern. Havel poses the "fundamental question" of the future of the Forum. He personally doesn't want to be a "chief," he says, or a professional politician. He wants to be a writer. Václav Malý says much the same thing, except that he wants to be—he is—a priest. Yet it is clear to everyone that Havel must carry on at least until the elections—and "in the elections," Dienstbier jokes. "I don't give you any chance!"

Someone else reports telephone calls complaining about undemocratic methods. Here is the familiar conflict between politics and morality, between the requirements of unity and democracy. The students insist on the need for unity, continuity, and Havel's leadership. But other voices are raised in favor of immediately founding political parties. A social democratic party will announce itself within the next few days. The Forum, everyone agrees, must not be a centralized, partylike organization. What is it then? How do you describe a civic crusade for national renewal?

* * *

Inevitably, the discussion swings abruptly between the great and small issues—from what to say to Adamec on Tuesday to what to say to the press in an hour's time, from socialism vs. liberalism to whether to go by car or by bus. In the midst of it, Václav Klaus, the glinting economist, suddenly starts to read an amazing document. It is called "What We Want" and subtitled "Programmatic Principles of the Civic Forum." It proposes a new Czechoslovakia with the rule of law guaranteed by an independent judiciary, free elections at all levels, a market economy, social justice, respect for the environment, and independent academic and cultural life. A normal country in the center of Europe. Three typewritten pages, prepared by the members of one of the commissions in a short weekend. First I saw them sitting up on the stage of the Magic Lantern, then sweating away in the dressing room. My friend Petr Pithart, a lawyer, historian, and author of one of the best books about 1968, who was reduced to doing menial work after signing Charter 77, just dropped in to the Magic Lantern to make a modest suggestion. Within minutes he was asked to work on the commission, writing the blueprint for a new Czechoslovakia.

When Klaus finishes reading there is a discussion. Václav Benda, a conservative Catholic and one of the original political brains of the Charter, says that although he helped to edit the text he doesn't agree with parts of it: the passage saying that Czechoslovakia will "respect its international legal obligations" (by implication, including the Warsaw Pact) and another saying the state should guarantee a social minimum for all. This is a tricky moment, for if the plenum plunges into a serious political discussion, then the deep differences that have been covered by the broad yet minimalist platform, first of Charter 77, now of the Forum, will surface with a vengeance. Fortunately the moment is saved by Petr Miller, who rises to his feet and says that although he has no higher education he can understand it all, finds it good, and thinks we should just adopt it. In effect: you intellectuals, stop blathering! Sighs of relief all around. A quick vote. Adopted with just three abstentions. Thank heaven for The Worker.

Of course the program contains passages of fudge: for example, on the Warsaw Pact issue, on the role of the state, and on the owner-ship question. On the last point, it talks of "real competition" com-ing about "on the basis of the parallel existence, with equal rights, of different types of ownership and the progressive opening of our economy to the world." This is a compromise formula, bearing in mind the sensibilities of the revisionists, social democrats, and even Trotskyists who are part of the Forum rainbow coalition, and who still believe in various forms of social(ist) ownership. In effect it says: let the best form win! But privately the economists have no doubt which kind of ownership will actually win out.

* * *

Yet the truly remarkable thing is not the differences about the program, but the degree of instant consensus. In 1968, even in 1977, it was almost unthinkable that there would be so much common ground. This is a Czech phenomenon. But it is not just a Czech phenomenon, for in different ways it is repeated all over East Central Europe. Take a more or less representative sample of politically aware persons. Stir under pressure for two days. And what do you get? The same fundamental Western, European model: parliamentary democracy, the rule of law, market economy. And if you made the same experiment in Warsaw or Budapest I wager you would get much the same result. This is no Third Way. It is not "socialism with a human face." It is the idea of "normality" that seems to be sweeping triumphantly across the world.

But that's enough philosophy. For in the next ten minutes they have to work out what to say to the prime minister—and to the world. At the press conference, they are of course asked about the fudging formulas on the alliances. Dienstbier says: we have to start from the existing situation, but our long-term objective is a Europe without blocs. Spoken like a foreign minister. As for the Soviet Union, this very evening Soviet television is broadcasting a program about the Prague Spring, including an interview with Dubcek. The Dubcek interview has been supplied by the samizdat *Videojournál.*

* * *

Day Eleven (Monday, November 27). The general strike is a success almost before it has begun. Television declares it so. Just before noon, the announcer demonstratively shows himself preparing to join in the strike. Then, from the stroke of noon, they show squares filled with people all around the country, in Prague, in Bratislava, in Brno, in Ostrava, wherever, and excited reporters describe the "fantastic atmosphere." A subtitle explains that reporting on the strike is the television crews' contribution to the strike. (Yet for the last twenty years they have been grinding out propaganda junk.)

* * *

Petr Miller drives me up to his factory, the large CKD electrotechnical works. Miller drives hair-raisingly fast in his sporty Lada. He enjoys hooting at traffic to let us through, shouting "Civic Forum!" "I'm just a very small figure in the opposition," he says, gesturing with his hand just a yard above the ground, to show how small. But in fact he is well on the way to being described as the Czech Walesa. On the road we pass an astounding sight: a line of taxis at least one mile long, taxi after taxi after taxi, crawling out up into the hills, wives or girlfriends in the passenger seats. It is the taxi drivers' strike.

In front of the factory gates, the workers are listening patiently to a long lecture on economics by the head of the Prognostic Institute, Dr. Valtr Komárek. "Komárek! Komárek!" they chant. The meeting ends with the singing of the national anthem at one thirty, so that everyone can be back at work by two. Miller says they will make up the lost work in unpaid overtime. On my way back there is, of course, not a taxi to be found.

4 PM. A celebration demo on Wenceslas Square. The organizers try to give the platform—or rather balcony—to a Communist. "Friends, comrades," he begins, but that is a terrible mistake. "Boo, boo," shout the crowd, and: "We're not comrades." Free elections and an end to the leading role of the Party are what people want to hear. Václav Klaus, now emerging as an opposition star, reads a statement announcing that the Civic Forum "considers its basic objective to be the definitive opening of our society for the development of political pluralism and for achieving free elections." The move-

ment is open to everyone who rejects the present system and accepts the Programmatic Principles. There will be no hierarchical structure, but there will be a "coordinating center." The coordinating center recommends the ending of strike action for the time being. Tomorrow they will submit their demands to the prime minister. If he doesn't respond adequately, they will call for the resignation of the government—"resignation, resignation!" cries the crowd—and the appointment of a new premier willing to assure the holding of a free election. "Free elections, free elections!"

Then comes the portly, goatee-bearded Dr. Komárek who delivers, very slowly and deliberately, what sounds like a prime minister's acceptance speech. There must be deeds not words, he says. "That's it," chants the crowd. There must be compromise between the new *de facto* situation and the old *de jure* one. The kids around me giggle at the professorial Latin, but they too shout, "Komárek, Komárek!" There should be a grand coalition government, a government of experts, men of competence and moral integrity (such as, we understand, Valtr Komárek). Then a girl student reads out, even more slowly and clearly, as if in school dictation, a letter from the students asking the president to replace Adamec with Komárek. "Pan Docent Komárek, *Dr. Sc.*," she says, has a program ready. The Forum stands behind him. "We too," cry the crowd, "we too!"

* * *

So to everyone standing on that square it is clear that the Forum—speaking for the people—has just proposed a candidate for prime minister. Go to the Magic Lantern, however, and you soon discover that the Forum didn't mean to do that at all. In the plenum at 6 PM, in the main auditorium now, there is confusion and consternation. Our position, says Havel, was that we would give Adamec a chance to meet our demands, before calling for his resignation. That was the statement Klaus read. The students jumped the gun. Why? There was a telephone call from the Lantern, say the students. "Disinformation!" someone says. "Provocation!" Or, more likely, just muddle. In any case, the question now is: What on earth are they to say in the negotiations with Adamec tomorrow? And who should be on the delegation? The Student. The Worker (Petr Miller). Ján Carnogurský, a lawyer and leading Slovak Catholic activist, just released from prison. Václav Malý. Perhaps Komárek? "On whose side?" someone asks. For Komárek is still a Party member. At this point Havel slips away off stage. He has to go and collect the Peace Prize of the German Book Trade awarded weeks before. (Four days ago he had to slip away to collect the Olof Palme Prize.)

7.30 PM. The press conference. Answers are delivered with great assurance to questions the Forum leaders have only just asked themselves, in this same room, a few minutes before. No matter. Make it up as you go along. Petr Miller says the strike committees still exist and will be maintained. Not only will the workers make up the time lost by the strike, they'll also work two free Saturdays—in the week when Czechoslovakia has free elections. Will there be a Green party? "This country needs all parties to be green," says Dienstbier. Well done, Jirí. Spoken like a foreign minister again. But now he has to dash. His boilers need stoking.

* * *

Day Twelve (Tuesday, November 28). At half past one a government minister, one Marián Calfa, gives the first account of the negotiations between the government/National Front team under Adamec and the Forum delegation under Havel. The meeting started in an "excited" atmosphere, he says. But then it settled down and ended in a "positive" spirit. The prime minister promised, by Sunday, December 3, to propose a new government based on "a broad coalition," a government of experts. The government will propose to the Federal Assembly that the clauses about the leading role of the Party, the closed, subordinate nature of the National Front, and Marxism-Leninism as the basis of education, should be removed from the constitution. The prime minister also promised that the City Council would provide the Forum with all necessary facilities.

According to people on the Forum side, Adamec actually blew his top on being confronted with the Forum's demands—a short digest of those raised by the students and the people over the last week. He called them "an ultimatum." After a break, Petr Miller once again defused the situation with some straight talking.

4 PM. Plenum. Perhaps two hundred people in the auditorium. Havel and other delegation members on stage. The main subject: the Forum's version of the meeting. As well as the three points accepted by the government, the demand was made that all political prisoners should be released by December 10 (UN Human Rights Day), and there was an expression of satisfaction at the establishment of a parliamentary commission to investigate the police and security forces' violence on November 17. The draft, read out by Radim Palouš, includes five more points. Of these the most immediately dramatic is the announcement that the Forum leaders are writing to President Husák, calling upon him to resign by December 10. The prime minister has until the end of the year to make clear the way in which his new government will create the legal conditions for free elections, freedom of assembly, association, speech, and press, the end of state control over the churches, etc. In addition, the People's Militia, the Party's private army, must be dissolved and all political organizations removed from the workplace (as in Hungary). If not, they will demand the prime minister's resignation, too.

* * *

After the draft is read, Havel says, "Now I leave you to discuss it," and scuttles off backstage, through the Minotaur's hole. In the course of a rather confused discussion, Petr Pithart sharply points out that they have not actually said anything about the composition of the new government. What about the crucial levers of power, the interior and defense ministries for example? From the platform comes the slightly sheepish reply: yes, but we can't really say something here that we didn't mention there. Somehow, in the rush and muddle, that point didn't get made. Ah well. Once again, Petr Miller ends the intellectual havering: let's accept it now, he says, we can always elaborate later.

Press conference. The final version of the communiqué—as edited by the two hundred!—is read out. So is the text of a letter to the Soviet authorities about the reassessment of 1968. This, they report, was accepted "with pleasure" by the Soviet embassy, who promised that it would promptly be sent to Moscow, by telex. Asked about the negotiations, Havel says they were complicated, fast, dramatic, and please don't expect all the details here. Altogether, he pleads to be left alone by the press. All questions to him, he says, he will gladly answer at an all-day press conference—after the revolution.

* * *

Day Thirteen (Wednesday, November 29). Television broadcasts the speech of the new Party secretary, Karel Urbánek, attempting to rally the faithful at an emergency *aktiv* in the Palace of Culture. He adopts a fighting tone. We will not sell out to foreign capital like the Poles! We cannot concede to demands to dissolve the People's Militia! (On Saturday, they will do just that.) The audience chants "Urbánek, Urbánek!" and "Long Live the KSC!" in the rhythms of the crowd on Wenceslas Square.

Then the Federal Assembly, the official parliament. The women with putty faces, cheap perms, and schoolmistress voices. The men in cheap suits, with hair swept straight back from sweaty fore-heads. The physiognomy of power for the last forty years. But at the end of the day they all vote "yes" to the prime minister's proposal, as agreed yesterday with the Forum, to delete the leading role of the Party from the constitution, and remove Marxism-Leninism as the basis of education. For years, for a life-time in some cases, they have been preaching Marxism-Leninism and the leading role of the Party. But not a single deputy votes against the change. Turn your coat, just like that. 4 PM. Plenum, in the auditorium. Havel and a delegation have hurried off to Bratislava, to speak in the Slovak National Theatre. It is vital not to let the authorities divide Slovaks against Czechs, as they have done so often in the past. Yesterday's communiqué about the meeting with the government underlined that this was a negotiation by the Civic Forum *and* the Public Against Violence (PAV), the sister organization in Slovakia. And the first item of today's communiqué records their joint resolution:

The common objective of the CF and the PAV is the changing of Czechoslovakia into a democratic federation, in which Czechs and Slovaks, together with other nationalities, will live in mutual friendship and understanding.

There are rocks ahead here. For the issue is not just democracy as such; it is also the degree of self-government to be enjoyed by the two nation(alitie)s within the federal state.

* * *

But before anyone can discuss this, a group of students come on stage, dressed comically as young pioneers: white blouses, red bows, the girls' hair in pigtails. It is the students' Committee for a More Joyful Strike. We have come, they say, to cheer you up—and to make sure that you don't turn into another politburo. Then they hand out little circular mirrors to each member of the plenum.

Back to business. Point three reads:

The prime minister in yesterday's negotiations with the CF said that he wished to discuss with us the members of the new cabinet. The CF does not aspire to any ministerial post, but would like to suggest to the prime minister that the minister of national defense be a civilian who has not compromised himself and is a member of the Communist Party of Czechoslovakia, while the minister of the interior be a person who has not compromised himself, is a civilian and is not a member of the Party. This suggestion was given to the prime minister in the course of this morning.

In fact the suggestion came, drafted by Havel, from his dressing room to the "crisis staff" dressing room, and was agreed on within a few minutes. A little afterthought: Oh, and by the way, you can't have the interior ministry any more!

Who wants to speak at the press conference? No takers. People have to be press-ganged to face the press.

Should we talk about this as a revolution? someone asks. For, after all, "in our linguistic context" the word "revolution" has a clear subtext of violence. A "peaceful revolution" sounds like a contradiction in terms. A rather academic point, you might think. But actually a great deal of what is happening is precisely about words: about finding new, clear, true words rather than the old, prefabricated, mendacious phrases under which they have lived for so long. The drafting committees try to ensure that from the outset the Forum's statements are in a new, plain language. Alas, they do not always succeed. The communiqués, with their repetition of abbreviations—CF and PAV— soon begin to sound a little like the old officialese.

7:30 PM. Press conference. The communiqué. News of the Federal Assembly vote. Václav Klaus smilingly reports a press interview with the deposed Party leader, Miloš Jakeš, in which he said that the Forum is well organized. "I'm sorry to say," Klaus comments, "that even on this point we can't agree with him." The issue of academics sacked after 1969. We are already drawing up a list of those who should be reinstated, says a student leader. But how would they find places for them? "I can assure you that we have quite enough very incompetent professors...."

* * *

Day Fourteen (Thursday, November 30). 4 PM. Plenum. The first topic is the internal organization of the Forum "coordinating center." Ivan Havel, whose subject is cybernetics, has produced a most impressive and logical plan, now displayed on a blackboard on stage. Suddenly the theater looks like a lecture room: the revolution has become a seminar.

One of the issues being discussed in the corridors is how to change the composition of the Federal Assembly. Once again, there is the conflict between the moral imperative of democracy and the political imperative of swift, effective action. There is a legal provision by which members of parliament can be "recalled," that is, removed, on a vote of the parliament itself, and replaced by new nominated—not freely elected—members. This method was used to purge the parliament after the Soviet invasion. Now Professor Jicinský, a constitutional lawyer who was himself removed from the parliament by this method, proposes to hoist the Communists with their own petard. Others say: but this is undemocratic, there should at least be free elections in the vacated constituencies (as, incidentally, has happened in Hungary). But this would take much longer, and time is what they do not have. They need a more representative assembly, now. So can you take an undemocratic shortcut to democracy?

* * *

Meanwhile, a Forum delegation has the first direct, bilateral meeting with Party leaders. The Party side is led by Vasil Mohorita, who, as head of the official youth movement, licensed the students' demonstration that started it all, and then agreed to a statement condemning the use of violence against the demonstrators. Perhaps he is the looked-for partner in the Party?

After the television news, there is a long interview with Zdenek Mlynár, a leading member of the Dubcek leadership in 1968. He was invited to Prague from his exile in Vienna by the new Party leader, Karel Urbánek, and rushed to a meeting with him after crossing the border in the dead of night. In their desperation, the Party leaders are turning for advice to, and hoping to win back, the old Communists, whom they expelled (some half a million of them) and defamed after the invasion. Mlynár is introduced on television as a "political scientist from Innsbruck." He gives a highly eloquent performance, stressing the importance of the international context, as at all the previous turning points in Czechoslovakia's history, in 1918, in 1938, in 1948, in 1968....What he does not spell out is the concrete steps needed to dismantle the Communist system. At the end of the interview you feel that he is still ultimately pleading, like Dubcek, for the concepts of 1968, for a reformed communism called "socialism with a human face"—in short, for an idea whose time has gone.

Later in the evening, I walk with the theater director Petr Oslzlý through the impossibly beautiful streets of the old town, to the small Theater on a Balustrade, where Havel's first plays were performed in the early 1960s. Today, like all the other theaters, it becomes the setting for an improvised happening. After a short talk by an economist, and a discussion with an exiled choreographer about how theaters are financed in the West, there is a Czech country-and-western group. In what might be called Czenglish they sing: "I got ol' time religion...."

* * *

Day Fifteen (Friday, December 1). Pavel Bratinka sits in his stoker's hut at the metro building site, with a huge pile of coal outside the door, a makeshift bed, junk-shop furniture, and he says: "On the whole I favor a bicameral legislature." He has been studying these issues for years, politics and law and economics, writing articles for the underground press, and occasionally for Western publications. With him, one has that rare experience of someone who has really thought his political views through for himself, not taking anything for granted. He is therefore unmatchably confident of the positions he takes up: positions which in American terms would be considered neoconservative. I have known him for several years, and always treasured his explosive intellectual wrath. But this conversation is unique. For while we still sit in the grimy hut, Pavel in his enormous, leather-reinforced stoker's trousers, I think that, within a few months, he will actually be sitting, in a smart suit, in the new lower house of a real parliament.

5 PM. Plenum. Several people have been nominated already for the "crisis staffs" over the weekend. Are there any more volunteers? This is a critical weekend, since Sunday is the deadline set by the Forum for the announcement of the new government, and they will then have to react to Adamec's list. Effectively, almost anyone from among this miscellaneous group could appoint himself to participate in the crucial decision. But everyone is simply exhausted after a fortnight of revolution. Their wives and children are complaining. And damn it, it is the weekend. So the list of volunteers grows only slowly.

The meeting wakes up when a burly farmer arrives, having just successfully disrupted an official congress of agricultural cooperatives. He reads out—no, he elocutes—a rousing statement, beginning, "We the citizens...," and calling for everything from freedom to fertilizers. Then he asks for speakers from the Forum to come out into the countryside. People in the country, he says, think Charter 77 is a group of former prisoners.

After seven, Havel and Petr Pithart return, also exhausted, from their five-hour-long negotiations with the Czech (as opposed to the federal) prime minister, František Pitra. Here, too, the central issue was the composition of a new government, and changes in those arrangements (e.g., for education) which are within the competence of this body. Finally they have agreed to a joint communiqué, after arguing for an hour over one word—"resignation." Havel says: You must understand what it means for these people to sign a joint communiqué with us, whom for twenty years they have regarded—or at least treated—as dangerous criminals.

* * *

The early hours. The king of Bohemia arrives back in his basement pub. "Ah, *pane* Havel!" cries a girl at a neighboring table, and sends over her boyfriend to get an autograph on a cigarette packet. Havel is a Bohemian in both senses of the word. He is a Czech intellectual from Bohemia, with a deep feeling for his native land. But he is also an artist, nowhere happier than in a tavern with a glass of beer and the company of pretty and amusing friends. Short, with light hair and moustache, and a thick body perched on small feet, he looks younger than his fifty-three years. Even in quieter times, he is a bundle of nervous energy, with hands waving like twin propellers, and a quite distinctive, almost Chaplinesque walk: short steps, slightly stooping, a kind of racing shuffle. He wears jeans, open shirts, perhaps a corduroy jacket, only putting on a suit and tie under extreme duress: for example, when receiving one of those international prizes. Negotiations with the government, by contrast, do not qualify for a suit and tie. His lined yet boyish face is constantly breaking into a winning smile, while from inside this small frame a surprisingly deep voice rumbles out some wry remark. Despite appearances, he has enormous stamina. Few men could have done half of what he has done in the last fortnight and come out walking, let alone talking. Yet here he is, at one o'clock in the morning, laughing as if he made revolutions every week.

* * *

Day Sixteen (Saturday, December 2). A shabby back room, with a broken-down bed and a girlie calendar on the wall. On one side, the editors of a samizdat—but soon to be legal—paper. On the other side, Havel, the head of the Stockholm-based Charter 77 Foundation, František Janouch, and, from Vienna, the chairman of the International Helsinki Federation, Prince Karl von Schwarzenberg, with tweed jacket and Sherlock Holmes pipe. Arrangements are to be made for the newly legal paper. The Prince takes note of their needs. At one point, there is talk of some fiscal permission required. Havel takes a typewritten list of names out of his bag, and finds the name of the finance minister. "Does anyone know him?" he jokes. Silence. Schwarzenberg says: "What kind of country is this, where one doesn't know the minister?"

Suddenly people have red, white, and blue badges saying "Havel for President." They are made, I am told, in Hungary. Havel shyly says, "May I have one?" and pops it into his pocket.

In the evening there is a ceremony on the stage of the Magic Lantern to thank the staff for their help, since on Monday they are to resume more normal performances. After short speeches, the lights go down, a fireworks display is projected onto the backdrop, and everyone joins in signing the Czech version of "We Shall Overcome," swaying from side to side with hands raised in the V-for-Victory sign. Then we drink pink champagne. Emerging from the auditorium, I see a solitary figure standing in the foyer, with half-raised glass, indecisively, as if pulled in four directions at once by invisible arms. It is Havel. We sit down on a bench and he rumbles confidentially: "I am just engaged in very important negotiations about…"—at which point a pretty girl comes up with another bottle of champagne. Then someone with an urgent message. Then another pretty girl. Then Prince Schwarzenberg. I never do get his account of those vital negotiations.

* * *

Day Seventeen (Sunday, December 3). Another stage, another founding meeting, this time of the new writers' union, in the Realistic Theater. Havel says a few words and is just slipping away when they haul him back on stage, and tell him he must be chairman of the new union. Elected by acclamation, he makes his racing shuffle to the microphone and says thank you, yes, thank you, and he is frightfully sorry but he really has to dash...which he does, for they are about to make known the proposed composition of Adamec's new government.

And a very bad composition it is too. Despite Adamec's solemn declaration about proposing a "broad coalition" government of experts, and despite the deletion of the leading role of the Party from the constitution, no less than sixteen out of the twenty-one proposed members of the government are Party members. Among them are almost no experts, but some very compromised figures, such as the foreign minister, Jaromír Johannes. Clearly this is unacceptable.

Crisis meeting in the smoking room. What is to be done? Some say that the Forum must go for what the people obviously want: a real government of experts led by Komárek. Others say that is impossible, and Komárek is not the right man. Professor Jicinský, the constitutional lawyer, points out that the Forum is in danger of painting itself into a constitutional corner: for if they don't accept the government, and demand the President's resignation by next Sunday, then they could end up with no constitutional authority in the land except the old and corrupt parliament. A confused discussion ends in general agreement that the Forum must demand the further reconstruction of the government, backing this up with a demonstration on Wenceslas Square tomorrow afternoon, and the threat of a general strike a week from Monday. Petr Pithart, now a central figure, is chosen to deliver the Forum's reaction on television this evening, along with a student, an actor, and Petr Miller, with the worker's muscle at the end. They hurry off down into the stuffy, overheated dressing rooms to draft the statements, together with the master draughtsman, Havel. Now there is no pink champagne and no laughter. It is too serious a business.

But later in the evening there is a moment, if not for laughter, then at least for a quiet tear. There is a concert "for all right-thinking people," a concert to celebrate the revolution. When Marta Kubišová comes on stage, the audience erupts in the kind of applause that usually only follows a brilliant performance. But they are not applauding her singing. They are applauding her silence. Years of silence. For Marta Kubišová, one of the most popular singers of the Sixties, has not been allowed to appear in public in her native land since she signed Charter 77. When the applause finally subsides, a girl presents her with a bunch of flowers, "one for each lost year." A fragile, gentle figure—now in early middle age—Marta Kubišová is so overwhelmed that she can hardly speak, let alone sing. "Thank you, thank you," she whispers into the microphone. Then, with a friend supporting her, she sings: "The times they are a changin'..." It is a moment of joy, but with an inner core of bitter sadness. For to most of her audience the songs she sings are ancient history—the sounds of the Sixties.

* * *

Day Eighteen (Monday, December 4). Three forty-five. Wenceslas Square. Despite the freezing cold, the demonstration will be huge, and a success. Of course it will. Everyone knows it. They file into the square slowly and matter-of-factly, as if they had been doing this for years. A few minutes before four, they start warming-up with the familiar chants, "Now's the time!" "Resignation!" and ringing the keys. "Long live the students" they cry—is there another city in the world where you would hear that? "Long live the actors."

Then come the official—that is, official unofficial—speakers, slowly reading rather complicated statements, full of "CF and PAV." "Long live the Forum!" they chant, nonetheless. Loud support for the general strike on December 11. A fine, theatrical performance by Radim Palouš, who reads out the proposal to recall compromised members of the Federal Assembly, such as—pause—and then, like a whiplash: "Jakeš." Whistles and jeers. And so on down the list of gibbering thugs: Fojtík, Indra, Bilak. "Let it be done," says the crowd. And from one corner: "Do it like the Germans!" (Meaning the East Germans, for this morning brought the news of Erich Honecker et al. being expelled from the Party, and placed under house arrest.) But "like the Germans" is how the Forum leadership does not want to do it. They want to do it like the Czechs, that is, gently, without hatred and revenge.

Finally, the bell-clear voice of Václav Malý reading the Forum statement: the demand for free elections by the end of June 1990 at the latest, with a new indication that the Forum will propose or endorse candidates; the formation of a genuine coalition government by next Sunday, otherwise the Forum will propose its own candidate; the Forum and the PAV declaring themselves to be the guarantors of the transition to a democratic state based on the rule of law. "Long live the Forum!" Then, in a last touch which verges on kitsch, the pudgy pop star Karel Gott (a housewives' darling) and the exiled Karel Kryl come out onto the balcony together, to lead the singing of the national anthem(s), the slow, heart-rending first verse in Czech, the sprightly, dance-rhythm second verse in Slovak.

Up the street to my hotel, where the television brings news of the successful Malta summit, of Gorbachev's subsequent meeting with Warsaw Pact leaders in Moscow, and then, separately, with Urbánek and Adamec. Then a report about the roundup of Communist leaders in East Germany. Later, a flash: the five Warsaw Pact states that invaded Czechoslovakia in 1968 have formally renounced and condemned this as an intervention in Czechoslovakia's internal affairs.

So every schoolboy can see which way the external winds are blowing. No doubt this will be a week of tense and tortuous negotiation. But it is hard to see what alternative the authorities have, other than to make further concessions. They are caught between the hammer of popular revolt and the anvil of a completely transformed external context, symbolized by the Malta summit and that Warsaw Pact statement: "From Yalta to Malta" for the world; from Husák to Havel for Prague.

A late-night walk through the old town, veiled in a mist. After twenty long years, the sleeping beauty of central Europe has woken up. The improvised posters on the shop windows deserve an article in themselves. "Unity is strength," they say. "People, open your eyes." And: "The heart of Europe cries for freedom."

5.

At this point the Forum had to leave the Magic Lantern, and I had, alas, to leave Prague. The next week was probably as important as the previous two, but someone else will have to chronicle its inner dramas. On Tuesday there were further, inconclusive talks with Adamec. On Wednesday he threatened to resign, and on Thursday he did so. His former deputy, Marián Calfa, a Slovak, was asked by President Husák to form a new government. The Forum said they might be able to come to an agreement with him, and made some "suggestions" for the new cabinet. (A week before they had said "the CF does not aspire to any ministerial post," but, as the British Prime Minister Harold Wilson once remarked, a week in politics is a long time. Above all, a week in revolutionary politics.)

There followed "round table" talks between representatives of all the official parties—crucially, of course, the Communists, headed here by Vasil Mohorita—and those of the Forum, headed by Havel, and of the Public Against Violence, headed by Jan Carnogurský. As in Poland, the "round table" really had just two sides. But in Poland, the round table took two months; in Czechoslovakia, two days. Precisely meeting the Forum's deadline, on Sunday, December 10, UN Human Rights Day, Gustav Husák swore in the new government, and then resigned as president.

Václav Havel read out the names of the new cabinet to a jubilant crowd on Wenceslas Square. Virtually all the Forum's "suggestions" were reflected in the agreed list. Jan Carnogurský was catapulted in the space of just a fortnight from being a prisoner of conscience. expecting a stiff sentence, to being one of two so-called "first vice-premiers" of Czechoslovakia, with partial responsibility for the security apparatus that had for so long harassed and persecuted him. In a compromise, since the two sides could not agree on an interior minister, he shared this responsibility with the Communist premier, Marián Calfa, and the other "first vice-premier," our old friend the chief Prognistic, Pan Docent Valtr Komárek, *Dr. Sc.*

Komárek would have overall responsibility for economic policy, with two other members of his institute under him: Vladimír Dlouhý (like Komárek, a Party member), and, predictably, the glinting economist Václav Klaus as minister of finance. (So now Prince Schwarzenberg could rest content: one *does* know the minister.) As if in a fairy-tale, Jirí Dienstbier went from stoker to foreign minister. Almost as remarkably, Miroslav Kusy, a well-known, Slovak philosopher and signer of Charter 77, expelled from the Party like so many others, took charge of the Federal Office of Press and Information. Petr Miller, The Worker, became minister for labor and social affairs. The formerly puppet, but newly independent, Socialist and People's parties got two seats each. Although the prime minister was still a Communist, only eight other ministers (out of a total of twenty-one) were Party members, and of these, two—Komárek and Dlouhý—were identified more with the Forum than with the Party.

It was an extraordinary triumph at incredible speed. The "ten days" actually took just twenty-four. Well might the factory sirens blow and church bells ring on the morrow, instead of the threatened general strike. Within the next week, Klaus and Carnogurský were already announcing fiscal and legal changes to start the country down the road to a market economy and the rule of law: the road conjured up seemingly out of nothingness in those steamy dressing rooms and corridors of the Magic Lantern just a fortnight before. The next Sunday, Jirí Dienstbier was cutting the barbed wire of the iron curtain on the Czechoslovak-Austrian frontier, holding the giant wire cutters with his colleague, the Austrian foreign minister, Aloïs Mock. The students held another demonstration, taking exactly the same route that they had on Day One, just a month before: along the embankment, right at the National Theater, up Národní Street into Wenceslas Square. This time they were not met by truncheon-wielding police, by white helmets or red berets, for this time the police were, in a real sense, under their control.

* * *

Of course there were countless difficulties ahead. One major outstanding issue was the election of a new president. The Forum quickly said that Havel was its candidate, for the transitional period to free elections, and that he should be elected as soon as possible by the Federal Assembly. The Party suddenly discovered a burning passion for "democracy," and suggested that the next president should be chosen by direct popular vote, which would take longer to organize, and which, it fondly hoped, Havel might actually lose. (Note, incidentally, that Hungary's Communists recently tried an almost identical wheeze.) There was also a side plot concerning a suitable position for Dubcek, with his threefold importance: as a historical symbol, a reform Communist, and, not least, a Slovak.

As this article goes to press, the (Communist) prime minister has formally endorsed Havel's candidacy at a session of the Federal Assembly, and it therefore seems likely that the playwright will indeed be elected by that body in the near future. But even if that important dispute is resolved by the time you read this, there are many more ahead, on the path to free elections to parliament in the first half of 1990. Barring a great disaster (external or internal), it nonetheless seems certain that Czechoslovakia is now launched down the same road as Poland and Hungary, as East Germany (in a special, complicated way), and perhaps as Bulgaria: the road from communism to democracy. The breakthrough has happened.

* * *

What I have recounted here is only a small part of the story, albeit a central part. There are many other vital parts that others will have to fill in: for example, the story from the Party–government side, and, indeed, the detail of the actual negotiations. It is too soon to draw any balance sheet. But a few tentative reflections may already be ventured.

Why did it happen in November? The real question is rather: why did it not happen before? Historically, Czechoslovakia was much the most democratic state in the region before the war. Geographically, Prague lies west of Vienna. Culturally, it is *the* Central European city. The Prague Spring was crushed by external force. But the river ran on underground. The gulf between the *pays réel* and the surreal, mendacious *pays légal*—Husák's kingdom of forgetting—grew ever wider. During the last couple of years, the number of those prepared to risk something in order to speak their real minds grew very significantly. There were the 40,000 who signed the "Several Sentences" Manifesto. There were the hundreds of thousands of believers who signed the petition for religious freedom. There were the students and the actors. Once the transformations began in neighboring Poland and Hungary, one had the feeling that it was just a matter of time before things moved in Czechoslovakia.

And so it was. But East Germany went first. And if one asks, "Why did things go so fast in Czechoslovakia?" the simple answer is "because the Czechs came last." East Germany was the final straw: seen, remember, not just on television but also in Prague itself, as the East German escapees flooded into the West German embassy. National pride was aroused. Rapid change was clearly possible, and allowed, even encouraged, by Gorbachev. From the members of the audience in the Realistic Theater on the first Saturday who immediately leapt to their feet in a standing ovation at the actors' demand for a general strike, to the crowds on Wenceslas Square chanting, "Now's the time," from the journalists who at once started reporting truthfully, to the workers who never hesitated about going on strike: everyone was ready. Everyone knew, from their neighbors' experience, that it could be done.

More than that, their neighbors had given them a few ideas about how it should be done. In a real sense, Czechoslovakia was the beneficiary, and what happened there the culmination, of a ten-year-long Central European learning process—with Poland being the first, but paying the heaviest price. A student occupation strike? Of course, as in Poland! Nonviolence? The First Commandment of all Central European oppositions. Puppet parties coming alive? As in East Germany. A "round table" to negotiate the transition? As in Poland and Hungary. And so on. Politically, Czechoslovakia had what economic historians call the "advantages of backwardness." They could learn from the others' examples; and from their mistakes.

Yet when all this has been said, no one in Prague could resist the feeling that there must also be an additional, suprarational cause at work. Hegel's *Weltgeist*, said some. Agnes of Bohemia, said others. "The world is moving from dictatorship to democracy," said a third, in a newspaper interview. How you describe the suprarational agency is a matter of personal choice—for myself, I'll stick with the angels— but on a sober enumeration of causes, the whole is definitely more than the sum of its parts.

* * *

If there were angels at work, there were also devils. One saw more than once how the devils of ambition, vanity, pride, the little germs of corruption, wriggled their way down into the bowels of the Magic Lantern. Taken all in all, however, the central assembly of the Forum in the Czech lands was an impressive body. It was as democratic as it could reasonably be, in the circumstances. It was remarkably good humored. It showed a genius for improvisation. Profound differences of political ideology, faith, and attitudes were generally subordinated to the common good. A reasonable balance was struck between the political and the moral imperatives. Above all, men and women who for twenty years had been deprived of the most basic possibilities of political articulation were able to get together and say, within a matter of days: "This is what we want, this is how the face of the new Czechoslovakia should look." And it is a face that bears examination.

All the same, they were lucky. Even compared with Solidarity in Poland nine years ago, this was the politics of amateurs. There were several moments in the second week when one felt they had lost their way in the tangle of demands, long and short term, moral, symbolic, and political. Thus, to forget about those crucial levers of power, the defense and interior ministries, might look, to a cold and critical observer, like carelessness. To toss in the demand next day, in a hastily drafted letter, might look, to the cold and critical observer, like theater rather than politics. But such was the tide of popular feeling (helped by the favorable external winds), and so clear the general direction, that it came right in the end. And in politics, as Disraeli observed, nothing succeeds like success.

* * *

"Unhappy the land that has need of heroes," cries Brecht's Galileo. Unhappy the land that has need of revolution. The twenty years, and in many respects the forty years, are really lost. Lives have been ruined. Damage has been done that can never be repaired. But if you must have a revolution, then it would be difficult to imagine a better revolution than the one Czechoslovakia had: swift, nonviolent, joyful, and funny. A laughing revolution. It also came without the accompanying (and precipitating) economic crisis of Poland or Hungary. What is more, because the change has been so swift—because Komárek, Dlouhý, and Klaus are already in government, taking the necessary steps—Czechoslovakia has a real chance of making the larger transition from dictatorship to democracy, and from planned to market economy, with relatively little economic pain: although I stress the word relatively.

So the parting images should be of happiness. Collective happiness, as seen in Wenceslas Square, but even more of individual happiness. I think of Pavel, designing the bicameral legislature in his stoker's hut. I think of Petr, given a new last chapter for his history of Czechoslovakia, which will be published legally, while he travels to Oxford. I think of Rita, preparing for her new job as ambassador to Washington. I think of Jiří, now making the foreign policy of the Czechoslovak (Socialist?) Republic. And I think of Václav—that is, Wenceslas—drinking a Christmas toast.

Sentimental? Absurdly so. But sufficient unto the day are the evils thereof, and God knows there will be evils enough in East Central Europe over the next decade: common, workaday evils of fragile polities and struggling economies. For a short while, at least, we may surely rejoice. After twenty years, the clocks have started again in Prague. The ice has melted. The most Western of all the so-called East European countries is resuming its proper history.

—January 18, 1990

14

Godot Comes to Sarajevo
Susan Sontag

What does one do, what can one do, when armed thugs, their heads filled with racist propaganda, start shooting at helpless people, at children running back from school, old men going for a coffee, mothers carrying groceries, actors, clerks, doctors, teachers trying to get to work? What do you do when these same thugs shell theaters, smash shops, blast schools? And all this in the name of an ethnically pure community, the antithesis of Sarajevo, a civilized European city with citizens from all manner of ethnic and religious backgrounds rubbing along fine.

One can call for the armed intervention of outside powers, to silence the sniping thugs with bombs. Or one can report meticulously and with personal risk on the atrocities taking place, so that crimes don't pass unnoticed, even if they remain unpunished.

But civilization is resilient. People still played music and went to the theater and educated children in the Warsaw ghetto too. Directing a performance of Waiting for Godot *is in this tradition. It upholds the standards of civilized life in the face of those who wish to destroy it.*

—I.B.

"Nothing to be done." "*Nista ne moze da se uradi.*"
—opening line of *Waiting for Godot*

I.

I WENT TO Sarajevo in mid-July to stage a production of *Waiting for Godot* not so much because I'd always wanted to direct Beckett's play (although I had), as because it gave me a practical reason to return to Sarajevo and stay for a month or more. I had spent two weeks there in April, and had come to care intensely about the battered city and what it stands for; some of its citizens had become friends. But I couldn't again be just a witness: that is, meet and visit, tremble with fear, feel brave, feel depressed, have heart-breaking conversations, grow ever more indignant, lose weight. If I went back, it would be to pitch in and do something.

No longer can a writer consider that the imperative task is to bring the news to the outside world. The news is out. Plenty of excellent foreign journalists (most of them in favor of intervention, as am I) have been reporting the lies and the slaughter since the beginning of the siege, while the decision of the western European powers and the United States not to intervene remains firm, thereby giving the victory to Serb fascism. I was not under the illusion that going to Sarajevo to direct a play would make me useful in the way I could be if I were a doctor or a water systems engineer. It would be a small contribution. But it was the only one of the three things I do—write, make films, and direct in the theater—which yields something that would exist only in Sarajevo, that would be made and consumed there.

Among the people I'd met in April was a young Sarajevo-born theater director, Haris Pasovic, who had left the city after he finished school and made his considerable reputation working mainly in Serbia. When the Serbs started the war in April 1992, Pasovic went abroad, but in the fall, while working on a spectacle called *Sarajevo in Antwerp*, he decided that he could no longer remain in safe exile, and at the end of the year managed to crawl back past UN patrols and under Serb gunfire into the freezing, besieged city. Pasovic invited me to see his *Grad* ("City")—a collage, with music, of declamations, partly drawn from texts by Constantine Cavafy, Zbigniew Herbert, and Sylvia Plath, using a dozen actors—which he had put together in eight days. Now he was preparing a far more ambitious production, Euripides' *Alcestis*, after which one of his students (Pasovic teaches at the still-functioning Academy of Drama) would be directing Sophocles' *Ajax*. Realizing suddenly that I was talking to a producer as well as to a director, I asked Pasovic if he would be interested in my coming back in a few months to direct a play.

"Of course," he said.

Before I could add, "Then let me think for a while about what I might want to do," he went on, "What play will you do?" And bravado, following the impulsiveness of my proposal, suggested to me in an instant what I might not have seen had I taken longer to reflect: there was one obvious play for me to direct. Beckett's play, written over forty years ago, seems written for, and about, Sarajevo.

* * *

Having often been asked since my return from Sarajevo if I worked with professional actors, I've come to understand that many people find it surprising that theater goes on at all in the besieged city. In fact, of the five theaters in Sarajevo before the war, two are still, sporadically, in use: Chamber Theater 55 (Kamerni Teater 55), where in April I'd seen a charmless production of *Hair* as well as Pasovic's *Grad*; and the Youth Theater (Pozoriste Mladih), where I decided to stage *Godot*. These are both small houses. The large house, closed since the beginning of the war, is the National Theater, which presented opera and the Sarajevo Ballet as well as plays. In front of the handsome ochre building (only lightly damaged by shelling), there is still a poster from early April 1992 announcing a new production of *Rigoletto*, which never opened. Most of the singers and musicians and ballet dancers left the city to seek work abroad soon after the Serbs attacked, but many of the most talented actors stayed, and want nothing more than to work.

Images of today's shattered city must make it hard to grasp that Sarajevo was once an extremely lively and attractive provincial capital, with a cultural life comparable to that of other middle-sized old European cities, including an audience for theater. Theater in Sarajevo, as elsewhere in Central Europe, was largely repertory: masterpieces from the past and the most admired twentieth-century plays. Just as good actors still live in Sarajevo, so do members of this cultivated audience. The difference is that actors and spectators alike can be murdered or maimed by a sniper's bullet or a mortar shell on their way to and from the theater; but then, that can happen to people in Sarajevo in their living rooms, while they sleep in their bedrooms, or fetch something from their kitchens, or go out their front doors.

But isn't this play rather pessimistic, I've been asked. Meaning, wasn't it depressing for an audience in Sarajevo; meaning, wasn't it pretentious or insensitive to stage *Godot* there?—as if the representation of despair were redundant when people really are in despair; as if what people want to see in such a situation would be, say, *The Odd Couple*. But it's not true that what everyone in Sarajevo wants is entertainment that offers them an escape from their own reality. In Sarajevo, as anywhere else, there are more than a few people who feel strengthened and consoled by having their sense of reality affirmed and transfigured by art. This is not to say that people in Sarajevo don't miss being merely entertained. The dramaturge of the National Theater, who began sitting in on the rehearsals of *Godot* after the first week, and who had studied at Columbia University, asked me before I left to bring some copies of *Vogue* and *Vanity Fair* when I return later this month, so she could be reminded of all the things that had gone out of her life. Certainly there are more Sarajevans who would rather see a Harrison Ford movie or attend a Guns n' Roses concert than watch *Waiting for Godot*. That was true before the war, too. It is, if anything, a little less true now.

And if one considers what plays were produced in Sarajevo before the siege began—as opposed to the movies shown, almost entirely the big Hollywood successes (the small *cinémathèque* was on the verge of closing just before the war, for lack of an audience, I was told)—there was nothing odd or gloomy for the Sarajevan audience in the choice of *Waiting for Godot*. The other productions currently in rehearsal or performance in Sarajevo are *Alcestis* (about the inevitability of death and the meaning of sacrifice); *Ajax* (about a warrior's madness and suicide); and *In Agony*, the first play of the Croatian Miroslav Krleza, who is, with the Bosnian Ivo Andric, one of the two internationally celebrated writers of the first half of the century from former Yugoslavia (the play's title speaks for itself). Compared with these, *Waiting for Godot* may have been the "lightest" entertainment of all.

* * *

Indeed, the question is not why there is any cultural activity in Sarajevo now after seventeen months of siege, but why there isn't more. Outside a boarded-up movie theater next to the Chamber Theater is a sun-bleached poster for *The Silence of the Lambs* with a diagonal strip across it that says DANAS (today), which was April 6, 1992, the day movie-going stopped. Since the war began, all of the movie theaters in Sarajevo have stayed shut, even if not all have been severely damaged by shelling. A building in which people gather so predictably would be too tempting a target for the Serb guns; anyway, there is no electricity to run a projector. There are no concerts, except for those given by a lone string quartet that rehearses every morning and performs very occasionally in a small room seating forty people, which also doubles as an art gallery. (It's in the same building on Marshal Tito Street that houses the Chamber Theater.) There is only one active space for painting and photography—the Obala Gallery, whose exhibits sometimes stay up only one day and never more than a week.

No one I talked to in Sarajevo disputes the sparseness of cultural life in this city where, after all, between 300,000 and 400,000 inhabitants still live. The majority of the city's intellectuals and creative people, including most of the faculty of the University of Sarajevo, fled at the beginning of the war, before the city was completely encircled. Besides, many Sarajevans are reluctant to leave their apartments except when it is absolutely necessary, to collect water and their UNHCR rations; though no one is safe anywhere, they have more to fear when they are in the street. And beyond fear, there is depression—most Sarajevans are very depressed—which produces lethargy, exhaustion, apathy.

Moreover, Belgrade was the cultural capital of former Yugoslavia, and I have the impression that in Sarajevo the visual arts were derivative; that ballet, opera, and musical life were routine. Only film and theater were distinguished, so it is not surprising that these continue in Sarajevo under siege. A film production company, SAGA, makes both documentary and fiction films, and there are the two functioning theaters.

In fact, the audience for theater expects to see a play like *Waiting for Godot*. What my production of *Godot* signifies to them, apart from the fact that an eccentric American writer and part-time director volunteered to work in the theater as an expression of solidarity with the city (a fact inflated by the local press and radio as evidence that the rest of the world "does care"—when I knew, to my indignation and shame, that I represented nobody but myself), is that this is a great European play and that they are members of European culture. For all their attachment to American popular culture, which is as intense here as anywhere else, it is the high culture of Europe that represents for them their ideal, their passport to a European identity. People had told me again and again on my earlier visit in April: We're part of Europe. We're the people in former Yugoslavia who stand for European values: secularism, religious tolerance, and multi-ethnicity. How can the rest of Europe let this happen to us? When I replied that Europe is and always has been as much a place of barbarism as a place of civilization, they didn't want to hear. Now, a few months later, no one would dispute such a statement.

* * *

People in Sarajevo know themselves to be terminally weak: waiting, hoping, not wanting to hope, knowing that they aren't going to be saved. They are humiliated by their disappointment, by their fear, and by the indignities of daily life—for instance, by having to spend a good part of each day seeing to it that their toilets flush, so that their bathrooms don't become cesspools. That is how they use most of the water they queue for in public spaces, at great risk to their lives. This sense of humiliation may be even greater than their fear.

Putting on a play means so much to the local theater professionals in Sarajevo because it allows them to be normal, that is, to do what they did before the war; to be not just haulers of water or passive recipients of "humanitarian aid." Indeed, the lucky people in Sarajevo are those who can carry on with their professional work. It is not a question of money, since Sarajevo has only a black-market economy whose currency is German marks; and many are living on their savings, which were always in deutsche marks, or on remittances from abroad. (To get an idea of the city's economy, consider that a skilled professional—say, a surgeon at the city's main hospital or a television journalist—earns three deutsche marks a month; while cigarettes—a local version of Marlboros—cost ten deutsche marks a pack.) The actors and I, of course, were not on salary. Other theater people would sit in on rehearsals not only because they wanted to watch our work, but because they were glad to have, once again, a theater to go to every day.

Far from it being frivolous to put on a play—this play or any other—it is a serious expression of normality. "Isn't putting on a play like fiddling while Rome burns?" a journalist asked one of the actors. "Just asking a provocative question," the journalist explained to me when I reproached her, worried that the actor might have been offended. He was not. He didn't know what she was talking about.

2.

I started auditioning actors the day after I arrived, one role already cast in my head. I remembered, at a meeting with theater people in April, a stout older woman wearing a large broad-brimmed black hat, who sat silently, imperiously, in a corner of the room. A few days later when I saw her in Pasovic's *Grad*, I learned that she was the senior actor of the pre-siege Sarajevo theater, and, when I decided to direct *Godot*, I immediately thought of her as Pozzo. Pasovic concluded that I would cast only women (he told me that an all-woman *Godot* had been done in Belgrade some years ago). But that wasn't my intention. I wanted the casting to be gender-blind, confident that this is one of the few plays where it makes sense, since the characters are representative, even allegorical figures. If Everyman (like the pronoun "he") really does stand for everybody—as women are always being told—then Everyman doesn't have to be played by a man. I was not making the statement that a woman can also be a tyrant—which Pasovic then decided I meant by casting Ines Fancovic in the role—

but rather that a woman can play the role of a tyrant. In contrast, Admir ("Atko") Glamocak, the actor I cast as Lucky, a gaunt, lithe man of thirty whom I'd admired as Death in *Alcestis*, fit perfectly the traditional conception of Pozzo's slave.

Three other roles were left: Vladimir and Estragon, the pair of forlorn tramps, and Godot's messenger, a small boy. It was troubling that there were more good actors available than parts, since I knew how much it meant to the actors I auditioned to be in the play. Three seemed particularly gifted: Velibor Topic, who also plays Death in *Alcestis*; Izudin ("Izo") Bajrovic, who is *Alcestis*'s Hercules; and Nada Djurevska, who has the lead in the Krleza play.

Then it occurred to me I could have three pairs of Vladimir and Estragon and put them all on the stage at once. Velibor and Izo seemed to me likely to make the most powerful, fluent couple; there was no reason *not* to use what Beckett envisaged, two men, at the center; but they would be flanked on the left side of the stage by two women and on the right by a woman and a man—three variations on the theme of the couple.

Since no child actors were available and I dreaded using a nonprofessional, I decided to make the messenger an adult: the boyish-looking Mirza Halilovic, a talented actor who happened to speak the best English of anyone in the cast. Of the other eight actors, three knew no English at all. It was a great help to have Mirza as my interpreter, so I could communicate with everyone at the same time.

* * *

By the second day of rehearsal, I had begun to divide up and apportion the text, like a musical score, among the three pairs of Vladimir and Estragon. I had once before worked in a foreign language, when I directed Pirandello's *As You Desire Me* at the Teatro Stabile in Turin. But I knew some Italian, while my Serbo-Croatian (or "the mother tongue," as people in Sarajevo call it, the words "Serbo-Croatian" being hard to utter now) was limited when I arrived to "Please," "Hello," "Thank you," and "Not now." I had brought with me an English-Serbo-Croatian dictionary, paperback copies of the play in English, and an enlarged photocopy of the text into which I copied in pencil the "Bosnian" translation, line by line, as soon as I received it. I also copied the English text line by line into the Bosnian script. In about ten days I managed to learn by heart the words of Beckett's play in the language in which my actors were speaking it.

The population of Sarajevo is so mixed, and there are so many intermarriages, that it would be hard to assemble any kind of group in which all three "ethnic" groups are not represented—and I never inquired what anyone was. It was by chance that I eventually learned that Velibor Topic (Estragon I) had a Muslim mother and a Serb father, though his name does not reveal that; while Ines Fancovic (Pozzo) had to be Croatian, since Ines is a Croat name, and she was born and grew up in the coastal town of Split and came to Sarajevo thirty years ago. Both parents of Milijana Zirojevic (Estragon II) are Serb, while Irena Mulamuhic (Estragon III) must have had at least a Muslim father. I never learned the ethnic origins of all the actors. They knew them and took them for granted because they are colleagues—they've acted in many plays together—and friends.

* * *

The propaganda of the aggressors holds that this war is caused by ageold hatreds; that it is a civil war or a war of secession, with Milosevic trying to save the union; that in crushing the Bosnians, whom Serb propaganda often refers to as the Turks, the Serbs are saving Europe from Muslim fundamentalism. Perhaps I should not have been surprised to be asked if I saw many women in Sarajevo who are veiled, or who wear the chador; one can't underestimate the extent to which the prevailing stereotypes about Muslims have shaped "Western" reactions to the Serb aggression in Bosnia.

In fact, the proportion of religiously observant people in Sarajevo is about the same as it is among the native-born in London or Paris or Berlin or Venice. In the prewar city, it was no odder for a "Muslim" to marry a Serb or a Croat than for someone from New York to marry someone from Massachusetts or California. Sixty percent of the marriages in Sarajevo in the year before the Serb attack took place between people from different religious backgrounds—a strong index of secularism. The Sarajevans of Muslim origin come from families that converted to Islam when Bosnia became a province of the Ottoman Empire, and they look the same as their southern Slav neighbors, spouses, and compatriots, since they are, in fact, descendants of Christian southern Slavs.

What Muslim faith existed throughout this century was already a diluted version of the moderate, Sunni faith brought by the Turks, with nothing of what could be called fundamentalism. When I asked friends who in their families are or were religiously observant, they invariably said: my grandparents. If they were under thirty-five, they usually said: my great-grandparents. Of the nine actors in *Godot* the only one with religious leanings was Nada, who is the disciple of an Indian guru; as her farewell present she gave me a copy of the Penguin edition of *The Teachings of Shiva*.

3.

Pozzo: "There is no denying it is still day."
(*They all look up at the sky.*)
"Good."
(*They stop looking at the sky.*)

We rehearsed in the dark. The bare proscenium stage was lit usually by only three or four candles, supplemented by the four flashlights I'd brought with me. When I asked for additional candles, I was told there weren't any; later I was told that they were being saved for our performances. In fact, I never learned who doled out the candles; they were simply in place on the floor when I arrived each morning at the theater, having walked through alleys and courtyards to reach the stage door, the only usable entrance, at the rear of the free-standing modern building. The theater's façade, lobby, cloakroom, and bar had been wrecked by shelling more than a year ago and the debris still had not been cleared away.

Actors in Sarajevo, Pasovic had explained to me with comradely regret, expect to work only four hours a day. "We have many bad habits here left over from the bad old socialist days." But that was not my experience; after a bumpy start—during the first week everyone seemed preoccupied by other performances and rehearsals or obligations at home—I could not have asked for actors more zealous, more eager. The main obstacle, apart from the siege lighting, was the fatigue of the malnourished actors, many of whom, before they arrived for rehearsal at ten, had for several hours been queuing for water and then lugging heavy plastic containers up eight or ten flights of stairs. Some of them had to walk two hours to get to the theater, and, of course, would have to follow the same dangerous route at the end of the day.

The only actor who seemed to have normal stamina was the oldest member of the cast, Ines Fancovic, who is sixty-eight. Still a stout woman, she has lost more than sixty pounds since the beginning of the siege, and this may have accounted for her remarkable energy. The other actors were visibly underweight and tired easily. Lucky must stand motionless through most of his long scene but never sets down the heavy bag he carries. Atko, who plays him (and now weighs no more than one hundred pounds) asked me to excuse him if he occasionally rested his empty suitcase on the floor throughout the rehearsal period. Whenever I halted the run-through for a few minutes to change a movement or a line reading, all the actors, with the exception of Ines, would instantly lie down on the stage.

Another symptom of fatigue: the actors were slower to memorize their lines than any I have ever worked with. Ten days before the opening they still needed to consult their scripts, and were not word-perfect until the day before the dress rehearsal. This might have been less of a problem had it not been too dark for them to read the scripts they held in their hands. An actor crossing the stage while saying some lines, who then forgot them, was obliged to make a detour to the nearest candle and peer at his or her script. (A script was loose pages, since binders and paper clips are virtually unobtainable in Sarajevo. The play had been typed once in Pasovic's office on a little manual typewriter whose ribbon looked as if it had been in use since the beginning of the siege. I was given the original and the actors the nine carbon copies, the last five of which would have been hard to read in any light.)

Not only could they not read their scripts; unless standing face to face, they could barely see one another. Lacking the normal peripheral vision that anybody has in daylight or when there is electric light, they could not do something as simple as put on or take off their bowler hats at the same time. And they appeared to me for a long time, to my despair, mostly as silhouettes. At the moment early in Act I when Vladimir "smiles suddenly from ear to ear, keeps smiling, ceases as suddenly"—in my version, three Vladimirs—I couldn't see a single one of those false smiles from my stool some ten feet in front of them, my flashlight lying across my scripts. Gradually, my night vision improved.

* * *

Of course, it was not just fatigue that made the actors slower to learn their lines and their movements and to be, often, inattentive and forgetful. It was distraction, and fear. Each time we heard the noise of a shell exploding, there was not only relief that the theater had not been hit. The actors had to be wondering where it *was* landing. Only the youngest in my cast, Velibor, and the oldest, Ines, lived alone. The others left wives and husbands, parents and children at home when they came to the theater each day, and several of them lived very close to the front lines, near Grbavica, a part of the city taken by the Serbs last year, or in Alipasino Polje, which is near the Serb-held airport.

On July 30, at two o'clock in the afternoon, Nada, who was often late during the first two weeks of rehearsal, arrived with the news that at eleven that morning Zlajko Sparavolo, a well-known older actor who specialized in Shakespearean roles, had been killed, along with two neighbors, when a shell landed outside his front door. The actors left the stage and went silently to an adjacent room. I followed them and the first to speak told me that this news was particularly upsetting to everyone because, up till then, no actor had been killed. (I had heard earlier about two actors who had each lost a leg to the shelling; and I knew Nermin Tulic, the actor who last year had lost both legs at the hip and now was the administrative director of the Youth Theater.) When I asked the actors if they felt up to continuing the rehearsal, all but one, Izo, said yes. But after working for another hour, some of the actors found they couldn't continue. That was the only day that rehearsals stopped early.

* * *

The set I had designed—as minimally furnished, I thought, as Beckett himself could have desired—had two levels. Pozzo and Lucky entered, acted on, and exited from a rickety platform eight feet deep and four feet high, running the whole length of upstage, with the tree toward the left; the front of the platform was covered with the translucent polyurethane sheeting that the UNHCR brought in last winter to seal the shattered windows of Sarajevo. The three couples stayed mostly on the stage floor, though sometimes one or more of the Vladimirs and Estragons went to the upper stage. It took several weeks of rehearsal to arrive at three distinct identities for them. The central Vladimir and Estragon (Izo and Velibor) were the classic buddy pair. After several false starts, the two women (Nada and Milijana) turned into another kind of couple in which affection and dependence are mixed with exasperation and resentment: mother in her early forties and grown daughter. And Sejo and Irena, who were also the oldest couple, played a quarrelsome, cranky husband and wife, modeled on homeless people I'd seen in downtown Manhattan. But when Lucky and Pozzo were on stage the Vladimirs and Estragons could join together, becoming something of a Greek Chorus as well as an audience to the show put on by the master and slave.

Tripling the parts of Vladimir and Estragon, and expanding the play with stage business, as well as silences, was making it a good deal longer than it usually is. I soon realized that Act I would run at least ninety minutes. Act II would be shorter, for my idea was to use only Izo and Velibor as Vladimir and Estragon. But even with a stripped-down and speeded-up Act II, the play would be two and a half hours long. And I could not envisage asking people to watch the play from the Youth Theater's auditorium, whose nine small chandeliers could come crashing down if the building suffered a direct hit from a shell, or even if an adjacent building were hit. Further, there was no way five hundred people in the auditorium could see what was taking place on a deep proscenium stage lit only by a few candles. But as many as a hundred people could be seated close to the actors, at the front of the stage, on a tier of six rows of seats made from wood planks. They would be hot, since it was high summer, and they would be squeezed together; I knew that many more people would be lining up outside the stage door for each performance than could be seated (tickets are free). How could I ask the audience, which would have no lobby, bathroom, or water, to sit so uncomfortably, without moving, for two and a half hours?

I concluded that I could not do all of *Waiting for Godot*. But the very choices I had made about the staging which made Act I as long as it was also meant that the staging could represent the whole of *Waiting for Godot*, while using only the words of Act I. For this may be the only work in dramatic literature in which Act I is itself a complete play. The place and time of Act I are: "A country road. A tree. Evening." (For Act II: "Next day. Same time. Same place.") Although the time is "Evening," both acts show a complete day, the day beginning with Vladimir and Estragon meeting again (though in every sense except the sexual one a couple, they separate each evening), and with Vladimir (the dominant one, the reasoner and information-gatherer, who is better at fending off despair) inquiring where Estragon has spent the night. They talk about waiting for Godot (whoever he may be), straining to pass the time. Pozzo and Lucky arrive, stay for a while and perform their "routines," for which Vladimir and Estragon are the audience, then depart. After this there is a time of deflation and relief: they are waiting again. Then the messenger arrives to tell them that they have waited once more in vain.

Of course, there is a difference between Act I and the replay of Act I which is Act II. Not only has one more day gone by. Everything is worse. Lucky no longer can speak, Pozzo is now pathetic and blind, Vladimir has given in to despair. Perhaps I felt that the despair of Act I was enough for the Sarajevo audience, and that I wanted to spare them a second time when Godot does not arrive. Maybe I wanted to propose, subliminally, that Act II might be different. For, precisely as *Waiting for Godot* was so apt an illustration of the feelings of Sarajevans now—bereft, hungry, dejected, waiting for an arbitrary, alien power to save them or take them under its protection—it seemed apt, too, to be staging *Waiting for Godot, Act I*.

4.

"Alas, alas…"/"*Ovai, ovai…*" —from Lucky's monologue

People in Sarajevo live harrowing lives; this was a harrowing *Godot*. Ines was flamboyantly theatrical as Pozzo, and Atko was the most heart-rending Lucky I have ever seen. Atko, who had ballet training and was a movement teacher at the Academy, quickly mastered the postures and gestures of decrepitude, and responded inventively to my suggestions for Lucky's dance of freedom. It took longer to work out Lucky's monologue—which in every other production of *Godot* I'd seen (including the one Beckett himself directed in 1975 at the Schiller Theater in Berlin) was, to my taste, delivered too fast, as nonsense. I divided this speech into five parts, and we discussed it line by line, as an argument, as a series of images and sounds, as a lament, as a cry. I wanted Atko to deliver Beckett's aria about divine apathy and indifference, about a heartless, petrifying world, as if it made perfect sense. Which it does, especially in Sarajevo.

It has always seemed to me that *Waiting for Godot* is a supremely realistic play, though it is generally acted in something like a minimalist, or vaudeville, style. The *Godot* that the Sarajevo actors were by inclination, temperament, previous theater experience, and present (atrocious) circumstances most able to perform, and the one I chose as a director, was full of anguish, of immense sadness, and toward the end, violence. That the messenger is a strapping adult meant that when he announces the bad news Vladimir and Estragon could express not only disappointment but rage: manhandling him as they could never have done were the role played by a small child. (And there are six, not two, of them, and only one of him.) After he escapes, they subside into a long, terrible silence. It was a Chekhovian moment of absolute pathos, as at the end of *The Cherry Orchard*, when the ancient butler Firs wakes up to find that he's been left behind in the abandoned house.

*   *   *

During the production of *Godot* and this second stay in Sarajevo it felt as if I were going through the replay of a familiar cycle. Some of the severest shelling of the central city since the beginning of the siege took place during the first ten days I was there. On one day Sarajevo was hit by nearly 4,000 shells. Once more hopes were raised of American intervention, but Clinton was outwitted (if that is not too strong a term to describe so weak a resolve) by the pro-Serb UNPRO-FOR command, which claimed that intervention would endanger UN troops. The despair and disbelief of the Sarajevans steadily mounted. A mock cease-fire was called, which meant just a little shelling and sniping, but since more people ventured out in the street, almost as many were murdered and maimed each day.

The cast and I tried to avoid jokes about "waiting for Clinton" but that was very much what we were doing in late July, when the Serbs took, or seemed to take, Mt. Igman, just above the airport. The capture of Mt. Igman would allow them to fire shells horizontally into the central city, and hope rose again that there would be American airstrikes against the Serb gun positions, or at least a lifting of the arms embargo. Although people were afraid to hope, for fear of being disappointed, at the same time no one could believe that Clinton would again speak of intervention and again do nothing. I myself had succumbed to hope again when a journalist friend showed me a dim satellite fax transmission of Senator Biden's superb speech in favor of intervention, twelve single-spaced pages, which he had delivered on the floor of the Senate on July 29. The Holiday Inn, the only functioning hotel in Sarajevo, which is on the western side of the central city, four blocks from the nearest Serb snipers, was crowded with journalists waiting for the fall of Sarajevo or the intervention; one of the hotel staff said the place hadn't been this full since the 1984 Winter Olympics.

* * *

Sometimes I thought we were not waiting for Godot, or Clinton. We were waiting for our props. There seemed no way to find Lucky's suitcase and picnic basket, Pozzo's cigarette holder (to substitute for the pipe) and whip. As for the carrot that Estragon munches slowly, rapturously: until two days before we opened, we had to rehearse with three of the dry rolls I scavenged each morning from the Holiday Inn dining room (rolls were the breakfast offered) to feed the actors and assistants, and the all-too-rare stagehand. We could not find any rope for Pozzo until a week after we started on the stage, and Ines got understandably cranky when, after three weeks of rehearsal, she still did not have the right length of rope, a proper whip, a cigarette holder, an atomizer. The bowler hats and the boots for the Estragons materialized only in the last days of rehearsal. And the costumes—whose designs I had suggested and the sketches of which I had approved in the first week—did not come until the day before we opened.

Some of this was owing to the scarcity of virtually everything in Sarajevo. Some of it, I had to conclude, was typically "southern" (or Balkan) mañana-ism. ("You'll definitely have the cigarette holder tomorrow," I was told every morning for three weeks.) But some of the shortages were the result of rivalry between theaters. There had to be props at the closed National Theater. Why were they not available to us? I discovered, shortly before the opening, that I was not just a visiting member of the Sarajevo "theater world," but that there were several theater tribes in Sarajevo and that, being allied with Haris Pasovic's, I could not count on the good will of the others. (It would work the other way around, too. On one occasion, when precious help was offered me by another producer, who on my last visit had become a friend, I was told by Pasovic, who was otherwise reasonable and helpful: "I don't want you to take anything from that person.")

Of course this would be normal behavior anywhere else. Why not in besieged Sarajevo? Theater in prewar Sarajevo must have had the same feuds, pettiness, and jealousy as in any other European city. I think my assistants, as well as Ognjenka Finci, the set and costume designer, and Pasovic himself were anxious to shield me from the knowledge that not everybody in Sarajevo was to be trusted. When I began to catch on that some of our difficulties reflected a degree of hostility or even sabotage, one of my assistants said to me sadly: "Now that you know us, you won't want to come back any more."

* * *

Sarajevo is not only a city that represents an ideal of pluralism; it was regarded by many of its citizens as an ideal place: though not important (because not big enough, not rich enough), it was still the best place to be, even if, being ambitious, you had to leave it to make a real career, as people from San Francisco eventually go to Los Angeles or New York. "You can't imagine what it used to be like here," Pasovic said to me. "It was paradise." That kind of idealization produces a very acute disillusionment, so that now almost all the people I know in Sarajevo cannot stop lamenting the city's moral deterioration: the increasing number of muggings and thefts, the gangsterism, the predatory black marketeers, the banditry of some army units, the absence of civic cooperation. One would think that they could forgive themselves, and their city. For seventeen months it has been a shooting gallery. There is virtually no municipal government; hence, debris from shelling doesn't get picked up, schooling isn't organized for small children, etc., etc. A city under siege must, sooner or later, become a city of rackets.

But most Sarajevans are pitiless in their condemnation of conditions now, and of many "elements," as they would call them with pained vagueness, in the city. "Anything good that happens here is a miracle," one of my friends said to me. And another: "This is a city of bad people." When an English photojournalist made us the invaluable gift of nine candles, three were immediately stolen. One day Mirza's lunch—a chunk of homebaked bread and a pear—was taken from his knapsack while he was on the stage. It could not have been one of the other actors. But it could have been anyone else, say, one of the stagehands or any of the students from the Academy of Drama who wandered in and out of the rehearsals. The discovery of this theft was very depressing to the actors.

* * *

Yet although a lot of people want to leave, and will leave when they can, a surprising number say that their lives are not unbearable. "We can live this life forever," said one of my friends from my April visit, Hrvoje Batinic, a local journalist. "I can live this life a hundred years," a new friend, Zehra Kreho—the dramaturge of the National Theater—said to me one evening. Both are in their late thirties.

Sometimes I felt the same way. Of course it was different for me. "I haven't taken a bath in sixteen months," a middle-aged matron said to me. "Do you know how that feels?" And of course I don't; I only know what it's like not to take a bath for a month. I was elated, full of energy, because of the challenge of the work I was doing, because of the valor and enthusiasm of everyone I worked with—while I could not ever forget how hard it has been for each of them, and how hopeless the future looks for their city. What made my lesser hardships and the danger relatively easy to bear, apart from the fact that I can leave and they can't, was that I was totally concentrated on them and on Beckett's play.

5.

Until about a week before it opened, I did not think the play would be very good. I feared that the choreography and emotional design I had constructed for the two-level stage and the nine actors in five roles were too complicated for them to master in so short a time; or, simply, that I had not been as demanding as I should have been. Two of my assistants, as well as Pasovic, told me that I was being too amicable, too "maternal," and that I should throw a tantrum now and then and, in particular, threaten to replace the actors who had not yet learned all their lines. But I went on, hoping that it would be not too bad; then, suddenly, in the last week, they turned a corner, it all came together, and at our dress rehearsal it seemed to me the production was; after all, affecting, continually interesting, well-made, and that this was an effort which did honor to Beckett's play.

I was also surprised by the amount of attention from the international press that *Godot* was getting. I had told few people that I was going to Sarajevo to direct *Waiting for Godot*, intending perhaps to write something about it later. I forgot that I would be living in a journalists' dormitory. The day after I arrived there were a dozen requests in the Holiday Inn lobby and in the dining room for interviews; and the next day; and the next. I said there was nothing to tell, I was still auditioning; and after that, the actors were simply reading the play aloud at a table; and after that, I said, we've just begun on the stage, there's hardly any light, there's nothing to see.

But when after a week I mentioned the journalists' requests to Pasovic, and my desire to keep the actors free from such distractions, I learned that he had scheduled a press conference for me and that he wanted me to admit journalists to rehearsals, give interviews, and get the maximum amount of publicity not just for the play but for an enterprise of which I had not altogether taken in that I was a part: the Sarajevo International Festival of Theater and Film, directed by Haris Pasovic, whose second production, following his *Alcestis*, was my *Godot*. When I apologized to the actors for the interruptions to come, I found that they too wanted the journalists to be there. All the friends I consulted in the city told me that the story of the production would be "good for Sarajevo."

* * *

Television, print, and radio journalism are an important part of this war. When, in April, I heard the French intellectual André Glucksmann, on his twenty-four-hour trip to Sarajevo, explain to the people of Sarajevo who had come to his press conference, that "war is now a media event," and "wars are won or lost on TV," I thought to myself: try telling that to all the people here who have lost their arms and legs. But there is a sense in which Glucksmann's indecent statement was on the mark. It's not that war has completely changed its nature, and is only or principally a media event, but that the media's coverage is a principal object of attention, and the very fact of media attention, sometimes becomes the main story.

While I was in Sarajevo, for example, my best friend among the journalists at the Holiday Inn, the BBC's admirable Alan Little, visited one of the city's hospitals and was shown a semiconscious five-year-old girl with severe head injuries, whose mother had been killed by the same mortar shell. The doctor said she would die in a few days if she could not be airlifted out to a hospital where she could be given a brain scan and sophisticated treatment. Moved by the child's plight, Alan began to talk about her in his reports. For days nothing happened. Then other journalists picked up the story, and the case of "Little Irma" became the front-page story day after day in the British tabloids and virtually the only Bosnia story on the TV news. John Major, eager to be seen as doing something, sent a plane to take the girl to London.

Then came the backlash. Alan, unaware at first that the story had become so big, then delighted because it meant that the pressure would help to bring the child out, was dismayed by the attacks on a "media circus" that was exploiting a child's suffering. It was morally obscene, the critics said, to concentrate on one child when thousands of children and adults, including many amputees and paraplegics, languish in the understaffed, undersupplied hospitals of Sarajevo and are not allowed to be transported out, thanks to the UN (but that is another story). That it *was* a good thing to do—that to try to save the life of one child is better than doing nothing at all should have been obvious, and in fact others were brought out as a result. But a story that needed to be told about the wretched hospitals of Sarajevo degenerated into a controversy over what the press did.

* * *

This is the first of the three European genocides of our century to be tracked by the world press, and documented nightly on TV. There were no reporters in 1915 sending daily stories to the world press from Armenia, and no foreign camera crews in Dachau and Auschwitz. Until the Bosnian genocide, one might have thought—this was indeed the conviction of many of the best reporters there, like Roy Guttman of *Newsday* and John Burns of *The New York Times*—that if the story could be gotten out, the world would do something. The coverage of the genocide in Bosnia has ended that illusion.

Newspaper and radio reporting and, above all, TV coverage have shown the war in Bosnia in extraordinary detail, but in the absence of a will to intervene by those few people in the world who make political and military decisions, the war becomes another remote disaster; the people suffering and being murdered there become disaster "victims." Suffering is visibly present, and can be seen in close-up; and no doubt many people feel sympathy for the victims. What cannot be recorded is an absence—the absence of any political will to end the suffering: more exactly, the decision not to intervene in Bosnia, primarily Europe's responsibility, which has its origins in the traditional pro-Serb slant of the Quai d'Orsay and the British Foreign Office. It is being implemented by the UN occupation of Sarajevo, which is largely a French operation.

I do not believe the standard argument made by critics of television that watching terrible events on the small screen distances them as much as it makes them real. It is the continuing coverage of the war in the absence of action to stop it that makes us mere spectators. Not television but our politicians have made history come to seem like re-runs. We get tired of watching the same show. If it seems unreal, it is because it's both so appalling and apparently so unstoppable.

Even people in Sarajevo sometimes say it seems to them unreal. They are in a state of shock, which does not diminish, which takes the form of a rhetorical incredulity ("How could this happen? I still can't believe this is happening."). They are genuinely astonished by the Serb atrocities, and by the starkness and sheer unfamiliarity of the lives they are now obliged to lead. "We're living in the Middle Ages," someone said to me. "This is science fiction," another friend said.

People ask me if Sarajevo ever seemed to me unreal while I was there. The truth is, since I've started going to Sarajevo—this winter I plan to return to direct *The Cherry Orchard* with Nada as Madame Ranevsky and Velibor as Lopakhin—it seems the most real place in the world.

* * *

Waiting for Godot opened, with twelve candles on the stage, on August 17. There were two performances that day, one at 2:00 PM and the other at 4:00 PM. In Sarajevo there are only matinees; hardly anybody goes out after dark. Many people were turned away. For the first few performances I was tense with anxiety. But there was a moment, I think it was the third performance, when I began to relax. For the first time I was seeing the play as a spectator. It was time to stop worrying that Ines would let the rope linking her and Atko sag while she devoured her papier-mâché chicken; that Sejo, the third Vladimir, would forget to keep shifting from foot to foot just before he suddenly rushes off to pee. The play now belonged to the actors, and I knew it was in good hands. And I think it was at the end of that performance—on Wednesday, August 18 at 2:00 PM—during the long tragic silence of the Vladimirs and Estragons which follows the messenger's announcement that Mr. Godot isn't coming today, but will surely come tomorrow, that my eyes began to sting with tears. Velibor was crying too. No one in the audience made a sound. The only sounds were those coming from outside the theater: a UN APC thundering down the street and the crack of sniper fire.

—October 21, 1993

15

The Nowhere City

Amos Elon

The violence of empires can destroy more than peoples and buildings; memories, histories, can be demolished too.

German-speaking peoples had lived in East Prussia, Silesia, Bohemia, Ruthenia, for many centuries. They were part of the European mosaic ripped apart in the 20th century by Hitler and Stalin, with some complicity of the Western nations too.

In 1945, German parts of Poland simply vanished, not just the people, and much of what they had built over the ages, but their histories. Memories were erased, new histories invented. Königsberg, the capital of Prussia, became Kaliningrad, part of the Soviet Union. After the collapse of the Soviet Union, in 1991, Kaliningrad became an orphan of history, a concrete mess with almost nothing left to remind people what came before.

—I.B.

I.

IN DAYTIME, THE main avenues of Kaliningrad—wide enough to allow ten tanks abreast to pass a reviewing stand—are half deserted. Traffic is sparse. Before the Russians took it over in 1945, this ice-free Baltic seaport was the ancient German city of Königsberg, the historic capital of East Prussia and one of the more attractive towns of the German empire. Recently there has even been talk of Germany taking the city back. But now the barren monotony and inhuman scale of Communist urban planning make Kaliningrad—the phantom of a city without any visible center—possibly one of the ugliest places in the world. Four hundred thousand inhabitants—70 percent transient sailors, fishermen, and members of the Russian armed forces and their dependents—live here in monotonous apartment blocks, crumbling mountain ranges of tar and cement and peeling plaster, gray on gray.

The public squares, as in most cities built by the Soviets after the war, are vast, each large enough to accommodate almost the entire population. Loudspeakers left over from the old Communist public-address system still dangle from their poles. There are no mass rallies nowadays and the loud-speakers are rarely if ever used. But the statue of M.I. Kalinin, a former president of the Soviet Union (he is said to have sent his own wife to the Gulag), is still standing in a vast square outside the railroad station. The city was named for him in 1945 after its capture by the Red Army in fierce street fighting with the Wehrmacht and its annexation by the Soviet Union. A giant statue of Lenin is also still standing on Ploshchad Pobedy (Victory Square)— the former Adolf-Hitler-Platz.

* * *

Founded in 1255 by knights of the Teutonic Order on rising ground above the river Pregel (now called Pregolya), Königsberg was the seat of a famous Lutheran university. In the countryside nearby were some of the largest and finest estates of the Prussian military aristocracy. In this quintessentially Germanic region the proverbial Prussian virtues of duty and discipline and austere living were cultivated in huts and manor houses, while in the city itself the dukes and the kings of Prussia were crowned. Immanuel Kant was born here in 1724, and he hardly ever left. At the university he taught not only philosophy, but geography and math as well. Johann Gottfried Herder, a Lutheran minister's son who also taught here, almost singlehandedly invented pan-German nationalism as the expression of the "spirit" of language and folksong and poetry.

Königsberg was an important garrison town, where generations of Prussian officers were trained in blind, ungrudging obedience to the word of command. Yet among young graduates of its military academy were also some of the spirited, if ineffective, aristocratic officers who conspired to launch the coup against Hitler's tyranny on July 20, 1944.

Driving through today's city, you would never guess how pretty Königsberg was. Old photographs show a scenic place, with a busy harbor, several fine churches, picturesque wharfs, and stately embankments and promenades along the river. On the hilltop stood the Prussian royal palace with its imposing crenelated towers. In the middle of the river was a densely built-up island whose narrow lanes, lined with medieval frame houses, led to the great brick Gothic cathedral in which the Prussian kings were crowned. Its grotesque ruin survives today in the middle of the completely empty island, with Kant's relatively well-preserved tombstone on the wall of the southwestern corner.

Nearly everything else has disappeared. When the Red Army stormed it in 1945, roughly a third of the old town was still standing and there were 120,000 remaining Germans. By 1947, the last of these had been deported to Germany or Kazakhstan, along with neighboring East Prussian farmers, many of whom died. Stalin ordered the old center of Prussian militarism bulldozed, leveled, and completely rebuilt as a model socialist city, to be resettled by Russians, Lithuanians, Georgians, Ukrainians, and other New Soviet Men and Women. Not all came voluntarily. Some were inmates of gulags ordered to settle in Kaliningrad after years of forced labor in the nearby swamps. The population today is still some twenty percent below its prewar level of 480,000.

* * *

The future of the Kaliningrad Province, or Oblast, one of Russia's thirty-nine increasingly autonomous provinces, is currently a matter of intense debate. The sudden collapse of the Soviet empire made Kaliningrad the last bit of territory (a mere 4,200 square miles) left over from Stalin's vast territorial gains in Eastern Europe during the Second World War. But Kaliningrad is now cut off from "mainland" Russia, to which it formally belongs, by hundreds of miles of newly independent Lithuanian, Latvian, and Belarus territory.

Only a few of the people I saw believe Kaliningrad should go on being governed directly by Moscow. They talk of Kaliningrad becoming an "independent" Baltic state, of "full autonomy" as a new "Republic of Prussia" within the Russian federation, of a joint German-Russian condominium, or of outright *Anschluss* with Germany. Like the officials of several other Russian regional governments, the local administrators here have become more independent of Moscow in recent months, and some are now actively courting virtually every prominent German businessman, journalist, or missionary who visits the city.

"Kaliningrad must become Königsberg again," I was told by Arsenij Gulyga, a prominent Russian philosopher who is now the leading Russian authority on Kant. Gulyga recalls with some irony that as a young Soviet officer in 1945, he had been one of the "liberators" of the city. Now, he says, "it would be the most natural thing in the world" if the city would revert to Germany again. Geographically, it is nearer to Berlin (400 miles) than to St. Petersburg (512 miles) or Moscow (more than 600 miles). Historically, it remains a German city, he says. Gulyga would also like to see the tsarist monarchy restored.

There is a persistent rumor in Kaliningrad, as well as in the Baltic countries, that an East Prussian "government in exile" has already been formed by right-wing German politicians. At the same time nationalists in both Warsaw and Vilnius are laying claim to parts of the Kaliningrad Autonomous Province, which they consider "historically" Polish or Lithuanian. In Warsaw last summer I saw leaflets calling for the return of Kaliningrad (Krolewiec) to Mother Poland; a few weeks later, in Vilnius, people were referring to the eastern parts of the Kaliningrad region as "Little Lithuania." The Lithuanian ambassador to Washington provoked a minor storm last year when he announced that Little Lithuania was an empty space and could be taken over by his country immediately.

Several people I talked to speculated that Russia might sell the former Königsberg to the Germans for money—a temptation which the Moscow English-language weekly *New Times* described last year as possibly "too strong to resist." According to one view of German politics, past and present—which by now may be a misleading stereotype—"Prussia" and "Königsberg" are central or permanent features of the German national psyche. "Can Kohl really refuse a Russian offer to restore Königsberg?" a Polish diplomat in Warsaw asked me. He may be overestimating Germany's wealth after reunification or the true extent of its economic or strategic designs in the East. President Yeltsin is thought to be sufficiently unconventional, and hard-pressed for Western currency, to entertain the idea of a sale for which there is a well-known precedent—the Russian sale of Alaska to the United States in 1872.

On the other hand, if Germany should reacquire East Prussia and Königsberg this might undermine the entire postwar border pattern in Eastern Europe and revive fears of German expansionism. "Poland will strongly oppose it," a Polish diplomat says. According to a joke circulating last summer, pessimists in Kaliningrad are taking lessons in Polish and optimists lessons in German, while realists are learning how to shoot Kalashnikov submachine guns. (In fact, nearly 75 percent of the students at the state university have signed up for German courses.)

* * *

The city's economy is in a state of collapse. The average monthly pay went down from sixteen dollars a month last summer to an estimated nine dollars a month now, and a Russian army major makes only slightly more than twice that amount. On the Lenin Prospect I saw soldiers in uniform selling gasoline from an army petrol tank to civilian motorists. There is a thriving black market in military equipment. Western diplomats claim that in Kaliningrad you can buy yourself a missile ("there are more missiles here than trees") or a tank, if you so wish, and perhaps even nuclear fuel or a nuclear device. A Western diplomat told me that dozens of nuclear devices formerly located in the Kaliningrad area remain unaccounted for.

The port's nuclear submarines have been transferred to the Arctic Sea or decommissioned, but there are many rumors—most of them ugly ones—about the condition and safety of these decommissioned nuclear submarines, and of the shorebased reactors that used to produce their fuel. The total amount of radioactive materials in them is said to be many times greater than that in the crippled unit at Chernobyl. In the Russian press there have been warnings of the danger of "dozens of Chernobyls" erupting in Russian naval bases in the Arctic and Baltic seas. One morning I visited Admiral Vladimir Yegorov, the officer commanding the Russian Baltic fleet, in his office on the outskirts of Kaliningrad. I asked if there was substance in these warnings. Or was the press perhaps exaggerating? "The situation is even more serious than as reported in the press," the admiral replied.

* * *

Early each morning, thousands line up outside the state-owned food shops where the shelves are often bare. There are long lines for the bus, which sometimes never arrives and often has no room for more passengers when it does. Lines of a different sort form every morning at some of the main intersections: hundreds of elderly woman and men, mostly state pensioners, stand about for hours with a little something in their hands they are hoping to sell: a bottle of Coke, a jar of preserved cucumbers, a handful of berries, a wilted cauliflower wrapped in a piece of torn newspaper.

Almost every night graves are dug up and robbed by thieves who come to the cemeteries with metal detectors, looking for rings and other valuables and for gold teeth which they pry off with hammers and pliers. The police seem to do nothing to prevent this. I visited the Kaliningrad police chief, Colonel Viktor Shoshnikov, in his office. A tough-looking man, with a habit of quoting Dostoevsky and Solzhenitsyn, he was sitting behind a large oak desk—before 1945 it may have served a German police chief—on which were many telephones. Keys dangled from his broad belt.

Shoshnikov began by lamenting that the crime rate in Kaliningrad had risen sharply since the beginning of glasnost and perestroika. Perestroika and the "Americanization of journalism" were inspiring permissiveness, pornography, prostitution, and capital crimes. The entire Kaliningrad region, he said, was infested by "a plague of Smerdyakovs," referring to the feebleminded, sinister half brother of the Karamazovs. People had never been afraid to go out at night, Shoshnikov said. Now they are.

At night, the streets are dim. Nearly all electric power is imported from neighboring Lithuania, which is threatening to charge hard currency for it soon. In the bluish uncertain light cast by neon and quartz street lamps, many of them damaged, the few souls still about throw weird shadows on the ground, and the atmosphere, grim and gloomy at best in daytime, is now even gloomier. On Prospekt Mira, outside the rickety old Hotel Moskwa where I was staying, drunks were hollering in the dark long after midnight. I watched them stagger over the potholes in the road, throwing bottles against the walls and shouting obscenities at one another. Drug addicts passed the night on the scraggly lawn nearby. According to a recent report in the liberal local newsweekly *Mirror*, a former samizdat publication, Kaliningrad is the "No. 1 drug city" in the former Soviet Union. When I asked Colonel Shoshnikov about that he said that Kaliningrad is number one on the list only because it is the only major city reporting true statistics; all the others were cheating.

* * *

One cannot escape an uncanny feeling of the existence of the old Königsberg, like the negative of a damaged photograph, lying ten to twenty feet underneath the city's surface, covered with rubble from the war and from Stalin's bulldozers. If the huge mass of debris were cleared away the old topography, now flattened out, would come into view, with its natural hills and dips, its landscaped river basins and embankments. Buried under the Lumumba and Friedrich Engels Sport Centers, under the Gamal Abdul Nasser Park and Oktober Revolution Housing Estates Nos. 1–9, the old town has survived only in the city's historical museum, where models of the 1945 street battles accompanied by sound effects convey an idea of the burning city's center, drowned in gunfire, at the moment of its capture by the Red Army.

Until the spring of 1991, Kaliningrad was a Soviet "security zone," known as the "Silent Swamp," since it was very difficult to visit and few people knew what was going on in the many military installations there. The region was closed to foreigners, except possibly spies, and even to most Russians except by special permit. Much of the rich farmland—before the war East Prussia was Germany's corn granary—lay fallow. Some three hundred abandoned German villages that had engaged in farming before the war were never resettled. During the early Sixties, oil was found east of the city but it was hardly developed. Nor was Kaliningrad's economic potential exploited, with its opportune geographic location at the westernmost point of the Soviet Union and its great port, as a link between Russia and Central Europe. Instead, the place was turned into one of the Soviet Union's main military and naval bases.

According to a report published last spring in *Moscow News*, if war with the West had broken out, the main task of the Soviet Baltic fleet would have been to capture the Danish Straits and seal off the Baltic Sea. Between 1945 and 1991, no Western cargo ship was allowed into either Kaliningrad waters or those of nearby Baltijsk (the former Prussian Pillau). The city is still a military fiefdom, headquarters of the 11th Army of the Guards, and seat of the admiral commanding the Russian Baltic fleet. The Baltic fleet, according to Admiral Yegorov, is expected nowadays to cover part of its maintenance costs by transporting civilian and foreign cargo and renting out ships to Western entrepreneurs and organizers of entertainments such as company anniversaries or wedding parties.

Throughout the city and its environs, the traffic on the streets is largely military. In the countryside, one drives past parked tanks and camouflaged installations behind seemingly endless barbed-wire fences. Since the withdrawal of Russian troops from Germany, Poland, and the Baltic states, there is an even greater military presence. According to one Western estimate, close to a quarter million troops are now stationed here. All this, according to a Western diplomat in

Warsaw, may reflect not only the difficulties of absorbing the army into Russia, but the extent of the Russians' self-consciousness and unease in this arch-Germanic spot.

* * *

Poland and the Soviet Union have treated the former German territories they took over after 1945 very differently. Many historic German cities in those territories suffered severe damage during the war. In the parts of Prussia (and Silesia) that fell under Polish rule (and from which some six million Germans were expelled) the Poles made a conscious effort to absorb the German past. Claiming that in these "regained Polish historical lands" Polish burghers and peasants had always been the majority, the Poles managed to make that past over into their own. Very carefully, even lovingly, and at great cost, they restored and in some cases rebuilt from scratch famous ancient German universities and Lutheran domed churches (they are now Catholic), castles, guildhouses, town halls, and Hanseatic burghers' mansions. The effort at rebuilding German ruins as Polish national monuments has been going on for decades; by now, the brand new Gothic or Baroque buildings have acquired their own patina and look genuine and old. Even that great symbol of German military colonialism in the East, the palatial castle of the Grand Masters of the Order of Teutonic Knights at Malbork (the former Marienburg) in East Prussia, has been restored as a major Polish historical landmark.[1]

The Russians, apparently for ideological reasons, including their

---

1. Until 1918 the castle was one of the Kaiser's official residences. Wilhelm II is said to have stayed in it more than fifty times. In an often quoted speech he delivered there on May 5, 1902, he referred to the Marienburg as Germany's "old bastion in the East...a monument that testifies to Germany's task [there]: Once again Polish insolence offends Germany and I am constrained to call upon the nation to safeguard its national inheritance." Quoted in *Der Letzte Kaiser*, catalog of an exhibition at the Historical Museum, Berlin (Berlin: Bertelsmann Lexikon Verlag, 1991), p. 314.

hostility to religion, and perhaps also from a sense of insecurity that the Poles did not share, systematically effaced nearly every remaining trace of German art and history in Kaliningrad. Churches, in particular, were the object of Soviet distaste. The Lutheran Kreuzkirche, which had survived the war almost intact, served until recently as a factory for smoked fish. The main Catholic church in the city was converted into a concert hall. Other churches were blown up or dismantled. In the outskirts, an old city gate was left standing, the scene of long-forgotten skirmishes with the Swedes during the Seven Years' War, last restored under "the gracious reign" of Wilhelm II in 1889, according to a still legible plaque on the wall; 1889, incidentally, was the year Hitler was born. A few medieval forts have also survived, as have some of the stately German villas in the suburbs, which are now occupied by high-ranking Russian army officers and members of the old Communist elite. With few exceptions, the major public monuments, including Kant's statue, were melted down.

In one case, a Prussian grand elector's headless torso was turned into a Russian monument by sticking Field Marshal Kutuzov's head on it; it can now be seen in the Oktober Revolution Quarter. Extensive remains of the former royal palace were still standing in 1969, and, according to Yuri Zabuga, a local architect, it could and should have been restored. Instead, it was bulldozed away. The bleak skeleton of a projected House of the Soviets has stood in its place unfinished for the past fifteen years, a monstrous eyesore twenty-two stories high, visible from nearly everywhere in the city. No trace is left of the many stone fountains that were still more or less intact after the war. "If I were dropped in this town by parachute, and asked where I was I would answer: perhaps in Irkutsk," wrote Marion Gräfin Dönhoff, publisher of Hamburg's liberal weekly *Die Zeit*, in 1989, on her first visit since 1945. She had grown up on an estate a few miles outside Königsberg. "Nothing, absolutely nothing, reminds you of the old Königsberg. At no point could I have said, this was once the *Paradeplatz* [where Kant's old university stood], or here stood the *Schloss*. It is as though a picture has been painted over; no one knows that underneath there had once been a different scene."

2.

In the former Paradeplatz, now an open space of cement blocks and tarred walks and a few dusty trees, I followed a group of German tourists down a flight of stairs into an underground bunker, now preserved as a war museum, where the last German commander of "Festung (fortress) Königsberg" capitulated to the Russians on April 9, 1945. Maps, photographs, and a diorama with toy soldiers and flickering lights recall the fierce fighting in the burning streets and the heavy casualties on both sides. A photocopy of the capitulation agreement is on view, and it stipulates, among other things, that each German officer is allowed to take into captivity as many suitcases as he and his servant are able to carry.

The German tourists spent a few minutes in the bunker and soon climbed back up to take their seats on their bus. A few young boys crowded the exit outside and shyly tugged at their sleeves. They pulled from their sleeves. They pulled from their shabby coat pockets little German medallions and other souvenirs dug up in the rubble, old silver spoons, combs, coins, military buttons, and rank insignia they were hoping to sell. There was also an elderly, one-armed Russian, who was offering Red Army battle medals, his own, he claimed, at thirty-five deutsche marks each. He had won one at Kiev, he said, and another in April 1945, outside Berlin.

* * *

The Hotel Moskwa, where I was staying, was a crumbling old hostel with dusty curtains and threadbare carpets on wooden floorboards that creaked underfoot. The seedy little rooms came with small radio loudspeakers screwed to the wall which could only be turned louder or softer, never completely off, and were wired to receive only one local station that endlessly repeated the hit tunes of a local rock group named American Boys. In the long corridors, the stale air smelled of cigarette butts and cleaning fluid.

On the walls were photographs of Kant's tomb and of the beaches at the nearby Baltic resorts of Zelednogradsk (the former Bad Crenz) and Svetlogorsk (Rauschen), where Thomas Mann is said to have vacationed in the Twenties and where high-ranking Russian naval officers now have their summer houses.

One day, coming out of my room on the second floor of the hotel, which was reserved for foreigners, I encountered an elderly German tourist from West Berlin who called out *"Guten Morgen"* and then told me in an assured tone that the Hotel Moskwa had been a German office building before the war, the headquarters of a big insurance company named Continental. This he knew for certain, he said. He himself was a Berliner but his wife was a native of Königsberg and knew the city. We walked down the stairs together and in a more casual tone he added that there was no doubt, no doubt whatsoever, that Königsberg would soon be German again. "It is in the stars," he said. "And in the books. As De Gaulle put it, everything in the world changes, except geography." The Russians themselves must be conscious of this, he said. "They can't really believe it possible for the city of Immanuel Kant to be a Russian city. It is an absurdity."

"It's happened before," I suggested. In the eighteenth century, after the Seven Years' War, when Königsberg fell briefly to the Russians, Kant himself and the entire university faculty voluntarily took an oath of allegiance to the "Illustrious and All Powerful Empress of All Russians, Elisabeth Petrovna etc etc" and to her heir, the future Peter III. I had just read that in a newly available English translation of Arsenij Gulyga's biography of Kant. He replied: "That doesn't count. The wars of the eighteenth century never affected ordinary people. And there was no nationalism then."

* * *

In Germany, in recent years, there has been a revival of interest in Prussia and Prussianism. The bones of Frederick the Great, which had been evacuated by the Nazis to West Germany to escape falling into Russian hands, were carried back to Potsdam in 1993 and, in the presence of Chancellor Kohl, ceremoniously reinterred next to the Emperor's greyhounds in the park of Sans Souci. Prussia continues to haunt the German imagination. It figures in all sorts of German myths, good and bad. The Prussian tradition of public service—the plotters against Hitler had been Prussian noblemen—is pitted against Prussian worship of discipline and authoritarianism. A powerful West German lobby advances the right of former Prussians to repossess the old *Heimat*, or at the very least, be compensated for lost property. The revival of interest in Prussia, highlighted recently also by three unusually extravagant exhibitions in Berlin—on Prussia in Europe, on Bismarck the Iron Chancellor, and on the last Kaiser, Wilhelm II—has been interpreted as possibly reflecting a revival of nationalism in Germany, especially since reunification.

In Kaliningrad I was told that since the city was opened to outsiders in 1991, some forty thousand German visitors had passed through, many of them former residents of Königsberg or members of former Königsberg families who wanted to see their Prussian homeland. The traffic was increasing all the time and was known in the trade as *Heimwehtourismus*—homesickness-tourism. To help German visitors find their way in the rebuilt city, a 1941 street plan, with its Herman-Goering-Strasse and Adolf-Hitler-Platz has recently been published, not by a German neo-Nazi but by an enterprising private printer in St. Petersburg.

When I joined a bus full of German tourists in Kaliningrad one morning, the Intourist guide on duty, a good-looking young woman borrowed for the day from the German department of Kaliningrad State University, systematically called out the names of old German streets—Hansaring, Steindamm, Junkerstrasse, Reichsplatz. Perhaps because the guide was so well informed, the tourists asked few questions. Like many young people in Kaliningrad today she referred to the city by its old name, Königsberg. She had never liked Kalinin anyway, she said. Kalinin had ordered that little children caught stealing a slice of bread be shot.

For many years, she said, talk about Kaliningrad's German past had been frowned upon. As recently as 1984, the Party newspaper would not publish an article, written by a colleague of hers, a philosopher, on the occasion of Kant's 260th birthday. She pointed resentfully into the empty air at long vanished landmarks. But, she said proudly, a number of concerned citizens of Kaliningrad had been successful in at least saving the ruined dome of the cathedral, even though Brezhnev himself, on a brief visit to the city in 1980, had given instructions to tear down the "rotten tooth."

* * *

During my stay I came to know some of the *Heimweh*-tourists who stayed at the hotel. They were fairly well-to-do people, most of them past retirement age. Self-conscious, even a little cowed, they wandered about the dilapidated city, complaining only of the smell everywhere of unclean lavatories and rotting food. Every morning around nine they walked out of the hotel in smart sports clothes, living advertisements for a free market economy, armed with the latest miniature video cameras and pocketfuls of deutsche marks in small change to hand out as tips as they went along. Shirtless little boys ran after them crying, "*Bitte, bitte! Eine Mark, Eine Mark, Bitte!*" They also toured the nearby countryside around Kaliningrad, which has changed the least. The roads, laid out long ago in seemingly endless straight lines by Prussian engineers, are lined with tall trees standing at exact intervals, like soldiers. Picturesque horse carts rattle on the old cobblestones and storks nest atop old telegraph poles. Flocks of white geese graze on the stubble fields. A woman from Düsseldorf said: "It's the world of yesterday. You don't see such sights any more in West Germany." The ancient trees that surrounded the noble estates outside the city still stand but the manor houses were burned down or have collapsed.

In Kaliningrad itself word has gotten around that the *Heimweh*-tourists are in no way anxious, as some local people had feared, to reclaim their former family houses that are now part of the squalid housing estates of Kaliningrad. Hence encounters between former and present day residents of Kaliningrad are often quite friendly and sometimes Germans and Russians get rather emotional. The Germans often come to visit their old houses with American cigarettes, six-packs of German beer, Würstel, cosmetics, and other small presents.

At the common breakfast table in the hotel the *Heimweh*-tourists discussed their experiences and impressions. They were hardly a cross-section of ordinary Germans. A middle-aged lawyer from Munich said he represented an organization called Union of Propertied Nobleman (Verband des Besitzenden Adels). But the same *Heimat*-polemics that one hears in Germany are also heard in Kaliningrad. When a man in his sixties, who said he had escaped from the small East Prussian town of Allenstein (today the Polish Olsztyn), complained of Russian barbarism, another man in the group told him not to forget that Hitler had been the principal reason for his loss and had, at the same time, condemned all of Eastern Europe to forty-five years of Communist tyranny. When a Berlin businessman said that *Realpolitik* made it imperative that Königsberg revert to Germany, a woman from Hanover, a retired school teacher, burst out: "*Realpoli-*

tik is just a nasty German word meaning the domination of the weak by the strong."

The new self-assurance of some Germans after reunification and the collapse of Soviet power in Eastern Europe was also evident. One man said: "In 1945 we left Königsberg totally defeated. Now we come back completely victorious. We'll just buy this place. How much do you think it'll cost us in real money?" A woman said: "We saw our house. It's in a terrible shape. The bathtub Father got shortly before the war is gone too." The businessman from Berlin was the most militant. I asked him why he was so insistent that the lost territories in the East be returned to Germany. Wasn't Germany a happier and more prosperous country nowadays than ever before in its history? "You don't need East Prussia," I said. He looked at me disdainfully. Then he said solemnly, as though reciting a wellknown text: "Need is not a historical category."

A woman born in the Rhineland said that in 1941, as a six-yearold child, she had been evacuated to her aunt's house in Königsberg because Königsberg was safer from air raids than Düsseldorf. When the Russians came she escaped with her aunt over the half-frozen Mazurian lakes. Her aunt fell through the ice and drowned. She said that she had now visited several times with the people who now occupied her aunt's house. They felt "guilty" about living in someone else's house, she said, but they were soulful, emotional people, and she was sentimental too and got along well with them. "We agreed," she said, "that we are all losers." Her *Heimat* was elsewhere now.

* * *

But *Heimat* continues to be a charged term in the German language. Even so liberal a writer as Marion Gräfin Dönhoff, who has devoted a lifetime to fighting right-wing romantic nationalism and to promoting responsible democratic citizenship, has cherished *Heimat* in her own way. The Federal Republic, she wrote in 1970, was well worth supporting and defending because it is a free and open society "but it is not *Heimat*." After diplomatic relations were established between Germany and Poland, with the implied recognition of the new frontiers, Countess Dönhoff, the former proprietor and heiress of vast estates in East Prussia, wrote:

> Farewell to Prussia, then? No, for the spiritual Prussia must continue to be active in this era of materialist desires, otherwise this state which we call Federal Republic of Germany will not survive.

When she publicly proposed last year the establishment of a Polish-Lithuanian-Russian-German condominium in Kaliningrad, the members of the editorial board of *Die Zeit*—including the former chancellor Helmut Schmidt—vehemently protested and, after reporting this reaction herself, she has not repeated her proposal in print.

"We call ourselves Russians, but we are not really Russians," the Kaliningrad writer Yuri Ivanov told me. Ivanov is the author of several books on Kaliningrad and head of the apparently well-endowed Kaliningrad Cultural Foundation. He and an increasing number of Kaliningrad intellectuals would like to free the city from what they call its "historical unconsciousness." Ivanov was born in Leningrad in 1929. He survived the German siege and famine there and arrived in Kaliningrad in 1945 as a sixteen-year-old soldier in the Soviet army and never left. "How could we be Russians, living where we do? I have no friends in Russia. We were never Soviets either. The so-called Soviet Man was an illusion. Our roots here are only forty-five years deep. We live in a historic German city. Those who lived here before us are our countrymen." Still, he adds, "We are not Germans either. Perhaps we are Balts."

Nevertheless he felt closer, he said, to Germans than to the highly nationalistic Lithuanians and other Balts. And he did not like Marion Dönhoff's plan of a Polish-Lithuanian-Russian-German condominium in Kaliningrad. "Who needs the Lithuanians?" he exclaimed. "I fear them much more than I fear the Germans." He envied the Poles who had rebuilt Danzig in all its past splendor. "It could have been done here too...Kaliningrad ought to be an autonomous republic within the Russian federation. We must get rid of the name. Kalinin was an evil man," Ivanov said. "As in Leningrad, we must bring back the old name of the city—Königsberg. It's a historical necessity."

* * *

In the countryside, German missionaries wander from town to town with mobile altars and electric organs and gift parcels from Germany. One Sunday morning, as I was passing through Chernyakhovsk (the former Insterburg), a small town near the Lithuanian border, I happened upon a German Apostolic Church revivalist meeting. Outside the old German Rathhaus some three hundred people were holding a prayer meeting. Many were young Russian soldiers in uniform. Electronic music wafted over a sea of bare heads. Banners and slogans hung between the dilapidated old buildings. The service was conducted in German from the back of a truck specially converted to serve as an altar and hold an electric organ. The minister paused frequently to allow for a Russian translation. Later, people lined up to receive small parcels filled with German biscuits or little plastic toys.

German Catholic missionaries are also active. They use as their headquarters an otherwise empty lot in the center of Kaliningrad where a priest and a dozen lay volunteers live in a few large metal boxes and prefabricated huts. Hans Schmidt, a layman from Wuppertal in West Germany, told me that they do social work in the city's hospitals. Several times a week they hold services in the villages and hear confessions in three languages, Russian, Lithuanian, and German. Tens of thousands of Russians who are ethnically German live in Kaliningrad, he said. More were arriving daily from Kazakhstan, where they had been deported from their historic villages on the Volga River by Stalin during the war. They hope that Kaliningrad will soon be restored to Germany or become an autonomous region. "We are here to reconcile Germans and Russians through Jesus Christ," said Mr. Schmidt. "If the industry of the Germans doesn't make them arrogant and if the Russians' naiveté—they are like children—doesn't lead them into mistakes, the love of God will cause the establishment here of an independent state. It will be modeled on the ancient Order of Teutonic Knights—not because the Knights were German but because, like us now, they spread the word of God in the pagan darkness of Königsberg."

* * *

The new magic words in Kaliningrad are Königsberg and Immanuel Kant. There are recurring calls for a referendum on going back to the city's former name. "We are all of us Kant's *Landsmänner,*" Ivanov said. He spoke Russian through a translator but he used the word *Landsmänner* in German. One of the first things a tourist sees upon landing at Kaliningrad's newly opened international airport is a big sign "Welcome to Kant's City."[2] At the tomb outside the ruined cathedral Kant is now venerated as a local saint. Newlywed couples go directly from the municipal Marriage Palace to the tomb to pose for photographs. (In the past, the preferred site had been the bust of Karl Marx in a nearby park.) A new monument to Kant, the copy of an original that was demolished after the war, was solemnly inaugu-

---

2. Another philosopher from a local family was Hannah Arendt, who grew up in Königsberg. No one I talked to had heard of her, including Vitaly V. Shipov, mayor of Kaliningrad, and Yuri Ivanov.

rated last summer in the former Paradeplatz by the heads of the city and regional government and a plane-load of distinguished West Germans. There was some talk of renaming the city Kantgrad and I saw a T-shirt inscribed "I ♥ Kant." Königsberg and Kant are, of course, also code names for German money. German power, German influence; Yeltsin's conservative opponents in the city, many of them Russian nationalists, know this. That is why N.A. Medvedev, the university rector, who says he sided with the instigators of the 1991 coup against Gorbachev, is against Kantgrad as a possible new name. "It's not pleasant to the ear," he says. Medvedev prefers a Slavic name that does not hark back to the German past, perhaps Baltijsk.

"Young people here don't know who they are," said Yuri Zabugin, the architect and a native of the city. "Or they want to be someone else. So would you," he told me, "if you had grown up under communism in this awful place." Zabugin is restoring old churches in the city with German money. He is also the curator of an exhibition on the history of Königsberg-Kaliningrad in the local museum. Put together by local arts and crafts students, it is the first independently conceived show in a museum that used to specialize in glorifying the Soviet petroleum or shoe industry. Its title is simply the number "236000," the city's zip-code. "It defines the city's existence," said Zabugin. In the catalog he described the city as a "spot on the map. Its historical name is not forgotten nor is it still valid. The new name is irrelevant and immaterial....Who are we?"

* * *

The regional Kaliningrad government issues warnings that Russia's sovereignty over Kaliningrad must not be questioned, but it is leading the efforts to form cultural and economic links with Germany. It wants Germany to open a consulate and a Goethe Institute in Kaliningrad, and is soliciting German public and private funds to finance industries, tourism, mining, and transportation. It has turned, among others, to Friedrich Christians, the chairman of the powerful Deutsche Bank and the most prominent German financier currently negotiating with the Kaliningrad authorities. A German diplomat in Bonn jokingly calls Christians the *Heimweh*-banker. Christians's connections with Königsberg go back to 1945 when, as a young German soldier, he saw the Red Army's final assault on the city. If Königsberg is rebuilt, he said recently, it "would no longer be a monument to cruel destruction. Rebuilt, it will reflect the hope for peace and reconciliation in Europe."

Mr. Christians has also put forward the idea of making Kaliningrad a free economic zone between East and West, a European Hong Kong or Singapore. The Russian Federation parliament has approved the idea in principle, but arrangements for abolishing customs duties remain to be worked out. The conservative bureaucracy opposes the scheme and the conservatives make up a majority in the regional Kaliningrad parliament. Some of them accuse Vladimir Matutshkin, the head of the regional administration who favors a free-trade zone, of being a "German agent." One of them told a local journalist recently: "If we are not careful we'll soon be governed by old SS men and Japanese samurai." The police chief, Viktor Shoshnikov, recently published an article in *Kaliningradskaya Pravda* claiming that the free-trade zone would only bring in more criminals and drugs.

The military, on the other hand, favors the free-trade zone, since, as Admiral Vladimir Yegorov, the officer commanding the Russian fleet in the Baltic, told me, "the free-trade zone will supply good jobs for retired officers." Few joint ventures with foreigners have been agreed upon. The most serious so far is the rebuilding of Hitler's old Autobahn connecting Königsberg with Berlin. (The Poles are unhappy about this project. Work has begun so far only north of the Polish border.) On the day I met the admiral, ceremonies were taking place on Russian ships in the Baltic celebrating the reintroduction of the old tsarist banner as the official flag of the Russian navy. "Everyone in Kaliningrad is looking forward to the free-trade zone," the admiral said. "Everyone looks forward to big *bizness*."

—May 13, 1993

16

Love and Misery in Cuba
Alma Guillermoprieto

So much hope was invested in Cuba, by people all over the world. Cuba was the romantic face of revolution. Handsome men in battle fatigues had fought against decadent despots who had turned their poor country into a giant brothel for rich capitalist gringos. They fought successfully and chased the despots out. And they promised self-respect, dignity, equality. They did not promise instant riches, but even a poor man can have his dignity.

But they turned out to be despots too, who chose to forget that there can be no self-respect without democratic rights. And when the money ran out with the collapse of their Soviet patrons, Cubans were forced to fall back on the old ways that once helped to spark the revolution. Once more Cuba is becoming a giant brothel, for tourists from richer countries who can afford to live like kings for a week.

And so the old promises have been betrayed. The best people have been silenced, or rot in jails. And women sell their bodies for a bowl of rice and beans.

—I.B.

FOR MANY OF the long years that the Revolution has been in power in Cuba much of it was off-limits to the potentially unfriendly gaze. Not only were all sorts of facts and procedures kept secret; all foreigners were barred from access to large portions of Cuba's territory and even Cubans were told where they could travel, and therefore where they could look. The reason stated for so much secrecy was the imperative of the cold war, but another reason was not given, and perhaps those who established the limits never formulated it clearly to themselves—it was simply understood that the way the Revolution was seen was critical to its survival. Its failures were hardly a secret but it was important that they not be visible.

So it comes as a double shock to arrive in Cuba as a tourist and see so much of it open to one's foreign stare, and to see also how brutal in many cases the new stare of the foreign visitor is. On a tour bus, the modest and articulate young woman who is our guide attempts to explain the currency system, but she is interrupted by a hefty middle-aged Mexican of some means who has been looking frankly at her body. "You're very good-looking, *Cubanita*," he says. "I like your hair." She thanks him less than graciously for the compliment, but he is unfazed. He makes a few comments about the pitiful state of the economy, and a short while later interrupts again. "Where can we see some table-dancing?" he wants to know.

Airports and airplanes, natural collection points for foreigners, are in other parts of the world centers of regimented behavior: no smoking, fasten your seat belts, step up to the counter. At the brand new international departures lounge in Havana these rules don't hold: hundreds of young men on charter tours—Mexican, Italian, and Spanish, on this occasion—sprawl on the floor, spill beer on the just-polished marble and throw the cans at each other, boast openly about their diminished supply of condoms after an Easter weekend sex holiday in sunny Havana, and blow cigar smoke in the face of the women at the check-in counter.

In the old days guerrilla apprentices from Brazil and Uruguay and El Salvador came here and treated each brick laid by the Revolution with reverence, and nevertheless were kept within strict boundaries during their stay. With an ordinary tourist visa provided with any charter tour package, however, the new type of foreigner can rent a car or buy a domestic plane ticket and travel just about anywhere he pleases in Cuba. On a decrepit plane that miraculously survives its daily run from Havana to Santiago and back, two Italians join the other tourists and Cubans who have already fastened their seat belts. They are late, it would seem, because they are less than coherent, or more than a little drunk. Convulsed with giggles, they make their way up the aisle, and then one of them decides that the jokey thing to do is to sit himself heavily in the lap of another traveler—a Cuban. "I'm sorry," the Italian slurs in deliberate English. He does not look at all repentant, and his friend is howling with laughter. Gently, the stewardess tugs the offender away from his victim and pushes him toward an empty seat.

* * *

To say that Cuba has opened itself up to tourism in this context has connotations that are unfortunately true: the island has become an established part of the world sex tour circuit. Of all the ways the Revolution could have looked for emergency money following the collapse of the Soviet Union, none was less predictable than this, and not only because the eradication of prostitution was one of Cuban socialism's proudest achievements—in the rhetoric, at least. Personified by Fidel Castro, the Revolution has craved nothing so much as respect, but prostitutes, who have given up the right to choose who they are possessed by, are generally not respected. They can be stared at by anyone, as if the stare itself were the equivalent of sexual commerce. Indeed, in Latin cultures the way a man looks at a woman—or at another man, for that matter—can be cause for conflict. A penetrating stare in the wrong direction may lead a man to feel that he needs to defend his honor. And yet in Cuba the brazen stare has replaced the old obsession with the respectful gaze.

Although there does not appear to be any official reference to the phenomenon in any government speech to date, the decision to tolerate, and even encourage, prostitution appears to have been deliberate. After all, once it was decided that only tourism could provide the emergency currency needed to keep the country afloat, how could Havana hope to compete with the likes of Martinique, Santo Domingo, Curaçao, or Cancún? Not on the basis of its shabby hotels, limited food supply, and terrible flight connections, certainly.

Five dollars, the young Mexicans standing with me at the departure line boast at the end of their sexual holiday, was enough to buy "a spectacular *mulata*" for the evening. They are happy. So was the businessman who checked in to my hotel on the same day I arrived. I had come to see what had changed in Cuba in the wake of John Paul II's January visit—how the euphoria of those days had carried over into everyday life during the Easter holidays.[1] Soon I was trying to solve the problems of my room—a fog of mosquitoes, the fact that if the windows were kept closed nothing could be seen of the outdoors, because for incomprehensible reasons the glazing had been varnished black—but the businessman had other concerns. Less than an hour after our joint arrival, I stepped into the hotel elevator and ran into him again. He had changed into tropical gear, and was now in the company of a woman who could, indeed, only be described as spec-

---

1. See "A Visit to Havana," *The New York Review*, March 26, 1998.

tacular: lithe, with skin the color of bitter chocolate, and dressed only in high heels and an electric-blue bodystocking.

Later that evening I saw him escorting the electric-blue woman and another marvelously beautiful woman into a taxi. The following morning he appeared at breakfast and rose to greet a different woman altogether. That evening he had changed partners again. The last time I saw him the woman in the bodystocking was back. He looked throughout earnest and busy, like someone with many important appointments to fit into an already crowded schedule.

At Twenty-third and Linea, Havana's central crossroads, young girls gathered from early in the morning in front of the Habana Libre hotel, dressed and painted for display. Passing them, I tried to convince myself that they were over sixteen. I was on the way to a weekly conference for foreign journalists that is held nearby, and I was struck by the fact that there seemed to be no attempt to zone prostitution, to restrict it to certain types of hotels or certain neighborhoods or otherwise hide it from view.

* * *

The press conference, attended by some fifty journalists, was different. There, nothing could be shown, no information could be revealed. To give the press officials credit, they seemed utterly relaxed about the fact that I was there as a reporter without the right kind of visa, and that, as I told them, I planned to look at what had become of the dissidents who were released from jail in February, following an appeal by the Pope. They were willing to let me look, but providing straightforward answers to the questions put to them by the gathered press corps was a different matter.

Was it true that a certain aged Colombian guerrilla leader had died not in Colombia last February, as was initially stated, but in a hospital in Havana, as a guerrilla defector was now claiming? The answer, compounded of careful evasions, was not even an explicit denial. Was it true that an important promoter of US investment on the island has been denied a visa? Again, the circumlocutions made nothing clear. The session ended without a sentence of real information being exchanged. The day's issue of *Granma*, the official newspaper, was again a model of obfuscation. None of the topics raised in the press conference were covered in the day's stories.

It is hard to understand just who is being protected by this censorship. True revolutionaries have presumably had time throughout these nearly forty years to develop an immunity to counterrevolutionary versions of the truth. The regime may have thought that it should protect from foreign influences the poor Cubans it described as "lumpen" and "scum" because they refused to accept revolutionary austerity. But as it happens, this is the group of people now most heavily engaged in prostitution and related black-market activities. They are, therefore, the very Cubans who are most in contact with the new type of foreigners, and who have the greatest access to the foreigners' contrasting versions of reality. Because they are also likely to be the significant breadwinners in some of the poorest Cuban households, their influence is probably great. And because these households are so poor, the effect of their commerce with foreigners is likely to be subversive. Under these circumstances the distinction between what the government does not wish to see and what it does not want others to look at seems, at the very least, arbitrary.

Perhaps it is nothing more than fear of the foreign gaze that is behind Cuba's perceived need to fill its jails with dissidents. Many who were in past years allowed to voice their unfavorable opinion of the socialist regime and wander the streets unsupervised were hustled into prison once they shared these opinions with a foreign journalist. Elisardo Sánchez, for example, founder of the Cuban Commission for Human Rights and National Reconciliation, spent two and a half years in prison after talking to Julia Preston, then a reporter with the *Washington Post*. Sánchez claimed that the relatives of prisoners who were executed in a notorious military trial in 1989 were not allowed to take the bodies home for burial. That the government brief against Sánchez virtually admitted this fact did not affect Sánchez's four-year sentence. José Angel Carrasco, founder of a movement whose acronym, AMOR, reveals a certain wistful romanticism rather than any violent impulse to take up arms against Fidel Castro, was sentenced to seven years after he gave an interview to *Le Monde*'s Bertrand de la Grange. (De la Grange was subsequently beaten and arrested before he left the island.)

One of the most striking cases is that of Dessi Mendoza Rivero, a doctor in Santiago, capital of Oriente province, who founded the College of Independent Physicians in 1994. Over the next three years he was called in regularly to the local State Security offices for questioning and scolding, and often spent a night in jail for good measure, but it was not until June of last year that he was arrested and charged with the crime of "enemy propaganda." The previous month he had held a few phone conversations with an assortment of foreign correspondents based in Havana. His statements were, if anything, moderate and cautious. Despite the best efforts of the government health authorities, he said, an epidemic of dengue fever was devastating his city. The first outbreak of the epidemic had been detected in January, and by May Dr. Mendoza's estimate was that between fifteen and thirty people had died. In addition, he thought that thousands of *santiagueros* had already been affected by the virus, which can turn lethal if the patient has suffered from dengue before or is undernourished or otherwise immune-deficient.

Dengue is generally transmitted by mosquitoes, and Dr. Mendoza may have been concerned that visitors to a scheduled trade fair in Santiago could be exposed to the virus. It may have been the government's concern that potential dollar-carrying visitors could be exposed to Dr. Mendoza's information and cancel their trip. Or it may have been that, once again, the Cuban regime's intense horror of a dissenting or irreverent gaze set off a reflex chain of actions and convinced the judge who presided over the trial that what Dessi Mendoza deserved for his *infidencia* was eight years in prison. This despite the fact that information on the epidemic that was essentially in agreement with Dr. Mendoza's figures was published by the official Santiago newspaper, *Sierra Maestra*, one month after his arrest.

Dissenters are invisible in Cuba, and inaudible. They have no access to the airwaves or the official press, and are not allowed to hold public meetings without permission, which in effect cancels out the possibility—so it seems inevitable that those who feel the need to protest should end up talking to foreign reporters.

* * *

When I sought out people who had been released from jail following the Pope's petition on their behalf, I asked them repeatedly if they were not afraid that talking to me might get them into trouble again. Their answer was generally a more or less pro forma statement in defense of freedom of speech—which was certainly sincere, and even heroic, in view of their histories. But it also struck me that there was something helpless about their situation when they were faced with an inquisitive foreigner. It was not so much that they made a decision to speak to me, but that they desperately needed to talk to anyone at all: they were lonely. They had stories to tell and opinions to give, and although neighbors might be friendly and friends might be supportive, any political conversation in Cuba is haunted by the terms of discussion enshrined long ago by the regime: *Dentro de la Revolución, todo. Fuera de la Revolución, nada.* Within the Revolution, everything: outside it, nothing—a radical restriction whose borders are impossibly vague. How much can you say, how closely can you look—even if the dissident before you is your best friend and you basically agree with the concrete points he or she is making—before you find that you have all unawares crossed over to the enemy side? Seeing becomes a fraught activity, and talking about what one observes can lead to ruinous disillusionment, or jail.

For the released prisoners, enforced silence seems a particularly cruel restriction, because people who have spent time in jail necessarily have terrible things they need to tell. I heard a story from a man who had served three and a half years of his seven-year sentence (again, for "enemy propaganda") before the Pope put his name on a list. He spent the months between the time of his arrest and final sentencing at the detention center run directly by State Security, the Villa Marista. He lost twenty-six pounds during those weeks, confined with four other prisoners to a cell whose only access to the outside world was a slot on the cell door. When a prisoner was taken from his cell and through the hallway, the slots were shut, which meant that no one was able to know who his fellow prisoners were.

The hallway was only wide enough for one person, and when a prisoner was let out of a cell for whatever reason, he had to march ahead of the guard, and was told to do so quickly and with his eyes to the floor, while the guard marched so closely behind him that the man I interviewed said he could still not forget the sensation of the guard's legs brushing his own at every step, forcing him forward. During these two months, he said, he was allowed out only once for an hour of sun and exercise, alone, on a patio, and this was the week before his transfer to the general prison at Combinado del Este. At the new prison he shared an overcrowded cell with men who, by and large, had been convicted of violent crimes, and were repeat offenders.

* * *

Prisoners serving harsh sentences at Combinado del Este are kept in galleys with forty to sixty other convicts, and, according to various sources, are fed so poorly that prison doctors classify their stage of undernourishment as either "moderate," severe," or "critical." The prisoners are allowed one two-hour visit by two family members every two months, and during these visits they can receive as much food as their relatives can carry (no canned goods, or items that require cooking). But many prisoners don't have good relations with their relatives, or else have relatives who are poor and live so far away that they cannot make the visits on a regular basis. The hunger they suffer is at the heart of the story that the man I talked to felt most compelled to tell, even though his wife gently tried to steer him away from the subject during our conversation.

This man is white. The cot above his in the overcrowded cell was vacated one day, and he began using this space to store the relatively bountiful supplies which his family lugged to prison every two months. Across from this cot was another, occupied by a young black man. My storyteller for some reason was specific about the youth's race, although he couldn't recall his crime, or didn't feel that it was relevant. One night, the man who slept in the cot above the young black man's (they were stacked in layers of four) discovered him stealing a small jar of preserves that belonged to the storyteller. As punishment, the young black man was severely beaten by the other prisoners. (I did not ask the storyteller what part he had in this.) The young man was taken away to the infirmary, and one month later he was dead. "Not as a result of the beating, you understand, but because he was so hungry. He died of hunger," my storyteller insisted. And then he repeated several times, in a tight voice, that what he could not get over was the fact that the young man was the same age as his son.

* * *

This man was released from prison after John Paul II's visit, and he is now awaiting an exit permit so that he can go abroad. (I do not mention his name or his other circumstances, not at his request, but out of my own fear that being quoted in an interview might send him back to prison rather than into exile.) According to a statement released by the Cuban government, seventy-five prisoners had already been freed before the Pope presented his list of 302 political detainees, and seventy "will not be liberated under any circumstances whatsoever." According to the Cuban Commission for Human Rights and National Reconciliation, 115 prisoners, out of the Pope's list of 302, were released in the days following his visit. But matters are not so simple. Gerardo Sánchez, brother of Elisardo Sánchez and president of the commission, has looked at the records available for these dissenters and found something interesting: a great many of them had already served either half or two thirds of their prison sentences, which is the point at which first and second offenders, respectively, are eligible for parole. Several knowledgeable Cubans confirmed to me that there was nothing unusual in this. As a matter of course, they said, political prisoners are detained long past their parole date, until some important person—Danielle Mitterrand, the Pope—comes to visit and speaks to Fidel on their behalf. No real amnesty is involved.[2]

Given the conditions under which the members of the Commission for Human Rights have to work, it is remarkable that they can collect or verify any information at all. As a former political prisoner himself, Elisardo Sánchez is not allowed to have a computer or a fax in the house he shares with his brother and several other members of the Sánchez family. Many other commission members or supporters don't have phones. Many relatives of men and women in jail who might like to give their names to a human rights organization probably don't know that the commission exists. (The government, of

---

2. Fidel himself would have fared poorly under this system. Captured in August 1953 following his assault on the Moncada army barracks, and sentenced to fifteen years in prison, he was freed by Batista less than two years later following an amnesty campaign in Cuba on behalf of the Moncada prisoners.

course, does not volunteer information on the individuals it chooses to keep in jail for crimes of opinion.) Thanks to new information provided by the recently released dissenters, Gerardo Sánchez said, they had only now been able to add to the list of prisoners the name of one man who has been in jail since 1993.

* * *

The Sánchezes' personal situation is difficult, too. Like every other person who has been a political prisoner, Elisardo will probably never be offered a job as anything other than a menial laborer by the government, which is still the only legal employer in Cuba. Gerardo was a union leader until the day in 1980 when they first arrested his brother and charged him with the all-purpose offense of enemy propaganda. He is also out of work. (Relatives living abroad are the main source of support for the Sánchez brothers, as well as most other dissenters, which may help explain why so many of them are white and middle-class.)

Elisardo has a right to a ration card, but what the card provides these days is not really enough to keep a person alive. (And even that is hard to come by for most former prisoners. Two months after his release, one man still had not had his card "reactivated.") Nevertheless, Gerardo says that over the last few years, conditions for those who disagree with the regime have improved somewhat, most likely as a result of Cuba's new need to be more responsive to international pressure. The total number of political prisoners has gone down significantly, Gerardo said, and State Security officers, who in the past have sometimes been regular visitors to the Sánchez household, lately have been leaving the brothers in peace. But Gerardo Sánchez insists that none of these changes are significant because the regime has always blown hot and cold on dissenters, and will have a legal justification for its repressive measures until there are fundamental changes in the Constitution and the legal system.

I asked Gerardo whether he thought that the US trade embargo had been a useful weapon against the regime. He shook his head. "Sometimes I have the impression that the embargo reflects a fear that this economic system might really work, that [the people who support the embargo believe] that if it were lifted today, tomorrow socialism would be viable. It probably couldn't be done overnight, but there should be some thought how to lift the embargo gradually. It would put an end to the regime's great excuse, which is to say that things are so bad here because of imperialism."

Thinking of how moderate the Sánchez brothers' politics are, and how useful the two might be as interlocutors to a regime suffering from severe interior decay and increasing distance from its subjects, I asked Gerardo if the government maintained any sort of regular contact with them: "Of course," he replied. "In the form of interrogations." It is hard to avoid the impression that the Revolution prefers the radical, invasion-prone opposition in Florida to the unarmed social-democrat and Christian-democrat activists within, as if Fidel and his comrades were grateful for the opportunity to present themselves—and see themselves—in a more flattering, heroic mold, facing enemy gunfire rather than snooping on people who want the right to register their organization as a fully legal political party.

* * *

If being outside the Revolution is difficult in Havana, it must be doubly so in Santiago, a small, sweltering seaport ringed by the hills of the Sierra Maestra, where generations of rebels, including Fidel Castro, have found shelter. Santiago is a fascinating place, but it is not the cosmopolitan center that Havana has been throughout its history. The visual landscape of Havana has remained pretty much unchanged since 1959, but the visitor to downtown Santiago has the impression of having traveled back in time straight into the nineteenth century: tile-roofed houses fronting on empty narrow streets, an ornate (but empty) *galería* of shops, and—one result of Cuba's ongoing fuel shortage—spindly carriages drawn by spindly horses. And if in Havana one is sometimes overwhelmed by the sensation that nothing ever happens—no news, no movie openings, no political changes—in Santiago the atmosphere of tedium is ever-present: a weary continuum of uneventfulness that was once happily interrupted by the bustle surrounding the Pope's visit.

In this small world nonconformists must feel particularly exposed to the glare of official disapproval. I would have liked to ask Dessi Mendoza Rivero, the physician who revealed the existence of a dengue epidemic in Santiago and was sentenced to eight years in prison as a result, how he came to see himself as outside the Revolution and what it was like to be a dissenter in Santiago; but it turned out that he was on the commission's list of political prisoners who were not released following the papal visit, even though his name was among those presented to the Cuban government on behalf of the Pope.

It may be that Dr. Mendoza was not released because he is considered a particular enemy of the people. What seems undeniable is that he did not overstate the extent or the dangers of the dengue epidemic. In Havana, I talked to a woman who lives in Santiago and whose husband was hospitalized during the epidemic. She says that the resources of the very large general hospital in Santiago were stretched so thin at the height of it that many dengue victims had to lie on cots on the lawns of the hospital grounds awaiting treatment. One morning when she arrived to visit her husband she found him in a state of great agitation. He begged her to take him away. "The young man in the bed on the other side of the aisle died last night. I don't want to die here," he said.

* * *

With some trepidation, I looked up Dr. Mendoza's wife, doubting that my visit to her would go unnoticed, or that she would be willing to expose herself by talking to me, but Caridad Piñón turned out to be a fearless woman. A physician herself, she told me that her husband had been fired from his hospital job in 1995, after he set up the College of Independent Physicians and joined the Human Rights Commission, and that from then until the day of his arrest he had contributed to the family income by selling fritters at the door of the crumbling nineteenth-century house the couple occupies with their three children.

Dr. Piñón is on maternity leave still (her youngest child was twenty days old when Dr Mendoza was arrested), but she knows that when she returns to work she too might lose her job, as outspoken relatives of political prisoners tend to. Still, she talked to me, and all of her answers to my questions seemed to come ringed in exclamation marks. "Me, afraid?" she said when I wondered aloud yet again why someone like her would talk to someone like me. "I told them [State Security] that I would say everything that happened. Imagine if I couldn't say what is happening to my husband!"

She went on. A few days earlier, her husband, who suffers from chronic heart problems, had spent five days in intensive care at the local hospital, undergoing treatment for severe hypertension. Even though she was wearing her hospital uniform and carrying her physician's credentials, she said, the guards at the door to his room did not allow her to see him, or even to deliver a basket of food. I could picture her giving the guards several pieces of her mind, loudly, and I decided that what I liked best about her was the sense that she did not feel impotent or inconsequential, the way so many people who disagree with the Revolution seem to. Of course, she had never spent any time in jail, but the fact remained that she was still trying to drive a hard bargain with the people in charge of keeping her husband behind bars.

"I tell them, you let him free and I won't say another word," she said in her exclaiming way, after mentioning that the State Security people had recently suggested that she might want to drop by their offices for a "constructive conversation." I asked her why she thought Dr. Mendoza had not been freed after the Pope's visit, and she said, for the first time looking worried and pained, that she didn't know. I thought to myself that it might have something to do with the fact that he will have to serve three and a half years of his sentence before he is eligible for the parole that authorities choose to present as "amnesty." If this is the case, he has more than thirty months to go.

I stared at the rain pouring in through the roof of the room where we were sitting while she saw to some urgent request of her youngest child. Everyone in the family looked healthy, and I wondered what miracles of thriftiness and hard barter were involved in making that possible. I had seen some ration cards for Santiago and other provinces, with the blanks showing that people had not received their allotted quotas of cooking oil, soap, or toothpaste for weeks on end; they were allowed, I saw, ten ounces of beans and one pound of meat substitute per person per month. Whatever food Caridad Piñón managed to acquire on the free market, at dollar prices, had to be stretched to provide for her husband as well; prisoners' ration cards are suspended, on the grounds that they are fed in jail. It was all so difficult it was a wonder that she did not throw up her hands in despair, or blame her husband for the mess he had gotten everyone into. I asked her if she thought Dessi Mendoza knew that he would pay for his statements about dengue with an eight-year prison sentence. "Are you crazy?" she said. "He wouldn't immolate himself like that. He's not crazy!" It had simply not occurred to him that talking about a public health epidemic to an unauthorized audience could be so wrong.

* * *

Later I sat on the terrace of the pleasant turn-of-the-century hotel where I was staying, which overlooks a leafy plaza and the Cathedral of Santiago. At the Cathedral the outspoken bishop of Santiago, Pedro Meurice, holds weekly support meetings for the relatives of prisoners. The hotel terrace, too, is a sanctuary of sorts, because on the streets that surround the hotel unaccompanied men or women like myself (and even, a Spanish couple told me, men held firmly by the hand by their wives) are targets for relentless hustling by women—or, in my case, men—hoping to obtain a few dollars in exchange for a little adventure. But because the money-seekers are not allowed on the terrace unless they are in the company of a hotel guest, a kind of tranquillity prevails there.

The just-formed Cuban-foreign couples who occupied so many of the tables around me were at peace: both partners had what they had come to find. And because Cuba is a place where fantasy and idealism and the pursuit of exoticism have always been intertwined, and because the women are so cheap that they are usually rented by the day, and because it is the hope of so many of the women who rent themselves out that one of their customers will want to keep her for good, the nature of the relationship between prostitute and customer was also different, I thought. A certain amount of trust had time to develop, along with the quest for romance and salvation involved on both sides. It seemed absurd that Dessi Mendoza should be in jail for talking to the foreign press while on the terrace hesitant conversations were taking place between the new couples—in sign language, or pidgin Spanish, or in whatever common language the two people had found.

I had spent some time talking with Bishop Meurice, and been struck by his arguments against the United States trade embargo, which he, like so many other Cubans, refers to always as "the blockade"—perhaps because the word more nearly conveys the besieged feeling of the island. "The Cuban Church has spoken out against the blockade in the past," Meurice said. "It is unjust. But the fact is that there are other realities that also affect the anguish lived by our people: unjust inequalities, state paternalism and centralism, limitations on civil society's ability to participate. The blockade depends on the United States, but the rest of it depends on us. In a situation as hard as the one the Cuban people are living, the truth must be said: the blockade doesn't help. On the contrary. It may prevent us from seeing those other realities."

—June 11, 1998

17

Tibet Disenchanted

Ian Buruma

Bombs and bullets are not the only ways to destroy a culture. Shared suffering can actually strengthen the sense of belonging, of being distinct.

To be bombarded with a kind of modernity, with new forms of consumption, and different sets of ideals and values, can be much more devastating than brute force.

At first the Chinese, assisted by Tibetan Red Guards, tore down temples and monasteries. Buddhist idols were pounded to dust. Monks were tortured and killed. But this did not destroy Tibetan culture. Then the Chinese tried something else. They brought new railways to the Tibetan lands, and built schools where Tibetans learn to be Chinese. They swamped Tibetan towns with Chinese merchants and stores. They did what all "good" imperial powers do in their colonies; forceful methods are justified by "progress."

Some Tibetans will benefit, lead more comfortable lives, have more material goods. But they will have lost what made them distinctive, what was uniquely theirs, their sense of themselves. They will no longer be Tibetans.

—I.B.

I.

THE FIRST TIME I visited Tibet, in the fall of 1982, scars of the Maoist years were still plain to see: Buddhist wall paintings in temples and monasteries were scratched out or daubed with revolutionary slogans. Now that new winds are blowing, these offending daubs have been scrubbed out in their turn. Chinese were around then, though not in large numbers, and almost all of them in military uniform. But the early 1980s were a time of relatively liberal policies. There was little sign of terror. And Tibetan towns still looked entirely Tibetan. Han Chinese influence was mainly confined to the barracks. Hotels hardly existed; restaurants were few and mostly bad. Even in the main cities of Lhasa, Gyantse, and Shigatse, there was little evidence of a modern economy.

Things have changed a great deal since then. Modernization replaced class struggle as the main form of propaganda, even though revolutionary dogma has not disappeared. Modernization is how many colonial powers before the Chinese justified their imperial rule in Asia, and elsewhere. And it is to a large extent how the Communist Party of China justifies its grip today. A huge amount of government money is being poured into the "Tibet Autonomous Region," and Chinese fortune hunters are flocking there in ever larger numbers. Stories I had been hearing of the results, from travelers and reporters, were disturbing and often a little fantastic: gambling casinos, gigantic discotheques, four-story brothels. These are not uncommon establishments in the wild frontier towns of Chinese-style capitalism, but it took some imagination to picture them in front of the Potala palace or the Tashilhunpo monastery. When I decided to have a look, it was less in a spirit of outrage, however, than of curiosity about who, among the Tibetans, might be benefiting.

* * *

I did not see a gambling casino in front of the Potala, but it is true that the road into Lhasa is lined with shabby little bordellos masquerading as karaoke bars, which means that customers are given the opportunity to sing before moving on to the main entertainment. That same road passes by a large, ugly sculpture of two golden yaks, which stands where the old West Gate of the city used to be until it was smashed by Red Guards in the 1960s. The golden yaks were a gift from the Chinese government to celebrate the fortieth anniversary of "peaceful liberation."

Orville Shell complains in his book *Virtual Tibet* that Lhasa looks "drab." I am not sure I agree. Much of the dilapidated charm of the old Tibetan city has gone, to be sure. Lhasa looks more like the market towns one finds around the borders of Thailand or in southern China—the East Asian versions of Dodge City in the old Wild West —teeming with Chinese carpetbaggers, hucksters, hookers, gamblers, hoodlums, corrupt officials, and other desperados lusting after quick cash. At the same time, as though from another planet, there are the Tibetan pilgrims, fingering their beads, spinning their prayer wheels, and moving their lips to endless prayers, and nomads with silver daggers and long hair tied up in red silk, and countrywomen in long skirts and striped aprons, and monks dressed in saffron and red. There is the constant din of Chinese and Hindi pop songs, market salesmen pitching their wares, and rattling machine gun fire from the video arcades (I saw a group of young monks staring in rapture at Tom Hanks stopping a tank in *Saving Private Ryan*). Weaving their way through all this hurly-burly with an air of imperial swagger are riot police in their green uniforms and the regular police in white— country boys with almost unlimited power speeding along in white jeeps, or cruising very slowly in unmarked Chinese-built Volkswagen cars. The general impression, then, is noisy, vulgar, raucous, and a little menacing, but drab it certainly is not.

One quickly gets a sketchy idea of the general divisions of labor.

The stores, restaurants, and most other forms of commercial enterprise are in the hands of Han Chinese, mostly from Sichuan, to judge from their accents and the preponderance of Sichuanese food. Petty traders, market salesmen, money-changers, and so on are often Muslims from the poor western provinces, such as Qinghai. They wear white caps and you see them hanging around the central market. Tibetans themselves tend to fall into two categories: country folk in traditional dress, who have come to the city to visit the holy places, and middle-ranking government employees, who sit around the Chinese fast-food restaurants, wolfing down plates of rice or noodles. Like many colonial people dependent on government jobs, they tend to run to fat.

I tried to see how the Tibetans fit into the brash new economy. At first sight it seemed that they did not, or at least only very few of them did. The pilgrims, nomads, and country people walked the same streets as the Chinese hustlers and traders, but they might as well have been in another country. They were also in a minority. More than half the people in Lhasa are Chinese, even though few of them stay there for very long, and almost none speaks Tibetan. This constant *va-et-vient* of fortune hunters is what gives Lhasa the impermanent, feverish atmosphere of a typical cowboy town. What makes it look more and more Chinese, apart from the people, is the new architecture, much of it gimcrack, most of it hideous, but of the same type you see all over the modern Chinese empire: squat white-tiled buildings with blue windows and kitschy, Chinese-style roofs.

The old Tibetan economy, before "liberation," had been, like so much else in Tibet, an integral part of religious life, for the monasteries were more than spiritual institutions; they managed real estate, acted as brokers and money-lenders, and ran schools and other public services. These functions have all been replaced by government institutions. There was once a Tibetan merchant class, too, trading mostly with India and Nepal, but I was told it had pretty much disappeared. Trade with India has been blocked by the Sino-Indian border problems, and by the government's successful policy of making Tibet dependent on China. Merchant families have either fled abroad or found jobs in the government.

* * *

In one of the Tibetan restaurants around the seventh-century Jokhang temple, where pilgrims and tourists mingle with hawkers of incense, jewelry, and religious objects ("hello, look look, cheap cheap!"), I met two Tibetan friends, both in their twenties. They spoke Tibetan in the way well-educated Indians speak Hindi, or Hong Kong Chinese speak Cantonese, spraying their native language with words, or even entire sentences, from the language of the colonial power. Chinese is the language of their education, their workplace, and some of their social life. Both were doing well working for Chinese financial institutions. One rode a fine Japanese motorcycle. They said it was people like themselves who benefited most from Chinese education, for it had opened up a wider world, of technology, economics, politics, and even some Western ideas. Tibetans in the countryside, they said, still led traditional lives, getting by on very little, and derived no benefit at all from China.

One of the men ordered a pizza, the other had Chinese noodles. Then, what had begun as a quiet conversation about the economy turned into an argument, in which I was merely a passive bystander. Perhaps for my sake, out of courtesy, they spoke Chinese, but with more and more Tibetan words thrown in. They disagreed about religion. The more studious of the two friends believed that religion was important. Without it, he said, the human spirit withers. He explained that without religion most Tibetans would never have survived the harsh conditions of living in arid, icy highlands, with little more to eat than dried yak meat and clumps of stamped barley. But affluence, he said, creates a thirst for religion too; you cannot live on materialism alone. I thought of Richard Gere and the other Hollywood Buddhists. But then his friend took the opposite, more conventional Chinese Communist line: religion was out of date; contemporary problems could only be solved by science. Science, in his view, had replaced religion.

It seemed to be a straightforward clash between a man of faith and an atheist. In fact, there was more to it than that. For the "atheist" was from a Muslim family. And although he didn't believe in religion himself, he still stuck to many of his family traditions. He did not eat pork, and said he would marry a Muslim girl. He even said he might go on a pilgrimage to Mecca one day, as his parents had done. It was a way to see the outside world. Religion to him did not carry the same meaning it did for his Buddhist friend. Muslims had been persecuted in the past by Tibetans who wanted to keep Tibet "pure," that is, purely Buddhist. Buddhism, to a Tibetan, cannot be separated from nationalism—to be Tibetan is to be Buddhist—which is why the Chinese government wishes to control it, and those from religious minorities view it with a sense of unease. In a way, Muslims occupy a position in Tibet similar to Jews in Poland under communism, when the Pope acted as the Dalai Lama of Polish nationalism.

* * *

Later that evening, the Buddhist and I repaired to a Tibetan nightclub. These are good places to talk. They are noisy, and there are few Han Chinese around. The décor looked vaguely Tibetan, with white curtains lined with blue, green, and red stripes, and the singers, some in traditional dress, sang Tibetan as well as Chinese songs. There are rules about this: the number of Tibetan songs and their content are strictly controlled, so as not to provoke unwelcome outbursts of nationalism. Video screens showed clips from Hollywood movies. I saw bits of *Titanic* and the burning of Atlanta in *Gone With the Wind*, as well as stock images of Tibet, copied perhaps from videos promoting tourism: the Potala, country dances, yaks grazing, monks blowing horns, and horse fairs. A reproduction of the Mona Lisa hung on the wall next to the plastic head of a bodhisattva.

I asked my friend what went through his mind when he saw how Tibetan folklore was presented at official celebrations in Beijing, those pumped-up occasions for endless parades on Tiananmen Square. Between the tanks and the missile launchers and the adoring schoolchildren, the fifty-five official "minorities," including Muslims, Mongols, Miao, and Tibetans, are always in attendance, dancing in colorful costumes for the leaders waving from their platform in front of Chairman Mao's portrait. He said it was both ridiculous, because many of the details were wrong, and outrageous, because it was so patronizing.

Despite the noise from the stage, where a woman in a red ballgown was singing a Chinese song in praise of the Tibetan mountains, my friend lowered his voice and studied his knees. The trouble was, he said, that it had become almost impossible to study Tibetan culture seriously, especially religious culture. And without the latter, you could not possibly understand Tibet. To take a serious interest in religion invited suspicion of political subversion. You might be denounced as a "splittist," a promoter of Tibetan independence, splitting the country from the "motherland." And the monasteries were no good anyway, because the monks were government employees who knew little about religion. Yet my friend wanted to know about his own culture and to be more literate in Tibetan as well. He spoke of his sense of shame at not mastering his mother tongue. The fact that he was compelled, because of his own education, to read about Tibetan Buddhism in Chinese made his situation even more galling. The Tibetan-language textbooks he had read at school were all about the glories of Chinese communism, and the few books he had studied about Tibet were written by Chinese. I glanced at the video monitor with its tourist images of yaks, horse fairs, and white mountains, and couldn't help wondering whether in the end Tibetan culture would be reduced to this: the commercial equivalent of the folk dancers on Tiananmen Square.

* * *

On another night, at a similar nightclub in Lhasa, this one with a small dance floor lit by a revolving ball reflecting speckles of blue light on the dancers, I got involved in another discussion about the Tibetan "identity." There were video screens showing the same stock images of Tibet as at the other club. A rather fey young man, dressed in the garb of a Tibetan herdsman, sang a folk song, prompting a female admirer to wrap a silk scarf around his neck in the traditional Tibetan manner of showing respect. After his act, he came up to me and told me in English that he was an art student. He sat down and I asked him what kind of art. Any kind, he said, oil painting, Western art, any kind. What about Tibetan art? He hesitated. Yes, he finally said, Tibetan art too. But he wanted to go to the United States, to work with computers. What about his art? I asked. He shrugged and said he couldn't express himself in art. I asked him why not. He drew closer and whispered in my ear: "Politics." He wanted to do Tibetan painting, but was not allowed to study religious art, and without that, Tibetan painting made no sense.

After the singer had gone back to the stage, where he started a comedy routine in Tibetan, which failed to provoke much laughter, I sat awhile nursing my glass of beer. Couples were dancing under the revolving ball, men with women, women with women, men with men, some of them going through well-practiced moves of Western ballroom dancing. I felt a tap on my shoulder. "Where you from?" asked a neatly dressed man of about thirty. He looked Han Chinese, which was indeed what he turned out to be. He had been living in Lhasa for three years and was almost due to go home. He wanted to know what I thought of the Tibetan situation. Not knowing who he was, I made a banal remark about every place having its problems. He nodded gravely. Then he asked what I thought of human rights in China. Again, I erred on the safe side. And what about democracy? Well, living in a democracy myself, I had to say I was rather in favor of it. He nodded, and said the one-party state was no good. There was too much corruption and abuse of power. China needed more political parties.

I was surprised to hear this, especially when he told me he was a Communist Party member and had been sent to Tibet by the government. But nothing had prepared me for the next question. Did I think Tibet was like Kosovo? I gulped, took a long sip of beer, recalled the nationalist fervor in China after the bombing of the Chinese embassy in Belgrade, and asked him whether he meant China was like Serbia. He looked me in the eye, and nodded quickly. That is what he meant. Living in Lhasa had opened his eyes to many problems, he said, problems of nationality and human rights. "In the West," he said, "people are allowed to chose their own governments. Here in Tibet, the government chooses its people."

I noticed another man, on my other side, who was straining to hear what was being said, a thin man with a dark brown complexion. He was a Tibetan friend of the Chinese official. Now it was his turn to talk. He cupped his hands around my ear and said in perfect Chinese that he was working for a Tibetan company. What did I think of human rights in Tibet? Once more, I played it safe: human rights were important everywhere, in the rest of China, as much as in Tibet. "No, no," he said, "we have a special problem in Tibet. We are losing our language, our religion is controlled, our culture is disappearing. You see, the forces of economic modernization are directly opposed to our own traditions." Still trying to be as bland as I could, I mumbled something about national traditions having survived modernization in other countries. This made him agitated. Surely all foreigners understood, he said, that Tibet was special: "As long as we are part of China, we cannot survive, we are like a man who is thrown into a lake without being able to swim. We are drowning. You foreigners must help us."

There was nothing much I could say. All three of us drank in silence. We all felt helpless in our different ways. The Chinese official had told me that others in the Party shared his views, but lacked the power to act on them, or even mention them in public. His friend just repeated that I should let the world know about Tibet. The world should come to the rescue. And I knew that the world would do no such thing.

* * *

The impression I got from these conversations in Lhasa was that the Tibetans who suffered most from Chinese cultural imperialism were precisely the most educated, the ones who benefited from economic modernization. The better you were able to function in Chinese, the more successful you were bound to be. Without Chinese, you were cut off from the urban economy. The man in the nightclub was right: Chinese-style modernization, with its eradication of the past, its official atheism, its consequent intolerance toward organized religion, and its emphasis, politically, philosophically, and economically, on materialism, is opposed to the Tibetan tradition. This does not mean that the Chinese-educated Tibetans all yearn for the revival of a Buddhist theocracy. Few, if any, want that. But to survive in the Chinese economy, Tibetans are forced to blot out their own cultural identity, and that leaves a sense of deep colonial humiliation.

The only Tibetan I spoke to who did not seem to care about the gradual replacement of the Tibetan language by Chinese, or the new dominance in urban areas of Chinese low life and pop culture, was the Muslim. He was able to speak like a true modernist. It was inevitable, he said, that traditions were hollowed out by modern life. It happened everywhere, in Europe and Japan as much as in Tibet. And if Chinese was more practical than Tibetan, why then people would speak Chinese, or English, or whatever. It was surely a waste of time to regret the past. After all, things were much better now; there were banks, and hospitals, and more schools. But it was easier for him to praise these developments than for his Buddhist friends, since the monasteries that used to perform some of these functions were not part of his spiritual tradition. The crude new cosmopolitanism of Lhasa was, on the contrary, part of his liberation.

2.

To leave Lhasa, or one of the few other cities, such as Shigatse or Gyantse, is in a sense to leave China, not officially, of course, but culturally. Little or no Chinese is spoken in the villages, let alone among the nomads who roam the vast, empty highlands which to most Han Chinese are as strange and intimidating as the surface of the moon. Where the outside world does happen to touch the life of a Tibetan village, economic transactions of the crudest kind take place.

There is only one road from Lhasa to Gyantse, the town to which Major Francis Younghusband, the commander of a British expedition to Tibet, was heading when he mowed down some seven hundred unruly Tibetans with a Maxim gun in 1904. It is a rocky, unpaved road that winds along some terrifying mountain passes with straight drops down to a glorious, deep blue lake. Jeeps and minibuses hired by tourists all stop at the same scenic spots, marked by Tibetan prayer flags fluttering from ceremonial piles of stones, or outside villages with whitewashed stone houses, inhabited by people in richly embroidered boots and coarse brown robes slung across their shoulders. The villagers are well aware of their photogenic appeal, and as soon as a tourist vehicle is sighted, women and children take up their positions together with a yak, whose long black hair contrasts prettily with red ribbons tied around its horns.

The tourists invariably stop, and are surrounded by children in states of remarkable squalor—long matted hair like old rope, green mucus clotted around the nose and mouth, various kinds of milky eye infections, and layers of hard, black grime on every inch of exposed skin. "Hello," cry the children, while rubbing their thumbs along the palms of their hands, "how are you, money, money!" An old man in dark rags and with a black face sticks out his pink tongue in the old-fashioned Tibetan gesture of obeisance to social superiors. One child dressed in a fine silk jacket is placed on top of the yak, and his mother holds up five fingers: five Chinese yuan for a photograph. Acting out a debased variation of themselves is the only way the villagers know how to make money from the tourist economy.

Few villages are on the tourist beat, however. Most villagers don't even have the occasion to beg. I visited a village several hours from Lhasa. It was actually less a village than a cluster of small, gray, stone huts in a beautiful green valley. The inhabitants herded yaks and sheep. The richest person had several hundred yaks, the poorest just a few. Only the village head, elected by the villagers, understood some Chinese. I was taken to the village by a man who was born there. He had not had any formal education; he called himself "a man without culture." But he had managed to leave the village and make a life in Lhasa by serving for a few years in the People's Liberation Army. It had not been a pleasant experience; the few Tibetan soldiers were harshly treated. But at least he had made some money and learned to speak Chinese. He was an intelligent, humorous person in his forties with the wrinkled, reddish-brown face of a much older man.

* * *

Most of the people in the village looked poorer than the ones I had encountered on the road to Gyantse. A few of the younger ones could read and write. There was a new school nearby. I was politely offered cup after cup of yak butter tea, which tastes a bit like very greasy soup, but keeps one's lips from cracking in the bone-dry air. One of the herdsmen reached inside his filthy shirt, tore off a chunk of dried raw meat, and kindly handed it to me. The meat was a year old. His hands were encrusted with dirt. My friend explained that most people suffered from intestinal diseases. The hard, raw meat tasted sweet, a bit like horse meat.

The poorest house consisted of one dark room, home to a family of six, but the richest was more sturdily built, and had a gate decorated with yak horns and had whitewashed walls. The inside was pleasantly furnished with painted wooden chests and sofas covered in carpets. On the wall were four religious paintings. One of them looked old and was quite finely drawn. The wooden ceiling beams were painted bright blue, apple green, and pink. The one thing both the rich and the poor house had in common was the open display of pictures of the current Dalai Lama, something for which a person in Lhasa would certainly be arrested. I also noticed a photograph of the Karmapa, the young lama who had recently escaped from China to India, to the acute embarrassment of the government in Beijing.

I asked my friend whether there was any risk in displaying these pictures. He made a dismissive gesture and said the officials hardly bothered to come to the villages. "They would not be welcome here," he said. Naively I then asked whether the villagers knew about the Karmapa's escape to India. "Of course," he snorted, "they knew before the government in Lhasa did. Every night, before going to sleep, they listen to the Voice of America."

It was clear from his account that the links between Tibet, even in the villages, and India had not been cut. People knew where the Dalai Lama was, and what he has been saying around the world. Young people still make their way to Dharamsala, despite border patrols and the risk of arrest. "They can't control what is in our heads," the driver said. It was not the first time I had heard that phrase in Tibet. He said: "They can make us say we love the Communist Party, but they can never make us hate the Dalai Lama."

Later, while having a picnic at the side of the river, my friend showed a sign of despair. He had told me before that he had thought many times of going to India, but had never had the opportunity. "It's all over for me now," he said. I said nothing. Then: "But maybe not for my son." He asked me where I was from. I said that I lived in England, in London. "Ah, yes," he replied, "you English. You English came here with guns and killed many Tibetans. When was it again?" I said it was in 1904. He smiled, as though it were a fond memory, and said: "If only you English would come here again, with many guns. Then we Tibetans would dress up in our finest clothes, and give you a warm welcome."

It was only a passing fancy, of course. He went on to talk of the hard times in the past, of the killings during the Cultural Revolution, and the destruction of temples and monasteries, often carried out by Tibetan Red Guards. They were the worst, he said. The Tibetan cadres were the most fanatical. "Long Live Chairman Mao," I said facetiously. He looked at me, and casually tossed an empty beer can into the clear blue river: "Bullshit!" he said. "Long live us, the people!" We could both drink to that.

3.

The Chinese are the last great power to try to run an empire, and they are finding it no easier than others did before them. They try to contain the discontents of the native elite by bringing them into the government (though never at the very top), and by pumping ever larger amounts of cash into the economy. Unlike many provinces of China, the Tibet Autonomous Region is almost entirely dependent on central government money, and has less autonomy as a result. Modernization will go on. There will be more schools, hospitals, post offices, banks, and better roads. These are the gifts of all successful empires. But as the influence of China slowly erodes what is left of Tibetan culture, first in the cities where most Han Chinese settle, then perhaps, far more slowly, in the rest of the country too, the discontent will fester. Colonial humiliation does not vanish with time. Even with the careful screening of reliable monks, the monasteries still erupt in protest on occasion. Horrifying stories emerge from the prisons where protesters are held, stories of torture, years in solitary confinement, and suicidal deaths of men and women who cannot take it anymore.

How, then, is the Tibetan problem to be solved? "Free Tibet!" cry the crowds at American rock concerts, organized in aid of good causes. Tibetan independence is what most Tibetans abroad want too. But what do they mean by "Tibet"? More than half the almost five million Tibetans in the People's Republic of China are living outside the Tibet Autonomous Region. If an independent Tibet should contain all those who speak Tibetan, eat stamped barley, and follow the Dalai Lama, large chunks of Sichuan, Yunnan, and Qinghai provinces would have to be torn off the PRC. Beijing, understandably, would never stand for that. If, on the other hand, Free Tibet were to be confined to the Autonomous Region, most Tibetans would be left outside, and the Tibetan government in exile cannot allow that. And neither, for that matter, will Beijing. Too much Chinese nationalism has been invested in the ideal of One China, including Taiwan and Tibet, for any Chinese government to let it go.

The dissident Wei Jingsheng believes that democracy is the only solution. It would certainly help. Under a democratic Chinese government there would be more civil liberties and fewer political prisoners. But even a democratic government is likely to tap into the deep reservoir of Chinese nationalism. At best, some kind of federation might be set up, which at least would allow Tibetans to run their own affairs, while the central government took care of foreign policy and defense. The Dalai Lama advocates this solution, and it is difficult to see how he could hope for more. Even so there would be problems: What about the Han Chinese and the Muslims who live in Tibet already? What about the role of the Buddhist institutions? And what about the Tibetan government abroad?

A Tibetan historian in London told me Tibet would be like Northern Ireland, a continuous conflict between peoples with incompatible aims. It is not unlike Kosovo either, a pawn in a brutal nationalist propaganda campaign. But at least the Albanians have their own independent state outside Kosovo, however wretched. As long as independence remains an impossible goal, Tibetans all over the world can only pray for better days, worship the Dalai Lama, and think to themselves, more in hope than expectation: Next year in Lhasa.

—July 20, 2000

18

AIDS: The Lesson of Uganda
Helen Epstein

The way people react to sickness, especially epidemics, is not just about medicine; it involves culture, religion, politics, economics. This is particularly true of AIDS, because the virus is so often sexually transmitted, and few aspects of human behavior are more fraught.

In Africa there is no consensus about the causes of AIDS. Like all devastating threats to human life that are ill-understood and seemingly uncontrollable, AIDS has given rise to forms of paranoia and delusion; conspiracy theories abound. Goodwill is an insufficient and sometimes counterproductive remedy: devout Christians, for example, who wish to help patients but forbid the use of contraceptives.

Uganda, more or less stabilized after years of man-made slaughter, has had more enlightened policies than many countries in the region. But even there, money and medicine will only go so far, as long as women continue to be brutalized by men. Viruses cause the disease, but human attitudes allow them to spread.

—I.B.

IN 1982, UGANDA became the first African country to identify patients suffering from the same disease that was killing homosexual men, heroin addicts, and hemophiliacs in Europe and the US. However, it soon became clear that AIDS in Uganda was different, because it seemed to affect everyone: housewives, businessmen, taxi drivers, hairdressers, teachers, small children, soldiers, policemen, civil servants, doctors, and nurses. Millions of people are infected with HIV in the United States, Russia, India, Thailand, and other countries, but in these places infection is associated with risky behavior, such as prostitution, intravenous drug use, and unsafe gay sex.

However, in Uganda, as in much of East and Southern Africa, few families have been spared. In such major cities as Kampala, Gaborone, Johannesburg, Harare, and Lusaka, between 10 and 40 percent of all adults carry HIV. Not only is sub-Saharan Africa in a class by itself when the global spread of the epidemic is considered, but HIV is creating new forms of inequality within particular countries. In this way, HIV has been seen as an indicator of social injustice, both globally and locally. It infests some of the most fragile nations on earth, and increasingly strikes the weakest men and women within them. Meanwhile, infected people and their families are now making up a new social class, excluded from the best jobs and schools and from the warmth of human relationships.

I first visited Uganda in 1993, when I went there to work on an AIDS vaccine project for an American biotechnology company. In 1995, when I left, Uganda was a hopeful, mostly peaceful country. Its president, Yoweri Museveni, came to power by force in 1986, after his National Resistance Army displaced the weak Tito Okello. Museveni promised to redress the corruption and brutality of the governments of Milton Obote and Idi Amin, and he did bring peace to most of the country, although fighting with rebels continues to this day in some northern districts. Museveni has forbidden campaigning by political parties other than his own National Resistance Movement, but he has encouraged limited forms of democracy. In 1989, parliamentary elections were held, and in 1997, Madeleine Albright hailed Museveni as one of Africa's "strong new leaders" who had brought order to one of the poorest countries in the world with one of the twentieth century's most brutal histories.

* * *

Uganda is one of the few countries where Structural Adjustment, the World Bank's economic program based on economic liberalization and privatization, civil service reform and reduced government spending, has been moderately successful.[1] The economy grew by about 6 percent a year throughout the 1990s, and Uganda is now exporting coffee, sesame seeds, fish, tea, cotton, and other commodities to the rest of the world. According to the World Bank and the Ugandan Bureau of Statistics, the number of people living in poverty in Uganda fell from 56 percent in 1992 to 35 percent in 2000. While these statistics have been questioned, and poverty in some rural areas may even be growing more severe,[2] for many people life in Uganda has been better in recent years than it has been for more than a generation.

Between independence in 1962 and Museveni's takeover in 1986, more than a million Ugandans were murdered in political violence and millions more died of starvation and disease. In *What Is Africa's*

---

1. See *AIDS and Reform in Africa: Lessons from Ten Case Studies,* edited by Shantayanan Devarajan, David Dollar, and Torgny Holmgren (World Bank, 2001); and E.A. Brett, "Responding to Poverty in Uganda: Structures, Policies and Prospects," *Journal of International Affairs,* Vol. 52, No. 1 (Fall 1998), pp. 313–337. See also my article "Time of Indifference," *The New York Review,* April 12, 2001.

2. The poverty level is defined roughly as US $1 per day, a severe criterion. Around half of Ugandan people still lack access to safe drinking water, sanitation, and health care. See *Human Development Report: Uganda* (UNDP, 1998); "Is Poverty Really Decreasing in Uganda?," Uganda Debt Network, April 9, 2001; "Dire Want Amidst Plenty Is Damaging M[useveni]'s Record," *The Sunrise,* April 13, 2001.

Problem?,[3] a collection of his speeches, Museveni describes how, in the early 1980s, packs of soldiers roamed from village to village, raping women and bashing the heads of crying babies. In Luwero district, where some of the most brutal fighting took place, skulls were heaped up in the forest. By 1986, most of the country's roads, hospitals, and cities were in ruins and consistent supplies of water and electricity were available almost nowhere.

The economy was run largely by thieves. Idi Amin, who overthrew Milton Obote and took power in 1971, appropriated much of the private capital in the country, including factories and shops, and these were soon destroyed. Uganda's only export was coffee beans, which were produced by rural farmers and then sold through government-owned companies. The foreign exchange earned through these companies was not used to develop the country but to import whiskey and transistor radios to bribe and placate the army. In the cattle-herding regions of the north, wealthy raiders used helicopters to locate cattle to steal. In the south, along the Tanzanian border, black-market traders got rich smuggling coffee out of the country and importing such essential goods as food and soap at highly inflated prices. Between 1970 and 1985, per capita GDP fell by half.

In 1995, the Kampala skyline still consisted of concrete buildings riddled with bullet holes and streaked with filth, church steeples, minarets, and construction cranes that, I was told, had not moved in more than a decade. There were building lots filled with rubble and piles of rotting banana peels, fed upon by giant marabou storks, scavengers with wings like black shrouds and bald, pink gullets shaped like the trap under a sink. These creatures were rarely seen in Kampala until the mid-1980s, when they came to feed on the detritus left behind by twenty-five years of corruption and war.

---

3. Kampala, Uganda: NRM, 1992; University of Minnesota Press, 2000.

* * *

Kampala has changed considerably since then. When I visited Uganda again in April 2001, I could see the entire city in its green basin from my hotel window. Mist from cooking fires hung over the slums, and a giant gray cloud sat on the rim of the surrounding hills. Once-derelict streets are lined with freshly painted shops and new hotels and glass office buildings had risen in the center of town. The paralyzed cranes were gone.

Perhaps Uganda's most noted success during the past decade has been its management of the AIDS epidemic. By the early 1990s, President Museveni became the first African leader to declare AIDS an economic and social catastrophe; a little reluctantly, because in public he is a puritanical man, he acknowledged that people should use condoms to protect themselves. He invited Western charities to establish prevention campaigns and Western researchers to study the epidemic. Condoms are available in most places, and there are radio programs that describe, in precise, even tedious, detail, how to use them. Surveys show that most Ugandans know what HIV is and what they should do to avoid it.

These efforts have been reasonably successful. In 1992, 16 percent of all adults in the country were HIV-positive, but by 1996, only 8 percent were. The proportion of HIV-positive people in Uganda has fallen far more slowly since 1996, and there were even indications that the infection rates rose slightly in rural areas in 1999.[4] But even if the decline in HIV prevalence has slowed, Uganda's relative success in dealing with HIV is unique in sub-Saharan Africa, and international health experts from the UN and other agencies

---

4. In 1996, the World Health Organization stopped supporting HIV surveillance activities in developing countries, so Uganda's HIV statistics since then are likely to be less reliable than those from the early 1990s.

have claimed that Uganda should be seen as a model for other countries.

However, questions have been raised about whether the fall in the number of HIV-positive people in Uganda really indicates that the epidemic is waning. To understand this, it helps to know the difference between what epidemiologists call "prevalence" and "incidence." Prevalence refers to the number of infected people in a population, while incidence refers to the rate at which people become infected. In an epidemic, it is incidence that must be reduced. Prevalence falls later, as people either recover or, in the case of HIV, die from AIDS. Incidence is much harder to measure than prevalence, and health departments seldom do it routinely. But epidemiologists conducting smaller studies of particular Ugandan populations have shown that even when prevalence is falling, incidence may still be high, or even rising. In fact, while some regions of Uganda have seen a fall in HIV incidence during the 1990s, others have seen little change.[5]

The Ugandan HIV epidemic probably occurred in two phases, and this could explain why incidence may be stable or even rising, even though prevalence is falling. The first phase occurred during the war and its aftermath in the 1980s. At the time, many cases of HIV infection probably resulted from what the authors of a recent study politely refer to as "one-off" sexual encounters.[6] Rape and prostitu-

---

5. See A.J. Nunn et al., "HIV-1 Incidence in Sub-Saharan Africa," *The Lancet*, September 21, 1996; Maria J. Wawer et al., "Control of Sexually Transmitted Diseases for AIDS Prevention in Uganda: A Randomized Community Trial," *The Lancet*, February 13, 1999, pp. 525–535; Anatoli Kamali et al., "Seven-Year Trends in HIV-1 Infection Rates, and Changes in Sexual Behaviour, Among Adults in Rural Uganda," *AIDS*, Vol. 14 (2000), pp. 427–434; and *The National Strategic Framework for HIV/AIDS Activities in Uganda*: 2000/1–2005/6, a report by the Government of Uganda, the Uganda AIDS Commission, the Joint United Nations Programme on AIDS, et al., March 2000.

6. See Noah Jamie Robinson et al., "Type of Partnership and Heterosexual Spread of HIV

tion, in particular, are well known to escalate during war. For example, it is estimated that virtually every woman who survived the Rwandan genocide was raped; at least 20,000 women were raped during the Bosnian war; and at least 250,000 were raped during the 1971 war of independence in Bangladesh. I could find no statistics on rape in Uganda during the civil war in the 1980s, but it is believed to have been very common.

At the time, Ugandan women also saw their families and livelihoods destroyed, and some were forced to exchange sexual favors to provide basic needs for themselves and their children. Since HIV prevalence rates among soldiers in East Africa tend to be very high, it is plausible that HIV first began to spread quickly in Uganda during the turbulent early 1980s. The second phase of the HIV epidemic in Uganda occurred during the relative peace of the 1990s. Today, most HIV transmission actually takes place in longer-term relationships. Indeed, those most at risk of HIV infection in Uganda now are married women who have sex only with their husbands.

The hypothesis that the HIV epidemic in Uganda occurred in two phases implies that HIV prevalence may have fallen in the 1990s because many people infected during the war in the 1980s died of AIDS. Nevertheless, HIV incidence rates during peacetime may still be quite high, although they are probably much lower than they were during the war.

2.

For more than a decade, charities and health ministries in many sub-Saharan African countries have established numerous HIV prevention

Infection in Rural Uganda," *International Journal of STD and AIDS*, Vol. 10 (November 1999), pp. 718–725.

343

programs like those in Uganda, but the results have been mixed. HIV prevention programs in Africa have been far less successful than those for gay men in Europe and the United States, and there has been much speculation about why.[7] Some programs have been moderately successful, but the epidemic is far from over anywhere in East and Southern Africa, including in Uganda.

When I was in Uganda in 1995, I myself wondered about the effectiveness of prevention programs. By then, it seemed clear that the vaccine I was studying did not work, and I knew it would be a decade, at the very least, before scientists found one that would protect people from HIV. But Uganda could not wait for a vaccine. At the time, one in five adults in Kampala was HIV-positive, and the virus was spreading along trade routes into the countryside and up into the poor and isolated villages in the north. The AIDS epidemic has concentrated attention on the circumstances in people's lives that increase the likelihood of unsafe sex, even when people know they should be careful. These circumstances are still poorly understood, but at least two schools of thought have emerged. Either people's beliefs about condoms, fertility, and disease prevent them from practicing safe sex or they are constrained by larger social conditions in their lives, such as poverty and unemployment, that result in a kind of resignation, a feeling that HIV infection is inevitable, and beyond one's power to prevent.[8]

* * *

Every African community has a medicine man or woman to whom an estimated 80 percent of African people turn in distress. These

---

7. See Paul Farmer, *Infections and Inequalities: The Modern Plagues* (University of California Press, 1999); and John Caldwell, "Rethinking the African AIDS Epidemic," *Population and Development Review*, Vol. 26, No. 1 (March 2000), pp. 117–135.

8. S. Leclerc-Madlala, "Infect One, Infect All: Zulu Youth Response to the AIDS Epidemic in South Africa," *Medical Anthropology*, Vol. 17, No. 4 (1997), pp. 363–380.

healers are part quack doctor, part psychiatrist, and through their rituals, stories, and medicine they preserve and hand down traditional African culture and beliefs. Perhaps it is through these healers, I thought, that I could understand the mysterious, persistent spread of HIV.

I knew of a charity that was working to train Ugandan traditional healers to become AIDS prevention counselors and I spent a few months working with them, tramping through villages and riding on bicycle taxis into the Ugandan countryside. I met a healer who cured his patients of diseases of the mind and body by placing live chickens on their heads, and another who did it by massaging the soles of their feet. Yet another inspected drops of his patients' saliva on the surface of a mirror. For many healers, the cure was the sacrifice of a white chicken or, in more serious cases, a goat. The healers told me how the human race had been created when the sun and the moon gave birth to the stars, and then to the earth and the gods. There were gods for love, jealousy, and malaria, but there was no god for AIDS. All of the healers knew about AIDS, but they said they didn't know where it came from, or how it could be cured. Many of them went to the training sessions the charity conducted, and learned to demonstrate how condoms are worn, and how to recognize when a patient probably has AIDS and should go to the hospital.

Once I went to the initiation ceremony of a traditional healer named Matthew. About thirty people gathered in an old barn in a village near Kampala. The ceremony lasted until dawn, and during the night different men and women fell one by one into mystical trances in which they reenacted the founding myths of the Buganda people, the largest tribe in the country.

During the daytime, Matthew was an accountant for an auto repair shop in Kampala, or he would have been if the company's owner had not emptied its bank account and gone to Kenya. Matthew still sat in his office all day reading newspapers and waiting for people to ask him to do their accounts. On the street where Matthew worked you could buy almost anything: furniture, chicken coops, spare parts for cars, machine tools, jerry-built appliances of all kinds. Pale green trucks with flimsy sheet-metal frames stood in the middle of the street piled high with bananas, foam rubber mattresses, chickens crammed in their cages, their feathers raining everywhere. The businesses spilled onto the sidewalk of broken paving stones, where women with enormous bundles on their heads and dusty, barefoot workers dressed in rags and stray goats and chickens mingled with the chaotic traffic in the street.

* * *

Matthew and I had an appointment, but he was not around. The workmen in the shop next door said that they had not seen him all week. A few days later, I came to look for Matthew again, and found him slumped in a chair, asleep. I startled him when I walked in, and he apologized for not showing up for our appointment. He was sorry, but there were problems at home. A girl had been raped, his niece. I had met her, she was the tall, shy one who had kneeled down when she brought me a cup of tea. She was all right, he said, bleeding a little. His wife, who was also a healer, had treated her with some traditional herbs. It happened at night, and Matthew knew who had done it, a man of about twenty who lived nearby.

In order to press charges, Matthew needed a document that had been signed by the local police commander requesting that the girl be examined by the police surgeon. Matthew had taken the girl to the police station, but when they got there, they had been asked to wait. He and the girl waited all afternoon. They were eventually told that the commander would not have time to see them that day.

The next day, Matthew went to the police station with the local government official. The police chief now had time to see them. He said, "Gentlemen, we have a problem in Uganda." The government had not paid the police surgeon, so what could they do? The police surgeon could not work without money. The form for the report would cost 50,000 shillings. Matthew refused to pay. He said he would call a lawyer. Rape was a serious crime.

I asked Matthew if he needed any help. I knew about a group of tough women lawyers in town who might take the case. No, Matthew said. He knew what to do.

The following week, I came to see Matthew again, and this time he was in better spirits. The situation has changed, he said. The mother of the boy came and prayed to us. She was worried. You know, the penalty for rape in this country is death.[9] The police would shoot her son if they caught him. His niece was OK. She had gone back to her father's village, about fifty miles away. She was not hurt so badly. He thought the hymen was already broken.

I wondered, but didn't ask, how much Matthew had been paid by the rapist's family. Fifty dollars? A hundred? Matthew was following traditional Ugandan law, according to which a woman is the property of her family. A woman's rights belong to her male relatives, so in cases of rape a woman cannot be wronged, but they can demand compensation. In many African countries, the crime of rape has only recently begun to be taken seriously. Now, because of the AIDS epidemic, rape and other forms of sexual coercion and abuse are drawing increasing attention from lawyers, researchers, and women's groups. The findings are alarming.

According to the UN, around 40 percent of Ugandan women have experienced some form of sexual violence in their lives, and the situation is probably similar throughout East Africa, and worse in

---

9. It is true that a person convicted of rape in Uganda is "liable to death," but such a harsh sentence is rarely carried out.

Southern Africa. This includes rape and coercion by husbands and boyfriends, as well as strangers. There are indications that sexual violence contributes enormously to the HIV epidemic. Recent studies from Tanzania and Uganda have found that young women who are HIV-positive, whether married or not, are seven to ten times more likely to have been beaten up or raped or otherwise coerced into sex in the past year, compared to women who are HIV-negative.[10] For epidemiologists, an increased risk of seven- to tenfold is very significant, like an archaeologist's "key find," the artifact that just might explain everything else.

Poor women in Africa often have very little control over their reproductive lives. How many children they have, and when to have them, and whether to have sex with a condom: these are decisions in which many poor African women have very little say. The long continuum between actual rape and the kind of persistent intimidation that makes women afraid to raise the issue of condoms with husbands they know are philandering contributes to a general climate of powerlessness. Police corruption and the weakness and poverty of justice systems (both exacerbated by World Bank–mandated cuts in public sector salaries and spending) only reinforce a prevailing disregard for women's rights and feelings.

It is not known why violence against women is more common in

---

10. See Maria A. Quigley et al., "Case-Control Study of Risk Factors for Incident HIV Infection in Rural Uganda," *AIDS*, Vol. 23, No. 5 (April 15, 2000), pp. 418–425; and Suzanne Maman et al., *HIV and Partner Violence: Implications for HIV Voluntary Counseling and Testing Programs in Dar es Salaam, Tanzania*, a report by the Population Council, 2001. I never learned whether Matthew's niece was infected with HIV as a result of her rape. In Uganda, most people do not discover they are HIV-positive until they become ill. The tests are expensive and since treatment is largely unavailable to the poor, there is little reason to take a test. It is estimated that only 5 percent of HIV-positive people in sub-Saharan Africa actually know that they are infected.

some societies than in others. In *World Mental Health*,[11] the anthropologist Robert Desjarlais and colleagues speculate that recent civil conflicts in developing countries may have more long-lasting effects on social life than the European wars of the early twentieth century did, because the nature of war has changed. The object of so many recent conflicts has been the control of populations, rather than territory, so civilians are not just bystanders but often targets of violence. During the two World Wars, the majority of casualties were soldiers, but during the wars of the past forty years, most casualties have been civilians, some of whom have died in particularly grotesque ways. When combatants cut off the heads of their victims and place them on stakes, or rape all the women in a village, the aim is not just to kill the enemy but to demoralize him. Such conflicts may particularly fuel men's rage by challenging their self-respect. At the same time, such conflicts destroy the very social ties that normally help prevent abuse of women.

It is difficult to make connections between larger social conditions and the personal behavior of individual men and women. But it is striking that in so many places where political violence has ended, apparently random acts of violent crime, particularly against women, continue and even increase. Writers have described how in Cambodia, Mozambique, Uganda, and El Salvador rape, domestic abuse, and intimidation of women are a feature not only of war itself, but of its aftermath as well.[12] In South Africa, while the political violence has died down, rape and other forms of violence have become a part of everyday life. An adolescent girl from Gauteng province recently told an interviewer, "They find you on the street and they

---

11. See Robert Desjarlais, et al., *World Mental Health: Problems and Priorities in Low-Income Countries* (Oxford University Press, 1995).

12. See C. Zimmerman, *Plates in a Basket Will Rattle: Domestic Violence in Cambodia* (Phnom Penh: Project Against Domestic Violence, 1995); and *What Women Do in Wartime*, edited by Meredeth Turshen and Clotilde Twagiramariya (Zed Books, 1998).

force you to go home with them so that they can have sex with you. It is rape, but we don't call it rape because they are our boyfriends."[13]

The authors of *World Mental Health* ask, "To what extent does domestic and street violence result from prolonged repression and conflict?" At the moment, they conclude, we don't know, nor do we know to what extent abuse of women is related to what the authors call "structural violence," which includes poverty, migrancy, inferior education, and other extreme forms of disadvantage.[14]

The causes of the African AIDS epidemic are complex, and sexual violence is not the entire explanation. Certainly not all African men abuse women. Far from it. Nor are all cases of HIV infection in the region to date likely to be the result of forced sex. But abuse of women by poor, frustrated, angry men has been a factor in making HIV as widespread as it is. Once HIV begins to spread in the general, hetero-sexual population, all such relationships become much riskier. In other words, violence against women might have been the spark that set off the blaze. Furthermore, as more people learn about how to protect themselves from HIV, those who remain most vulnerable to infection will likely be those who suffer most from injustice, an-ger, and abuse. For these reasons, the results of prevention programs may continue to be disappointing, unless the rights of women are strengthened at the same time, and unless sub-Saharan African countries can provide young men with an alternative to poverty and hopelessness.

---

13. See Catherine MacPhail and Catherine Campbell, "'I Think Condoms Are Good but, Aai, I Hate Those Things': Condom Use Among Adolescents and Young People in a South-ern African Township," *Social Science and Medicine*, Vol. 52 (2001), pp. 1613–1627.

14. War and its aftermath have not contributed to the spread of HIV everywhere in South-ern and East Africa. Botswana, Zambia, and Tanzania have high rates of HIV infection, but have also been largely peaceful since independence. However, all these countries have high rates of rural poverty and migrancy, which may take a similar toll on social life.

3.

What is the future of AIDS in Uganda? The answer may well depend on whether the country remains at peace. But all was not well when I returned there in April. Since 1996, Uganda's army has been fighting various factions in the Congo war, first the Hutus who fled from Rwanda after the genocide in 1994, and then the government of Laurent Kabila and his supporters from Zimbabwe, Namibia, and Angola, and now the army of Rwanda, which, confusingly, was until recently Uganda's ally. The war has been a drain on Uganda's economy, and has increased tensions among the nation's many ethnic groups. In April, the UN released a report accusing high-level Ugandan army officers, including Museveni's brother, Salim Saleh, of systematically looting gold, diamonds, timber, coffee, livestock, elephant tusks, automobiles, and private property, exporting them from the Congo to Uganda, and then reselling them through his own companies to buyers all over the world who have chosen not to ask questions about where the goods come from. Some of these goods were allegedly stolen, and some allegedly bought with counterfeit Congolese francs and US dollars.[15]

Salim Saleh has also been involved in several dubious privatization deals, in which state-owned companies and banks were sold off for far less than they were worth to companies he owns. In one disturbing account,[16] businessmen who attempted to buy a government-owned hotel said they were threatened with death because they refused to pay a bribe to Museveni's brother. Smuggling and extortion are hardly unknown in Africa, but in Uganda it is creating a tiny,

---

15. *Report of the Panel of Experts on the Illegal Exploitation of Natural Resources and Other Forms of Wealth from the Democratic Republic of the Congo*, United Nations, April 2001.

16. Roger Tangri and Andrew Mwenda, "Corruption and Cronyism in Uganda's Privatisation in the 1990s," *African Affairs*, Vol. 100, No. 398 (January 2001), pp. 117–133.

corrupt wealthy class with very close ties to the President, and this seems all too familiar to those who recall the country's terrible past.

* * *

In March 2001, Uganda held presidential elections. There were six candidates, one of whom, a medical doctor and retired colonel from Museveni's National Resistance Army, was a serious challenger to Museveni. Kizza Besigye fought alongside Museveni during the war in the 1980s, and later joined his government. He decided to run against Museveni because he believed the President had been in power for too long, and had become complacent and corrupt. Besigye has been critical of Uganda's involvement in the Congo, and of increasing human rights abuses within Uganda itself. He also supports multiparty democracy, while Museveni believes the country should remain in the hands of his own National Resistance Movement. During the months leading up to the election, there were numerous episodes of violence, kidnapping, and torture.[17] By far, most offenses, according to newspaper reports, and according to Human Rights Watch,[18] were carried out by Museveni supporters, including Museveni's personal guards, the Presidential Protection Unit, against Besigye supporters. Besigye challenged the election results in court, alleging that two and a half million ghost votes had been cast in Museveni's favor. The Supreme Court decided, by a vote of 3–2, not to annul the elections, and Museveni was recently sworn in to another presidential term.

---

17. Museveni is also harassing Besigye's wife, Winnie Byanyima, who is a very popular and articulate member of parliament. Both Byanyima and Besigye had their passports suspended, and Byanyima has been charged with sedition. Byanyima has been actively challenging corruption in Museveni's government. Parliamentary elections are also due to be held in July, and it may be in Museveni's interest to interfere with her campaign.
18. See "Uganda: Not a Level Playing Field: Government Violations in the Lead-Up to the Election," *Human Rights Watch*, March 2001.

It is widely believed, however, that the Court had originally decided that the elections had not been legitimate, but that the evening before the ruling, Museveni threatened the judges that he would call in the army if they did not revise their decision.[19] Besigye has decided not to challenge the election results again, and, despite the fact that the election was clearly flawed, this is good news for Uganda. If he did, the pre-election violence might well escalate into yet another civil war. In that case, it seems clear, no HIV prevention program could prevent another surge in infection rates.

4.

AIDS threatens African development because it kills and disables adults of working age and leaves children without parents. Societies lose teachers, doctors, bureaucrats, soldiers, businessmen, and other workers, and the rest of the world loses consumers. But AIDS is as much a symptom of social crises as it is a cause of them. Rural poverty, corruption, political mischief, human rights abuses, and a pointless war are reviving tensions that linger from Uganda's brutal past and could contribute to further spread of HIV. There are already signs of increased insecurity. Kampala is still one of the safest cities in Africa, but there are reports that violent crime rates have risen in recent years, after a long decline since 1986, and I heard people talk casually about crime in a way they did not before. During the past few years, Kampala has been hit by a spate of bomb attacks and eight students at Makerere University have been murdered, but the killer has never been found. There are stories in the newspaper about

---

19. Charles Onyango-Obbo, "'Crown Prince' Museveni, and 'Queen' Janet," *The Monitor*, May 9, 2001. The Supreme Court has yet to issue its written judgments in the case. Such delay is unusual.

traditional healers kidnapping and sacrificing children, because chickens and goats no longer do the trick. There are also many accounts of domestic violence, which remains an endemic problem.

Recently the UN, a group of concerned Harvard academics, and other advocacy groups have been campaigning for an AIDS fund for developing countries that, they hope, will amount to up to $10 billion per year. There is considerable debate about how this money should be spent, if it actually materializes. Lack of AIDS treatment and inadequate funding for prevention programs in Africa are increasingly seen as grave injustices. However, injustice itself, and the many forms it takes in Africa, are a fundamental cause of the growth of the epidemic, and unless that changes, even the most well designed prevention programs may not make much headway.

* * *

In the meantime, thousands of Ugandans are dying every year from AIDS, and there is a desperate need for better treatment. But that is not all they need. In April I accompanied a nurse from the charity Hospice Uganda on a visit to a woman who was dying at home, in a village outside of Kampala. In the small, dark room, the patient's skeletal outline was barely perceptible among the wrinkles in the bedcovers. Sun shone through holes in the iron roof, so that the patient got soaked when it rained. "We would fix it if we had the money," the woman's sister said. Family members gathered in the room and asked the nurse questions as she dispensed antibiotics and painkillers. Small children came and went, and one little girl, about four years old, with a bald head and tiny shoulders, stared at me. This was the patient's daughter. Her uncle, a man of about twenty, leaned over and asked me a question: "The other children go to school, but not this one. She keeps getting sick. What do you think is the matter with her?" I did not have the courage to tell him what he already knew.

There is much explicit information in the newspapers and on the radio in Uganda about how to use a condom, and the feelings, manners, and techniques of romance and sex; but there is far less open discussion about what it is really like to live in a family affected by HIV. There is an odd silence surrounding these people, who now number in the millions, if you include those whose wives, husbands, parents, siblings, or children are HIV-positive.

The family I visited was relatively lucky. The nurse comes once a week. But Uganda needs much better salaries for more people like her, and also for better medications and health centers for the roughly 50 percent of its people who have no access to health care at all.

While I was in Uganda, I learned that these people also need not just health care, but protection from cruel and discriminatory treatment as well. I met a woman named Milly Katana, who runs an organization that monitors AIDS-related discrimination. She explained to me how, in the early days of the epidemic, people used to gossip whenever someone died. People didn't want to sit next to someone whose children or husband was known to be sick, and schoolchildren would tease classmates whose parents had died. At funerals, rumors would go around: "If that one died, well, so-and-so is next." But according to Katana, Ugandan communities soon realized that anyone could die from AIDS, and these cruel attitudes are slowly changing. Now, she says, a new form of discrimination is emerging, in businesses, the civil service, and other institutions. President Museveni has made a negative HIV test a requirement for promotion in the army, and the US embassy had a similar policy, but it ceased this month, after journalists accompanying Colin Powell on his recent African tour drew attention to it.

Being HIV-negative is also an unspoken criterion for employment in many businesses. During the past ten years, under Uganda's World Bank– sponsored reform program, state-owned businesses have been privatized and government jobs have been cut. As a result, many workers and civil servants have been laid off. According to Katana, workers whose wives, husbands, or children have died, and who are therefore suspected to be HIV-positive—what her HIV activist friends call "the so-called sick"—are usually the first to go.

People may live with HIV for years or even decades without AIDS symptoms, and human rights groups have long argued that HIV infection should be treated like any other "latent" affliction, such as diabetes or high blood pressure. Uganda has no laws against unfair hiring practices based on HIV status, but they are in clear violation of international guidelines established by the UN Commission on Human Rights.[20]

* * *

Before I met Katana, I attended a speech given by President Museveni on the subject of AIDS. Museveni is a large man, with a great bald head like polished brass, and a deep voice that carries very far, like the roar of a lion. In his speech, he told a rather strange story, tracing the origins of the AIDS epidemic in Uganda to the arrival of Europeans in the nineteenth century. Before that, Ugandan society had strict moral codes. For example, if an unmarried girl became pregnant, "the punishment then for the boy and girl was death; the girl would be tied in dry banana leaves, set on fire, and rolled down a cliff, and the boy speared. But when the Europeans and Christians came they said it was barbaric, and put a stop to it. So the tribal regime broke down into a permissive society."

Press reports provide further insights into the President's attitude toward people with HIV. For more than a decade, rebels based in

---

20. For reasons that are not clear, UNAIDS makes no mention of "institutional discrimination" in its report on HIV discrimination in Uganda. See *HIV and AIDS-Related Stigmatization, Discrimination and Denial: Forms, Contexts and Determinants*, Research Studies from Uganda and India, UNAIDS, July 2000.

Sudan have launched attacks on villages and towns in northern Uganda. More recently they have been abducting Ugandan children and forcing them to join their armies, or in the case of girls, to work as slaves. The parents of 12,000 of these children have been complaining that the Ugandan government has not been doing enough to get their children back. Museveni has responded by saying that these children were by now HIV-positive anyway, so they were "no longer an issue."[21]

Shortly before polling day in March 2001, Museveni told an American journalist that his main opponent, Kizza Besigye, had AIDS.[22] Later he repeated his remarks to the Ugandan press. "State House is not a place for invalids," Museveni said. In the court case challenging the election results, Besigye denied that he had AIDS, and claimed that Museveni was spreading false rumors to dissuade voters from supporting him. But Museveni's lawyers argued that since Besigye's first wife and child had died in the early 1990s, it was fair to assume that he had AIDS. AIDS support groups in Uganda have claimed that Museveni's statements were an outrageous and cynical attempt to use the stigma surrounding HIV to further his campaign, and to promote discrimination against people whose lives have been affected by AIDS.

In Uganda, the loyalty and strength of Ugandan families and the perseverance of HIV prevention workers and AIDS treatment advocates are continually undermined by war, corruption, and injustice. HIV struck Europe and the US just as gay men were organizing to confront discrimination against them, and the struggle against AIDS became part of the greater struggle for gay rights. By and large, the

---

21. "Abducted Children's Parents Angered by Museveni's Words," *The Monitor*, February 23, 2001.

22. Marguerite Michaels, "Three's a Crowd in Love and Politics," *Time*, March 12, 2001.

people of sub-Saharan Africa have yet to assume their rights. Until the status of women improves, something that is linked to the improvement of rights for all people, regardless of tribe, political connections, or HIV status, the most generous funding for AIDS in Africa will not go nearly far enough.

—July 5, 2001

19

Arrested in China

Kang Zhengguo

Chairman Mao ruled over a poor and almost entirely walled society. Oppression in Mao's China was brutal and often murderous. Now that China has opened up to the world, and the Chinese economy has been transformed from a Communist autarky to a form of (Party) crony capitalism, different methods must be used to keep the population in line.

Since the 1980s, individual freedoms have been expanded; wealthy or well-connected Chinese citizens can travel or study abroad, where they have access to information that is unavailable inside China. It will no longer do to murder dissidents or "class enemies" in savage campaigns. Not all information that is unwelcome to the authoritarian rulers can be wiped off the Internet.

Enforced self-censorship and conformism is now preferred —through threats and intimidation, through examples of harsh punishment, and through social ostracism. By instilling enough fear in the Chinese, including those who live abroad, Chinese order will prevail. Or so the authorities hope.

—I.B.

A YEAR AGO, after my classes teaching Chinese at Yale were over and the students had left, I set out for my old home in Xi'an, China, to visit relatives. Early in the morning on June 15, the fifth day of my stay in my mother's house, I had a rude awakening. Before I had gotten out of bed, eight plainclothes agents of the local State Security Bureau burst in, tersely stated their purpose, and forced me to leave with them immediately.

They said they wanted me to take part in a "returnee interview"—which was a standard thing, they said, and nothing for me to be upset about. It was just that my mother's house was not the most convenient place for a chat, so they would need to use the sedan they had parked in a corner of the compound to bring me to a more suitable place to ask a few questions. The car made a number of turns and then raced toward the guest house of the nearby Electric Power Institute. First I had breakfast with eight agents in the downstairs dining room; then they brought me up to the seventh floor to a room that had been prepared for me. From time to time I noticed other agents heading downstairs toward the dining room. It seemed as if they had moved in during the previous evening to get things ready for me, and now were just finishing their night duty. Agents kept popping in and out of the room, as if taking part in some scheduled deployment.

Their first item of business was to inspect my documents. The agents took my Chinese passport and my US green card, and said they would keep them for the time being. This little move, both they and I knew, was in fact like attaching to me an invisible leg iron. Every Chinese who goes home and gets into trouble knows that once your documents are gone, they've got you. Even if they let you go, you can't move. So there I was, still groggy from sleep, under comfortable detention in a guest house.

* * *

They called it a "chat," but it was a formal interrogation—it just started gently. In order to create a more relaxed atmosphere, they explained, they had specially recalled an old acquaintance of mine, a man who had interrogated me for six months after the Tiananmen events of 1989. I understood the terms of such interrogations, because I had been through them before. The questioner begins from the assumption that you are guilty of many, many crimes and that the police already know the details of all of them. He does not say what the crimes are; it is up to you to show your sincerity and earn forgiveness by confessing. The purpose of this approach is to get as much out of you as possible. If you fall for the promise that "confession brings lenience" and spill everything you know, you only get yourself and your friends more deeply into trouble. So I began by stating my own ground rules: since this was a "returnee interview," not an interrogation, there would be no need for me to volunteer anything. Their side would have to initiate the questions from start to finish. I would answer what I could.

They began by asking about letters I had exchanged with friends in Xi'an after I had left for the West. Then they asked about my contacts in the US with Liu Binyan and Hu Ping, two well-known critics of the Chinese government. They wanted to make clear their especially profound distaste for an essay called "The Crime of Counterrevolution and the Mendacity of Dictatorship" which I had published in the Hong Kong *Ming Pao Monthly* in 1995 after Wei Jingsheng had been sentenced to a second lengthy prison term. But both they and I knew that none of this added up to "endangerment of national security" and that my responses were unlikely to yield much of value to them. Hence they were obliged to play their trump card, which revealed more directly why they had arrested me.

They had, they said, concrete evidence that made it necessary for them to talk to me. They had searched the home of an elderly friend of mine the day before, and had confiscated all of the letters, magazines, and newspaper clippings that I had mailed to him after moving to America. Now they had some questions: What publications had I mailed to this friend? How many, all together? To whom else had I mailed similar publications? How many? On whose instructions had I mailed these banned publications into China? And so on. So now things were coming clear: my article supporting Wei Jingsheng had sparked their interest, and their raid on my friend's house had delivered the goods.

This elderly friend of mine was retired, lived at home, and had time on his hands. But he maintained a lively interest in public affairs, and he kept up a steady correspondence with me after I went abroad. He was always eager to learn, and wanted to use me as a way to get hold of information and opinions that were prohibited inside China. I was over fifty years old, had already been through enough political battles, and perhaps should have put him off. But I thought that, well, if I can supply the needs of an old friend for information and at the same time send some uncensored materials to China, those are things one simply ought to do. So I began to buy magazines like *Democratic China* and *Beijing Spring*, which published independent comment on Chinese society, and to mail them to China. The police specifically asked about Liu Binyan because I had given the address of my elderly friend to Liu, who in turn had mailed some writings directly to him. They had asked about Hu Ping because another friend had sent me an article that he wanted to have published, and I had sent it to Hu Ping's magazine *Beijing Spring*.

After a full day of questioning, certain things dawned on me. During all that time that I was mailing materials to my elderly friend, we thought nothing was amiss because all of them got through. In fact, though, the police had been reading the mail from the beginning and had let things pass on purpose. They wanted to catch bigger fish; they would cut me some slack, let me pile up a bad record, and then deal with everything at once when I came back to Xi'an to visit relatives. Now their day of reckoning had arrived. First they raided the home of my elderly friend and took away what they would need for their case; one of the confiscated items, as it happened, was the issue of *Beijing Spring* that contained the article by my friend which I had sent to the magazine. I now realized why they had asked me about Liu Binyan and Hu Ping at the beginning of the day. They wanted me to confirm and perhaps say more about matters that, from months of reading my mail, they already knew.

* * *

My "returnee interview" lasted into the evening. When it was over my handlers made it clear that I would remain on the seventh floor of that guest house while they prepared to spend the night with me.

In the morning they tightened the noose. The section chief who was in charge put on a stern face and said I would have to submit a written self-criticism. They would not let me go home until I put in writing that I admitted my crimes and promised never to mail this kind of publication again. I tried two or three drafts and each was rejected. The two main points at issue were: (1) my statement that "I viewed my mailings of these materials from the standpoint of my context overseas, where, with press freedom and legal guarantees of private correspondence, such mailings violated nothing"; and (2) my insistence that the police had not just happened to discover my mailings during their raid on my friend's house the day before my arrest, but had long been building their case by opening my mail. This monitoring of my mail, I wrote, gave me a sense of having been entrapped.

During the entire second day, the relevant section chief and department head took turns delivering harsh warnings to me. So long as I did not delete those two items from my written confession I would continue to be held. At one point the section chief adopted a pose of offering friendly advice: even if I were right about the protracted opening of my mail, he said, this was permissible under security law. I could think what I wanted about my mail; I just mustn't write it down in black and white. In any case, so long as I persisted in my two points, I would never pass muster with their superiors.

And sure enough, during the afternoon of the second day things escalated. They took out a document that they had prepared in advance and read me an official "summons": within twelve hours my status would shift to that of "legal detainee." I went to bed under that cloud.

Early the next morning, before dawn, I was suddenly awakened by one of the handlers. Half-asleep, I saw before me a security agent whom I had not met before. He was using the last moments of my twelve-hour "summons" period to read me a decision on "supervised residence." The gist was that, from this moment on, I could be held for interrogation for up to six months; I would, moreover, be responsible for my own room and board expenses.

It was well known that the methods for persecuting people had shifted in recent years and that economic punishments now had been added to the others. I suspected that the security agents were planning a shakedown, and so refused their request that I sign my name agreeing to "supervised residence." They responded that the decision would take effect anyway, with or without my signature.

It emerged that their entire plan to "interview" me had run into some interference. This happened because, as soon as I had arrived in the guest house, I had called home and had asked my family to notify my friends and relatives in New Haven that I had been detained. The response from the US, including the State Department, had been quick, and had quickly reached high levels in Beijing, from where, it seems, word went down to Xi'an Security to be careful. As I look back now, all those procedures about "summons," "supervised residence," and whatnot seem likely to have been precautionary measures that the police resorted to after their plan to hold me had run into difficulty. The third day was the beginning of a weekend, and they told me that my case would have to be resolved before the end of the work day. They kept urging me to write a new statement. Since I did want to go home, I decided to relent and open the way to a solution. I deleted the two points that I had been insisting upon, and yielded to the demand that I acknowledge the crime of which I was accused: I had violated the state security law that prohibits the "production, distribution, or reading of materials that endanger state security." This self-criticism worked. About 6 PM they announced that "supervised residence is ending at this point."

* * *

I returned to my mother's house in a foul mood, feeling sour and violated. The three days of detention had swept away my zest for visiting relatives. I lay on the bed and replayed for myself, scene by scene, the various political tests I had faced in my life, beginning with the "reactionary statements" I had made during my student days right through to that protest poster that I had put up after the Tiananmen Massacre and that had almost got me arrested. Like other "troublemakers," I had over the years made more than a few specious "self-criticisms" in order to get past the interrogators. I lived in America now, and by staying there I could have ended all contact with these functionaries; but the threads that pulled me toward family and hometown would not let go.

So here I was, with no one to blame but myself, back for more—more humiliation by experts in "Chinese-style" self-criticism. It's been several decades now, and we Chinese are stuck with the same old question: Why aren't people allowed to talk, write, and read what they want? The Party and state won't tolerate free expression on the part of the people they rule. The naively optimistic intellectuals recurrently hope that China will turn a corner, that *this* time we're really going to get things on the right track. But then it always emerges that nothing fundamentally changes and we start over again. For people like me, writing self-criticism feels like falling into a very old rut.

During the Cultural Revolution I was sentenced to reeducation through labor for my "reactionary thinking." Later I was exonerated, but I still suffered a recurring nightmare. In it I saw myself rearrested and sent back to the labor team to begin serving another sentence. As the intensity of the nightmare increased, I would awake with a start. For years this dream attacked me at night, over and over, like a ghost clinging to my body. Its spell remained in force until I moved with my family to the US. Then I thought I was finally rid of it. But no. Now, here in Xi'an, it had ambushed me again, and this time in broad daylight. My three days in detention had left my family shocked and exhausted and had worried many of my old friends. Everybody was afraid that if I stayed in Xi'an longer something else might happen, and that things might get out of hand. They urged me to go back to America while I still could. So I decided to cut short my visit to my mother. I changed my air ticket to an earlier flight back to the US.

* * *

Any Chinese who gets detained during a trip home to China also normally receives "send-off instructions" just before being released. Your handlers tell you to seal your experiences inside yourself, just as you might seal exposed film inside a light-impenetrable canister. And they back this up with a threat: should you ever dare mention anything to the media, your next visit home will be even more rocky—in fact you might just forget about being allowed back into the country at all. This is the reason why, even though hundreds and thousands of people get harassed in things like "returnee interviews," so few are willing—or dare—to tell what has happened to them once they reach the outside world.

On the day I was released, the State Security department head who had worked on me suddenly discovered that we had gone to the same school. Now she wanted to invite me to a grand banquet to celebrate the end of her department's interrogation. At this dinner the agents' admonitions and warnings now took on the flavor of a word game, since their duty to harass me was clearly behind them. Now they wanted me to join them in acknowledging their patriotic enterprise; it all made me feel that I had somehow become an accomplice in their mission to turn me inside-out.

The whole thing was, moreover, a fitting sign of the officially sponsored commercialism of recent years; even an episode of arresting and then releasing somebody was ending in a little orgy of corrupt consumption. Of course, the messages that got passed along amid the clinking of glasses were sharply pointed. For example, when you go back to the US, you should take care to protect the positive image of State Security; everything that's happened here should be kept under wraps—let's not have any loose tongues; and so on. And then some intimate advice, delivered in a voice intended to convey sympathetic feeling: your mother's getting up there in years, remember; someday you'll need to come back for those final duties of a filial son. The underlying message was clear enough: so long as I had reason to come back to Xi'an, they could do more to me if they wanted.

I had been given some intimidating warnings, and they were part of the reason why I held my tongue for nearly a year after returning to the US. But there were other reasons as well. The well-intentioned reproach and counsel of my friends and relatives came to be in some ways a bigger psychological problem than the intimidation tactics of State Security. Both in Xi'an and back in the US there were people—including my wife—who made fun of my naive behavior. Why spend good money to mail magazines to China? I had asked for trouble, and had ended by getting it. The root cause of my humiliation was my own stupidity. I hadn't known how to protect myself.

At one point when the police were pressing me to admit that I had harmed China's national security, I became exasperated: "I didn't organize any violence. I didn't steal national military secrets or sell any economic intelligence—in what way did I harm national security? Is national security all that fragile? A few articles criticizing the judiciary, or the passing around of some things that the authorities don't want people to read—things like that really threaten security?" The police found my efforts to reason with them laughable, of course. Yet still, even now, I feel the need to make my point: they can look up in their little books whatever empty rule they like, but I did nothing whatever to endanger national security. If "national security" means the security of a nation's citizens, then the state is the biggest threat to national security.

For the person who lives in a country without legal protections, under an unmoving cloud of intimidation, the best one can often do is to go along, angling for small benefits as best one can. When the price becomes prohibitive even for something like reading an overseas magazine, what other recourse does one have? If we look at my three-day detention, we see that State Security may have failed to change my thinking, but its goal of intimidation has largely been achieved. I am not afraid to mail *Beijing Spring* to China again, but I no longer know of anyone willing to receive it, and I no longer have the same desire to get in touch with them. The whole episode affected a good many other people besides myself. It also brought disaster down on that elderly friend of mine. I can sense that the Chinese who were hurt or even just tainted by my case feel a certain resentment toward me, and want to keep their distance. They apparently feel that I have become a serious threat to their own security.

* * *

So why my delay in writing about my experience? A gross act of persecution can elicit a direct response of indignation. That much is easy. But when you have been persecuted the people around you distance themselves from you, or criticize you, and you lose your self-confidence. It can leave you feeling helpless and frustrated, almost paralyzed, even if still full of rage. When you realize that you have caused trouble to other people, or when people close to you express disappointment at your stubbornness, your resolve to fight back starts to melt away, whether you like it or not. Last year at Christmas and New Year's I received almost no cards or greetings from Xi'an. The detention episode had put my relations with people there into deep freeze, and had cut me off from my hometown and roots. I feel now that the place where I was born and grew up has been lost to me forever.

I have never had any interest in the kind of attention that can come from telling one's troubles in public, and for that reason, too, I had no plan to rush into print with my story. But human rights conditions in China are worsening. Over the past year it seems to have become an "open season" on Chinese scholars—some of whom are American citizens—who return to China to visit relatives or do research. Several have been arrested and many others have canceled trips for fear of trouble.

I cannot expect that my voice by itself will do anything to improve the human rights situation in China, but perhaps others can learn something from my account about how to handle it. If you are detained, for example, be sure to try to get word to the outside world as soon as possible; don't just hope you can quietly plea-bargain your way out. Doing so only gives the other side what it wants: the chance to use pressure in secret. And don't go along with the other side's encouragement to confess your mistakes or guilt in detail. You may find no alternative to signing a brief statement to get yourself released; but if the purpose of the authorities is to extract from you the very materials they need in order to nail you, then you only trap yourself by talking.

Here in the US I can speak out, but it's like shouting at a fire from the other side of a river. The moment a Chinese person steps out of China, he or she is largely separated from the struggles of the people back home who, while lacking both rights and power, somehow hope to sweep away falsity and create a secure system that will use law to serve the true interests of everyone.

After returning to New Haven I applied for American citizenship. The terrifying and absurd experience had ruined my ties to my homeland. The poet Wei Zhuang (836–910 AD) has written:

Until you grow old, do not return home; Going back only breaks your heart.

My own sadness might be captured by changing the first line to "Once you go out, do not return home."

Translated from the Chinese by Perry Link
—September 20, 2001

20

With the Northern Alliance
Tim Judah

This time the Western powers should surely have learned their lesson. Invading Afghanistan with foreign forces has never been a good idea. Britain and the Soviet Union found that out to their cost. Tribal tensions make Afghanistan almost impossible to rule under the best circumstances. Wars make those tensions far worse. And so it was hoped, in 2001, after Osama bin Laden's bloody enterprise in downtown Manhattan and Washington DC, that the only Western superpower and her allies would be cautious about unleashing another war.

There was hope that Ahmad Shah Masoud, a Tajik, might overcome the mostly Pashtun Taliban. But Masoud was assassinated by suicide bombers.

When this article was written, there was still some hope that Masoud's United Front might bring unity and some justice to the country. This, too, was in vain. The US did invade, there was another war, and soon the foreign invaders will follow their predecessors in a hasty, and most probably messy, re-treat.

—I.B.

Khoja Bahaudin, northern Afghanistan

A FEW WEEKS ago President George W. Bush said something to the effect that he didn't want to fire off $2 million missiles to hit $10 tents in Afghanistan. Well, I think he said that, but I can't check, because now I am living in a $10 tent in northern Afghanistan. There is no electricity, no clean water, no paved roads, not much food, and it is only the aid agencies that are staving off famine here. In this part of opposition-controlled northern Afghanistan, close to the border with the former Soviet republic of Tajikistan, it has barely rained for three years and choking dust swirls everywhere, entering every pore.

I arrived in the early hours of the morning after a five-day journey from London. On the banks of the Amu Darya, the Oxus River of legend, which marks the frontier between Tajikistan and Afghanistan, Afghan and Russian officials pored over everyone's documents. Although Tajikistan has been independent for more than a decade, it has fought a war against Islamic insurgents and thousands of Russian troops help guard its frontiers. On the other side, after more document checks, and haggling with pickup-truck drivers, my colleagues and I got to the little town of Khoja Bahaudin. There we were directed by Afghan officials of the Northern Alliance to spend our first night in the country on the concrete veranda of a small building.

When I woke up I noticed that the windows of half the building were boarded over and that the ceiling was black. In fact it looked as if there had been a fire or explosion inside. My suspicions were quickly confirmed. I was sleeping just outside the room where the first deaths of this new war had happened. On September 9, two Moroccans posing as journalists had set up their television camera inside the room to interview the legendary Afghan Mujahideen commander Ahmed Shah Masoud. One of the Moroccans asked, "When you get to Kabul what will you do with Osama bin Laden?" Masoud took a breath to answer but before he did so the Moroccan set off the bombs strapped around his waist; he was shredded, and body parts were scattered around the room. The second suicide bomber survived and ran down to the nearby river, where he was killed. According to one version, Masoud died in a hospital six days later. Another has it that he died within hours but that his death was covered up for six days so as to ensure a smooth succession.

Of course it is impossible to prove a link between the murder of Masoud and the attacks on New York and Washington two days later, but people here have few doubts about it. Osama bin Laden, they feel sure, was giving his Taliban hosts the head of their most implacable foe before moving on to bigger things.

I.

Ahmed Shah Masoud, an ethnic Tajik, was born in 1956, the son of a military officer. He attended Kabul's French-run Lycée Istiqlal. In 1975 he fled to Pakistan because he had been involved in trying to begin an Islamic movement along with others, such as the engineering student Gulbuddin Hekmatyar. After the Soviet invasion in 1979 he became one of the founders of the Mujahideen resistance along with Hekmatyar and others. With Western backing, they were able to force the Soviet occupiers to retreat and thus played a major part in the collapse of the Soviet Union. Following the Soviet pullout the Russian-backed regime of President Mohammad Najibullah clung to power until 1992, when Masoud made a deal with General Rashid Dostum, a powerful ethnic Uzbek in Najibullah's army, to switch sides and join his troops to Masoud's against Najibullah. After that Kabul fell.

Michael Griffen, a British writer and journalist who is the author of the excellent *Reaping the Whirlwind: The Taliban Movement in*

Afghanistan, quotes from an interview given to a US reporter by Najibullah just before the end:

> We have a common task—Afghanistan, the USA and the civilized world—to launch a joint struggle against fundamentalism. If fundamentalism comes to Afghanistan, war will continue for many years. Afghanistan will turn into a center of world smuggling for narcotic drugs. Afghanistan will be turned into a center for terrorism.

The rival Mujahideen commanders and their armies now turned on one another. In 1993 the new president, Burhanuddin Rabbani, an Islamic scholar and poet, opposed Hekmatyar. Between January 1994 and February 1995 Masoud fought Dostum and Hekmatyar for control of Kabul, which had not been seriously damaged during the war with the Soviet Union but was now largely turned to rubble. Some 50,000 people are estimated to have died in these battles. Masoud was eventually forced to retreat from Kabul to the heartland of his support, the Panjshir Valley, the southernmost tip of which lies roughly thirty miles north of the capital. Rabbani also fled north from the Taliban.

Then Masoud formed a new alliance with Dostum and others because they had a new common enemy, the Taliban. According to Ahmed Rashid, the widely respected Pakistani journalist and author of *Taliban: Militant Islam, Oil and Fundamentalism in Central Asia*, Masoud's reputation was at its peak in 1992, but "four years in power in Kabul had turned Masoud's army into arrogant masters who harassed civilians, stole from shops and confiscated people's houses, which is why Kabulis first welcomed the Taliban when they entered Kabul."

The Taliban sprang from the *madrasas*, or religious schools, which flourished among the Afghan refugees in Pakistan during the years of the Soviet occupation and indeed ever since. "These boys," writes Rashid,

> had no memories of their tribes, their elders, their neighbours nor the complex ethnic mix of peoples that often made up their villages and their homeland. These boys were what the war had thrown up like the sea's surrender on the beach of history.... They were literally the orphans of war, the rootless and restless.... Their simple belief in a messianic, puritan Islam which had been drummed into them by simple village mullahs was the only prop they could hold on to and which gave their lives some meaning.... Ironically, the Taliban were a direct throwback to the military religious orders that arose in Christendom during the crusades to fight Islam.

The main Taliban leaders came from the southern city of Kandahar. The driving force behind them was Mullah Mohammad Omar, who lost his right eye fighting the Soviets. Born in 1959, he came from a family of landless peasants and supported his family after his father died by becoming a village mullah and opening a *madrasa*. Different legends circulate about how Omar founded the Taliban because he was outraged by the sexual behavior of Mujahideen commanders; but we will probably never know exactly what prompted him to gather the religious students into a fighting force of their own, which would then go on to seize most of Afghanistan and subject it to its extreme version of Islam. What is clear is that religion here is entwined with the delicate ethnic politics of Afghanistan, which in turn is a factor manipulated by the country's neighbors and others.

* * *

Today there are probably some 20 million or so Afghans, but of course, after twenty-two years of war no one can be sure. According to the 1973 census, the last to be carried out, 43 percent were Pashtuns (also known by the anglicized name of Pathans), mostly Sunni Muslims, who live mainly in the south. The border, known as the Durand line, which was drawn in 1897 to demarcate the frontier with then British India, now of course, Pakistan, divides the Afghan Pashtuns from their Pakistani brothers. Pakistani governments have always felt the need to keep their Pashtun population of some 20 million happy; their enduring nightmare is a revival of Pashtun nationalism, which would seek to carve a Pashtun state out of Pakistan and Afghanistan.

Curiously, in view of the fact that Britain's Royal Air Force has been bombing Afghanistan "shoulder to shoulder" with the US, it was this border question that was the reason for Britain's last bombing of Afghanistan in 1919. After an Afghan-inspired attempt to raise a revolt among Pashtuns over the border, the RAF bombed Jalalabad (near the present Pakistan border), while a single plane made it to Kabul and bombed the royal palace and an arms factory. Martin Ewans, a former British diplomat who is the author of a highly readable new primer, *Afghanistan: A New History*, quotes a letter that an Afghan leader sent in 1919 to the viceroy of India; it sounds curiously reminiscent of the statements of Taliban and other Muslim leaders today:

> It is a matter of great regret that the throwing of bombs by Zeppelins on London was denounced as a most savage act and the bombardment of places of worship was considered a most abominable operation, while now we can see with our own eyes that such operations were a habit which is prevalent amongst all civilized people of the West.

Pashtun ethnic loyalty continues to be strong in Afghan politics today. The Taliban themselves come from the Pashtun heartlands and all but a few of their leaders are Pashtuns, some of whom do not even speak Dari, the Persian lingua franca of Afghanistan.

* * *

Many ordinary Afghans, of whatever ethnicity, at first supported the Taliban because, after years of war and mayhem, they expected them to bring peace and law and order. But after the fall of Najibullah it had rankled Pashtuns that the new authorities in Kabul were dominated by Masoud and Rabbani, who were both Tajiks, and by an Uzbek general, Dostum, while Hekmatyar, the main Pashtun Mujahideen, had lost out. According to the 1973 census, Tajiks, whose language is close to Persian, made up 24 percent of the population. They are concentrated in the north, where the old border of the tsarist Russian Empire had cut them off from their cousins in what is now Tajikistan. Uzbeks make up 6 percent of the population, and are likewise cut off by the old Russian and then Soviet border from their cousins in what is now Uzbekistan. The next-largest ethnic group are the Hazaras, who live in the center of Afghanistan, and who are set apart from most other Afghans in that they are Shia Muslims, like Iranians. Their broad faces and slanting eyes also make it clear that their origins must lie far to the east, and some believe they are, at least in part, the descendants of Genghis Khan's Mongol Hordes. Other Afghans have tended to look down on the Hazaras, and in turn there is no love lost between them and the Pashtuns in particular. In 1995 Masoud drove the Hazaras out of Kabul.

Even if Afghanistan did not have strategic importance for all of its neighbors, it is clear that these ethnic and religious links would have drawn the surrounding states into the country's politics anyway, either for their own reasons or to help their ethnic or religious kinfolk. Iran has helped the Hazaras. Tajikistan and Uzbekistan have helped the Tajiks and Uzbeks, and still do. And of course Pakistan wants to support the Pashtuns. Russia too has its interests; its chief concern had been to stop the spread of Islamic fundamentalism. Iran has made it clear it wants a weak and divided Afghanistan which could not threaten it. Pakistan has wanted Afghanistan to have a strong central government, dominated by Pakistan of course, which would then ensure open trade routes to Central Asia and allow the building of valuable gas and oil pipelines across Afghanistan and then into Pakistan. These were major considerations when Pakistan's security services, the Inter-Services Intelligence (ISI), poured money and arms over the border to build up the Pashtun Taliban.

2.

What the Taliban did when they took Kabul and indeed some 90 percent of Afghanistan is by now well known. They prevented women from working, closed schools for girls as well as many nonreligious schools for boys. They debated whether homosexuals should be killed under falling walls or whether another type of punishment was appropriate. They banned music, television, and just about any other type of entertainment. They also played host to Osama bin Laden, the rich Saudi dissident who had fought with the Mujahideen and who, after US troops were stationed in Saudi Arabia, declared a jihad against the United States. Bin Laden is believed to have been a major source of funding for the Taliban, along with Pakistan and Saudi Arabia. But until last spring the Taliban also financed themselves through the production of opium for heroin, which was deemed acceptable because only infidels, i.e., non-Muslims, became heroin addicts. (For their part, the health authorities in Pakistan say that their country has a major heroin addiction problem.)

As the Taliban took towns that lay outside Pashtun areas they became more and more brutal, committing massacres against civilians, especially Hazaras and Uzbeks. In return, thousands of Taliban prisoners were treated badly. The Taliban hope was not just to take all of Afghanistan, but to foment Islamic revolution throughout Central Asia and beyond. For this reason they welcomed thousands of Arab fundamentalists, as well as Chechen rebels and extremists from Uzbekistan and Tajikistan, and from among China's Muslim minorities. However, even with their foreign legions, the Taliban were never able to dislodge Masoud. They chased Dostum from his base at Mazar-e-Sharif, less than fifty miles from the Uzbekistan border, but could not crush resistance there either; nor could they defeat several other groups connected with the Tajiks and Uzbeks in at least half a dozen enclaves. Over the last year the front lines have not moved much but these groups fight under the common banner of what is widely called the Northern Alliance, although technically they should be known as the United Front. Most of these groups are not Pashtuns. When Masoud was killed, the Taliban's leaders must have hoped that the troops led by the man they dubbed the Lion of the Panjshir would be so demoralized that the Northern Alliance would no longer be able to resist a knock-out blow. What they had not bargained for then was that the events of September 11 would set in motion a series of events which seem, thus far at least, to have had precisely the opposite effect.

3.

While you can see Masoud's picture everywhere up here in the north, the curious thing is that people don't talk about him unless you ask. After he was killed, a *shura*, or traditional council, of his commanders was called. They decided that they had to carry on the struggle or face death. Masoud's successor as minister of defense for the Northern Alliance is Masoud's deputy, General Mohammad Fahim, a man who had fought by his side since the days of the war with the Soviets. By all accounts, and by appearances here, Fahim is doing a good job coordinating all the disparate semi-autonomous commanders and their troops that make up the armies of the Northern Alliance.

If the World Trade Center and the Pentagon had not been bombed then perhaps things would have been different. As it is, these small forces fighting in faraway Afghanistan are now being courted by the United States, with Russia and the Central Asian states all promising more aid. The US is mounting daily air strikes against their mortal foes. And just because Masoud has gone, this does not mean the Northern Alliance is unable to take advantage of the new situation. Evidence of preparations for an offensive are everywhere. By the banks of the Amu Darya, I came across hundreds of soldiers who had just been brought north from the Panjshir Valley to prepare to fight up here.

I went to Ai Khanoum, a majestic natural escarpment at the confluence of the Amu Darya and the Kokcha rivers. In 1963 French archaeologists discovered the remains of a fabulous and wealthy Hellenistic city, complete, Martin Ewans writes, "with a citadel, palace, temples and a gymnasium," that "appears to have been sacked and burnt at the end of the second century BC." It is once again in the middle of a war. Soldiers wait for the offensive to begin while a tank, dug into position, fires off odd rounds at the Taliban about a mile away. This is a rear position, but significantly the soldiers here, as everywhere else along these front lines, are both Tajik and Uzbek plus a sprinkling from other Afghan ethnic groups, including Pashtuns who have turned against the Taliban. They also include old enemies. I met former members of Mujahideen groups who were now fighting next to Afghans who had themselves years ago fought with the Soviets against the Mujahideen.

I caught a ride on the back of a truck loaded with soldiers going to their positions. Some were in uniform but others were wearing baggy pajama-style outfits, with pinstriped or checked waistcoats. The sturdy Russian truck lumbered across the Kokcha River and took us first to another escarpment at Kuruk. Here a spotter was directing fire on Taliban positions from artillery on another hill. "Down a hundred meters! That's it!"

Then I drove for miles down the dusty track that lies behind the Kalakata hills. Here the front line is strung along the hilltops. It was eerily quiet except for the desultory exchange of the odd tank or artillery shell. It was also clear that almost everything was now in place for a major push to try to break Taliban lines. In otherwise empty mud-brick villages hundreds of soldiers were living in small barracks compounds which would not have looked out of place on the set of a 1920s film about the French Foreign Legion. At the barracks of Mazar-e-Sharif 01 ("zero-one") Brigade, the soldiers, refugees from Taliban-controlled territory, were making eight-foot-long rakes. When the offensive comes, the first troops to advance will be armed with these, which they will use to clear Taliban mines lying in their path. All of these men are full-time soldiers. They are housed and fed and paid between $12 and $20 a month.

As dozens of his soldiers crowded around General Abdul Manon, the leader of the 01 Brigade sat cross-legged on the floor. "We have been fighting the Taliban and terrorism for six years, but the world did not know about their dangers. Now we hope that the UN and the whole world will fight against them and soon peace will come." On the wall behind him a slogan was written in charcoal: "We are waiting for tomorrow's victory over the Taliban! Our Taliban brothers, the traitors, have sold our country to the foreigners!" General Manon said that his hope was that the US air strikes would "destroy their army—then only bin Laden will be left. He will be alone and have nowhere to hide."

General Manon, who fought on the side of the Russians during the Soviet war, said he believed that desertions were diminishing Taliban ranks, a statement which was of course impossible to verify. "They want to fight America," he said, "but they don't have antiaircraft guns or good enough weapons." Ten minutes' walk from his head-quarters, his men have set up positions at the top of a very steep hill. They have dug trenches and sandbagged their bunkers in readiness for action. Peering across the valley, you can see a landscape pock-marked with shell craters.

Less than a mile away two figures could be seen moving on the top of a facing hill. "*Dushman! Dushman!*" (Enemy! Enemy!) the sol-diers shouted before loosing off rounds from heavy machine guns. Barely a minute later the Taliban fired back. As I sprinted for shelter and fell into the deep dust of the trenches, the crowd of thirty or so accompanying soldiers broke out in hysterical laughter, before taking cover themselves. As the firing died down they ran back down the hill to safety, whooping and screaming like kids plunging down a roller coaster at a funfair.

If they survive the coming storm General Manon says that he and his men, some of whom, like himself, have been fighting for the last twenty-two years without a break, want to go home to Mazar-e-Sharif. And then, he says, "if people agree, I hope we will have a good government. Our people are hungry for peace. We hope that then we will be able to put our guns away and grow food, build roads, build schools, and build hospitals."

4.

For the last few weeks there has been speculation by Western ana-lysts about whether the US and Britain will try to invade Afghani-stan, using bases in Uzbekistan and Tajikistan. An invasion with sizable ground forces seems unlikely and may be doomed to repeat the lessons of history, which in this part of the world can be summed up, "Don't invade Afghanistan." I met a man who said, "Are your soldiers coming here to Afghanistan? They can help us for a while, OK, but not if they come to live here." A well-informed Afghan intellectual, who asked not to be named, said, "I don't think these soldiers will come. It would completely change the dynamic of the situation and it would bring people together to fight the foreigners."

Before I left London I had called Tom Carew, who led missions into Afghanistan for Britain's special forces, the SAS, during the war with the Soviet forces, and asked him about the prospects of US and British troops. Carew is the author of the highly readable and revealing book called *Jihad: The Secret War in Afghanistan.* He said, "You can't even look at an Afghan woman so you can imagine what it would be like bringing in your average squaddie [ordinary soldier] to Afghanistan! All the Afghans would go: 'Whoa! Here come the infidels again,' and all get together and jump on them."

Chris Stephen, a friend of mine who writes for *The Scotsman,* and who shares the $10 tent with me, has been saying, "This is the first postmodern conflict because we are definitely at war but we don't know who the enemy is." If the aim of the war is to get rid of the Taliban, as opposed to trying to shut down Osama bin Laden's network and camps, and arrest him, then it would seem that the Northern Alliance members are the West's strategic allies. The Alliance is clearly ready to fight; but it is not certain if it is strong enough to take on even a weakened Taliban army spread out across the country. After all, the last time the people who lead the Alliance were in control, the country descended into bloody chaos, a fact that worries Western planners too. As for the size of the Northern Alliance forces, the estimates I heard—including one of ten thousand soldiers—are unreliable. Everyone over fourteen years old seems to have a gun;

there is no clear distinction between soldiers and civilians. In any case, no one can say how many fighters are being added to the expanding local units.

What the Alliance leaders and at least some of the Western strategists are hoping for is that after a couple of military defeats Taliban commanders will begin to defect with their troops, either because they want to be on the winning side in the war or because they would be well paid. Throughout the last decade money has had as important a part as force of arms in determining who wins and who loses. Once one or two commanders defect, runs the theory, then their fellow commanders will follow like dominoes. Indeed the hope here is that once that happens, the northern territories will fall first, followed by much of the rest of the country, where there will be no major fighting at all; there would instead be local coups to overthrow the Taliban leaders and take over the province.

According to the Northern Alliance, this is already starting to happen. On October 13 I got through to General Dostum by satellite phone. He is fighting south of Mazar-e-Sharif, far away across Taliban territory. He claimed that within the last twenty-four hours a Taliban commander called Kazi Abdul Hai had defected to him, bringing his four thousand men with him. This is probably a highly inflated figure. Still, if it proves to be true then it is possible that the strategy is working. If Mazar-e-Sharif falls, it is widely assumed that the Alliance will take control of the rest of the north, including the north–south road leading from Kabul to Uzbekistan, where US and British troops are reportedly being deployed.

"Of course," says the Afghan intellectual I've mentioned, "when it is all over no one will admit to having been a Taliban. It is easy to shave off your beard and take off your turban. Actually I know several people who were not mullahs but who grew beards and now they are big mullahs."

The opposition and the West could face a disaster if the Taliban are willing to continue fighting and don't collapse; or if the Taliban is forced to retreat from non-Pashtun areas but stand firm in their ethnic heartlands, bolstered by support from the Pakistani Pashtuns. If that happens it is impossible to predict what the outcome might be, but then, as my Afghan intellectual source says, "It is impossible to predict what is going to happen in this country in an hour."

5.

Who is running the Northern Alliance and what would happen if they did take over the country? In mud-built Khoja Bahaudin you will not find much by way of a reasoned answer. The Northern Alliance is, formally at least, the legitimate, internationally recognized government of the "Islamic State of Afghanistan," which just happens to have been kicked out of Kabul in 1995. It still controls the country's UN seat and most of its embassies abroad. Officially Burhanuddin Rabbani is still president, living in Faizabad, about forty miles from the Tajikistan border, but he is seldom heard from. On October 11, however, he said at a press conference in Dushanbe, the capital of Tajikistan, that representatives of all Afghanistan's peoples should help determine the nation's fate, "except terrorists and those who are up to their elbows in blood," i.e., bin Laden and his organization and his Taliban allies.

Rabbani did not say so, but we often hear of the plan for a future government headed by the former king of Afghanistan, Zahir Shah, who is eighty-six, was overthrown in 1973, and lives in Rome. He is keen to return, and, crucially, he is a Pashtun, although his first language is Dari. There is a chance that this might work, especially now that Masoud, who loathed the monarch and was opposed to his having any political position, is dead. Zahir Shah's advantage is that he can claim to be above politics and is not associated with the internecine bloodletting of the past decade.

In mid-October Northern Alliance officials gathered in the Panjshir Valley to select sixty delegates to attend a *shura* with sixty partisans of the King; this meeting is supposed to select delegates to a Loya Jirga, or grand council, that would discuss the future shape of any post-Taliban government. The Northern Alliance now say that they are holding the door open to collaborating with at least a part of the Taliban if they defect now. What the Northern Alliance resists however is pressure from Pakistan, which in turn is pressuring the US, to accept what Pakistani President Pervez Musharraf wants, which is a broad-based government "including moderate Taliban elements." Pakistan is of course terrified that a hostile Northern Alliance government will come to power in Kabul and take revenge on Pakistan for supporting the Taliban.

When, on October 16, Dr. Abdullah Abdullah, the urbane Northern Alliance foreign minister, came to Khoja Bahaudin he said there was no such thing as a "moderate Taliban element," adding: "Their objective is terrorism and fanaticism so who could expect us to join such a government with such people? This is against the objective of the international alliance against terrorism." But Dr. Abdullah accepted that a future government did have to have a broader base than the Northern Alliance, which is code for saying that it did need to include some significant Pashtun representation.

Another senior leader in northern Afghanistan is General Atiqullah Baryolai, the deputy minister of defense. He says the "original" Taliban, that is to say Mullah Omar and his cronies, can have no say in the future of the country because they are nothing but Pakistani agents. "They brought foreigners here to kill Afghans. They educated boys of thirteen or fifteen in Pakistan to destroy our history, our museums and our archives." Like the Afghan intellectual I met, General Baryolai believes that there are many who became Taliban for opportunistic reasons and, especially if they defect now, they should be able to participate in decisions on how the country should be run. Of course it is difficult to divine what will happen from Khoja Bahaudin, but it is possible that the UN will be drawn into a diplomatic process by which it would oversee a transitional phase in Afghanistan just as it did in Cambodia. The UN, which has its own special representative for Afghanistan, has formed a task force to consider this and other possibilities, but it is too early to say whether foreign governments would commit troops to bolster any such operation.

The Afghan intellectual told me he was "quite optimistic" about the prospects of the Northern Alliance leaders. As for the slaughter they committed when they were in Kabul, which leaves their popularity in doubt, he said: "I think now they understand very well. If there is no cooperation [with Pashtuns and other groups] they will lose everything."

I saw Dr. Syed Kamil Ibrahim, who is the acting minister of health. He told me: "Our aim is an Islamic democracy. It is freedom for the Islamic religion, but not by force. Yes, we will have Sharia [Islamic] law but not like the Taliban. Women will have rights to study and work. They will be equal." This was echoed by Dr. Abdullah, who claimed that women would have a say in determining the future of the country.

Here in the north of Afghanistan, however, women are not equal. They have no part in decision-making. But girls go to school and they can work. In this deeply conservative society you rarely see women outside their homes and when you do they are veiled. In the camp of Lalla Guzar, which houses ten thousand refugees from Taliban-controlled territory, I visited a new school, which was built by a French aid group called ACTED and funded by the Turkish government. It has space for less than half of the children in the camp, but it is a start. Boys go to school in the morning, girls in the afternoon. When I went I saw four classrooms full of eager girls chanting the alphabet, doing arithmetic, and having a religion class. I asked them what they wanted to be when they grew up and almost all of them said they wanted to be either a teacher or a doctor, the only jobs they ever see women doing. They also knew that in Taliban-held territory girls are banned from school and women not allowed to work. Lalimoh, aged twelve, said that girls were being prevented from going to school in Taliban-held areas because the Taliban "are not educated and that is why they don't allow schools."

I wanted to ask if anyone wanted to become an astronaut but the director of the school said that this was absurd since "they don't know what an astronaut is." In this land without electricity there is no television either. Everyone lives in tents or mud huts, yet despite their tough life these refugee girls were full of energy and smiles. Bucking the trend among her schoolmates, Zokira, aged ten, said: "If I try, I will become a minister!"—she meant in a future government. Such are the glimmers of hope in northern Afghanistan.

—November 15, 2001

21

The Suicide Bombers
Avishai Margalit

Palestinians were not the first people to engage in suicidal violence. There have always been individuals deranged enough to do so. Suicide bombing has been used as a military tactic before, and as a form of political terrorism too. Palestinian suicide bombers began to adopt this method of killing about two decades ago.

One way to read suicide bombing is as a sign of weakness, a last resort of a desperate people with no other means to inflict damage on a detested and more powerful enemy; propaganda by acts of spectacular violence. And yet, there have been many desperate people who never resorted to suicidal murder.

One of the horrors of suicide bombing is the sense of total helplessness it inflicts on the citizens at large. The bomber looks like you or me and can strike at random. Fear for one's own life, the normal human brake on public killing, is no longer operational. Not only has the suicide bomber lost his or her fear to die, but death is actively desired. More perhaps than the wish for vengeance, or the fanaticism of religious faith, it is this love of death that is makes suicide bombers into such a terrifying weapon.

—*I.B.*

389

IN ITS OFFICIAL count of the number of "hostile terrorist attacks," the Israeli government includes any kind of attack, from planting bombs to throwing stones. By this count suicide bombings make up only half a percent of the attacks by Palestinians against Israelis since the beginning of the second intifada in September 2000. But this tiny percentage accounts for more than half the total number of Israelis killed since then. In the minds of Israelis, suicide bombing colors everything else.

According to B'tselem, the Israeli Information Center for Human Rights in the Occupied Territories, the number of Israelis killed by Palestinians between September 29, 2000, and November 30, 2002, is 640. Of those, 440 are civilians, including 82 under the age of eighteen. Some 335 were killed inside Israel proper, the rest in the West Bank and the Gaza Strip. The Palestinians also killed 27 foreign citizens during this period. The number of Palestinians who were killed by Israelis between September 29, 2000, and November 2002 was 1,597, 300 of them minors. Since March there have been no accurate numbers for the occupied territories; B'tselem estimates that during Sharon's operation "Defensive Shield" in March and April 2002, some 130 Palestinians were killed in Jenin and Nablus alone.

From the signing of the Oslo agreements in 1993 until the beginning of August 2002 we know of 198 suicide bombing missions, of which 136 ended with the attackers blowing up others along with themselves. This year has seen by far the greatest concentration of the attacks, about one hundred by the end of November.

In other attacks by Palestinians—called "no-escape" attacks—the chances of staying alive after, say, firing on an army position or a settlement are next to zero. Over forty settlers were killed by such attacks this year. The no-escape fighters strike mainly targets in the occupied territories; the suicide bombers are most likely to attack targets inside Israel's pre-1967 borders. In the willingness to sacrifice their own lives there is very little difference between the suicide bombers and the no-escape attackers. But the impression a suicide bombing leaves on Israelis is very different from a no-escape attack. The suicide bombers make most Israelis feel not just ordinary fear but an intense mixture of horror and revulsion as well.

* * *

In this conflict practically every statement one makes is bound to be contested, including the description of the attackers as suicide bombers and the victims as civilians. Islamic law explicitly prohibits suicide and the killing of innocents. Muslims are consequently extremely reluctant to refer to the human bombers as suicide bombers. They refer to them instead as *shuhada* (in singular: *shahid*), or martyrs. Palestinians are also reluctant to use the expression "Israeli civilians," which implies that they are innocent victims. Even if they are Israeli dissidents they are not regarded as such. In a recent attack by Hamas at the campus of the Hebrew University of Jerusalem, one of the victims, Dafna Spruch, had been active in one of the most fearless peace protest groups in Israel, Women in Black. Hamas dealt with this simply by claiming that she belonged to Women in Green, a ferocious anti-Palestinian right-wing organization. As such, she was not innocent.

Spokesmen for Hamas justify the killing of civilians by saying it is a necessary act of defense—the only weapon they have to protect Palestinian women and children. "If we should not use" suicide bombing, the Hamas leaders announced this November, "we shall be back in the situation of the first week of the Intifada when the Israelis killed us with impunity."

A report by Amnesty International in July 2002 summarizes the arguments cited by the Palestinians as reasons for targeting civilians. The Palestinians claim that they are engaged in a war against an occupying power and that religion and international law permit the use of any means in resistance to occupation; that they are retaliating against Israel killing members of armed groups and Palestinians generally; that striking at civilians is the only way they can make an impact upon a powerful adversary; that Israelis generally or settlers in particular are not civilians.[1]

The report finds these reasons unacceptable. It considers Israeli violations of human rights so grave that many of them "meet the definition of crimes against humanity under international law." But it also concludes, "The deliberate killing of Israeli civilians by Palestinian armed groups amounts to crimes against humanity."

* * *

Throughout the twentieth century the nineteenth-century taboo on targeting and killing civilians has been eroding. In World War I only 5 percent of the casualties were civilians. In World War II the figure went up to 50 percent and in the Vietnam War it was 90 percent. Amnesty International is making an admirable effort to restore the prohibition against targeting and killing civilians. Its report, rightly, does not make any moral distinction between those who kill themselves while killing civilians and those who spare themselves while killing.

My concern with the suicide bombers here is to understand what they do and why they do it and with what political consequences. To put the matter briefly, it is clear that there will be no peace between Israel and Palestine if suicide bombings continue. It is not clear that there will be peace if they stop, but there would at least be a chance for peace.

I.

In the Middle East, suicide bombing was first used by the Hezbollah

---

[1]. *Without Distinction: Attacks on Civilians by Palestinian Armed Groups* (Amnesty International, July 2002).

in Lebanon. From November 1982, when a suicide bomber destroyed a building in Tyre, killing seventy-six Israeli security personnel, through 1999, the year the Israelis withdrew from Lebanon, the Hezbollah carried out fifty-one suicide attacks. In October 1983 it took only two suicide explosions—one killing 241 American servicemen, mostly Marines, and the other killing 58 French paratroopers—to force the Americans and the French out of Lebanon. It wasn't until ten years later that the first Palestinian suicide bombing took place.

In other parts of the world, soldiers of one army—the Japanese kamikaze, or the Iranian basaji—have been willing to commit suicide in bombing another army. Some of the Tamil Black Tigers of Sri Lanka have killed themselves in attacks on politicians and army installations, and they have done so with utter disregard for the lives of civilians who happened to be around. But the Palestinian case is the only one in which civilians of one society regularly volunteer to become suicide bombers who target civilians of another society. They may be chosen by Hamas or Islamic Jihad to carry out a suicide bombing mission, but for the most part the volunteers have not been active members of these organizations.

We can see how the practice of suicide bombing evolved. The Palestinians started using suicide bombers as a weapon not to emulate the Hezbollah strategy in Lebanon but in reaction to a specific event. According to *Ha'aretz*'s Daniel Rubinstein, the most authoritative Israeli commentator on the Palestinians, the bombing began with the so-called "war of the knives." On October 8, 1990, hundreds of worshipers came out of the al-Aqsa mosque throwing stones at the Israeli police and at the Jewish worshipers praying by the Wailing Wall nearby. The Israeli police reacted by firing on them. Eighteen Palestinians were killed by Israelis in the clashes that day (in comparison, four were killed in the skirmishes that started the current intifada). Hamas called for jihad, or holy war, but no organized response followed.

However some Palestinians tried to seek revenge on their own. The first, Omar abu Sirhan, came with a butcher's knife to my neighborhood in Jerusalem and slaughtered three people. He later said he had little hope of surviving his self-appointed mission. After he was caught, he said he saw the Prophet in his dream and was ordered by him to avenge those who were killed in the al-Aqsa mosque. Hamas immediately adopted abu Sirhan as a hero. It sensed the potential of such avenging attacks and soon transformed that potential into organized human bombers.

* * *

The one thing that Palestinian suicide bombers have in common is that they are all Muslims. No Christians have been involved. Hamas and Islamic Jihad, for their part, say that suicide bombing is a religious duty and these two Islamic organizations for years monopolized the bombings. They would have nothing to do with Christians and they have long been hostile to the Palestinian nationalists of Arafat's Fatah movement. But the monopoly ended once the nationalists of the al-Aqsa Martyrs Brigade, which is affiliated with Fatah, joined in. It is unclear whether those who act under the auspices of the al-Aqsa Brigade, who have in the past emphasized nationalism, not Islam, as central to their movement, would now also regard their missions as religious acts of martyrdom.

In the account of the struggle against Israel given by political Islamists there are two elements. One is the holy war, jihad, which suicide bombers consider not just a war against the oppressive occupation of Palestinian land but one fought in defense of Islam itself. The other element is martyrdom: those who sacrifice themselves in the holy war are martyrs. From the many statements by the suicide bombers themselves, it is the idea of the martyr, the *shahid*, rather than the idea of the jihad that seems to capture the imagination of the suicide bombers. The idea of the jihad may give the struggle an Islamic content; but the idea of the *shahid* seems more powerful.

While the language used by the bombers and their organizations is always distinctly Islamic, the motives of the bombers are much more complicated, and some mention more than one motive for their act. Mahmoud Ahmed Marmash, a twenty-one-year-old bachelor from Tulkarm, blew himself up in Netanya, near Tel Aviv, in May 2001. On a videocassette recorded before he was sent on his mission, he said:

> I want to avenge the blood of the Palestinians, especially the blood of the women, of the elderly, and of the children, and in particular the blood of the baby girl Iman Hejjo, whose death shook me to the core.... I devote my humble deed to the Islamic believers who admire the martyrs and who work for them.

In a letter he left for his family he wrote, "God's justice will prevail only in jihad and in blood and in corpses." Such references to jihad are not as common as references to revenge. Having talked to many Israelis and Palestinians who know something about the bombers, and having read and watched many of the bombers' statements, my distinct impression is that the main motive of many of the suicide bombers is revenge for acts committed by Israelis, a revenge that will be known and celebrated in the Islamic world.

Most of the suicide bombers say as much themselves, but it is impossible to generalize about them. At first, when Hamas and its military branch, the Izz al-Din al-Qasam Brigade, and the Palestinian Islamic Jihad took responsibility for sending virtually all of the suicide bombers, the bombers were young unmarried males. But since December of last year, when the al-Aqsa Martyrs Brigade joined in, the bombers have included both men and women, villagers and townspeople, bachelors and married people. The bombers are young and not so young, educated and not educated, from poor families and from relatively well-off ones. Still, most of the bombers are young unmarried men, between seventeen and twenty-eight, and more than half of them come from refugee camps, where the hatred of Israel is strongest. From the accounts of them in the press and the statements by those who know them, the suicide bombers are not what psychologists call suicidal types—they are not depressed, impulsive, lonely, and helpless, with a continuous history of being in situations of personal difficulty. Nor do they seem driven by economic despair. A study conducted by the Israeli army analyzing the background of eight bombers from the Gaza strip showed that they were relatively well-off.[2] I have never seen a public or private statement by a suicide bomber that mentions his own economic situation or that of the Palestinians generally as a reason for his action.

* * *

It is often said that the bombers are driven by their own feelings of hopelessness and despair about the situation of the Palestinians; but this seems open to question. It is true that the Palestinian community is in a state of despair, but this does not mean that each and every person, in his or her personal life, is in despair—any more than the fact that the US is relatively rich makes each American rich. The despair in communities explains the support for the suicide bombers, but it does not explain each person's choice to commit suicide by means of a bomb.

Hussein al-Tawil is a member of the People's Party, formerly the Communist Party, in the West Bank. His son Dia blew himself up in Jerusalem, in March 2001, on a Hamas mission. Amira Hass, an Is-

---

2. Amos Harel, *Ha'aretz*, January 22, 2002.

raeli journalist for *Ha'aretz* who has intimate knowledge of life in the occupied territories, talked to friends of the father, former Communists, and some of the son's friends, who are members of the Hamas group at Beir-Zeit University. The two groups of friends don't mix. The father's friends claim that Dia was "brainwashed" by Hamas, causing great pain to a father who loved him and did what he could to send his son to the university to study engineering. For Dia's friends from Hamas, who chanted at his funeral, on the other hand, he is a heroic martyr to the Islamic cause.

Their reaction resembles that of Raania, the pregnant wife of the Hamas militant Ali Julani and a mother of three. Her husband took part in a no-escape attack in Tel Aviv. "I am very proud of him. I am even prouder for my children, whose father was a hero. I want to tell the Israelis that I support my husband and I support people like him." Was she angry with him for leaving his children fatherless? "He left us in the mercy of God. He was raised as an orphan and the way he was raised so his children will be raised."[3] A man named Hassan, whose son blew himself up in a Tel Aviv discotheque, had a similar reaction: "I am very happy and proud of what my son did and I hope all the men of Palestine and Jordan will do the same."[4]

Most families seem to be similarly proud of their kin who become *shuhada*. According to a verse in the Koran that is quoted often by the *shahid*'s family and friends, the *shahid* does not die. From a religious point of view, a crucial element in being a *shahid* is purity of motive (*niyya*), doing God's will rather than acting out of self-interest. Acting because of one's personal plight or to achieve glory are not pure motives. Most of the families of the *shuhada* accordingly want to present their suicides in the best possible light. To honor and admire the family

---

3. Gideon Levy, *Ha'aretz*, August 17, 2001.
4. *Ha'aretz*, June 4, 2001.

of a *shahid* is a religious obligation and the family's status is thus elevated among religious and traditionalist Palestinians. In addition families of *shuhada* receive substantial financial rewards, mainly from Gulf countries and especially from Saudi Arabia, but also from a special fund created by Saddam Hussein. So far as I know, no one who has followed the history of the *shuhada* closely believes that money is what makes their families support them, although it helps.

2.

According to statements by Hamas and Islamic Jihad, the suicide bomber is willing to die as an act of ultimate devotion in a "defensive" holy war. There are two senses of jihad: a holy war to spread Islam, and a defensive holy war that takes place when what is perceived as the domain of Islam is threatened by invaders. From a radical Islamic point of view, Israel itself, as a Jewish state, is an invasion of the domain of Islam. Worse, according to the platform of Hamas, Israel is a state composed of heretics established on land that has been divinely granted to Islam (*waqf*). Battling Israel is one of the most urgent tasks of the defensive *jihad*. It is a duty that should be undertaken by any Muslim, man or woman, and it overrides any other obligation. The idea of defensive *jihad* can easily be understood as carrying out the national goal of "freeing the land" from the presence of the invaders.

In October, Iyaat al-Haras, a high school student from Bethlehem, explained on a videocassette that her suicide mission was an act in defense of both the mosque of al-Aqsa and of Palestine. This message can be interpreted both in national and in religious terms. Judging solely from her video it is hard to tell whether religion or nationalism is the stronger motive. But since she was dispatched by the nationalist group associated with Fatah, and since the organization would have taken part in formulating her statement, we can surmise that the message was deliberately ambiguous. Whether suicide bombers act for national or for religious reasons or from different mixtures of both is often difficult to tell. The predominantly nationalist and predominantly religious groups are eager to keep it that way, both for the sake of Palestinian unity and because each camp is trying to gain popularity within a community that is made up of both Islamists and nationalists.

As I have said, the main motivating force for the suicide bombers seems to be the desire for spectacular revenge; what is important as well is the knowledge that the revenge will be recognized and celebrated by the community to which the suicide bomber belongs. In many cases the bombers say they are taking revenge for the death of someone quite close to them, a member of their family or a friend. In May 2002, Jihad Titi, a young man in his twenties from the refugee camp of Balata near Nablus, collected the shrapnel of the shell that killed his cousin, a Fatah commander in the camp whom the Israeli army had targeted and killed. Titi stuffed the shrapnel pieces into the containers of TNT he carried and killed an elderly woman and her granddaughter while blowing himself up. In the early morning of November 27, 2001, Tyseer al-Ajrami, a man in his twenties, blew himself up, killing an Israeli policeman in a building used as a gathering place for Palestinian workers. Ajrami was from the Gabalia refugee camp in the Gaza Strip, married and a father of three. In his will he explained his deed as, among other things, a retaliation for the killing of five children in Khan Yunis the week before.

It is in fact a common practice among the bombers to mention a very specific event or incident for which they take revenge. Darin abu-Isa, a student of English literature who blew herself up in March 2002, lost her husband and her brother in the current intifada; her family says that she did it to avenge their deaths.

The bombers seek vengeance not just by killing Jews, but by

instilling fear in them as well. Anwar Aziz, who later blew himself up in an ambulance in Gaza in 1993, said: "Battles for Islam are won not through the gun but by striking fear into the enemy's heart." The writer Nasra Hassan, a Muslim from Pakistan, was told by a dispatcher that spreading fear is as important as killing. But the urge for revenge in itself does not explain why people become suicide bombers. After all there are other, more conventional, ways of taking revenge without taking one's own life. Vengeance through suicide bombing has, as I understand it, an additional value: that of making yourself the victim of your own act, and thereby putting your tormentors to moral shame. The idea of the suicide bombing, unlike that of an ordinary attack, is, perversely, a moral idea in which the killers, in acting out the drama of being the ultimate victim, claim for their cause the moral high ground.

* * *

In preparing the *shuhada* for their mission, the idea of winning an instant place in paradise used to have a major part. In a remarkable account, Nasra Hassan talked to a member of Hamas who described to her how people are given instructions on how to act as a *shahid*: "We focus his attention on Paradise, on being in the presence of Allah, on meeting the Prophet Muhammad, on interceding for his loved ones so that they, too, can be saved from the agonies of Hell, on the *houris*"—i.e., the heavenly virgins. When she talked to a volunteer who was ready to carry out his mission, but for some reason stopped, he told her about the sense of the immediacy of paradise: "It is very, very near—right in front of our eyes. It lies beneath the thumb. On the other side of the detonator."[5]

In the current intifada, the time spent in instructing volunteers has apparently become much shorter than in the past. Tabet Mardawi, a

---

5. "An Arsenal of Believers," *The New Yorker*, November 19, 2001.

dispatcher for Hamas, says that there is never a lack of volunteers now. "We do not have to talk to them about virgins waiting in paradise."[6] Talking of the promise of paradise, a skeptical young man in Gaza said to Amira Hass, "If it were true, why is it that the experts and the leaders of the Islamic movements are not all running out to be killed themselves and are not sending their own children on these missions?" But I do not necessarily see the dispatchers as manipulative cynics who dupe confused youngsters into believing something that they themselves do not quite believe. Whatever their Islamic belief or suspension of disbelief, they seem to have too many other motives for acting as they do against the Israelis, whom they perceive as the hated conquerors of the land.

If it is easy to question whether being a *shahid* secures an immediate entrance to paradise, no one can doubt that being a *shahid* secures instant fame, spread by television stations like the Qatar-based al-Jazeera and the Lebanon-based al-Manar, which are watched throughout the Arab world. Once a suicide bomber has completed his mission he at once becomes a phantom celebrity. Visitors to the occupied territories have been struck by how well the names of the suicide bombers are known, even to small children.

Before the bombers are sent on their mission, all the dispatching organizations make videotapes in which the would-be *shuhada* read a statement describing their reasons for sacrificing their lives. They do this while wearing the organization's distinctive headcovering and often with something in the background identifying the organization—for example, a picture of the al-Aqsa mosque, a copy of the Koran, and sometimes a Kalashnikov. The video may be conducted as an interview, with a masked member of the dispatching organization asking questions. We are told in some published accounts that

---

6. *Ha'aretz*, April 23, 2002.

before setting off, the volunteers watch their video again and again, as well as videos of previous *shuhada*. "These videos encourage him to confront death, not to fear it," one dispatcher told Nasra Hassan. "He becomes intimately familiar with what he is about to do. Then he can greet death like an old friend."

On the day of the mission the video is sent to television stations to be broadcast as soon as the organization takes responsibility for the bombing. Posters and even calendars are distributed, with pictures of the "martyr of the month." The *shahid* is often surrounded by green birds, which are an allusion to a saying by Muhammad, that the martyr is carried to Allah by green birds.

* * *

While resentment of the extreme economic misery in which Palestinians live, especially in Gaza, partly explains the support for suicide bombing among the Palestinian population, suicide bombings have only further devastated the Palestinian economy. Some 120,000 Palestinian workers, over 40 percent of the Palestinian work force, were employed in Israel in 1993. The suicide bombings of 1995 and 1996 then led to the decision of the government to close off the territories and drastically reduce the numbers of Palestinians working in Israel. Many of them were eventually replaced by foreign workers from Thailand, Romania, and various African and other countries. By 2000 the Palestinian workers were back at work in Israel, many of them as illegal workers. Their number is estimated to have reached about 130,000, which by then was a lower percentage of the Palestinian work force than it was in 1993.

The second intifada, and especially the recent wave of suicide bombings, once again reduced drastically the number of workers from the territories. It also stopped the flow of goods and services to and from Israel, the only serious market for Palestinian exports. The result has been devastating for the Palestinian economy. The Palestinian Authority, which subsists on donations from abroad, is the only remaining employer to speak of.

Although there is much talk about the corruption within the Authority, I doubt that it is more corrupt than many post-Communist or third-world countries. But in trying to create an economy that could lay the foundations for Palestinian independence, the Authority has failed miserably. The Palestinians are almost completely dependent on Israel, not only for jobs but for the only large market for their produce. Moreover, in a desperate response to the suicide bombings, Israel is now erecting a fence separating Israel proper from the occupied territories. This will likely leave the Palestinian economy crippled beyond repair since a large proportion of Palestinian workers will be cut off from any jobs.

Both Hamas and Islamic Jihad want to convey the message that Islam has been divinely endowed with the entire land of Palestine, which includes all of Israel, and that this sacred endowment is not subject to negotiation. Sending suicide bombers into Israel proper rather than confining them to the occupied territories gives a clear signal that the two Islamic organizations do not accept the distinction between the pre-1967 land of Israel and the land that was conquered by Israel in 1967. All of it belongs to the Palestinians. Arafat's Fatah accepted the distinction in 1988, and it was subsequently incorporated in the Oslo agreements of 1993. Once the Fatah organization, which had since its inception been a secular, national movement, joined forces with the Islamists at the end of 2001 in sending suicide bombers into Israel proper, the question arose whether its leaders had begun to share the message of erasing the distinction between the pre-1967 land and the land conquered in the 1967 war.

The Palestinian mantra "end to the occupation" has thus become equivocal about what is under occupation. According to the interpretation of Hamas and other Islamic groups, the entire state of Israel is essentially an occupation and Israel should therefore be annihilated. Thus, while many Palestinians would probably welcome a separate state of their own, the religious belief in jihad may have prepared the way for some nationalists, and especially for militants who are not politically minded, to subscribe to the belief that all of Palestine is under occupation; hence an end to the occupation means the end of Israel.

* * *

A major question concerning the dispatchers of the suicide bombers is where they stand in their own organization and who gives them orders, particularly the dispatchers who belong to the two organizations associated with Arafat, the al-Aqsa Martyrs Brigade and the Tanzim. If leaders, especially Arafat, decide that suicide missions must stop, will the dispatchers obey them?

In December 2001, Arafat delivered a speech in which he called for the terror to stop. He had done this several times before, but always with what seemed a wink. On that occasion, he seemed serious. In the aftermath of September 11, Arafat, according to many reports, was desperate not to repeat his mistake of the Gulf War, when he sided with Saddam Hussein. When Colin Powell called for the future establishment of a Palestinian state, his speech was seen as an achievement for Arafat, at least among his followers. I have heard from well-informed Palestinian and Israeli sources that Arafat's loyalists believed that Arafat wanted in December last year to regain control and to stop the suicide bombings. People close to Arafat also believed that this was clear to the Americans and to the Israelis.

Three weeks of calm followed. Then Sharon ordered the "targeted killing" of Arafat's popular lieutenant, Raad Karmi, and Palestinian protests erupted throughout Israel and Gaza. Arafat's activists became convinced that there was no way that they could reach even a limited understanding with Sharon; the only way to fight was to adopt Hamas's tactic of using suicide bombers. It was at that point, my Palestinian sources told me, that Arafat's people joined in the deadly game of dispatching suicide bombers into Israel proper. Arafat himself, they say, most likely went along with his activists so as not to lose his control over the Palestinian Authority. At the same time it seems likely that he lost control over the al-Aqsa Brigades. In its recent report, Human Rights Watch blames the Palestinian Authority for not acting to stop the terror strikes when it could—that is, before its security apparatus was destroyed by Israel in 2002.[7]

The suicide bombing got out of control—so much so that even Hamas became worried. There was outrage among Palestinians when Hamas started sending children on no-escape missions in the Gaza Strip. "I am going to be a *shahid*," said fourteen-year-old Ismail abu Nida to his mother. She did not take him seriously but the child meant what he said and he was killed while taking part in an attack. The same happened to Yussuf Zakoot, fourteen, and Anwar Hamduna, thirteen. Hamas sensed, however, that the families were angry and, according to reports in the Palestinian press, it changed its recruiting tactics.

There was also a debate in 2002 between Sheikh Tantawi, a Cairo mullah whom most Palestinians consider the highest religious authority, and Sheikh Yassin, the spiritual and political founder and leader of Hamas. Sheikh Tantawi publically raised the issue of women suicide bombers after Arafat's organization first began using them. He endorsed the participation of women in the suicide missions, saying that for the purpose of becoming *shuhada* they are, if

---

7. *Erased in a Moment: Suicide Bombing Attacks Against Israeli Civilians* (Human Rights Watch, October 2002).

their mission required it, allowed to disregard their roles as wives and mothers, not to mention to disregard the code of modesty. Sheikh Yassin did not contradict him on religious grounds, but he claimed that there was no need for women since there was already a surplus of male volunteers. The Palestinians I talked to said that they believed Yassin was worried not just that Hamas would lose its near monopoly of control over suicide bombing once the Fatah movement joined in; he also feared that suicide bombing would get out of hand and no longer serve a clear political purpose. So maintaining control over the people who actually dispatch the suicide bombers is a concern not just of Arafat but of Hamas as well.

* * *

If revenge is the principal goal, the suicide bombers have succeeded in hurting Israel very badly, and not just by killing and injuring many civilians. A more far-reaching success is that Israel's leaders, in retaliating, have behaved so harshly, putting three million people under siege, with recurring curfews for unlimited periods of time, all in front of the world press and television, with the result that Israel may now be the most hated country in the world. This is hugely damaging to Israel, since the difference between being hated and losing legitimacy is dangerously narrow. Throughout the world, moreover, the suicide bombings have often been taken more as a sign of the desperation of the Palestinians than as acts of terror.

Israel claims it is fighting a war against the "infrastructure of terrorism," but in fact it is destroying the infrastructure of the entire Palestinian society, not only its security forces and civil administration but much else as well. Many of the Israeli countermeasures are not only cruel but also irrational. As Ian Buruma recently reported in these pages, at the height of the olive-picking season, Israeli settlers have prevented Palestinian villagers from tending their own olive trees, fully aware that producing olive oil is one of the major activities of the Palestinian economy, the main source of income for many Palestinian villagers, and a source of pride as well.[8] To make matters worse, settlers have not only been preventing the Palestinians from picking their olives but have been stealing them for themselves. This is simply one small example of a policy that is not just bad but also irrational.

Still, even when it is clear that Israeli policies toward the Palestinians are evil and irrational, it is far from clear how to confront the suicide bombers in ways that are rational and effective, as well as morally justified. This is why the moderate left is in trouble in Israel. The public is scared and in despair, and has no use for moralizing comments. It wants strategic solutions for stopping the suicide terror.

The members of the Israeli center-left, the only people who could secure for the Palestinians a state alongside Israel, used to believe in two propositions. First, the occupation since 1967 has been a moral and social disaster for Israel, let alone for the Palestinians, and it has to end. Second, if Israel withdrew to pre-1967 borders this would end the conflict. The second intifada convinced more and more Israelis, including many on the right, of the truth of the first proposition; the occupation cannot go on. On the other hand, the suicide bombers have convinced more and more Israelis, including many in the center-left, that the end of the occupation would mean neither an end to the conflict nor, more important, an end to the terror. In order to deal with an enemy organization you must assume that it cares about the lives of its own people. The suicide bombers convey to the Israelis the message that the resentment of the Palestinians, or at least of a good many of them, cannot be alleviated by Jews and that their demands cannot be met. This, at least, is the message that Hamas wants to send; but for a national movement like Fatah, if it still has national goals, it is suicidal to send such a message to Israelis.

---

8. "On the West Bank," *The New York Review*, December 5, 2002.

Israelis and Palestinians take it as a foregone conclusion that there will be a war against Iraq. What the Palestinians fear—as Arafat has said publicly—is that Israel might use the smokescreen and confusion of a war to force as many Palestinians as it can to leave the West Bank, perhaps for Jordan. This is not an irrational fear, especially since the Labor ministers are no longer in the government, and Sharon presides over an ultra-right-wing cabinet. Should Palestinians be seen celebrating Iraqi missile strikes on Israel, and should a particularly destructive suicide bombing occur roughly at the same time, Sharon, in my view, would be quite capable of taking the opportunity to expel masses of Palestinians. In the meantime, as long as the Palestinians keep fighting, especially by attacking civilians, Israel will make the lives of the Palestinians even more miserable than they are now. Over 100,000 Palestinians have already left for Jordan since the beginning of the second intifada. If many more are forced to leave, that would suit Sharon just fine.

—January 16, 2003

22

Delusions in Baghdad
Mark Danner

Operation Iraqi Freedom was launched in March 2003 with so much idealistic hyperbole: first there would be democracy in Iraq, then in the rest of the Middle East. One dictator after another would be shocked and awed into submission, and the American destiny to bring freedom to the world would be fullfilled to the adoring cheers of the liberated Arab peoples.

On May 1, 2003, President George W. Bush, standing tall on the deck of the USS Abraham Lincoln, assured the nation that the mission was accomplished.

However, stuff happens. The mission was far from accomplished. The dictator was gone, but millions of Iraqi civilians had to flee their homes, or were blown up by car bombs, by nervous US soldiers, or in revenge killings stirred up by tribal, religious, and political demagogues.

Mark Danner wrote his report in December 2003. The mission was not accomplished then. It still isn't.

—I.B.

I.

AUTUMN IN BAGHDAD is cloudy and gray. Trapped in rush-hour traffic one October morning, without warning my car bucked up and back, like a horse whose reins had been brutally pulled. For a jolting instant the explosion registered only as the absence of sound, a silent blow to the stomach; and then a beat later, as hearing returned, a faint tinkling chorus: the store windows, all along busy Karrada Street, trembling together in their sashes. They were tinkling still when over the rooftops to the right came the immense eruption of oily black smoke.

Such dark plumes have become the beacons, the lighthouses, of contemporary Baghdad, and we rushed to follow, bumping over the center divider, vaulting the curb, screeching through the honking chaos of Seventies-vintage American cars, trailing the blasting horns and screaming tires for two, three, four heart-pounding moments until, barely three blocks away, at one end of a pleasant residential square, behind a gaggle of blue-shirted Iraqi security men running in panic about the grass, shouting, waving their AK-47s, we came upon two towering conflagrations, rising perhaps a dozen feet in the air, and, perfectly outlined in the bright orange flames, like skeletons preserved in amber, the blackened frames of what moments before had been a van and a four-wheel drive.

Between the two great fires rose a smaller one, eight or nine feet high, enclosing a tangled mass of metal. Pushing past the Iraqis, who shouted angrily, gesturing with their guns, I ran forward, toward the flames: the heat was intense. I saw slabs of smashed wall, hunks of rubble, glass, and sand scattered about, and behind it all an immense curtain of black smoke obscuring everything: the building, part of the International Red Cross compound, that stood there, the wall that had guarded it, the remains of the people who, four minutes before, had lived and worked there.

* * *

"Terrorism," the US Army lieutenant colonel had told me ruefully the week before, "is Grand Theater," and, as a mustached security man yanked me roughly by the arm, spinning me away from the flames, I saw that behind me the front rows had quickly filled: photographers with their long lenses, khaki vests, and shoulder bags struggled to push their way through the Iraqi security men, who, growing angrier, shouted and cursed, pushing them back. Swinging their AK-47s, they managed to form a ragged perimeter against what was now a jostling, roiling crowd, while camera crews in the vanguard surged forward. Now a US Army Humvee appeared; four American soldiers leaped out and plunged into the crowd, assault rifles raised, and began to scream, in what I had come to recognize as a characteristic form of address, "GET. THE FUCK. BACK! GET. THE FUCK. BACK!" Very young men in tan camouflage fatigues, armed, red-faced, flustered; facing them, the men and women of the world press, Baghdad division, assembled in their hundreds in less than a quarter of an hour: in the front row, those who, like me, had had the dumb luck to be in the neighborhood; behind them network crews who had received a quick tip from an embassy contact or an Iraqi stringer, or had simply heard or felt the explosion and pounded their way up to the hotel roof, scanning the horizon anxiously, locating the black beacon, and racing off to cover the story—or, as Lieutenant Colonel George Krivo put it bitterly, to "*make* the story. Here, media is the total message: I now have an understanding of McLuhan you wouldn't believe. Kill twenty people here? In front of that lens it's killing twenty thousand."

Behind the flames and the dark smoke, amid the shattered walls and twisted metal, a dozen people lay dead, many of whom had been unlucky enough to find themselves passing the front of the

International Red Cross compound when, at half past eight in the morning, a man later claimed to be of Saudi nationality drove an ambulance with Red Cross markings up to the security checkpoint and detonated what must have been several thousand pounds of explosives, collapsing forty feet of the protective wall and sending a huge sandbag barrier cascading forward.[1] The Red Cross compound, with its security wall and sandbags and manned checkpoints, was a "hardened target"—as were, indeed, the three Baghdad police stations that, within the next forty-five minutes, suicide bombers struck, in the neighborhoods of al-Baya'a, al-Shaab, and al-Khadra.

In the rhetoric of security, all of these attacks failed dismally. "From what our indications are," Brigadier General Mark Hertling told Fox News that afternoon, "none of those bombers got close to the target." In the rhetoric of politics, however, the attacks were a brilliant coup de théâtre. In less than an hour, four men, by killing forty people, including one American soldier and twenty Iraqi police, had succeeded in dominating news coverage around the world, sending television crews rushing about Baghdad in pursuit of the latest plume of smoke and broadcasting the message, via television screens in a hundred countries, first and foremost the United States, that Baghdad, US official pronouncements notwithstanding, remained a war zone.

Within a week, as members of the Red Cross left Iraq and many of the few remaining international organizations followed close behind, the attackers had set in motion, at the "highest levels" of the Bush administration, a "reevaluation" of American policy. Within two weeks, even as President Bush went on vowing publicly that the United States "would not be intimidated," he abruptly recalled L.

---

1. For the Saudi claim, see Mohammad Bazzi, "Saudis Suspected in 2 Iraq Attacks," *Newsday*, November 11, 2003.

Paul Bremer, the American administrator in Iraq, who rushed back to Washington so hurriedly he left the prime minister of Poland, one of America's few major allies in Iraq, waiting forlornly for an appointment that never came.

After two days of intensive consultations, administration officials unveiled a new policy. They decided to discard what had been a carefully planned, multiyear process that would gradually transform the authoritarian Iraqi state into a democracy—seven clearly defined steps intended to allow democratic parties, practices, and institutions to take root, develop, and grow, eventually leading to a new constitution written and ratified by the Iraqi people and, finally, a nationwide election and handover of power from American administrators to the elected Iraqi politicians it produced. The administration put in its place a hastily improvised rush to "return power to the Iraqis." In practice, this meant that in seven months the United States would hand over sovereignty to unelected Iraqis (presumably those on the American-appointed Governing Council, many of them former exiles, who had been pressing for such a rapid granting of power since before the war). Elections and a constitution would come later.[2] Despite President Bush's fervent protestations to the contrary, this was clearly a dramatic change in his policy of "bringing democracy to Iraq"—and, by extension, of making Iraq the first step in what he recently described as his "forward strategy of democracy in the Middle East."

* * *

If victory in war is defined as accomplishing the political goals for which military means were originally brought to bear, then eight months after it invaded Iraq, the United States remains far from

---

2. See Susan Sachs, "US Is Set to Return Power to Iraqis as Early as June," *The New York Times*, November 15, 2003.

victory. If the political goal of the war in Iraq was to remove Saddam Hussein and his Baathist regime and establish in their place a stable, democratic government—then that goal, during the weeks I spent in Iraq in late October and early November, seemed to be growing ever more distant.

When I arrived in Baghdad, Iraqi insurgents were staging about fifteen attacks a day on American troops; by the time I left the number of daily attacks had more than doubled, to thirty-five a day. Though military leaders like General Ricardo Sanchez, the overall commander, have repeatedly denigrated the attacks on his troops as "strategically and operationally insignificant," those attacks led the CIA to conclude, in a report leaked in mid-November, that the "US-led drive to rebuild the country as a democracy could collapse unless corrective actions are taken immediately."[3] The United States fields by far the most powerful military in the world, spending more on defense than the rest of the world combined, and as I write a relative handful of lightly armed insurgents, numbering in the tens of thousands or perhaps less, using the classic techniques of guerrilla warfare and suicide terrorism, are well on the way toward defeating it.

"What we have here," Lieutenant Colonel William Darley told me, "is basically a constabulary action. I mean, this is pretty much the Old West here. Peacekeeping. Where are the regiment on regiment, division on division engagements? We've seen almost nothing above the squad level. Basically this is not a real war." I heard this view, in various versions, expressed by American military men all over Iraq, from staff officers to combat commanders to lieutenants on the ground. Most of these men I found deeply impressive: well

---

3. See Jonathan S. Landay, "CIA Has a Bleak Analysis of Iraq," *Philadelphia Inquirer*, November 12, 2003.

trained, well schooled, extremely competent. What joined them to-gether, as the war grew steadily worse for American forces, was an inability, or perhaps a reluctance, to recognize what was happening in Iraq *as a war.*

"There's a deep cultural bias in the United States that if a military doesn't resemble ours, it's no good," the military strategist George Freidman of the private intelligence company Stratfor told me. "We have the strongest conventional forces in the world. So no one fights us conventionally. They fight us asymmetrically."

In Iraq, asymmetric warfare has meant a combination of guerrilla attacks on US and other coalition forces and terrorist attacks on a variety of prominent nonmilitary targets, including hotels, embas-sies, and international organizations. Beginning late this spring, the guerrilla attacks were centered in Baghdad and the so-called "Sunni Triangle" north and west of the capital but, since mid-autumn, they have increasingly spread to the north and, more slowly, the south of the country. Since late summer, highly effective terrorist attacks, in-cluding suicide bombings, have grown steadily more audacious and sophisticated, particularly in their use of the international press to multiply their political effect. In responding to both lines of attack, US intelligence—the "center of gravity" in any guerrilla war—has seemed poor or nonexistent.

* * *

The guerrilla attacks have built on, and worsened, the American oc-cupation's unpopularity among many Iraqis, capitalizing on, among other things, the US military's failure to provide security during the early weeks of the occupation and the daily humiliations and occa-sional brutalities that come with the presence of an occupying army. The terrorist attacks have served to consolidate and then worsen the international isolation the Americans have labored under since the catastrophic diplomatic decisions that led up to the war and have succeeded in depriving the coalition of additional military forces and international help in rebuilding the country.

Terrorism is certainly—as the lieutenant colonel put it—Grand Theater. Or to put it a slightly different way, terrorism is a form of talk. To hear what is being said, one must look at the sequence of major bombings in Iraq over the last several months:

August 7, Jordanian Embassy: A suicide car bomber kills nineteen people.

August 19, United Nations Headquarters: A suicide truck bomber kills twenty-three, including the UN's chief envoy in Iraq.

September 22, UN Headquarters: A suicide car bomber kills two and wounds nineteen.

October 9, police station: A suicide car bomber kills ten.

October 12, Baghdad Hotel: A suicide car bomber kills eight and wounds thirty-two.

October 14, Turkish Embassy: A suicide car bomber kills two and wounds thirteen.

October 27, Red Cross Headquarters and four police stations: Car bombers kill about forty and wound two hundred.

November 12, Italian Carabinieri Headquarters, Nasiriya: A truck bomber kills thirty-one.

Behind these attacks—I list only the major ones—one can see a rather methodical intention to sever, one by one, with patience, care, and precision, the fragile lines that still tie the occupation authority to the rest of the world. Suicide bombers struck at the countries that supported the Americans in the war (Jordan), that support the occupation with troops (Italy) or professed a willingness to do so (Turkey). They struck at the heart of an "international community" that could, with increased involvement, help give the occupation both legitimacy (the United Nations) and material help in rebuilding the country (the Red Cross). Finally they repeatedly struck at Iraqis collaborating with occupation authorities, whether as members of the American-selected Governing Council (several of whom lived in the Baghdad Hotel) or as policemen trained and paid by Americans.

By striking at the Jordanians, the bombers helped to ensure that no Arab country will contribute troops to support the occupation. By striking at the Turks, they helped force them to withdraw their controversial offer to send soldiers. By striking at the United Nations and the Red Cross, they not only forced the members of those two critical institutions to flee the country but led most other nongovernmental organizations, who would have been central to supplying expertise and resources to rebuilding Iraq, to leave as well. And by striking at the homes of several members of the Governing Council (wounding one member and, in a separate incident, assassinating another), they forced those officials to join the Americans behind their isolating wall of security, further separating them from Iraqis and underlining their utter political reliance on the Americans.

"Signs and symbols," the Italian security officer said. "Terrorism is nothing but signs and symbols." He looked at the sandbags and barbed wire, the rows of concrete Jersey barriers and armed guards that surrounded his embassy. "None of this will matter," he told me. "If they want to hit us, they will, and though they won't get to the building, it will still be a victory because it will kill people and make news. Terror," he said, "is quite predictable." What, I asked, did the signs and symbols mean? He spoke matter-of-factly: that anyone who helps the Americans will be a target; that the Americans cannot protect their allies and provide security to Iraqis; that the disorder is growing and that deciding to work with the Americans, who in their isolation are looking like a less-than-dominant and in any event ephemeral presence, is not the most prudent of bets; that the war, whatever fine words President Bush may pronounce from his aircraft carrier, is not over. Terror, he said, has a logic of its own. Two weeks after we spoke a suicide bomber killed nineteen Italians at Nasiriya.

2.

Autumn in Baghdad is sunny and bright. Drive about the bustling city of tan, sun-dried brick and you will hear the noise of honking horns and see crowded markets, the streets overwhelmed by an enormous postwar expansion of traffic, the sidewalks cluttered with satellite disks and other new products flooding into the newly opened Iraqi market. During the last several months, however, a new city has taken root amid these busy streets and avenues, spreading rapidly as it superimposes itself over the old tan brick metropolis: a new grim city of concrete. It is constructed of twelve-foot-high gray concrete barriers, endless roadblocks manned by squads of men with Kalashnikovs, walls of enormous steel-reinforced bags of earth and rubble and mile upon mile of coiled razor wire, and studded here and there with tanks rooted behind sandbags and watchful soldiers in combat fatigues. This city has a vaguely postmodern, apocalyptic feel, "a bit of Belfast here, a bit of Cyprus there, here and there a sprinkling of West Bank," as one network cameraman put it to me.

Many streets, including several of the grand ceremonial avenues of Saddam's capital, are now entirely lined with raw concrete a dozen feet high, giving the driver the impression of advancing down a stone tube. Behind these walls entire chunks of Baghdad have effectively vanished, notably the great park and building complex that had housed Saddam's Republican Palace and now comprises the so-called Green Zone—a four-and-a-half-square-mile concrete bunker that has at its heart the headquarters of the Coalition Provisional Authority.

* * *

To enter the palace you must secure, first, an appointment—hard to get, and made immeasurably harder by the fact that most members of the CPA are difficult or impossible to reach by telephone—and then make your way down several hundred yards of sidewalk lined with razor wire. Your journey will be broken by three checkpoints, two military (concrete cordons, sandbags, machine guns) and one civilian. At two of these you present two identifications and submit to full body searches, standing with your legs parted and arms extended and staring straight ahead, in a ritual I found myself repeating, on a busy day in Baghdad, a dozen or more times. Finally, after securing an identification badge, you must wait for a military escort to drive you to the palace, where yet another series of checks and searches will be performed.

Inside Saddam's Republican Palace—his huge likeness in the central atrium is discreetly masked by a large blue cloth—you will find, amid the dark marble floors and sconces and chandeliers, a great many Americans striding purposefully about, some in uniform but many in casual civilian clothing: chinos, jeans, sport shirts. They look bright, crisp, self-assured, and extremely young; they look, in other words, like what they are: junior staffers from Washington, from the Capitol, the departments and various agencies and think tanks. After all the combat fatigues on the city streets ("During my two weeks here," an oil industry contractor told me, "I've not seen one American who wasn't in uniform"), it is a bit of a shock to find this great horde of young American civilians secreted in Saddam's marble-lined hideaway, now become Baghdad's own Emerald City.

I spoke to one young expert from the Governance Department at some length about the Americans' "seven-point plan" to install democracy in Iraq, which was then stalled at point three: writing the constitution. (To summarize very crudely, the Shia, the majority on the Governing Council and in the country, were insisting that the writers of the constitution be chosen in a nationwide election; the others, fearing the Shia's numerical dominance, were pushing for the writers to be "selected" under various methods. This deadlock over the constitution is a precise reflection of the larger "governance problem" in Iraq—beginning with Shia numerical dominance—that would need to be resolved if Iraq is ever to become a working democracy.) I found myself impressed with the young woman's knowledge and commitment. In general, the CPA members seem dedicated and well-meaning—they'd have to be, to come to Baghdad; they are also entirely isolated, traveling twice daily by military-driven bus within the bunkered compound from their places of work in the bunkered palace to their places of rest in the bunkered Rasheed Hotel.

Or rather they made that trip until October 26, when, just before six in the morning, a person or persons unknown towed a small blue two-wheeled trailer—to any observer (including, presumably, the soldier manning the checkpoint a couple hundred yards away), it looked like a generator, a common sight in electricity-starved Iraq—up to the park across from which the Rasheed stood resplendent behind its impressive concrete barriers, quickly opened the trailer's doors, turned it around, and directed it toward the hotel, and ran off, no doubt looking back to gaze in satisfaction a few moments later when a dozen or so converted French-made air-to-surface missiles whooshed out of their tubes and began peppering the rooms in which the Americans running the occupation slept, wounding seventeen people, killing one (a lieutenant colonel), and coming within a few yards of killing the visiting Paul L. Wolfowitz, United States deputy secretary of defense and mastermind of the Iraq war.

My friend in Governance was thrown from her bed and, finding her door jammed shut by the blast damage, and taking "one look at the smoke coming from under that jammed door and realizing if I didn't get out of there I was going to die," she climbed out on the ledge and crept along it, ten floors up, to the room next door and the smoke-filled, chaotic hallway beyond. The Rasheed was evacuated and many of its former occupants found themselves sleeping on quickly assembled cots in Saddam's palace. As for my friend's "seven-point plan," two weeks later President Bush decided to abandon it. Instead of confronting the problem that had blocked the writing of a new Iraqi constitution—the question of how the fact of Shia numerical dominance, and other unresolved conflicts in the Iraqi state, would be integrated into a functioning Iraqi democracy—the President, faced with mounting attacks from Iraqis opposed to the new political dispensation he had declared himself committed to create, decided to abandon the effort.

* * *

Security underlies everything in Iraq; it is the fault line running squarely beneath the occupation and the political world that will emerge from it. As I look back, perhaps my most frightening moment in the country came not at the Red Cross bombing, or at an ambush on the highway between Falluja and Ramadi where five civilians were killed, or at various other scenes of violence of one kind or another, but at a press conference the afternoon of the Rasheed attack, when General Martin E. Dempsey, the impressive commander of the First Infantry Division, characterized the rocket launcher—the cleverly disguised weapon that some unknown persons had used to pierce successfully the huge security perimeter around the Rasheed and thereby kill and wound, under the noses of tens of thousands of US soldiers, the Americans who were supposedly running Iraq, and nearly kill the deputy secretary of defense—as "not very sophisticated . . . a science project, made in a garage with a welder, a battery, and a handful of wire." What frightened me was the possibility that General Dempsey—a sophisticated man who no doubt had read the literature on counterinsurgency and knew well "the lessons" of the British in

Malaya and the French in Algeria and the Americans in Vietnam, but who, like almost every other impressive American commander in Iraq, had been trained to fight with, and against, large armored formations—was aware of the condescension evident in his tone.

"The idea behind these stay-behind insurgent groups is that they're *clandestine*, they use what's *available*—an old drainpipe, whatever," said a private security officer working for an American television network who, like many of the security professionals in Iraq, was a veteran of Britain's elite Special Air Service. "They don't need to be sophisticated, they need to be *effective*—and that device that hit the Rasheed was very effective." Raymond Bonner, a *New York Times* reporter, made a somewhat broader point: "The good news is it was a science project put together in a garage. The bad news is it was a science project put together in a garage."

Ten days later, when a colleague, a strong advocate of the United States' invasion, declared to me with some impatience, "The United States will not *lose*. The United States has *absolute military superiority in Iraq!*,"[4] I remembered Bonner's comment. In view of the progress of the war against the US coalition—the spreading activities of the opposition, the growing sophistication of their methods, the increasing numbers of Americans being killed—is the fact that the United States has "absolute military superiority" in Iraq good or bad news? All differences aside (and there are a great many differences), people commonly made the same point about Vietnam; but if it is true that "the United States had absolute military superiority in Vietnam," then what exactly do those words mean—and what do they tell us about those who utter them?

---

4. Christopher Hitchens made the comment, in a debate with me at the University of California at Berkeley on November 4. See "Has Bush Made Us Safer? Iraq, Terror and American Power," at webcast.berkeley.edu/events /archive.html.

3.

Fall in Falluja is dusty and bright. Here, on an average day in late October, insurgents attacked American soldiers eight times, twice the rate of a month before, according to General Chuck Swannack, commander of the 82nd Airborne Division. The method of choice was IEDs—"improvised explosive devices," in military parlance— planted, presumably, by FRLs, or "former regime loyalists." On the road leading into town, just emerging from the cloverleaf off the main highway, I saw the aftermath of one such attack. Late that afternoon, as an American armored convoy rumbled up the highway into the city, someone set off what the general described as a very sophisticated device, three barrels of flammable material rigged to a triggering mechanism, using a remote-controlled trigger. As our squad was clearing the cloverleaf, the individuals set off the device, killed a paratrooper, and then some individuals directed fire at us with AK-47s from the houses.

General Swannack's men dismounted, returned fire, stormed the houses, and arrested several civilians, leading them roughly away in flex cuffs. It was a typical day in Falluja, with a typical score: one dead American soldier, two dead civilians, several civilians wounded, several arrested, with an indeterminate number of family members, neighbors, and friends of those killed, wounded, and arrested left furious at the Americans and nursing strong grievances, which tribal honor, an especially strong force in Falluja, now demanded they personally avenge—by killing more Americans. As for the handful of "individuals" who had set off the device and opened fire on the Americans, they managed—as they do in all but a few such ambushes—to get away clean.

As I write, 423 Americans have died in Iraq since the United States invaded in March and more than 2,300 have been wounded there, many grievously; and the rate at which Americans are being killed and wounded is increasing. But while these tolls are having a discernible effect on President Bush's popularity among Americans, the major goal of this kind of warfare is not only to kill and wound Americans but to increase Iraqi recruits, both active and passive, who will oppose the occupation; its major product, that is, is *political*. "The point," said General Swannack, "is to get the Americans to fire back and hopefully they'll get some Iraqi casualties out of that and they can publicize that."

After first estimating the guerrilla strength in and around Falluja at 20,000, the general revised his figure: "Probably about a thousand people out there really want to attack us and kill us and another nineteen thousand or so really really don't like us." Such estimates vary wildly around Iraq, depending on whom you ask. General Sanchez recently put the total number of the opposition nationwide at five thousand. Whatever the numbers, the guerrillas' main business is to make them grow, particularly the number of strong sympathizers; and all evidence suggests that thus far they are succeeding.

* * *

Saddam's Iraq was a national security state dominated by the interlocking intelligence services of the government and the elite security units of the army, all of it rooted in the enormous Baath Party, a highly elaborated structure that over a half-century spread and proliferated into every institution in the country and that originally grew from a complex network of conspiratorial cells of three to seven members. Saddam's elite Republican Guard numbered 80,000; his even more select Special Republican Guard numbered 16,000; his Fedayeen Saddam, a paramilitary force—in effect, Saddam's brownshirts—numbered 40,000. The Mukhabarat and the various intelligence services, of which there were perhaps a dozen, numbered thousands more. All of these men were highly trained, well armed, and tested for their political loyalty. Few of them died in the war.

In May, in an astonishing decision that still has not been adequately explained, American administrator L. Paul Bremer vastly increased the number of willing Iraqi foot soldiers by abruptly dissolving the regular Iraqi army, which had been established by King Faisal I in 1921, and thereby sent out into bitter shame and unemployment 350,000 of those young Iraqis who were well trained, well armed, and deeply angry at the Americans. Add to these a million or so tons of weapons and munitions of all sorts, including rockets and missiles, readily available in more than a hundred mostly unguarded arms depots around the country, as well as vast amounts of money stockpiled during thirty-five years in power (notably on March 18, when Saddam sent three tractor trailers to the Central Bank and relieved it of more than a billion dollars in cash), and you have the makings of a well-manned, well-funded insurgency.

During the months since the fall of Baghdad in April, that insurgency has grown and evolved. Its methods have moved from assassinations of isolated US soldiers, to attacks on convoys with small arms, to increasingly sophisticated and frequent ambushes of convoys with remote-controlled explosives and attacks on helicopters with rocket-propelled grenades and missiles. While there seems to be some regional coordination among groups, it is clear that the opposition is made up of many different organizations, some regionally based, some local; some are explicitly Saddamist, some more broadly Baathist, some Islamist, and some frankly anti-Saddam and nationalist. "I don't see a vision by these disparate groups of insurgents or partisans," said Ahmed S. Hashim, a professor at the Naval War College who has closely studied the opposition. "But at this stage they do not need one. They are making our stay uncomfortable, they have affected our calculus and are driving a wedge between us. What I know is the coalition is losing ground among Iraqis." Within and among these groupings a competitive politics now exists, an armed politics that will evolve and develop, depending on how successful they are in attacking the Americans and forcing them to adjust their policies and, eventually, to leave the country.

* * *

By now much evidence exists, including documents apparently prepared by Iraqi intelligence services, to suggest that this insurgency, at least in its broad outlines, was planned before the war and that the plan included looting, sabotage, and assassination of clerics.[5] Particularly damaging was the looting, in which government ministries and other public buildings, including museums, libraries, and universities, were thoroughly ransacked, down to the copper pipes and electrical wiring in the walls, and then burned, and the capital was given over to weeks of utter lawlessness while American soldiers stood by and watched. This was an enormously important political blow against the occupation, undermining any trust or faith Iraqis might have had in their new rulers and destroying any chance the occupiers had to establish their authority. Most of all, the looting created an overwhelming sense of insecurity and trepidation, a sense that the insurgents, with their bombings and attacks, have built on to convince many Iraqis that the Americans have not achieved full control and may well not stay long enough to attain it.

All of this is another way of saying that if security is the fault line running beneath political development in Iraq, then politics is the fault line running beneath security. By now the failures in planning and execution that have dogged the occupation—the lack of military police, the refusal to provide security in the capital, the dissolution of the Iraqi army—are well known.[6] All have originated in Washing-

---

5. See Michael Hirsh, Rod Nordland, and Mark Hosenball, "About-Face in Iraq," *Newsweek*, November 24, 2003; and Douglas Jehl, "Plan for Guerrilla Action May Have Predated War," *The New York Times*, November 15, 2003.
6. See Mark Fineman, Robin Wright, and Doyle McManus, "Preparing for War, Stumbling

ton, many born of struggles between the leading departments of government, principally the State Department, the CIA, and the Pentagon, which the White House has never managed to resolve. (The most obvious product of these struggles was the President's decision, barely two months before the invasion, to discard the year of occupation planning by the State Department and shift control to the Pentagon, which proved itself wholly unprepared to take on the task.)

In Iraq, after the Big Bang of the American invasion, a new political universe is slowly being born. Part of this Iraqi political universe is called the Governing Council, and it does its work behind the concrete barriers of the Green Zone. Another part works at the level of nascent local government throughout the country. Still another works in the mosques of the south and among the Shiite religious establishment known as the Hawza. And yet another part—now a rather large and powerful part—is armed and clandestine and is making increasingly sophisticated and effective use of guerrilla warfare and terrorism, hoping to force the Americans from the country and claim its share of power. The Americans seek to define the armed claimants as illegitimate—essentially, as not part of the recognized universe at all. But in order to enforce that definition—to confine the game to the actors they regard as legitimate—the Americans must prove themselves able to make use of their power, both military and political, more effectively.

As I write, on November 19, US military forces in Iraq are conducting Operation Iron Hammer, striking with warplanes and artillery bases thought to be occupied by Iraqi insurgents. American television broadcasts are filled with dramatic footage of huge explosions illuminating the night sky. In Tikrit, Saddam's political base

---

to Peace," *Los Angeles Times*, July 18, 2003; and David Rieff, "Blueprint for a Mess," *The New York Times Magazine*, November 2, 2003.

and a stronghold of the opposition, the Americans staged a military show of force, sending tanks and other armored vehicles rumbling through the main street. "They need to understand," Lieutenant Colonel Steve Russell told ABC News, "it's more than just Humvees we'll be using in these attacks."

The armed opposition in Iraq seems unlikely to be impressed. However many insurgents the Americans manage to kill in bombing runs and artillery barrages, the toll on civilians, in death and disruption, is also likely to be high, as will damage to the fragile sense of normalcy that Americans are struggling to achieve and the opposition forces are determined to destroy. Large-scale armored warfare looks and sounds impressive, inspiring overwhelming fear; but it is not discriminate, which makes it a blunt and ultimately self-defeating instrument to deploy against determined guerrillas. In general, the American military, the finest and most powerful in the world, is not organized and equipped to fight this war, and the part of it that is—the Special Forces—are almost entirely occupied in what seems a never-ending hunt for Saddam. For American leaders, and particularly President Bush, this has become the quest for the Holy Grail: finding Saddam will be an enormous political boon. For the American military, this quest has the feel of a traditional kind of war not wholly suited to what they find in Iraq. "We are a hierarchy and we like to fight hierarchies," says military strategist John Arquilla. "We think if we cut off the head we can end this."

Whatever the political rewards of finding Saddam, they will not likely include putting a definitive end to the insurgency in Iraq.[7] "The

---

7. See Ahmed S. Hashim, "The Sunni Insurgency in Iraq," *Middle East Institute Policy Brief*, August 15, 2003, who notes that the "elimination of Saddam and his dynasty may demoralize pro-regime insurgents but may actually embolden anti-regime and anti-US insurgents who may have held back in the past...because of the barely submerged fears that the regime could come back."

Americans need to get out of their tanks, get out from behind their sunglasses," a British military officer, a veteran of Northern Ireland told me. "They need to get on the ground where they can get to know people and encourage them to tell them where the bad guys are." As I write, operations on the ground seem to be moving in the opposite direction. In any event it is difficult to impress an opponent with a military advance plainly meant to cover a political retreat.

President Bush's audacious project in Iraq was always going to be difficult, perhaps impossible, but without political steadfastness and resilience, it had no chance to succeed. This autumn in Baghdad, a ruthless insurgency, growing but still in its infancy, has managed to make the President retreat from his project, and has worked, with growing success, to divide Iraqis from the Americans who claim to govern them. These insurgents cannot win, but by seizing on Washington's mistakes and working relentlessly to widen the fault lines in occupied Iraq, they threaten to prevent what President Bush sent the US military to achieve: a stable, democratic, and peaceful Iraq, at the heart of a stable and democratic Middle East.

—December 18, 2003

23

Left Out in Turkey

Christopher de Bellaigue

The first decade of the twenty-first century was the time when ghosts of the old Ottoman Empire began to stir once more. The empire was not exactly reconstituted; Cairo and Damascus are not ruled from Istanbul. But there is much leftover business, some of it historical: the Armenian genocide; and some very current: the Kurdish question.

The ghosts were stirring just as, the secularist state, established in the 1920s by Mustafa Kemal Atatürk, was beginning to be challenged by a new wave of religious populism led by Prime Minister Erdogan. Ethnic and religious differences could no longer be ignored or suppressed. It was no longer possible to silence the unhealed grievances of history. Atatürk and his successors had frozen their vision of Turkey, secular, monoethnic, into place. Now the ice is beginning to melt.

—*I.B.*

I.

"IN TURKEY WE have no minorities," the leading official in a poor district in one of the poorest provinces of eastern Turkey told me in April. The official was in his late twenties; he had studied public administration at a Turkish university, then received training in Ankara and spent a few months at a language institute in England's West Country. He enthusiastically practiced his English on me. There was not much use for it in his district, where most people speak one of two Kurdish tongues, Kirmanji or Zaza, and many of the old people do not know Turkish.

The Kirmanji speakers in the district are Sunni Kurds, of which there are at least 10 million in Turkey. The Zaza speakers are members of Turkey's roughly 12-million-strong Alevi community, heterodox Shiites of Turkmen and Kurdish lineage. Neither of these groups, the official went on, should be called a minority; that would imply that there is discrimination against them, which is not the case. He told me this with the assurance of someone who knows that he, and his view of the world, enjoy the sanction of a large and powerful state. You can find young men like him throughout Turkey sitting in government offices, where a cast of the death mask of Kemal Atatürk, the republic's founder, is hanging on the wall behind them.

The Turkish Republic's attitude toward minorities only makes sense if you have an idea of the contribution that the nationalism of those minorities made to the decline of the Ottoman Empire. Starting in the eighteenth century, Europe's Christian powers assumed the role of protectors of their coreligionists in the empire. By the nineteenth century, they were promoting nationalist movements among them and protecting the newly independent states that had been created from former Ottoman territories, such as Greece, Serbia, and Romania. The process of making new nations was lethal for the empire and very often for those Muslims who were caught up in it; millions of Muslims were forced out of those newly independent states (besides the new autonomous territory of Bulgaria) and fled to Anatolia, the empire's heartland. By the eve of World War I, Anatolia had become a refuge for dispossessed Muslims from the Balkans and from the Caucasian territories that Russia had won during the Russian–Ottoman War of 1877–1878.

But Anatolia also had large non-Muslim minorities, including the Orthodox Greeks and mostly Gregorian Christian Armenians. These minorities looked to outside Christian powers for protection, especially to Greece (in the case of the Greek Orthodox) and Russia (in the case of the Armenians). Many of them were uneasy about the Ottoman decision during World War I to side with Germany against their own protectors, while the Ottomans viewed them as potential fifth columnists.

* * *

In 1915, following severe military defeat at the hands of the Russians and an Armenian uprising in the eastern city of Van, the Ottomans ordered the deportation of Armenians from Anatolia. Well over one million are thought to have died in what many historians consider to have been a premeditated act of genocide. In the Treaty of Lausanne, which was signed in 1923, Turkey pledged to protect its non-Muslim minorities, but the Turkish delegates at Lausanne succeeded in preventing Muslim minorities such as the Kurds and Alevis from being mentioned; and they emerged from Lausanne protected only by general commitments to linguistic and religious freedom, commitments that, in many cases, the Turks went on to disregard. In 1925, around one million Anatolian Greeks were sent to Greece under a population exchange that was managed relatively humanely and cleansed Anatolia further of non-Turkish minorities.

Atatürk presented his new state as an increasingly monolithic entity. Regardless of their ethnic identity, Muslim citizens of the republic were henceforth to be considered Turks. The glorious national history taught in schools was supposedly pure in its Turkishness—it starts with an epic migration from the Central Asian steppe, follows the Turks as they assume leadership of the Islamic community, and ends as they triumphantly embrace modern European civilization. "Happy is he who calls himself a Turk" became Atatürk's most famous saying, and everyone was encouraged to agree.

It is well known that millions of Kurds, whose ancestors inhabited parts of Mesopotamia and eastern Anatolia well before the Turks turned up, resented being designated as Turks, and that on several occasions they took up arms to demand autonomy or independence. (The most recent separatist rebellion, by the Kurdish Workers Party, whose Kurdish acronym is PKK, lasted from 1984 to 1999 and cost at least 30,000 lives.) But the most striking thing about the Turkish identity promoted by Atatürk is just how many citizens of the new state enthusiastically accepted it. Few of today's Turks are descended from the original Central Asian migrants. Atatürk himself was not the "Father of the Turk" that his self-conferred surname suggests, but was probably descended from Slavic converts to Islam. Many of the people I spoke to in Turkey this spring told me that their ancestors had fled from the Balkans, the Caucasus, or Ottoman Mesopotamia during the empire's collapse. I met others who were assimilated Kurds; they had, they said, no sympathy for Kurdish nationalism.

What has induced these people to embrace Atatürk's national identity? As Muslims under the Ottoman Empire traumatized by the loss of their former lands whether in the Balkans or elsewhere, their forebears found refuge in Anatolia. In the face of new threats to their security, not least Allied attempts at the end of World War I to carve up Anatolia and create new Armenian and Kurdish countries, the only thing for them to do was to assimilate. Most forgot their Balkan or Caucasian languages and traditions; their children became model Turkish citizens, diligently learning at school about allegedly Turkish skull types and memorizing the poems of Ziya Gokalp, an exponent of Turkish nationalism who wrote much of his poetry in the first quarter of the nineteenth century. And so modern Turkishness, while theoretically springing from a common racial heritage, actually means something more and less than that. It was born in response to irredentist Balkan nationalisms of the nineteenth century and it became a means of uniting people against hostile states trying to divide up Anatolia at the end of World War I.

Atatürk chose Turkishness, and not Islam, to bind the citizens together because he had decided that Turkey should be a secular state, and hoped that Islam, which he felt retarded modern development, would lose its influence over people's daily lives. In the words of the Turkish historian Taner Akcam, who has written extensively about Turkey's self-image, particularly in connection with the atrocities committed against the Armenians, the national identity "developed together with the fear of extermination, of extinction" by predatory enemies.[1] For the Armenians, of course, the fear of extermination turned out to be real; but many modern Turks concur with the words of Talat Pasha, the chief vizier who ordered the deportations: "If I had not done it to them, they would have done it to us." Any attempt to dismantle Turkishness, even now, is bound to revive old fears.

2.

In April, I visited the eastern city of Erzurum, 150 miles from the Turkish border with Georgia and a thousand miles to the east of

---

1. *Turk Ulusal Kimligi ve Ermeni Sorunu* (*The Turkish National Identity and the Armenian Problem*) (Istanbul: Iletisim Yayinlari, 1994).

Ankara. Commanding both the headwaters of the Euphrates and a vital corridor for a foreign army seeking to invade Anatolia from the northeast, Erzurum has a tumultuous history of acquisition and loss, of resistance and vulnerability. You feel the weight of this history when you visit the city's medieval mosques, which more closely resemble fortresses than places of worship. From the hills overlooking the city, you can see the plains from which the Russians approached when they conquered Erzerum three times in less than a century. And you learn quickly about ethnic conflict. When H. F. B. Lynch, a British writer and statesman, visited Erzurum in the final years of the nineteenth century, the city's Turkish and Armenian inhabitants were complaining of attacks by Kurdish militias that the Ottoman government had unwisely armed—militias that embarrassed local officials described as "brigands, disguised as soldiers."

Erzurum lies on the boundary of the heavily Kurdish southeast. Kurds are said to make up about 25 percent of the population of Erzerum province, but the place is better known for its Turkish nationalism. Some two hundred young men from the province were killed while suppressing the PKK revolt, which ended after the 1999 capture of the PKK leader, Abdullah Ocalan, and the PKK's subsequent cease-fire and withdrawal into northern Iraq. After that, Turkish nationalists became worried as the Kurds, having lost the war, began to win the peace. The nationalist Turks were dismayed when the current, mildly Islamist government of Recep Tayyip Erdogan released hundreds of jailed PKK members, legalized Kurdish-language broadcasting, and allowed private Kurdish-language schools to open.

That it was previously against the law for the Kurdish language to be used anywhere in public suggests one source of the deep Kurdish resentment that developed over the years. Turkish nationalists are well aware of the Kurds' bitterness and fear its consequences. They felt uneasy when the main Kurdish party, the Democratic People's

Party (DEHAP), with its close but informal links to the PKK, won control of fifty-six municipal councils in the 2004 local elections. In March, Turkish nationalists across the country, including several thousands in Erzurum, turned out in the streets to protest the actions of some Kurdish youths who had been captured on television trying to set fire to the Turkish flag.

* * *

For many Turks, the PKK insurgency was horrendous for its violence, but at least there was no room for uncertainty about opposing Kurdish nationalism; this is no longer the case. Last summer, the PKK, which for a time changed its name to Kongra-Gel but now calls itself the PKK again, resumed its armed struggle in response to the government's refusal both to end Ocalan's solitary confinement and to offer an amnesty to around 3,500 rebels. But despite an increase in PKK attacks, most Kurdish nationalists now see their future in a Turkey that is in the EU; they are not drawn to the camps that train Kurdish insurgents in northern Iraq. For the state, this is both an opportunity and a challenge.

In April, speaking to both Turkish officials and Turks on both the left and the right, I sensed an apprehension that the government in Ankara is losing control over the Kurdish issue, an apprehension that cuts through traditional political differences between left-wingers and right-wingers. The anxiety that arose when the PKK started acquiring a political presence has sharpened as ordinary Turks have learned more about the concessions to minorities that the European Union will demand when negotiations over Turkey's admission begin in October. In the words of Mesut Yegen, a columnist at *Radikal*, one of Turkey's few sizable liberal newspapers, the Kurds are increasingly seen by Turks as a community that is being emboldened from outside the country to resist Turkification.... In the eyes of the people, the Kurds are increasingly becoming like the Greeks and Armenians.

In other words, the Kurds have become a minority that looks to outsiders, not to its own government, to protect its interests.

In the Erzurum branch of the Association of Martyrs' Families, which cares for the next of kin of Turkish servicemen killed during the PKK rebellion, Hatem Tetik, the branch head, articulated the widespread Turkish skepticism about the EU's intentions. He said he doubted the wisdom of a government plan to lower the parliamentary threshold, currently 10 percent of the vote, that parties must exceed to gain representation in the Ankara chamber. He said, "It's clear that the EU wants DEHAP to be represented in parliament." (DEHAP won 6.3 percent of the vote at the last general election, and currently has no deputies.) Tetik complained about last summer's release from prison of a prominent Kurdish nationalist and spoke resentfully of European pressure on Turkey to safeguard the property rights of non-Muslim religious foundations. He was aghast at the idea that the European Court of Human Rights would soon rule on whether or not Ocalan's trial in Turkey for treason had been conducted fairly, a decision that could prepare the way for a retrial.[2]

Surrounded by the framed photographs of dozens of fallen soldiers, including his own twenty-year-old son, I sensed that Tetik was struggling to understand a great irony. Having spent fifteen years fighting to protect the nation's sovereignty, Turkey was now preparing to relinquish it voluntarily.

* * *

As we spoke of the Kurds, I was reminded of government officials whom I had met in the Kurdish region of southeastern Turkey. They had disparaged the "mentality" of the people whose lives they ran, without bothering to understand that mentality; they never seemed

---

2. In May, the ECHR ruled that Ocalan's trial "was not tried by an independent and impartial tribunal," and called for a retrial.

to ask themselves why many Kurds remain deeply hostile to the Turkish state. The armed forces, guardians of Atatürk's republic, have done little to improve relations. Following the attempt by Kurdish youths to burn the flag, the General Staff castigated the "so-called citizens" who "breathe [the country's] air, drink its water and fill their stomachs, and then dare to lay a finger on that country's most sacred shared national value, its flag." The statement says as much about the state's view of Kurdish nationalists as ungrateful tenants as it does about the generals' readiness to encourage Turkish chauvinism. Tetik's reply to my question about Kurdish nationalists was in the same vein. "They eat the same bread as us, they marry our daughters, and then disparage the country. I don't understand it."

In the past, Turkish governments usually came to power speaking of reconciliation; they soon felt obliged, by a combination of PKK atrocities and pressure from the generals, to announce their faith in a "military solution" to what was presented as a simple problem of terrorism. Now, things have changed. With Erdogan in power, the generals must deal with a popular prime minister whose AK Party argues that a shared religion that does not deny ethnic differences will be sufficient to bind Turks and Kurds together. When I met Abdulrahman Dilipak, a militant Turkish Islamist based in Istanbul, he called for a "unitary state of many communities," i.e., for according the Kurds some recognition.

For the first time in years, the place where the most adventurous opinions about Turkey's future are being ventured is the Kurdish southeast. In the past, the representatives of Kurdish parties spoke circumspectly, fearing that they might be arrested or their party banned, but the climate is now freer. In Mus, an overwhelmingly Kurdish province, the local Human Rights Association representative, a supporter of the Kurdish cause, told me that "the number of people coming to me to complain that they have been tortured has gone down to virtually zero." This reflects well on Erdogan and his policy of "zero tolerance" toward torture, which had indeed been widespread, but the atmosphere has emboldened Kurdish nationalists to articulate their aspirations with a new frankness. In Mus, when I asked the representative of DEHAP whether the Kurds wanted minority rights, he replied, "First we want the privileges that are afforded to minorities, and then we want to go beyond that."

For many Kurds that probably means exploring Ocalan's recent announcement from prison that he was setting up a "democratic federation" that would bind together the Kurds of Turkey, Iraq, Iran, and Syria, but without splitting them from their host countries. How he would manage that, he did not say. Others envisage a new constitution that recognizes the Kurds as equal partners with the Turks and that provides explicitly for Kurdish instruction in state schools. The DEHAP mayor of Varto, a town in Mus province, spoke to me of bringing about a "transformation" in attitudes and forcing the state to evolve toward full recognition of Kurds.

The EU process has elicited fears that the Alevis, too, will seek special status. As heterodox Muslims, the Alevis were often treated shoddily by the Ottomans. Many welcomed Atatürk's secular republic because it seemed to offer an end to discrimination. More recently, the heterodox Shia Alevis have felt threatened by Turkey's Sunni revival and by the state's desire to regulate the revival. No room has been made for Alevi beliefs and practices; at school, Alevi children are instructed in orthodox Sunni Islam alongside their Sunni peers. In Ankara, Kazim Genc, who heads the Pir Abdal Culture Association, a big Alevi group, demanded that religious instruction be removed from the national curriculum and that the state provide help in building Alevi prayer halls, just as it helps the benefactors of Sunni mosques. Genc wants the Alevis to be elevated to their rightful status as a "founding element of the Turkish Republic."

A new constitution, recognition for the Alevis, protection for non-Muslim religious foundations—for millions of Turks, these are frightening ideas, and they are all the more frightening because they are being articulated at the same time as the move toward EU entry, the stated goal of the Turkish state. This paradoxical situation seems now to be provoking among some Turks a reevaluation of the wisdom of seeking EU entry, and recent polls suggest a decline in support for that goal and a rise in nationalist feelings.[3]

3.

Having lived in Turkey during the late 1990s, when most Turks admired Bill Clinton, I was startled by the anti-American feeling that I observed when I was there in April. George Bush's invasion of Iraq and his support for Ariel Sharon have alienated the devout. America's current patronage of the Kurds of northern Iraq has convinced many Turks that the US is prepared to tolerate an independent Kurdish state there—a state that could be seen as a model by Turkey's Kurds. Some Turks believe that the US wants to take revenge for the Ankara parliament's refusal to allow American forces to use Turkey as a launching pad for the Iraq invasion. Many Turks believe that, far from trying to control PKK units in northern Iraq, the US is abetting them in order to destabilize Turkey.

This background helps to explain the success of *Metal Storm*, a Turkish novel describing Turkey's invasion by US forces which has been a runaway best seller, with a print run, huge by Turkish standards, of 350,000 to date. Polls suggest that many Turks regard such

---

3. That decline is bound to be accelerated by the crisis that was precipitated by the rejection by French and Dutch voters of the new EU constitution. Now Turks have even less of an idea than they did of what sort of EU they might eventually join—or, indeed, whether rising anti-Turk sentiment in member states might keep them out.

an invasion as a distinct possibility. At the end of 2004, the US embassy in Ankara had to deny Turkish newspaper reports claiming that the Asian tsunami had been caused by American underwater explosions designed to kill large numbers of Muslims.

Traveling through Turkey I was struck by a tendency among the people I met to look for villains. In Mus, for example, right-wing activists told me there had been a rise in Christian missionary activity, a claim for which they were unable to provide evidence. Some Turks are passionately opposed to the proposed reopening of a Greek Orthodox seminary near Istanbul. They regard this tiny concession to Turkey's few remaining Greeks as a serious threat. Most improbable of all, many Turks say they fear the Sabbataians, a Jewish sect that probably no longer exists.

In the seventeenth century the Sabbataians were followers of Sabbatai Zevi, an Ottoman Jew who proclaimed himself the Messiah. After Zevi was induced by the Ottomans to embrace Islam, thousands of his followers followed his example, but continued to practice Judaism in secret. During the past two decades, some writers, most of them Islamist, have received some attention by challenging without any serious evidence the conventional account of what happened next—namely, that the Sabbataians' descendants became integrated into Muslim Turkish society. On the contrary, these writers maintain, the Sabbataians multiplied, maintained their secret faith, and now exert a sinister stranglehold over Turkey's political and economic life.[4]

---

4. *Yahudi Turkler, yahut Sabetaycilar* (*Jewish Turks, or Sabbataians*) (Zvi-Geyik Yayinlari, 2000), a collection of articles on the subject by Mehmed Sevket Eygi, a prominent Islamist columnist, contains the assertion that "a few thousand Sabbataians control the country's affairs," but provides no evidence that this is the case. He says that Istanbul contains "secret synagogues" where Sabbataians worship, but does not say where they are. Like other writers on the subject, Eygi makes no attempt to distinguish between sincere

This is the idea behind Soner Yalcin's current best seller, *Efendi: The White Turks' Big Secret.*[5] The book is a detailed historical account of a powerful and tentacular Izmir family, the Evliyazades, many of whose descendants are well known in Turkey today. Yalcin follows the extended family from the late nineteenth century as its members make fortunes, arrange advantageous marriages, achieve high office during the imperial and republican periods, and are occasionally defeated by politics or jealousy. In the book's last paragraph, Yalcin tells his readers his book was written with the aim of lifting the veil on a secret that remains taboo in Turkey.... Sabbataiism is our reality. We cannot write our history if we ignore it.

And yet the alleged Sabbataiism of *Efendi* is not based on any evidence; it is suggested by innuendo for the initiated. Yalcin does not say outright that the Evliyazades are Sabbataians; he only implies that they are. He does not flatly contradict the Evliyazades' account that the family originally came from Anatolia, but he hints that they are descended from Jewish converts. Once this is accepted, everything else falls into place: the Evliyazades' business partnerships with foreigners; their supposedly effete, Western style of life; their association with sinister institutions like the Rotary Club and the Miss Europe competition (the 1952 winner, Gunseli Basar, apparently married an Evliyazade). Yalcin's point is that the Evliyazades and people like them deserve the honorific "Efendi," a word meaning "gentleman" or "leader," that was often used to refer to non-Muslims during the Ottoman period, and that Yalcin seems to be using ironically. These "white Turks," he seems to be saying, can hardly be considered Turks at all.

---

converts to Islam and Sabbataians, which further weakens his assertion that Sabbataiism is a thriving sect. It seems no more than a scurrilous anti-Semitic label.

5. *Efendi: Beyaz Turklerin Buyuk Sirri* (Dogan Kitap, 2004). With fifty-six reprints to date, *Efendi* is one of Turkey's most successful nonfiction books of recent years.

In a recent issue of a left-wing Turkish magazine, Rifat N. Bali, a Turkish Jew, sees *Efendi* as part of the tradition of Turkish anti-Semitic writing.[6] He describes Islamist journalists who try to "out" famous Turks as being Sabbataian. He points out several passages in which Yalcin implies that Sabbataians have intervened during Turkish history to the benefit of their own (and Israel's) interest, and to the detriment of Turkey's. Without any factual basis for doing so, Yalcin ascribes a discriminatory tax imposed on the capital of well-to-do non-Muslims in the 1940s to a plot by pro-Israel Jewish converts in the Turkish government to persuade Turkish Jews to migrate to the new state. Whatever the reason for their departure, Yalcin concludes, the Jews who eventually left showed "disloyalty" to Turkey. In the eyes of Turkish nationalists, disloyalty and ingratitude are common traits among minorities.

4.

I arrived in Istanbul on Sunday, April 24, ninety years to the day since the Ottomans began arresting prominent Armenians in the city, an event that for Armenians marks the beginning of the genocide. A large Armenian church that I visited in European Istanbul was packed with worshipers who lit candles in memory of those who had died. Some local Armenians, along with a few liberal Turkish journalists and historians, had flown to Armenia to participate in a commemoration there and to support demands that Turkey recognize the events of 1915 as genocide.

Turkish newspapers had much to say about those events. Columnists and celebrities presented themselves in the press as experts on history. Could the deportations of 1915 have been avoided? No, ar-

---

6. *Birikim*, June 2004.

gued Sukru Elekdag, a handsome former ambassador turned politician, "the Ottoman government went to great pains" to protect the Armenians during the deportations, but "due to contagious diseases, severe weather conditions and limited resources there were losses on both sides." On April 25, *Hurriyet*, Turkey's most slavishly pro-establishment paper, announced that "today, for the first time, fully ninety years after the events of 1915," Talat Pasha, the Ottoman grand vizier who ordered the deportations, "speaks, joining the debate with hitherto unpublished documents from his personal archive!" During the next few days, a series of articles taken from Talat's journal purported to show that the chief vizier, who was assassinated by an Armenian in 1921, had been much concerned for the welfare of the deportees.

The evident purpose behind this display of opinion was to promote the Turkish version of events. The Armenians, so the Turkish argument goes, were deported because the Turks credibly feared that they would link up with the advancing Russians and seize parts of Anatolia. The deportations could not have been better managed because the Ottoman Empire was at war and in chaos. Most of the massacres were committed by brigands who acted without state sanction. And some of the worst massacres were committed against Turkish villages by Armenian gangs withdrawing from eastern Anatolia along with the Russians after the Bolshevik Revolution.

During the past two decades, several Turkish historians have made careers by developing this thesis, and also by dismissing as inflated claims that 1.5 million Armenians lost their lives during the deportations. These historians have been supported by Turkish diplomats, but they have had little success. Few foreign historians and, perhaps more important, no foreign countries feel confident defending the Turkish thesis. Turkish newspapers like *Hurriyet* carried triumphant headlines after George Bush avoided using the word "genocide" in a statement of condolence to the Armenians on April 24, but throughout the world, the opinion of politicians and historians is decidedly against the Turks. The parliaments of more than a dozen countries have recognized the events of 1915 as genocide and a resolution has been submitted to the European Parliament demanding that "genocide recognition" be made a precondition for Turkish entry to the EU.

* * *

Many Armenians agree that Turkey must recognize the events of 1915 as genocide. Turkish officials vigorously resist a label that, they rightly fear, will result in their being associated with horrors comparable to the Holocaust and may expose them to class-action lawsuits. It is hard to argue that the writing and understanding of history have benefited from the bitter controversy over the word "genocide." Many individual Turks accept that the Ottomans committed an appalling crime, but the same Turks violently react against suggestions that the crime was genocide.[7] The attitude of these Turks, in turn, enrages many Armenians, for some of whom it is the label of genocide that counts—more so than an appropriate show of contrition or even an honest appraisal of the past.[8] So a distorted "debate"

---

7. In his statement on April 24, Bush referred to the "mass killings of as many as 1.5 million Armenians during the last days of the Ottoman Empire." This contradicts Turkish claims that there were no mass killings and that only a fraction of that number died. Although Bush was accusing the Ottomans of an appalling crime, the fact that he did not use the word "genocide" was presented in Turkey as cause for celebration.

8. Some people contend that, unless Turkey recognizes that a genocide took place, no appraisal of the past can be considered complete. I am not so sure. It is unlikely that Turkey's justice minister would have reacted so aggressively to the proposed conference at Bosporus University if he did not fear that the event would be useful to those who advocate recognition of genocide. His reaction, naturally, was strongly attacked by such advocates, including a group called the Campaign for Recognition of the Armenian Genocide. It is hard to imagine that the experience of Bosporus University will encourage other Turkish institutions, especially ones that value academic integrity, to stage conferences of their own. They would inevitably get caught up in the dispute between proponents and opponents of

is taking place in the shadow of Turkey's bid for EU membership. Some Turks, many of them writers and academics, dare to put their heads above the parapet, and try to discuss the issue in a dispassionate manner, but they are not always allowed to do so. In May, academics at Istanbul's respected Bosporus University felt obliged to cancel a conference on the history of the Armenian deportations after the Turkish justice minister obliquely referred to the event as "treason," and "the spreading of propaganda against Turkey by people who belong to it."

When Orhan Pamuk, Turkey's best-known novelist, made the unremarkable observation last year that one million Armenians were killed in Turkey, his words provoked a protest demonstration in the streets. Under Turkey's new penal code, it is not clear that referring to Armenian genocide constitutes "anti-national activity"—a crime that is punishable by ten years' imprisonment. (The law's original footnote, which suggests that it does, has officially been erased, but this may not have much effect in practice; many copies of the new penal code that have been circulated contain the offending footnote, raising fears that lawyers and judges will apply it.) If saying the Turks committed genocide is a crime, this is surely as flagrant an affront to intellectual freedom as the recent decision by the Swiss judiciary to launch an inquiry into Yusuf Halacoglu, the head of the Turkish History Organization, on the grounds that his denial of the genocide during a speech he gave in Switzerland may amount to illegal racism. That court decision was denounced not only by members of the Turkish establishment, but also by pro-Armenian Turkish historians such as Sabanci University's Halil Berktay, who says that the events of 1915 constitute a "proto-genocide." Etyen Mahcupyan, a prominent

---

genocide recognition—a dispute that often has the result of drawing a semantic veil over the Armenian tragedy of 1915.

Turkish Armenian writer and journalist, also criticized the Swiss decision, saying that he agreed with "none of Professor Halacoglu's views," although he defended his right to express them.

In the offices of the weekly *Agos*, a paper published for Istanbul's roughly 60,000 Armenians, Karin Karakasli, the newspaper's general coordinator, told me that despite the controversy over official recognition of the killings as genocide, the conditions that Turkey's Armenians live under are getting better. Only a few years ago, Karakasli recalled, the Armenian community was being accused of cooperating with the PKK; what the government calls "minority affairs," including relations with Armenians, were supervised by the police. Until the cancellation of the Bosporus University conference, it had seemed as though Erdogan and his government were showing a softer and more tolerant attitude. The picture is now less clear—and members of the Turkish establishment, including top army commanders, have yet to show any sign that they would endorse such a softening. All the same, *Agos* has benefited from a relaxation in laws and attitudes concerning freedom of expression. Minority affairs are now supervised by the Interior Ministry. Karakasli told me that dozens of Armenian memoirs, novels, and history books are now being published in Turkish, part of a trend toward greater pluralism in publishing.[9] For the first time that she can remember, there is no general desire among Istanbul's Armenians to emigrate.

---

9. In Turkey, it is now possible to buy books arguing that genocide took place in 1915, as well as memoirs, written by Armenians who survived the deportations, that describe appalling behavior by the Ottomans. The success now being enjoyed by Fetiye Cetin's story of her Armenian grandmother, who was rescued by Turks, has prompted others to admit that they, too, have Armenian antecedents. In fashionable Istanbul bookshops, it is possible to find, on the same shelf as Soner Yalcin's *Efendi*, novels that celebrate the Ottoman cosmopolitanism that Yalcin finds so objectionable. Such books sell less than the chauvinist ones, Karakasli concedes, but that they are largely available is new and important. "In the past, you only heard one view."

* * *

Although Istanbul's Armenians agree that the events of 1915 amounted to genocide, more immediate practical matters, such as Turkey's continuing refusal to reopen its land border with Armenia, seem more important to many of them than the issue of whether genocide is officially recognized. Justifying its decision to keep the border closed, Turkey cites Armenia's occupation of territory belonging to Azerbaijan, a Turkish ally, and Armenia's claim to parts of eastern Anatolia. But Erdogan has said that he wants improved relations with Armenia and he recently called for a joint commission of Turkish and Armenian historians to review the events of 1915. Etyen Mahcupyan has advised the Turkish parliament that Turkey should reopen relations with Armenia; if it does, Turkish acknowledgment of the genocide will, he believes, become less important. He, Karakasli, and other prominent Turkish Armenians criticize the efforts of diaspora Armenians to persuade foreign parliaments to pass resolutions denouncing the genocide. "They seek to protect their identity by generating hatred," Karakasli said, "and they end up poisoning themselves.... They have no contact with the Turks. We live among them."

Of all Turkey's minorities, recognized or not, Armenians have the most tragic past. They may also have the brightest future, since most of them live in Turkey's only cosmopolitan city. In more remote and conservative parts of the country, such as Erzurum, it is harder to envisage a smooth accommodation of minority demands, still less the sharing of ideas that would help facilitate the transition. This is why a recent work on Turkey's minorities, by Baskin Oran, a political scientist at Ankara University, is so important.[10]

---

10. *Turkiye'de Azinliklar: Kavramlar, Teori Lozan, ic Mevzuat, Ictihat, Uygulama* (*Minorities in Turkey: Notions, Theory, Lausanne, Internal Regulations, Interpretation, Implementation*) (Iletsim Yayinlari, 2004).

In his scholarly and exhaustive book, Oran examines the Treaty of Lausanne, the consequences of Atatürk's exclusive conception of Turkishness, and the repressive laws that have been enacted in the name of both. He contends that Turkey's foundations could be strengthened, and many inconsistencies resolved, simply by changing the official designation of the Turkish citizen from *Turk*, or Turk, to *Turkiyeli*, which means "of Turkey." It is an ingenious answer both to Turkish nationalists and also to demands by Kurds that their special status be recognized, for it convincingly assumes that no one should have special status. In Oran's Turkey, everyone is a *Turkiyeli*. Of course, Oran's ideas amount to more than semantic invention. They challenge the way that the state regards its citizens. In the words of an EU diplomat based in Ankara, the state has hitherto organized itself in order to "protect itself from its citizens, rather than the other way around."

Last November, a condensed version of Oran's book was issued by a panel—of which Oran was a member—that had been asked by the government to examine minority questions. The result was an uproar of objections. To show his opposition to Oran's views, another member of the panel snatched it from the jurist who was reading it aloud, and ripped it up. Later on, Oran's suggestion was attacked by Turkey's second most senior general, and denounced by Turkish nationalists. Startled by the reaction, the government disowned Oran's ideas.

At least Oran was not charged with any crime or fired from his job at the university, as he might have been a few years ago. He and other progressives realize that attempts to change Turkey will set off reactions, not least from a reactionary and ultra-cautious establishment. Still, a transformation is underway in Turkey, and a central part of it involves Turkey's still troubled relations with its minorities.

—July 14, 2005

24

The Battle for Egypt's Future
Yasmine El Rashidi

It was still springtime in Cairo. The people had spoken in Tahrir Square. They had defied the intimidation of a panicked police state. They had booed and hissed the wooden, uncomprehending, patronizing words of the man who ruled them for thirty years. Mubarak's dictatorship was over.

But what then? Political transitions from authoritarian rule are never easy and always messy. Elections, even if free and fair, are not enough. Democracy needs institutions to safeguard the liberty of its citizens; it needs independent judges, trade unions, political parties, mass media.

Without such institutions, conflicts of interest and struggles for power cannot be resolved in peace. Liberal democrats are seldom the winners in the aftermath of revolutions. Still, Egypt might be lucky. Too much optimism would be foolish, but so would giving up on hope.

—I.B.

TO JUDGE BY the streets of Cairo on the morning of March 19, it seemed that a good chunk of my city's 19 million residents were taking part in the constitutional referendum. The roaring old school buses that rattle my windows when they pass in the morning were not to be heard, there were hardly any cars on the usually clogged streets, and the daily flood of people making their way through the dense web of thoroughfares and alleyways was absent. The only signs of traffic or crowds were around the hundreds of designated polling stations. It had been nearly five weeks since protesters in Tahrir Square had brought down President Hosni Mubarak, and Egyptians throughout the country were voting on an all-or-nothing package of nine constitutional amendments. A win for the yes votes promised to lead to parliamentary elections as early as June, returning power to a civilian government following the military's temporary takeover. If the no votes prevailed, it might start the process of political reform over again, or it might cause the military to pursue a different strategy.

After decades of oppressive rule, in which elections had been pro forma exercises marked by violence and fraud, Egyptians were elated that their ballots would finally count. Many were voting for the first time in their lives. When the results were announced the next day, they seemed unambiguous: 77.2 percent had voted for the amendments—ostensibly an endorsement for reform—and just 22.8 percent had voted against them. The reality, as I had discovered in the days leading up to March 19, was far more complicated. Only 18 million of Egypt's eligible 45 million voters participated (though, as many have reported, this was the country's highest turnout on record). In fact, most of the activists who had had a leading part in the revolution dismissed the referendum as cosmetic, when what was needed, they felt, was an entirely new constitution. Moreover, many who voted yes had little sense how these amendments were going to change the country's political life.

The referendum had been conceived by the Egyptian armed forces as part of its response to the youth protesters, who were pressing for sweeping reforms to the political system that had sustained Mubarak in power. After it formally assumed power on February 11, the day Mubarak stepped down, the military had suspended the 1971 constitution and appointed a constitutional committee to address these demands. Instructed by the military to "get this over with" as soon as possible, the eight members of the committee—among them a member of the Muslim Brotherhood, two professors of law, and a respected judge—had been given a free hand to redraft any of the constitution's 211 articles and select a referendum date. Key priorities for the protesters were the abolishment of the emergency law, the revision of all articles concerning presidential elections and executive power, and a redrafting of Article Two concerning the state and religion, as well as of other articles concerning the rights of citizens.

Despite pressure by activists for a complete overhaul of the constitution, however, the commission's recommendations—arrived at seemingly in a matter of days—were far narrower: on February 26, the military announced only nine proposed amendments, to be voted on three weeks later. From the start it was clear where the emphasis lay. While leaving many of the protesters' demands—such as the electoral process—unaddressed, the proposed changes revealed some of the recurring concerns of the military, such as the fear of "foreign" interference in the country's affairs.

The most significant of the amendments would limit presidents to two four-year terms, allow independent candidates to campaign, and bar from office anyone who holds a foreign passport or, oddly, has a "foreign" spouse (Mubarak's wife, and President Anwar Sadat's wife before her, both had British mothers). It also would establish new legislative powers, providing for a subsequent revision of the constitution by a committee chosen by the new parliament.

Although military leaders had met privately with activists before the announcement of the referendum, protest leaders were quick to denounce the amendments as inadequate. "To us, the regime was a failed one, which means that its constitution too is failed," the activist Esraa Abdel Fattah told me. Esraa, who had been jailed under Mubarak's regime for organizing a nationwide protest on April 6, 2008, in solidarity with striking laborers, was one of the planners of the January 25 protest that started the revolution. She had been meeting with the military and the interim cabinet on a regular basis, and was among those who proposed appointing Essam Sharaf, a civil engineer and former transport minister who had participated in the Tahrir uprising, as interim prime minster, which the military leadership did following the resignation of old-regime holdover Ahmed Shafiq on March 3.

Esraa was also one of the handful of activists and policymakers who were invited to meet US Secretary of State Hillary Clinton during her visit to Cairo on March 15. The weekend before, I found Esraa in her office at the Egyptian Democratic Academy, an organization that uses social media to promote democracy and human rights, flipping through her recently recovered state security file. She told me that Clinton

> has to understand the proposed amendments are completely inadequate. We are not ready for elections. We need a transitional three-person presidential council, comprised of two civilian leaders and an army one. We need at least a year to raise awareness and prepare the people for elections. Political awareness and engagement is currently lacking. If the United States wants to help, there needs to be a balance between military aid and that to civil society. We need help with this coming phase. Talk is not enough.

After the meeting, Esraa called me. "Hillary responded positively to what I had to say," she said. "Although she didn't have firm responses, she took general criticism well."

In the weeks leading up to the referendum, there had been a few further moments of victory for the revolution. On March 5, crowds of activists overran state security bureaus across the country, including the state security headquarters in Cairo. For many, the *Amn al-Dawla*, or State Security Investigation Service, had been one of the darkest forces behind the Mubarak regime—known for its random arrests and the torture of activists, and for keeping surveillance files on millions of people—and its sacking seemed to consummate the defeat of the old order.

Yet at the same time, the protest movement had fragmented. There were widespread reports of robberies and lawlessness; tensions between Muslims and Copts had reignited; the army had released Islamist political prisoners, including those accused of assassinating Sadat in 1981; and stories of detentions and torture were continuing to surface. At a women's rights demonstration on March 8, thugs stormed the crowd in an attack reminiscent of the pro-Mubarak violence against the Tahrir uprising a month earlier. The police, meanwhile, were still largely absent from the streets, while the army and its tanks seemed to be just standing by. Amid this growing sense of unease, many who had taken part in the uprising thought the referendum was hasty and ill-conceived, and activists like Esraa drew on all their political connections to try to pressure the military to postpone it.

Meanwhile, the debate on how to vote in the referendum intensified on social network sites and TV talk shows. Even the popular youth radio channel 104.2 Nile FM—whose young hosts spin popular Western tunes and invite guests to talk about dating, love, and movies—was discussing the constitution. Yes and no camps swiftly took shape. Activists and the members of the upper-middle class were calling for no; they wanted a new constitution and more time to raise political awareness among the nation's 80 million people. Those who felt the referendum was taking place too soon—a group of reformists that included presidential hopeful Mohamed ElBaradei—hinged their argument on readiness. None of the opposition coalitions and movements had secured the resources or organization to mobilize large numbers in an effective way, and their supporters worried that a yes victory would result in a parliament divided between the Muslim Brotherhood and members of Mubarak's old patronage network. Moreover, such a parliament would then be free to redraft the constitution to its liking. "Bad news," one activist told me. "We'll all be dead."

But the limited Cairo- and Alexandria-based campaigns of the no advocates had little chance of winning over the broader public. The Muslim Brotherhood, the ultra-conservative Salafis, and groups affiliated with the former party of Mubarak, the National Democratic Party (NDP), were endorsing the amendments and targeting their efforts at the working classes—laborers and farmers. The Muslim Brotherhood—the largest and most organized movement apart, perhaps, from the remaining political network of the former regime itself—initially distributed flyers urging the yes vote as a religious obligation. But activists and the media quickly got wind of this strategy—stirring up long-standing suspicions about an underlying Brotherhood agenda to turn Egypt into an Islamist state—and the Brotherhood adopted the more palatable slogan "Yes is a vote for stability." The day before the referendum, around noon, I could hear from my desk the distant sound of an imam promoting yes-for-stability in his Friday sermon; there were reports that the same was taking place at mosques across the country.

When Saturday came, there was only one place to vote in my neighborhood, a public school, and by the time the polls opened at 8

AM, the lines of voters—parallel ones for men and women—ran down a narrow side street, past the post office and an art gallery, around a corner by a flower shop, and all the way down to the Bahraini and Algerian embassies a mile away. My mother, who is in her sixties and had never voted, woke up at 6 AM, eager to make it to the voting station early. By 8:05 AM, tweets were already coming in from those who had cast the first ballots, and from others standing by as election monitors. "I went to vote in Zamalek," tweeted the telecom tycoon Naguib Sawiris, who had been an active mediator between the youth and the regime during the revolt. "At 8 o clock the line was endless. My body shivered of happiness." Many seemed hopeful, if not for the immediate results, than certainly for the future.

After an hour, I decided to head to a polling station near parliament, a few minutes from Tahrir Square, where Amr Moussa—the departing secretary-general of the Arab League who had taken an active part in the protests and was considered a leading candidate for president—had earlier voted no. (Moussa said that the proposed amendments were not in line with the democratic ambitions of the Egyptian people, arguing that a temporary constitution should be created instead to provide for presidential elections followed by a more full-scale, independent redrafting of the constitution in the coming year.) When I got there, I saw Cairo's governor, Abdel Azim Wazeer, jump the line with a large entourage and cast his ballot. One man watching, furious, screamed, "Some things never change," and several hundred voters erupted into the familiar chant "*Irhal*" (Depart). "What does he know about order and standing in lines," a woman beside me said. "He's part of the old regime. We can't expect anything better from him."

The Muslim Brotherhood had been campaigning hard all week, and by 10 AM, I was getting reports that its followers were congregating outside voting stations around the country to press for yes votes. They had already distributed thousands of bags of sugar and other staple goods off the backs of trucks—another of the social services they have provided for years, winning them followers—and some of their members were reportedly preventing "no" voters from entering polling stations. I was curious about this, and along with a friend—the artist and photographer Lara Baladi—hailed a cab and headed to Shubra, a largely working-class and Coptic area. Our taxi driver, a man in his forties, said he was voting yes. "This won't do anymore. We need a parliament. We need a president. We need life to get back to normal and for business to pick up again."

I had spent much time with Coptic protesters downtown following the destruction of a church by thugs on March 5, and expected to find many of them in Shubra, voting no for fear of an Islamist takeover. But they were nowhere to be seen and we were met instead by Muslim Brothers—bearded men and women covered in black from head to toe, with only small eye-slits revealing slivers of skin.

At the first polling station we entered, we were followed by guards—familiar state security types—and the police, soldiers, and even the judges overseeing the ballots did little to calm things when dozens of voters started screaming at us to get out. As we left, we tried to speak to some people at the exit, asking them, "Why yes?" Their arguments were all the same: "stability."

Around the corner, at another Shubra polling station, we were met with even more hostility. A Muslim Brother manning the door took our IDs and walked away. When we asked for them back, saying we would leave, he refused, gripping them harder, refusing to explain why. When we vigorously protested, the crowd started yelling that we were "'no' people." We finally grabbed our IDs from the man's hand and quickly left.

In the week leading up to the referendum, pro-democracy activists and supporters had accused the military of cutting a power-sharing deal with the Brotherhood to preserve its hold on power. The armed forces had not explicitly taken a position on the amendments, but they sent text messages telling people that participation in the referendum was a vote for "democracy." And while they left Brotherhood members to freely campaign for yes, they harassed youth activists who were calling on people to reject the proposed amendments, arresting several the day before the vote.

Still, the former MP Mona Makram Ebeid—who served on the council designated to negotiate between the youth and the military—was skeptical about claims of military collusion with the Islamists. "They are keen to get back to the barracks," she told me when I saw her at a downtown polling station the morning of the referendum. Former army generals, pointing to the ominous state of the region and the threat of instability along Egypt's border with Libya, had also told me that the military needed to return to its normal job. Even the widely disliked Army Field Marshal Hussein Tantawi seemed reluctant to meddle for long in Egypt's daily affairs. (A December 2009 diplomatic cable disclosed by Wikileaks described Tantawi as saying "that any country where the military became engaged in 'internal affairs' was 'doomed to have lots of problems.'")

More plausibly, military leaders view the Brotherhood as the devil they know; even in the event of a large Islamist representation in parliament, they would understand what they were getting and how to deal with it. The Muslim Brotherhood, which had previously announced it would run for 30 to 40 percent of parliamentary seats, has said it is now reconsidering that ratio, and may compete for more. It is also expected that other Islamic factions will campaign for seats independently, including the recently legalized Islamist al-Wasat party. A parliament of young revolutionaries could threaten the military's position. Since the military has been the backbone of the system for decades, many also believe that there is corruption of significant scale to be uncovered in the history of the army's dealings. "You have to understand," the activist Basem had told me earlier, "the military is not a radical institution—why would they support us? They only responded to our demands when we were a critical mass." At the time, that mass included the Brotherhood and people from the working class.

I visited several other ballot stations on Saturday, and nowhere else did I experience the hostility we found in Shubra. But a report had come in that thugs had prevented ElBaradei from entering a polling station, and a picture was circulating that showed his car window smashed, splintered glass covering the seats. Contacts in the Coptic community (almost 10 percent of the population) were also reporting that Copts were being harassed into voting yes by polling station staff, or simply prevented from voting at all. A Coptic priest in the southern town of Naga Hammadi—where gunmen killed eight Copts as they were exiting church following Christmas prayers last year—said that Christian voters were being obstructed. In some towns with large Coptic communities there were reports that election officials, or their minders in the military and police, had apparently left voting stations closed.

Despite such reports, however, the referendum was perhaps the most legitimate poll the country has seen. "They were clean," the law professor Amr Shalakany told al-Jazeera. "But they weren't fair." Amr was right—few people I had spoken to in the streets had a firm grasp of what a yes or no vote really meant. Yes, most people thought, meant a quick solution to the country's economic woes. Even the design of the ballot seemed to encourage the notion: the yes circle was a bright, promising green color; the no circle was black.

By Sunday morning, preliminary returns suggested that 65 percent of the estimated 18 million voters had voted yes. Among those who cast votes were the former prime minister Ahmed Shafiq and many of the former president's much-hated men, including former Speaker of Parliament Fathy Sorour. According to reports, the presidential family voted too—in the seaside resort of Sharm el-Sheikh. Later, when the official results came in with even more in the yes tally, reactions varied. In some neighborhoods people celebrated with fireworks. In others, they were simply celebrating the right to vote democratically. It was mainly on Facebook and Twitter that disgruntled voices were airing grievances: about reports of fraud, about the "dirty tricks" of the Islamists, and about the "absolute insanity" of the military. "This is crazy," one wrote. "We're going to have another NDP government, this time filled with Islamists too."

By Monday, the Brotherhood had already begun preparing its parliamentary campaign, and a video of hip-looking young Brothers—each featured answering the question "Why are you with the Brotherhood?"—was circulating on Facebook. A prominent Salafi sheikh announced that religion had won the yes vote, saying people had effectively declared "yes to religion." In response, activists and friends started making an urgent appeal to regroup their supporters and ponder their next steps. A widely circulated post by the blogger Sandmonkey advised, "Start organizing yourselves into an offline grassroots movement, Zenga Zenga style.... Start reaching out to Imams and Priests now.... Know thy enemy."

With parliamentary elections around the corner—the military leadership has said they will take place in September—many political hopefuls are talking about forming parties, though just how easy that will be remains unclear. Despite the military leadership's announcement on March 28 that religiously based political parties will continue to be prohibited, the Muslim Brotherhood will likely still form a party under its previously announced "Freedom and Justice" banner. Moreover, even if the Brotherhood is not legalized under the new party formation law—which reformists have dismissed as cosmetic—

its members can campaign as independents, and they already have the support of a considerable swath of Egyptian society. Esraa had told me recently that she planned to campaign for a parliament seat herself, but now, with just a few months to prepare and much other work to be done, it's looking less likely.

Elsewhere, Mubarak loyalists are busy planning their next steps too—few doubt that many familiar faces will emerge when parliamentary campaigning gets underway. There are already rumors that some of Mubarak's closest associates will run themselves, and while there isn't much apparent popular support for the NDP, the party has pockets of strength and many loyalists are businessmen with huge stakes in the national economy. Even some of those now in jail continue to employ tens of thousands of people in factories and industries, and could wield outsize influence in a future election.

No one seems to know what a parliament dominated by former NDP members and Islamists might mean. What will become of the youth activists and their movement for change? What will happen to sometime leading figures in the uprising like Amr Moussa and the Google executive Wael Ghonim? May the army, as many fear, crack down on more radical calls for change? Already in late March, the cabinet took steps to outlaw protests and strikes, which the army swiftly used as a warrant to force its way into Cairo University and disperse student protesters with Tasers on the following day. Those with grievances, though, remain undeterred—activists and labor movements protested again in late March, and were calling for a million-man march on April 1.

In the meantime, a member of the Muslim Brotherhood has said he is considering running for president, an Islamist activist has confirmed he is preparing to campaign, and there are reports that Salafists have been inciting violence against secularists, women, and Copts. They have also been distributing antidemocracy flyers arguing for an Islamic state. Despite the army's promise to hand over powers to a new president within six months of Mubarak's departure, it is evident that the presidential elections will be postponed. Loyalists of the former president's son, Gamal, have now announced that they are forming a political party.

—April 28, 2011

25

An Exclusive Corner of Hebron
Jonathan Freedland

A chilling aspect of life in Israel today is the way average, well-meaning, law-abiding Israeli citizens can ignore the violence and humiliation visited upon Palestinians by other Israelis.

What goes on around the Israeli settlements on the West Bank, where black-hatted zealots wreck the harvests and seal the water wells of Palestinian farmers, where the children of these zealots throw stones at elderly Palestinian women, and where Palestinian families are driven from homes owned by their families for generations, and all this in full sight of the Israeli army, can be safely ignored if you live in Netanya or Tel Aviv.

More corrosive to Israeli society than the sometimes violent oppression of Palestinians is this cocoon of civil indifference. Security is a valid concern. Terrorists can do great damage to a country. But so can turning a blind eye to injustices done in that country's name.

—I.B.

IF YOU EXCLUDE Jerusalem, Hebron has the largest population of any Palestinian city in the West Bank. It is, along with Nablus, a commercial center, and what serves today as its thronging market square brims with life and trade, noise and fumes. There are stores selling groceries and electronics, as well as sidewalk stalls consisting of simple tables laid out with fruit and vegetables, toys, trinkets, and children's clothes. Those are concentrated especially by the bus station, with its yellow public buses, and by the ranks of taxis and private minibuses, many of them heading north to Bethlehem. Palestinian police, in Palestinian uniforms, direct the traffic. If you walked no further, you would assume that Hebron, home to an estimated 175,000 Palestinians, is a thriving Arab city.

Until, that is, you got close to the crossing point that marks the de facto border between the Palestinian-controlled 80 percent of the city, known as H1, and the Israeli-controlled remainder, known as H2. Not everyone can cross. Since the start of the second intifada, Israeli citizens have been forbidden by their own government from entering H1, just as they are barred from entering the wider Palestinian-controlled Area A of the West Bank. The ruling is based on security grounds, Israel concluding that visible Israelis, especially settlers, would likely be attacked and the Israel Defense Forces insisting that it can guarantee the security of Israeli citizens only in those areas it controls.

For those who are permitted, however, crossing the line that separates H1 from H2 is to cross into another realm entirely. For H2, which consists of a substantial eastern chunk of the city, combined with what looks on the map like a wide, stubby finger jabbing westward, includes the historic heart of Hebron. This strip, the finger on the map, might account for no more than 3 percent of the total geographic area of Hebron, but it is here that you find the sites that have made it a place revered by both Muslims and Jews, indeed ranked by

Jews alongside Jerusalem, Tiberias, and Safed as one of Judaism's four holy cities. It is here too that you find an eerie, emptied ghost town whose once-thriving markets stand shuttered and deserted, its Palestinian population subject to a policy of separation and restriction that makes the city the place where Israel's forty-four-year occupation of the West Bank shows its harshest face.

You can hear the battle for supremacy between the approximately 30,000 Arabs and eight hundred Jewish settlers who live in Israeli-controlled H2 even before you see it. On the crisp, bright morning I visited, there was Hassidic-style klezmer music playing loudly from the Gutnick Center, an event hall that welcomes Jewish visitors from around the world and especially the United States, offering both refreshments and tours, its website reassuring any nervous customers that "all buses are bullet-proof." Minutes later, those melodies of old Ashkenazi Europe were joined by the traditional muezzin, singing the Muslim call to prayer. The two tunes continued, at full volume, filling the ancient square with dueling, discordant noise. This is Hebron's so-called loudspeaker war.

Any visit usually begins at the Tomb of the Patriarchs, the magnetic core of Hebron's religious power. Judaism deems the site, recorded in the Bible as the Cave of Machpela, purchased by Abraham, as second in sacred value only to the Temple Mount, that part of ancient Jerusalem on which the First and Second Temples were built. Inside are caskets said to contain the remains of Jacob, Isaac, and Abraham himself, revered as a forefather by the three ancient monotheistic faiths.

As the Jews of Hebron remind visitors, including the busload of African Christians that pulls in, for seven hundred years Jews were barred by the city's Mameluke, Ottoman, British, and Jordanian rulers from entering this holy site; they were allowed to ascend only the first seven steps toward it. In 1967, when Hebron and the rest of the

West Bank were conquered by Israel in the Six-Day War, Jews could at last walk the eighth step, and the fifty-odd more, and enter.

Today, there are separate entrances to the tomb for Jews and for Muslims. But what is more striking is the road approaching the site: it is divided according to nationality, with three quarters of the thoroughfare available to Israelis, and the narrow remainder set aside for Palestinians. Concrete blocks separate the two parts. The Israelis are given the greater portion because they are allowed to drive down this road, a right denied to Palestinians.

On Israeli military maps, this shows up as a green road, which means that no Palestinian cars are allowed. Blue is for those streets where no Palestinian cars are allowed and no Palestinian shops are permitted to open. Then there are roads that are more restricted still: on those, no Palestinian is allowed to set foot. The Israel Defense Forces refer to such a road as a *tzir sterili*, literally a sterile road.

Most of the H2 Palestinians unlucky enough to have their homes on a *tzir sterili* have had their front doors sealed shut. To leave, they have to use a back door, which often means climbing out onto the roof and down via a series of ladders: inconvenient for those who are young and fit, difficult if not impossible for those who are old or infirm. Later I will see an elderly man, a bag of cement resting on his shoulder, walking with a boy I take to be his grandson. When he reaches a-Shuhada Street, once the main artery through central Hebron and a "sterile road" since 2000, he turns off and begins to ascend a steep series of rough-hewn steps, necessary in order to walk around rather than on the street. This will lead him through a series of unpaved, dusty paths, a longer, indirect alternative route to a-Shuhada Street. This is so neither his feet nor those of the little boy will touch the forbidden road—ensuring it remains *sterili*.

The street is lined with what used to be shops, now permanently closed behind green metal shutters. They are all covered by graffiti.

In a short walk I see "Arabs out!" and "Death to the Arabs" as well as the less familiar "You have Arabs, you have mice," which has been painted over but is still legible. So too is "Arabs to the crematorium," close to the Muslim cemetery. (One notorious message, daubed in English but covered over a few years ago, read "Arabs to the gas chambers.") The clenched fist symbol of the Kach party of the late Rabbi Meir Kahane, the founder of the Jewish Defense League once ostracized as a fascist, appears in several places. But the most recurrent image is also the most shocking. It is the Star of David. Utterly familiar to Jewish eyes, it nevertheless is a shock to see that symbol—associated with Judaism itself and with the long history of Jewish suffering—used as a crude declaration of dominance, used, in fact, as an insult.

We walk down the center of the road. There is no need to use the sidewalk because the place is empty, like an abandoned film set. My guide, Yehuda Shaul, a *kippa*-wearing, black-bearded Orthodox Jewish Israeli—who will later mutter the traditional *bracha*, or blessing, before taking a bite of a sandwich—is intimately familiar with Hebron, having served two extended tours of army duty in the city, spanning the second intifada, first as a regular soldier in 2001–2002 and then again as a commander and company sergeant in 2003. Indeed, he was on patrol when IDF engineers sealed up those front doors, welding them shut, in 2001.

He recalls too the instructions he had not to touch the settlers, who were subject to Israeli law and therefore under the jurisdiction of the Israeli police rather than the army, even though he could see that they were engaged in a campaign of harassment of the local population, throwing stones, cutting water pipes, or severing electricity cables. A soldier has testified to the Breaking the Silence organization—founded by IDF reservists determined to alert their fellow Israelis and Jews around the world to the everyday reality of military occupation—that a sign hung on the briefing wall of his unit, spelling out their mission: "To disrupt the routine of the inhabitants of the neighborhood," whether through house searches, physical checks, or sudden, surprise checkpoints established in apparently arbitrary locations.

Shaul is not in uniform today but is here as part of his work with Breaking the Silence. He is armed with "before" photographs of central Hebron, dating from 1999, that show a fruit market bustling with people, with produce, and with life. The "after" shot is right in front of me: the very same place, now desolate and silent. What used to be here has been relocated to H1, some of it, at any rate. The teeming marketplace I saw on the other side of the crossing point is in fact part of Bab a-Zawiya, once just a neighborhood of Hebron, now its substitute downtown. Some of those traders in Bab a-Zawiya used to live and work in what is now H2. They once owned shops. They now sell their wares on tables.

Nor is this a mere impression. A study by the Israeli human rights group B'Tselem shows that 1,014 housing units—apartments or houses—have been abandoned by their occupants, some 42 percent of the total in this core part of Hebron. One estimate suggests that this amounts to eight or nine thousand people who found that life under such restrictions was no longer viable or bearable. Eventually, I see one of the rare people who have held on, remaining inside H2. An Arab woman is hanging laundry on her balcony on a-Shuhada Street. She is caged on all sides by a mesh of metal wire, including above her head. This is not because of any law or regulation; she has put herself in what looks like a small chicken coop for her own protection, to avoid the stones that would otherwise be thrown at her by settlers.

The roof of the cage is, indeed, weighed down with stones.

B'Tselem, which has given cameras to some of the Palestinians of Hebron, has posted several videos showing settlers, including young children, throwing stones at the Arabs in their midst—unrestrained by the Israeli soldiers standing close by. One particularly disturbing film shows a female settler repeatedly hissing the word *sharmuta*, or whore, at her female Arab neighbor.

Close by is the chicken market, now behind tall concrete slabs. Next comes the old bus station, now in service as an IDF base that doubles as the home of six settler families who have moved in. And then, around the corner, behind a rusting gate, is a scrapyard, filled with junk, weeds, and coils of barbed wire. Shaul produces a photograph that reveals that this dumping ground used to be Hebron's jewelry market. (A few individual jewelers now ply their trade in Palestinian-controlled H1, but the market itself has not been reconstituted.) On the other side of the street is a yeshiva.

It is this—Jews and Arabs living next to each other—that makes central Hebron exceptional, at least outside Jerusalem. While Jewish settlements are found throughout the West Bank, they are usually on hilltops adjacent to, or overlooking, Palestinian towns and villages. But in this part of central Hebron, they are found within, in four clusters referred to as settlements but that often amount to just a few houses and buildings surrounded by Palestinians. Three of them are on or just off a-Shuhada Street; the fourth is a short walk away.

And so you only have to take a few steps away from the emptied fruit market to walk into Avraham Avinu—literally, Abraham, Our Father—the largest of the Jewish enclaves in Hebron, home to some forty families. Inside it is another country. The walls are made of a scrubbed, flat stone that contrasts with the dust and age outside. There is a children's playground, with young Orthodox mothers, their heads covered, playing with their kids, the latter apparently unaware that there are approximately six hundred IDF soldiers around, chiefly for their protection. There is a rack for bicycles and in the air the distinct aroma of chicken soup. It could be any of the more well-heeled neighborhoods of West Jerusalem. There are plaques everywhere, a sight not uncommon in Jerusalem—except almost all of these are in memory of people killed by "Arab terrorists." The benefactors thanked are Jewish families from New York, London, and elsewhere.

This division of Hebron into H1 and H2 was the result of the Hebron Protocol of January 1997, signed by Yasser Arafat and Binyamin Netanyahu, then in his first term as prime minister. Special arrangements were deemed necessary for the sake of the few hundred Jewish settlers inside Hebron, whom Israel believed it had to protect with its own forces. In the years since, protection has come to mean a series of ever more stringent steps to keep the Jews and Arabs apart by restricting the Palestinians' ability to move within H2. Every time there has been a terror attack on the Jewish settlers—the most notorious being the murder of a ten-month old baby, Shalhevet Pass, by a sniper's bullet in 2001—the settlers have demanded and usually won either a further tightening of Palestinian movement or Israeli state permission for expansion or both. Bit by bit, central Hebron has been emptied, the Palestinians hemmed in ever more claustrophobically, so that the settlers can move freely and without fear, their safety guaranteed by the IDF.

It is probably fruitless to attempt to define the beginning of this situation. For the Jewish community of Hebron, the last hundred years are a mere interlude, the decisive event coming several thousand years ago when Abraham made his purchase of Machpela. Still, many light upon 1929 and the massacre of sixty-seven Jews by Arabs in Hebron as the pivotal date. They believe that that traumatic event reveals an essential truth about the conflict with the Palestinians: that the Arab objection to Jews predates, and therefore has little to do with, the establishment of the State of Israel in 1948 or the occupation of the West Bank in 1967. To the settlers, the 1929 massacre shows that the Arabs have a murderous intolerance of Jews in their midst. If a heavy military presence and onerous security measurements are necessary, then that is why.

Until 1929, Jews had lived in significant numbers in the city. In the immediate aftermath of the massacre, British forces evacuated the surviving Jews to Jerusalem, though a year later the Arab leaders of the city invited them back. Some thirty or so families accepted the invitation, then left again during the disturbances of 1936. One Jew, a milkman, is said to have stayed on until 1947, but after that, for two decades, there were none. Still, when Hebron was captured by Israeli forces in 1967 it was, say the settlers, only natural that Jews should return. Their presence there now is, they insist, no foreign, colonial enterprise, but rather a homecoming, delayed for too long.

The manner of the return is certainly susceptible to mythmaking. For the first Passover after Hebron's "liberation," a group of eighty-eight Orthodox Jews, led by the charismatic Rabbi Moshe Levinger, checked into the city's Arab-owned Park Hotel to hold a seder. They stayed and refused to leave. Eventually, Israel's Labor-led government suggested a compromise: the squatters would be allowed to move into a nearby IDF base where homes would be built for them. Thus was born Kiryat Arba, now a city of more than seven thousand next to Hebron, the first step in the entire West Bank settlement project. Levinger would go on to be a founder of Gush Emunim (Bloc of the Faithful), later serving jail time for shooting dead a Palestinian store owner. But Hebron was where he took his first stand.

His heirs today do not feel any need to justify the effects of their presence on the Palestinians who live in H2. On the contrary, the Jewish community in Hebron regards itself as the victim. "People say there's apartheid here," says David Wilder, their New Jersey–born spokesman. "I agree, there is—but it's not against them, it's against us." He points to the fact that the Casbah, inside H2, is a closed military zone and therefore off-limits, save for a few hours on the Sabbath, to Jews. He argues that, in effect, Jews have access to only 3 percent of the city—where the Israeli security presence is sufficiently intense—while Arabs have access to all the rest. Sure, he concedes, there's one street, maybe a kilometer, a kilometer and a half, that the Arabs can't walk on. Does he mean a-Shuhada Street? "I don't know what they call it. We call it David Ha'Melech [King David] Street." That road used to be open, until the second intifada, says Wilder—in fact, save for a few months the road was barred to Palestinian cars from 1994—"but they started shooting at us" from the nearby hills.

Still, he insists, he and his fellow Jews have "never said that for us to live here, no one else can live here," whereas he believes that the Palestinians will permit no Jewish presence in Hebron in a future Palestinian state. It is the Jews who are the tolerant ones. As for the graffiti, he says, "We're not particularly fond of it," but he refuses to condemn it, calling it an "outlet" for settler youth "frustrated by terror attacks and the activities of the Israeli government against them."

Wilder's message—that if the Palestinians stopped threatening the settlers with violence, the restrictions could be eased—runs counter to experience. When, for example, the US-born Baruch Goldstein killed twenty-nine Palestinian Muslim worshipers in the Tomb of the Patriarchs in 1994, Israel imposed new restrictions—not on the settlers but on Hebron's Arabs. The vegetable and meat markets were closed, and the ban on Palestinian cars on a-Shuhada Street introduced. (It's striking that, far from being reviled as a terrorist and murderer in Hebron, Goldstein is buried in the Meir Kahane Memorial Park, which comes under the auspices of the Kiryat Arba municipal authority.)

Still, and despite the twenty-four-hour armed protection they are given—Shaul testifies that as a soldier his orders were very clear: "We're here to protect the settlers"—Hebron's Jews appear to regard the Israel Defense Forces and the Israeli state as their adversary. A poster in the Bab al-Khan neighborhood in H2, emptied of all but a handful of its former Arab residents with its gates to the Old City now sealed and bolted shut, declares in Hebrew: "Here's where the ghetto begins. No entry for Jews." Elsewhere, a spray-painted slogan denounces what it regards as the godless state of Israel: "We have no faith in the regime of the infidels, we follow the path of Torah." Another seeks a regime governed by religious law: "We want a *halacha* state of Judea now." Still another urges, "Death to the traitors of the King," the King being God.

In this dispute, with the settlers hostile to an Israeli government that denies them the run of Hebron in its entirety, the Palestinians are caught in the middle. They dismiss the settlers' suggestion that it is only a small fraction of the city from which Palestinians are barred, a relatively modest imposition on their lives. Issa Amro, thirty-one years old and active in organizing nonviolent protest in Hebron, says, "H2 is the center of the city.... All the markets were there: the vegetable market, the fruit market, the camel market, the meat market, the blacksmith market, all the markets were in H2. It is the heart of the city. And if your heart is sick, your whole body will be affected."

He explains that the restrictions, even if applied to a superficially narrow area, have a far-reaching effect. Families are split between H1 and H2, making it hard for relatives to see each other, especially those who live on H2 streets barred to Palestinian cars or pedestrians. And it has a wider impact: if you want to drive north to south through Hebron, you have to take a long, convoluted route on congested roads. Shaul imagines the equivalent move in Jerusalem, shutting down Jaffa Street and the Old City. It might only account for less than 1 percent of the municipal territory, he says, but it would include the main road and the historic monuments. "What's the impact that has on a city?"

Some admit that what one sees in central Hebron is ugly, but console themselves that it is an extreme case typical only of itself. For others, though, Hebron is an intense, distilled version of the wider Israeli occupation. Yehuda Shaul places himself, reluctantly, in the latter camp. "This is a microcosm," he tells me. "Walk here and you understand how the West Bank functions: the separation, the land grab, the sterile roads, the violence." Nor does he reassure himself that Hebron is the handiwork of a few hard-core settlers. The presence of the IDF shatters that delusion, as does the plaque from the Housing Ministry on the settler building of Beit HaShisha, a seal of government approval that dates back to 2000, when the supposedly center-left leader Ehud Barak was prime minister. Twenty-one buses depart every weekday, more than one an hour, from the Jewish settlements inside H2 to Jerusalem, offering cheap, government-subsidized fares. Shaul's grievance is not with the settlers alone, but with the state.

For people like Shaul, proud Israeli patriots and conscientious Jews, Hebron poses a more profound challenge than can be captured by the bland diplomatese of "obstacles to peace" and the like. For them it is about more than a fault line in a bitter, territorial dispute. "What's being done here is in the name of God and in the name of my state," he says, in a voice much older than his twenty-eight years.

Shaul has become well known in Hebron. On the steps of the Tomb of the Patriarchs, a settler spots him and shouts, several times, that he is a traitor to his people. But there is a face better known than his and I see it within two minutes of arriving in Hebron. In a wheelchair, the consequence of a stroke in 2007, is a white-haired old man in a Panama hat, being pushed by a young, devout caregiver. He is Moshe Levinger, the man who started it all, out for his daily dose of fresh air. I catch up and ask whether, when he holed himself up inside the Park Hotel all those years ago, he ever imagined it would lead to this, the center of Hebron cleared and emptied for the sake of his fellow settlers. "No," the rabbi says, he foresaw no such thing. He points a finger toward the sky. "It is a blessing of God."

—February 23, 2012

26

A Farewell to Haiti
Mischa Berlinski

Haiti is one of those countries where everything always appears to go wrong; it is isn't the cruelty, incompetence, or venality of man that does the place in, it is nature that inflicts one of her periodic horrors.

Dismissing Haiti as a permanent basket case is not a helpful or adequate response. But nor are the patronizing views of people from more fortunate countries who refuse to see anything but sweetness and light. Clear eyes that see with compassion are what is needed.

The ways of other peoples may seem incomprehensible, twisted by violent oppression, perverted by histories gone violently wrong, but they are still people, like us, and when they are pricked, they bleed.

—I.B.

I.

I CAME TO Haiti in the spring of 2007 when my wife found a job with the United Nations Peacekeeping Mission there. She was assigned to the southern seaside town of Jérémie, a place where donkeys outnumbered cars on the streets. Jérémie was just 125 miles or so from Port-au-Prince, but only a single dirt road linked the two, and the trip overland could take fourteen or fifteen hours. Otherwise, the only connection to the capital was by propeller plane, if one had the money; or, for the poor, the night ferry, the *Trois Rivières*.

About a week after we arrived in Jérémie, the *Trois Rivières* ran aground leaving the wharf. It had been loaded badly, its cargo heavy and high on the bow and its passengers perched precariously above the cargo. Another ship soon came to its assistance. Crew members ran lines between the two boats and the assisting ship reversed its engines. The *Trois Rivières* did not budge, listing instead under the tension of the ropes until its flank was at a sharp angle to the horizon. Then the lines snapped and the *Trois Rivières*, rolling fast back to the vertical, flung its passengers and goods into the shallow bay.

Eighteen travelers drowned. The bodies were gathered from the wharf and rushed to the Hôpital Saint-Antoine where in the middle courtyard they were tossed into a promiscuous heap—face down, face up, mouths streaked by weird smiles of sputum and sea foam. The next day or the day after that, the tides shifted and the *Trois Rivières* proceeded normally to Port-au-Prince. Several days later, the last of the drowned travelers was found on the wharf being eaten by a pig.

Here then was my introduction to Haiti, a classic Haitian tragedy: the careless, criminal incompetence; the gratuitous grief inflicted on the poorest of the poor; the absolute lack of accountability, on the part of both the boat's owners and the bureaucrats responsible for overseeing maritime safety. In his new book, *Haiti: The Aftershocks of History*, the historian Laurent Dubois laments that "when Haiti appears at all in the media, it registers largely as a place of disaster, poverty and suffering, populated by desperate people trying to escape." This is, he says, a "negative stereotype."[1] But Haiti appears this way in media accounts because in my experience it is the truth. It is not the whole truth about Haiti but it is surely the most important truth about Haiti. The newsman, traveler, or historian who ignores Haiti's suffering to focus instead on its lovely beaches, its remarkable folk culture, or its brilliant and ingenious art might well be accused of having an awfully cold heart.

The local explanation for the grounding of the *Trois Rivières* was this: the owner of the vessel had made an enemy—the details were obscure. The enemy had secured the services of a *boko*, or sorcerer, who had employed magical means to curse the ship. The accident was thus a punishment, the dead bystanders caught up in a private feud. In my time in Haiti, I would hear stories like this over and over again, from every level of society. The dean of the civil court in Jérémie refused to settle cases because he feared the losing party to his decisions would punish him with magic; manila folders settled on his desk in a dusty heap. The richest man in town was said to owe his fortune to human sacrifice. The failure of a merchant in the market was only the result of the supernatural intervention of her competitors.

The Haitian world was like the world famously described by E. E. Evans-Pritchard in his ethnology of the Azande: "Witchcraft participates in all misfortunes and is the idiom in which Azande speak about them and in which they explain them." The details of Haitian life differed radically, of course, from Azande life. But Haitians, like the Azande, lived in a world where everything that went wrong went wrong for a reason: the door of fate in Haiti, not always but very

---

1. Metropolitan, 2012, p. 3.

often, swung on a hinge of sorcery. Happenstance, coincidence, sheer bad luck—these were all bit players in the drama of Haitian life. The chain of causation inevitably led back past magic to one's enemies, real or imagined; magic was something commissioned or desired, an overt act of hostility. Feud with your neighbor today, a child falls sick tomorrow: one has surely caused the other. There is to this principle a bitter converse: your child falls sick, surely your neighbor was at fault. Every death is, in a fashion, a murder.

A magical world is a world in which things make sense, where cause provokes effect. It is a rational world. It is a world without existential despair. It is a world in which one is never wholly responsible for one's misfortunes. But it is also a world that supposes that one's neighbors are vicious and predatory; that suffering is directly the result of somebody else—somebody in your community, somebody close to you—wishing you ill.

The January 12, 2010 earthquake was too large—too dramatic—to be considered the result of simple witchcraft. In its drama and horror and grotesque scale, it was outside common experience and the ordinary system of life. The consistent explanation offered to me for the earthquake was this: God had been angered by the inability of the Haitian people to live together harmoniously. In my experience, Haitians were no more fractious than any other people and quite possibly less. My Haitian friends, however, told me that I was naive. The earthquake, in their way of thinking, was the just response of a wrathful God to the mistrust, suspicion, and cruelty that, they argued, pervaded Haitian society.

2.

The Haitian worldview allowed multiple causes for the grounding of the *Trois Rivières*. Sorcery motivated by a personal grudge was a necessary condition for the accident; in the absence of black magic, the ship might have sailed tranquilly. It had after all sailed without incident under similar conditions so many times before. But the effectiveness of the sorcery required bad governance. The ship was old and in poor shape and still on the seas; it sailed from port without inspection; the owners were assured of legal impunity should an accident happen; the wharf was too shallow for a ship the size of the *Trois Rivières* and required dredging; there was no decent road to Port-au-Prince—all of this was subsumed in the phrase *gouvman pa bon*, by now almost a Creole proverb: the government isn't good.

The phrase as used by Haitians describes not only the chronic political instability of the capital and the weakness of the state but also the inability of Haitians to take collective action. Haiti is not only anarchic at the top, at the level of the presidency, where power has historically passed from hand to hand by revolution and coup d'état; it is anarchic at every level of society. From village to town to city to state, community resources are poorly managed; what worked once has fallen apart.

"Examples abound of the reticence, not to say incapacity, of rural communities to take charge of the global relationship to the environment, which can only be collective by nature," writes the Haitian anthropologist Gérard Barthélemy. "Thus, water from the source is not captured...; thus, the only irrigation canal that survives is underground; thus, the road network that supposes a collective will of travel and maintenance is not cared for while it exists."[2]

I frequently visited the rural town of Carrefour Charles, about five kilometers from the nearest spring. The town was effectively divided into two castes: the upper caste consisted of those families who could

2. Gerard Barthélemy, *Le Pays en Dehors* (Port-au-Prince: Éditions Henry Deschamps/CIDIHCA, 1989), pp. 49–50 (translation mine).

afford to hire the vastly larger lower caste to haul water for them, at five gourdes, or about 15 cents, per bucket. Lack of water dramatically aggravated poverty: children failed to attend school because they needed to fetch water; local gardens depending exclusively on rainwater failed to yield cash crops.

I spoke with a local engineer who estimated that it would cost about US$15,000, between pipes, pumps, cement, and labor, to build a rudimentary aqueduct to transport water to the town center. Even in a place as poor as Carrefour Charles, this was economically feasible, should the enterprise be undertaken collectively. I learned later that the project had been broached numerous times, but the community had been unable to reach consensus on how to proceed. The lack of clean water in Carrefour Charles was essentially a political problem, not a problem of poverty. The aqueduct in Carrefour Charles, like any action in Haiti that required an effective institutional structure, was doomed from the outset.

It is the custom in Haiti, when commencing some charitable intervention, to erect a large wooden placard at the site of a proposed project. On these placards is written the name of the project, the bureaucratic entity responsible for the project's completion, and the *bailleur de fonds*, the foreign donor whose generosity will make possible the proposed work. These hand-painted signs line the roads of rural Haiti, an unmistakable feature of the landscape, one after the other, every several hundred meters or so. So on the road to Dame Marie, we see a scheme to help farmers affected by hurricanes, paid for by the government of Japan and executed by the World Food Program. A kilometer down the road, there is a pilot project to protect the banks of the Grand'Anse River, paid for by the European Union. In a large open field, the Inter-American Development Bank was proposing to fund the construction of sixty latrines. The project was scheduled to begin in May 2005, and would last four months.

The field was still barren and rocky years later. I could continue this list for some considerable time. Haiti has not suffered the indifference of the world.

These projects are almost all specific in their intent, limited in scope, and created by institutional bodies staffed by transient employees. They all attempt to remedy some specific failure of Haitian government, grafting a foreign idea onto a community profoundly resistant to foreign intervention, even an idea as desirable as clean drinking water. When they work with local governments, the foreign sponsors are working with governments in no way representative of the will of the people; and when they work with the national government, they work with people considered as alien as Tibetans. Some of these projects work; some don't. They are valuable insomuch as they ameliorate suffering for as long as they endure.

I saw only one foreign intervention in my corner of southern Haiti that was fundamentally transformative. The Haitian Health Foundation has been working in Haiti for almost three decades and now provides basic health care to over a quarter of a million peasants. This admirable enterprise succeeds precisely because it is not a project, scheme, idea, or proposal, but rather an enduring institution. It remedies the weakness of the state by replacing the state. The success of the intervention owes to the decades' long involvement of its founders, and their ability to coax Haitians themselves to work within an effective institutional structure. Such dedication requires a transcendent personal engagement on the part of its organizers. It is no surprise to discover that they are motivated by the most serious religious commitments.

To the tendency toward radical independence there is a countervailing tendency in the Haitian character that makes survival, no matter how tenuous, possible. Haitians have remarkable qualities of personal generosity and an instinct, in informal groups, toward intense solidarity. Haitians will work the fields together, take in one another's children in times of need, or without hesitation share meager resources—these are considered primary social obligations. That this exists contemporaneously with so much fear, mistrust, and suspicion suggests only the complexity of the human heart.

In the immediate aftermath of the earthquake, the people of Port-au-Prince displayed admirable cohesion. A strange calm, beautiful and moving, reigned over the ruined city. People who knew each other only glancingly and whose lives had been reduced to the fact of their continuing existence and nothing more lived together side by side in remarkable harmony; what people still had, they shared. Almost in an instant the vast numbers of children who had been orphaned seemed to find sheltering hands. How different and superior this was to my own instinctive reaction, which was to hoard what I had, and to be fearful and mistrustful of my neighbors! It was as if two hundred years or more of Haitian life had exquisitely prepared this people for this moment, when everything would be stripped away but their own internal fortitude and discipline. In that moment, I saw that Haitians for all their myriad faults were a great people.

3.

I could be wrong about Haiti—my sense of its people could be entirely mistaken. One of the strangest things about life in Haiti is how mysterious a place it still is; how little the foreigner ever knows about Haitian life. Haiti is a nation where information consists chiefly of rumor, and where story dominates over fact. The structure of the society is opaque. Who is in power? Who makes decisions? To what ends? It is a place whose complexities increase over time: I'm leaving Haiti after five years with the dismaying sensation that I understand it only marginally better than when I arrived.

Some part of this necessarily owes to the language. Haitian Creole employs a vocabulary almost entirely derived from French overlaid upon a substructure of phonology and grammar inherited from a number of West African languages. It is the only language in which most Haitian people can communicate comfortably. Creole's short, pithy sentences, almost Latinate in their concision and powerful in their emotional force like slaps, make it ideal for rousing orations, jokes, and storytelling; every sentence in Creole is like an apothegm or proverb. The small vocabulary means that words come to serve double or triple duty, and new words are added to the Creole vocabulary as needed: *goudougoudou* is how Haitians refer to the great earthquake, the invented word suggesting the rumbling of the earth; when food prices rose, the phenomenon was described as *klorox*, as in the brand of bleach, so corrosive was the ensuing hunger.

Because the Creole system of tense, case, and gender is radically simple compared with French, and because the vocabulary is small, foreigners, myself included, often make the mistake of supposing the language easy to learn. Not so: the difficulties have simply been displaced elsewhere. Full comprehension of the language seemed to recede from me always, particularly when I was far from the Francophone city, into a morass of proverb, neologism, and allusion.

But language is not the only obstacle to comprehension. Haiti remains also, from an ethnographic point of view, an understudied country. This is strange, given its accessibility, its celebrity, and the vast sums of foreign aid that have been invested in recent decades. But large swathes of Haitian life remain unexplored. In the aftermath of the earthquake, for example, Port-au-Prince was seized by a wave of panic: the *loup-garou*—usually translated inadequately as the werewolf—had descended on the city. These *loups-garous* were said to fly through the night sky shooting flames from their anuses, feasting on small children.

The *loup-garou* is every bit as dominant a fear in Haitian society as the zombie; yet it remains largely undiscussed in the ethnographic literature. Equally mysterious were the secret societies that proliferate through the Haitian countryside. In the small corner of rural Haiti that I came to know, their influence and power were profound: they dominated daily life. No one can discuss governance or justice in Haiti without coming to terms with the importance of these societies; but they remain—as they surely wish to be—largely unknown.

Travesty in Haiti is the American anthropologist Timothy Schwartz's remarkable memoir of ten years in the north of Haiti as an ethnologist and aid worker.[3] His work is chiefly concerned with the microeconomics of poverty. The theme of his book is just how little was understood by foreigners about the country that they proposed to aid. Why did Haitians have large families? Surely, he suggests, one must understand this before one can propose family planning measures. How much money and food do ordinary Haitian peasants actually have? Who lives in orphanages and who benefits?

After the earthquake, Schwartz was the author of a controversial USAID-funded report that concluded that mortality from the earthquake was substantially lower than government estimates. He has also argued that many residents of the tent cities did not lose their homes in the earthquake, but rather had migrated to the tent cities to take advantage of the services offered by the international aid organizations. I was convinced myself by Schwartz's reasoning—but the essential point is not how many died, but the miasma of confusion that surrounds even the most basic facts of Haitian life.

So pervasive is the experience of being culturally adrift in Haiti

---

3. *Travesty in Haiti: A True Account of Christian Missions, Orphanages, Fraud, Food Aid, and Drug Trafficking* (Booksurge, 2008).

that Barthélemy, the canniest of observers, has proposed that it is an essential cultural trait. Dissimulation, he argues, is a deliberate strategy employed by the Haitian peasant to protect himself from the outsider—whether the foreigner or just the visitor from Port-au-Prince. Barthélemy gives us the example of the "technical expert" trying to introduce himself into rural Haiti. One feels he is speaking here from much personal experience. Once arrived, the expert will find an abundance of apparent structures: health committees, water committees, road committees, farmers' committees, work-for-food committees, committees for conserving the soil, committees for the young, and committees devoted to reforestation.

"It is not structure that is lacking, but rather their credibility," writes Barthélemy. "In all that, where does the ultimate power lie? Who are the truly representative men? Where are the effective authorities?" Only the most sensitive observer, he claims, would suppose that the docile and self-effacing old man with whom he is talking is in fact the real power—"the sagacious observer judging, in the name of the group, the degree of naiveté, of real power, and usefulness of his interlocutor from the exterior."

In the end, Barthélemy concludes, "the essential always remains hidden." This is true as well of national politics. The great foreign institutions—the United Nations, the European Union, the World Bank, the American embassy, and USAID—are all in the position of Barthélemy's technical expert, engaging with the apparent structures of national government and ignoring the effective authority. The Haitian politician negotiates with foreigners never revealing that he only represents his wealthy benefactors. The judiciary, ostensibly independent, is in fact beholden to the executive. Nobody admits to power; nobody denies that he has power. The most successful Haitian politicians are masters of a certain crafty smile somewhere between a wink and a glower that suggests they are in fact far more powerful than they can reveal. To employ such a smile is inevitably to reveal that one has no power at all.

The dean of the civil court in Jérémie found a separate peace from the demands of his position in literature: he sat in his shady office all through the long judicial work day and read the Latin classics.

4.

For ethnologists, friendship is the most impenetrable of social institutions. They frequently admit that having spent however many years studying some remote people, they leave having formed no intimate friendships at all; they wonder if for such a people, the institution of friendship, as understood in the West, actually exists. Friendship, after all, like marriage or kinship or blood brotherhood, is a culturally conditioned institution. The ethnologists wonder if simple affection can ever transcend the vast social abyss between the observer and the observed; between rich and poor; between the one who can leave at will and the one who must remain.

In leaving Haiti, I find myself in very much the opposite situation. The Haitian people seem to have a particular capacity for friendship. "With all of their ineptitude for certain concepts that the Anglo-Saxon holds sacred, the Haitian people have a tremendous talent for getting themselves loved," wrote Zora Neale Hurston, who visited Haiti in the 1930s. I can say that I also succumbed. I left behind a number of Haitian friends for whom I feel only the warmest and most sympathetic emotions.

Barthélemy, the most cynical of observers, proposes that *la séduction* is simply another tactic of the Haitian peasant to disarm the potentially aggressive outsider; the charm, the vivacity, the wit, and the kindness of my Haitian friends just some "strategy of dissuasion" meant to keep me always at a remove. I have found in my Haitian friends, he argues, only the interlocutors that I was seeking, their apparent friendship nothing but a "shining veil" obscuring the violent, unknowable Haitian heart.

Barthélemy might well be right—it is his country, after all. We know our own family in a way no interloper ever will: we see in a transient gesture what a foreigner will never see at all. A Haitian proverb says, "When the dog smiles, he's not happy." The Haitian smile might only be so many bared and yellow teeth. But wouldn't it be lovely to imagine that, just this once, Barthélemy is wrong? I was the recipient in Haiti of a tremendous amount of kindness and generosity, and was the witness to many remarkable displays of courage and grace. For all of that I remain enduringly grateful.

—March 22, 2012

27

Is Libya Cracking Up?
Nicolas Pelham

Sometimes it is better just to enjoy the party. The fall of Muammar Qaddafi was reason enough to rejoice. So was the release from dreadful captivity of countless men and women who were tortured for no other reason than that they spoke their minds, or just happened to annoy someone in power, or were unlucky to be in the wrong place at the wrong time. State terror is often random.

Benghazi escaped from possible annihilation. Tripoli was freer than it had ever been before. Good men were trying to establish a better order in Libya.

But once the party is over, the problems begin to appear. Wars have consequences, and can spill across borders. Order is hard to establish in a country riven by factions and clans. Revolutionaries do not willingly surrender their arms. Qaddafi was lynched by a violent mob, not a harbinger of justice and peace. Less than three months after this article was written voicing concern about potential violence in Libya, four US citizens were killed as a result of an attack on the US diplomatic mission in Benghazi. Among the dead was US Ambassador J. Christopher Stevens.

—I.B.

EIGHT MONTHS AFTER Muammar Qaddafi's overthrow, journalists seeking wars in Libya have to journey deep into the Sahara and beyond the horizons of most Libyans to find them. A senior official of Libya's temporary ruling body, the National Transitional Council (NTC), flippantly waved away an invitation to leave his residence at the Rixos, Qaddafi's palatial Tripoli hotel, to join a fact-finding delegation to Kufra, a trading post 1,300 kilometers to the southeast, near Sudan and Chad. "Isn't it Africa?" he asks.

Yet for Libya's new governors, the turbulent south—home to Libya's wells of water and oil—is unnerving. Since Mustafa Abdel Jalil, the NTC chairman, declared an end to the civil war last October, the violence in the south is worse than it was during the struggle to oust Qaddafi. Hundreds have been killed, thousands injured, and, according to UN figures, tens of thousands displaced in ethnic feuding. Without its dictator to keep the lid on, the country, it seems, is boiling over the sides.

Kufra, some six hundred kilometers from the nearest Libyan town, epitomizes the postwar neglect. Several on the NTC's nine-man mission I accompanied in late April were making their first visit there. The air of exuberance we felt flying aboard Qaddafi's private jet and breakfasting on salmon-filled omelets cooked by his dashing stewardess, clad in a scarlet uniform, vanished as we began our descent. How much protection could we expect from the two members of the mission who had been included to protect the group and who had been recruited for the journey from the Kufra's two fighting tribes—the Arab Zuwayy and the black Toubou? A NTC official criticized the pilot for approaching the runway from the town, where we made an easy target, not the desert. The airfield was deserted.

"We have a tradition of welcoming our guests," said the Zuwayy's tribal sheikh, Mohammed Suleiman, in less than welcoming tones, once we had found his mansion. "But we're cursing this government for abandoning us to the Africans." A room full of sixty tribesmen echoed his rebuke; since the revolution, members of the Toubou tribe had swarmed into the town and were threatening to wrest control of the oil fields nearby, he said. For the sheikh, the only solution was to expel them.

The catalyst for the fighting had been the NTC's appointment of a Toubou leader to guard the Chad frontier, thus putting him in control of trans-Saharan smuggling, apparently as a reward for his support in the revolution. Gasoline, which in Libya is cheaper than water, subsidized flour, and guns go out; whisky and migrants come in. Though the Zuwayy had ten times as many Mercedes trucks as the Toubou, their incomes had plummeted. As animosities rose, the two tribes divided their mixed town of Kufra into fortified zones and fired mortars at each other's houses. In fighting that followed this spring, 150 were killed.

After a communal meal of lambs' heads served on vast tin trays, we crossed town to the Toubou quarter. Red-tiled Swiss-style villas gave way to African cinder-block shanties, some blackened by bombing. Tarmac roads led into sandy tracks. Where the Zuwayy had served us a feast on thick blood-red carpets, the Toubou poured glasses of goat yogurt. The Zuwayy had chandeliers; the Toubou had a flickering neon strip and sporadic blackouts. "The air-conditioning is broken," their spokesmen apologized. The NTC delegates, who sat silently during the Zuwayys' browbeating, now seemed like feudal lords chiding troublesome peasants; as we left they said the Toubou border guards were outlaws. The next day fighting flared. At a gathering of Libya's many militias in Benghazi, nearly a thousand kilometers to the north, startled UN officials ducked for cover as Zuwayy and Toubou gunmen faced off in the corridors.

* * *

Some nine hundred kilometers west of Kufra as the crow or plane flies—for there are no roads—Sabha, the provincial capital of the southwestern Fezzan, also suffered from ethnic strife. On March 27, in the midst of a heated session of a local military council meeting to discuss the allocation of payments to former fighters, the representative of the Awlad Suleiman, another Arab tribe, shot three Toubou councilors dead. As the fighting spread, Arab snipers took to their villa rooftops and lobbed Katyusha rockets across the tin wall separating their neighborhood from the Toubou shantytown of Tayuri. Footage on their mobile phones shows tribesmen parking their tanks at Tayuri's entrance and shelling its shacks. When the firing subsided three days later, the Toubou counted seventy-six dead in the shantytown alone. Scores more were killed on the roads.

Like the Toubou, North Africa's indigenous Berbers—or Imazighen as they prefer to call themselves—depict Qaddafi's rule as four decades of unremitting Arabization. To erase their ethnicity, they say, Qaddafi labeled them mountain Arabs, replaced their historic place-names with Arab ones, and suppressed the Ibadi school of Islam that many Imazighen follow on account of its more egalitarian bent. Unlike Sunnis, the mainstream Ibadi school opens up leadership of the Muslim community to all ethnic groups, not only the Quraish, the Prophet Muhammad's Arab tribe. Qaddafi accused mothers who spoke the Amazigh tongue, Tifinagh, at home of feeding poison to their children.

While the Toubou number several tens of thousands, Amazigh leaders estimate—somewhat optimistically—that they make up 25 percent of Libya's six million people. From the desert in the south, where they are called Tuareg, to the Berber town of Zwara on the coast, they have been more successful than the Toubou in sloughing off Qaddafi's lingering Arabization. In Zwara, the brightly colored Amazigh flag flies from the lampposts and shops sport freshly painted signs in Tifinagh, their hitherto illicit script. Zwara's Berber militias have seized control of the nearby Tunisian border and rampaged through Riqdaleen, a neighboring Arab town where the shopfronts remaikn stubbornly green, the color of Qaddafi's regime. After Qaddafi's son Khamis fled Tripoli at the head of his praetorian guard, the 32nd Brigade, in mid-August last year, he briefly found a safe haven in Riqdaleen. Even today, only 30 percent of the town supported the revolution, a member of the local council told me. He works as a Total oil field manager.

Riqdaleen's Arabs have tried to fight back, not least for their border and its contraband profits. Last month, fighters in Riqdaleen captured twenty-nine Zwaran militiamen patrolling the border and beat them up, claiming they were trespassing. Only after the two towns had engaged in the ritual of lobbing missiles at each other's houses, killing a few dozen people, and only after marauding Zwarans had destroyed Riqdaleen's engineering college and torched several shops, did Zwara secure their release.

Both sides speak of arming for the battle ahead. Photographs of mutilated cadavers displayed on mobile phones ensure that the scars remain open. The graffiti that raiding Zwarans left on Riqdaleen's walls threatened to turn the town into a "second Tuwagha," the site inhabited by pro-Qaddafi black Libyans that militiamen from Misrata, further east, ethnically cleansed in the fall. "We don't see a new Libya," the Riqdaleen town councilor told me. "We're starting to regret. The Berbers want us out."

In what Riqdaleen fears is a precedent, Zwarans have evicted some seven hundred Arab workers from the housing compound of their chemical factory, Abu Kammash, saying the workers were complicit in Qaddafi's plot to wipe their Berber town off the map. Since its opening in the 1980s—atop what Zwarans say is an old Amazigh graveyard—the plant employing these workers had spewed mercury and acid into the sea, poisoning the Zwarans' fishing waters and population. The compound's few remaining Arab residents cower from the Zwaran squatters who have taken over the empty houses, and wonder when their turn for eviction will come. They say Zwarans —violating Muslim law—spend their nights drunk on contraband whisky and frolicking with Tunisian prostitutes, as well as firing their guns into the sky. "They claim they are revolutionaries and therefore untouchable," explains a teenage boy. Nasr, a former factory technician who has found refuge in Riqdaleen, says he has nightmares about Berber militiamen sleeping in his bed and wearing his clothes. "If this is the price we have to pay for freedom, it's not worth it," he says.

While separately none of the communal battles alone poses an immediate threat to Libya's unity, the border skirmishes risk stirring broader upheavals that could pick apart Libya and its neighbors. Riqdaleen sees itself as a potential bridgehead for tens of thousands of Qaddafi supporters who have sought refuge in Tunisia and may return. Kufra's feuding parties are attracting supporters from opposite ends of the Sahara, from the Mediterranean to the northern scrub land of Chad. Arab militiamen in Benghazi see a cause and an opportunity to fly the Prophet Muhammad's black flag of jihad; the Toubou in Chad are anxious to repel an Arab attack on their fellow tribesmen. As the contents of Qaddafi's armories spread across the region, gun markets are sprouting across middle-class Tunisia and fueling the low-level insurgency that Sinai's Bedouin are waging against their Egyptian overseers. Equipped with their extensive bullion, Qaddafi's surviving children—his son Saadi in Niamey, Niger, and daughter Aisha, in Algiers—stir up their old followers. Libya's turmoil is acquiring continental significance.

* * *

Of all the ethnic movements that have surfaced since Qaddafi's overthrow, that of the Imazighen has the greatest reach. In two months of travels across North Africa I repeatedly crossed paths with Fathi Khalifa, a highly articulate Berber from Zwara, wearing a silver suit and tie, who heads the World Amazigh Congress, a Paris-based organization promoting a pan–North African Berber revival. At an Amazigh gathering in Morocco I heard him advocating the revival of Tamazgha, the fabled Amazigh homeland stretching from the Canary Islands to Siwa, an Egyptian oasis. In Tripoli's Martyrs' Square, I met him leading a rally celebrating Tafsaweet, the Amazigh spring, and demanding official recognition of Tifinagh, the Amazigh language, by the new Libya. At a tribal feast in Sabha, I found him wooing the Warfalla, Libya's largest tribe—estimated at one million strong—with an etymological lesson on the Amazigh roots of their name.

Despite the obvious threat to their preeminence, many Arabs appear remarkably tolerant of ethnic rivals. Arab civil servants hire private teachers to learn Tifinagh. Arabic radio stations invite Khalifa to appear on chat shows. A civil rights movement staging an anti-militia protest at the same time and place as Khalifa's rally in Tripoli invited Amazigh activists onto the podium to show their flags and address their supporters. Even when a protester cried (in Arabic) that one day Libyans would speak no tongue but Tifinagh, the hosts cheered. At one of Khalifa's lectures in a public hall in Sabha, garlanded in Amazigh flags and pictures of such Berber icons as the Algerian soccer player Zinedine Zidane, Arabs almost outnumbered Imazighen.

Even so, there are limits. When Kha-lifa described Arabism as a foreign implant, there were gasps. When he described the seventh-century advent of Islam as a *ghazu*, or invasion, some walked out. Several heckled after he called the Islamic crescent on Libya's flag "a relic of Turkish colonialism" and proposed replacing it with a trident, an Amazigh symbol. His backing for the Amazigh declaration of a separate homeland—Azawad—in northern Mali sparked fears that he had similar plans for Libya. Though he denied it, his Tuareg bodyguard told me that the arms he smuggled to Mali would one day help to push the borders of his Azawad homeland from Timbuktu north via Sabha to Spain. "Can't you put your dreams on hold while we all get Libya back on its feet?" asked one of five imposing Arabs who confronted Khalifa as we sat in a Tripoli café sipping macchiatos.

* * *

If the periphery is fraying, the center, at first sight, has taken serious steps to set up an authority that its architects hope will sooner or later radiate out to the provinces. As under Qaddafi, Tripoli displays the best that revolutionary Libya has to offer. Utilities work. Air-conditioners cool tempers. Civil servants clock in at ministries. Banks have lifted wartime restrictions on cash withdrawals. International airlines unload their cargoes of oil prospectors and businessmen for the latest trade fair. Government coffers are flush with oil revenues of $5 billion a month. Unlike Baghdad's quick turn to insurgency after the US ousted Saddam Hussein, Tripoli has resumed business. Tripolitanians fail to understand their bad press.

The presence of militiamen is receding as well. The checkpoints manned by irregulars that once crisscrossed the capital are gone, and their heavy weapons have fallen silent. Tripoli's professionals nervously speak of the last of the Misratans, the militia from the large town of Misrata that fought in Tripoli. Despite the prevalence of weapons—some 20 million guns are estimated to be circulating in Libya—crime levels in Tripoli are said to be lower than in many Western capitals. Store managers have whitewashed away the obsessive green, the color of the book Qaddafi wrote to reveal his Third Universal Theory, perhaps the world's wackiest personality cult. Salafis troop into the former cathedral, now a mosque, for a lecture on the virtues of polygamy. Otherwise, for a moment, it might be Europe.

In the People's Congress where delegates waited for the Great Leader to raise his hand before voting, the halls buzz with a plethora of community organizations criticizing the NTC's management. New radio stations offer traffic updates, a novelty in a country where Qaddafi banned reports of car accidents and traffic jams lest they stain his utopia. On Ozone Radio you hear, "Sexy girl, I like the way you're grooving"—another novelty, since Qaddafi also banned Western pop. In place of a melodramatic megalomaniac, the country has for a leader a soft-spoken professor, Prime Minister Abdurrahim al-Keib. When I talked with him on his arrival from the United Arab Emirates in Tripoli in August 2011, he shed some tears in a handkerchief when the rebel victory became clear. Later he offered to be my guide, driving me around the capital. So long had he spent in exile that he had to stop to ask for directions to the Corinthia Hotel, the capital's bulkiest landmark.

For all his kindness, al-Keib's self-effacing nature makes him vulnerable. For many Libyans, he seems too small and retiring to step into the Great Leader's shoes. That he has no accompanying goons around him only makes him seem weak. In addition, a rapid changeover of governments has confounded efforts to make plans. Ministers say their only mandate is to prepare for the ballot for an elected assembly in June. Officials use the formula "not before the elections," insisting that only an elected authority would have the legitimacy to undertake substantial change.

The result is that the part of the bureaucracy that continues to function largely belongs to the old Qaddafi order. Visas remain as hard to come by for foreign journalists as under Qaddafi. And minorities detect signs in government ministries that the colonel's promotion of the Arab cause is making a comeback. Only after a month of protests did the government appoint an Amazigh minister. The old ways persist. The NTC has been under heavy pressure from workers striking to uphold their right to elect their own bosses, in accordance with the Third Universal Theory. Children at birthday parties still clamor for green balloons. Revolutionaries struggle—often in vain—to coin a post-Qaddafi terminology and method for their new institutions.

"Revolutionary committees" continue to exercise sway as part of a shadow government. *Katibas*, or brigades of paramilitaries, remain beyond the control of the formal military chain of command. "After forty years Qaddafi lives in our minds," I was told by the minister of industry.

Where the state does not function, there are impulses toward anarchy. Drivers head the wrong way up a one-way street shouting *Libya Hurra*—Libya's Free. A mild-mannered bank clerk tells me he drives to work repeating the mantra "kill or be killed." A taxi driver pulls out a brochure for German guns and recommends that I purchase one called a Viper Desert. Looters are still active; some cite Koranic verses justifying their rights to *ghanima*, the spoils of war. The words "holy property" are scrawled on mansion walls all over the capital. "From the garage or God?" Libyans ask friends driving new sports cars.

* * *

Reestablishing law and order has proved to be the hardest task, not least because many militias want to provide an alternative. The government has succeeded in cajoling the militiamen to make a formal decision to leave the capital's airports. But whole units have simply switched uniforms and painted their cars the red and white of security vehicles. "We call them policemen," a security official tells me; but the new Libya still has no criminal justice system, because judges are too nervous to issue verdicts, and the police too powerless to enforce them.

In their absence, the militias offer what little rough justice exists. They maintain their own makeshift detention centers with an estimated five thousand captives, all held without prospect of trial. "Tripoli is safe only as long as the rebels are here," says Faraj Sweihli, an eccentric militia leader from Misrata who has refused to hand over his headquarters in Tripoli's military college for women despite government requests to leave. While I am talking to him, he threatens to arrest me for not having a government press card. (He did the same to two English journalists a month earlier.) A friend in Tripoli calls the uprising Libya's "rebelution."

The arrival of private security companies, primarily from London, further undermines the government's hope of regaining a monopoly on the use of force. Soldiers and veterans of Baghdad and Kabul, they are the "West's Afghans"—a counterpoint to the movement of global jihad, chasing the world's crises to sell their mercenary services. Though they carry arms, few are registered, and none are regulated. They open safe houses in Tripoli while they solicit contracts to guard oil installations and establish a multibillion-dollar border force. The EU delegation made a deal for its protection with G4S, a company that helps secure Ofer, an Israeli prison for Palestinians in the occupied West Bank.

With "security" in so many competing hands, many fear violence will only get worse. Security officials attempting to instill some method into this madness estimate that some 15,000 fighters took part in the battle to topple Qaddafi. Of these, they say, thousands have returned to their previous jobs, from car mechanics to psychiatrists. But the authorities' attempt to forge a new security apparatus out of the remnant has hit an impasse in part of their own making. Enticed by government handouts of 4,000 dinars for married men who took up arms against Qaddafi's regime and 2,400 for bachelors, as well as the chance to cover up their history of involvement with Qaddafi, hundreds of thousands more have registered as "revolutionaries," proclaiming their loyalty to some sixty militias. "The truth is no one knows how many there are," I was told by Mustafa Rugbani, the labor minister and former Paris-based IBM manager responsible for vetting recruits.

The authorities claim to have established a 78,000-strong security force that is independent of the militias. A few hundred officers and men—primarily professionals from Qaddafi's old army—have been dispatched to the south to set up buffer zones between the feuding forces. Although cease-fires have largely held, there are a good many exceptions and the army is too stretched to do more than curb the most egregious bloodletting. The army set up a zone of twenty kilometers at the western borders from which militias were to be excluded. It remains unenforced. An April 2 deadline for the dissolution of militias has come and gone. So have predictions by spokesmen for the transitional council that militias would largely disappear from Libya by mid-May. With sporadic attacks on the prime minister's office, even in Tripoli the government can seem more ephemeral than the militias.

Elections for a two-hundred-seat assembly scheduled for mid-June remain the best chance to replace the militias with the legitimacy of the ballot box. Behind the scenes, Ian Martin, the UN's special representative in Libya, drawing on his experience overseeing elections in East Timor and Nepal, has been trying to get the NTC to keep to its timetable. Voter registration has proceeded remarkably smoothly, even in the south. According to the UN more than two million of Libya's estimated three million voters registered within the first two weeks.

But it is unclear whether the forces working against the elections will allow them to proceed on time. Reluctant to relinquish their golden goose, members of the NTC say there mustn't be hasty elections. Communal and tribal politicians favor holding local elections first in order to buy time to build up regional power bases. Above all the militias are afraid that an elected government will strip them of their authority and revolutionary credibility. Daw Ahmed al-Mansouri, a teacher on a reconciliation committee in the town of Sabha, told me he is still deciding whether to run for office. "Any militia unhappy with the results can use its stockpile of heavy weapons to shell a polling station or kill a candidate," he says.

* * *

Nowhere are the militias stronger than in Benghazi, the eastern city where Libya's "rebelution" began. After a year of paralysis, the goodwill that still keeps the wheels of central authority turning in Tripoli has evaporated here. The courthouse, beneath which tens of thousands gathered to hail the new rulers in the first days of the uprising, is boarded up. Its leaders have long since left for the plusher world of Tripoli, lured by free accommodation in the marble decadence of the city's Rixos Hotel. Left behind, Benghazi languishes, as before the revolution, in a perpetual *ghayla*—the siesta that Lib-yans take between the midday and late afternoon prayers. The dirt and dust of abandonment coat the city along with smoke from a thousand burning refuse piles. "At least there was a system before," I was told by a middle-aged soccer fan, whose al-Ahli team shut down after its chairman fled to Egypt with the company's proceeds. "Now there is nothing."

Strikes are the exception in Tripoli but they have become the norm in Benghazi. The war wounded have set up a roadblock along the coastal road to force the government to pay for their medical treatment abroad. Gasoline haulers demanding pay hikes park their trucks outside garages. The headquarters of Agoco, the national oil company's eastern subsidiary, which functioned for the first months of the revolution and through which much of the country's oil flows, was closed for four weeks in April and May. On the day that I visited, picketers had barricaded its gates. "We protected the company from

Qaddafi with our lives and it gave us nothing back," says a protester. He said he was a cleaner fired earlier this year to make way for newly arrived and cheaper Bangladeshis.

With the collapse of central authority, militias rule in and around Ben-ghazi. The day I arrived there hundreds of militia members had converged on the city for a congress aimed at unifying their ranks and reclaiming what they see as their rightful inheritance from the NTC and whatever elected authority might follow. "Benghazi paid the price, and Tripoli takes the profits," declared the organizer, as he spoke from the podium after the militiamen had feasted beneath a golden canopy, regaling each other with past exploits.

Paraplegics paraded their untreated injuries, shouting war cries and accusing the health minister of pilfering the funds for their treatment. A skinhead in jeans and a camouflage jacket pranced across the stage, claiming he had killed Qaddafi, only to be denied his prize money. "I was a taxi driver before, and I'm a taxi driver now," I was told by Ahmed Sweib of the Lions of Libya Brigade. (He drives a blue-metallic two-door Daewoo with the word PUNISHER stenciled on the back window in Gothic capitals, and black flames painted on the side. The car has a German license plate.)

Many of the former militiamen appear as mentally battered as the buildings they fought for in the eight months of bloodshed. "They returned from the front line, from war, to find no one wanted them," I was told by a psychiatrist who ran a soup kitchen on the front. "They thought they were heroes, and were treated as troublemakers. That's why they act so boisterously and aggressively. That's why they say Libya needs another revolution."

Their capacity for being spoilers is substantial, whether of the electoral process or the system of government. "Revolutionaries have to lead the country of the revolution," says Hussein bin Ahmed, an oil engineer turned general coordinator for preventative security, who acted as host for the militias' congress in his headquarters. In their concluding session, delegates resolved not to hand over weapons "to those who killed us"—that is, the NTC's formal army, which they see as recruited from old regime forces—and some delegates drew up plans for a united militia to protect the revolution.

Some at least seemed prepared to use force to defend their powers. When the UN's Ian Martin arrived outside an Interior Ministry office in Benghazi to discuss plans for security sector reform, someone hurled a gelignite stick under his armored car. Two NTC members have been kidnapped for supporting—in view of widespread fraud—the cancellation by the council of handouts for militiamen. On May 8, two hundred militiamen opened fire on the prime minister's Tripoli office with anti-tank guns, forcing the unfortunate al-Keib to briefly take flight.

Against such pressures, there are signs that the NTC is buckling. It has agreed to establish a Patriotism and Integrity Commission, a star chamber for de-Qaddafization, which will vet all appointments from officials to electoral candidates. Abdel Hafiz Ghoga, a Benghazi lawyer who announced the NTC's formation in the early days of the uprising, lost his NTC post amid accusations of being an associate of Qaddafi's son Seif al-Islam. Some want Mustafa Abdel Jalil, Qaddafi's justice minister who replaced him, and his first prime minister, Mahmoud Jibreel, another of Seif's appointees, to suffer a similar fate.

More sober voices caution that the root-and-branch elimination of all remnants of the old civil service and security forces will precipitate the country's collapse, as happened for some years in Iraq. A poet I met at the Amazigh rally in Tripoli told me, "Everyone blames the vestiges of the old order for their woes, as if they had no association with it. But the truth is we were all complicit. We had to survive." A Salafi car dealer, who spent years in Qaddafi's torture chamber of Bu Salim and has a job in the Interior Ministry, warns of repeating the mistakes of France's postrevolutionary reign of terror. Quoting an eighteenth-century revolutionary who was subsequently guillotined, he warns, "Like Saturn, the revolution is devouring its children." And then he adds, "A small country cannot afford such a loss of qualified staff."

—June 21, 2012

ABOUT THE AUTHORS

ROBERT B. SILVERS and the late Barbara Epstein are founding editors of *The New York Review of Books*, which this year celebrates the fiftieth anniversary of its first issue in 1963. Before he was a co-founder of *The New York Review*, Mr. Silvers was Paris editor of *The Paris Review* and then associate editor of *Harper's* magazine. In 2006, together with co-editor Barbara Epstein, Mr. Silvers was recognized by the National Book Foundation with the Literarian Award for Outstanding Service to the American Literary Community. In 2012 he was awarded an inaugural New York City Literary Honor by Mayor Michael Bloomberg for his contributions to the literary life of the city. He has edited several books for *The New York Review*.

* * *

CHRISTOPHER DE BELLAIGUE has written widely on political developments in the Middle East and the Indian subcontinent. Among his books are *In the Rose Garden of the Martyrs: A Memoir of Iran*, *Rebel's Land: Among Turkey's Forgotten People*, and *The Struggle for Iran*.

MISCHA BERLINSKI lives in Rome. His first novel, *Fieldwork*, was a finalist for the 2007 National Book Award.

CAROLINE BLACKWOOD (1931–1996) was an Anglo-Irish writer. Among her books are the novels *Great Granny Webster* and *Corrigan*; *On the Perimeter*, an account of the women's anti-nuclear protest at Greenham Common; and *The Last of the Duchess*, about the final years of the Duchess of Windsor.

IAN BURUMA is the Henry R. Luce Professor at Bard College. Educated in Japan and the Netherlands, Buruma has written extensively on East Asian literature and history and, more recently, on globalization. His books include *Murderer in Amsterdam: The Death of Theo van Gogh and the Limits of Tolerance*, *Taming the Gods: Religion and Democracy on Three Continents*, and the novel *The China Lover*.

MARK DANNER is an American journalist and scholar of American foreign policy. He teaches at the University of California, Berkeley, and Bard College. Danner's books include *The Massacre at El Mozote: A Parable of the Cold War*; *Stripping Bare the Body: Politics Violence War*; and *Torture and Truth* (New York Review Books).

JOAN DIDION is an American novelist and critic. She has received the National Book Award and the National Book Foundation's Medal for Distinguished Contribution to American Letters. Among Didion's novels are *Play It As It Lays* and *A Book of Common Prayer*; her nonfiction works include *Slouching Towards Bethlehem*, *The White Album*, *Miami*, *The Year of Magical Thinking*, and *Blue Nights*.

ROSEMARY DINNAGE is a British essayist, playwright, and literary critic. Her books include *One to One: Experiences of Psychotherapy*, *Annie Besant*, *Alone! Alone! Lives of Some Outsider Women*, and the one-act play *The Ruffian on the Stair*.

AMOS ELON (1926–2009) was an Israeli journalist, historian, and essayist. Born in Vienna, he emigrated in 1933 to Palestine; he devoted much of his career to the history of European Jewry and of Zionism. His final book was *The Pity of It All: A Portrait of Jews in Germany, 1743–1933*.

HELEN EPSTEIN is an American writer and scholar of public health. She has devoted much of her career to the HIV/AIDS crisis in the developing world. *The Invisible Cure: Why We Are Losing the Fight Against AIDS in Africa* recounts her experiences as a medical researcher in Uganda in the early 1990s.

JONATHAN FREEDLAND is a British journalist. He writes a weekly column for *The Guardian* and a monthly article for *The Jewish Chronicle*. Freedland is the author of *Bring Home the Revolution: How Britain Can Live the American Dream* and *Jacob's Gift*, as well as numerous best-selling thrillers published under the pseudonym Sam Bourne.

TIMOTHY GARTON ASH is Professor of European Studies and Isaiah Berlin Professorial Fellow at St. Antony's College, Oxford, and a Senior Fellow at the Hoover Institution at Stanford University. Among his books are *The Magic Lantern*, an eyewitness account of the velvet revolutions of 1989, and *Facts Are Subversive: Political Writing from a Decade Without a Name*.

NADINE GORDIMER is a South African writer and political activist. An unwavering critic of racial and economic injustice in her homeland, Gordimer was awarded the Nobel Prize in Literature in 1991. Her novels include *Burger's Daughter*, *The Conservationist*, and *No Time Like the Present*.

ALMA GUILLERMOPRIETO is a Mexican journalist. She has written extensively on Latin American culture and politics for *The New Yorker* and *The New York Review of Books*. In 2001 Guillermoprieto received a George Polk Award for the anthology *Looking for History*. Among her other books are *Samba*, an account of her time at a samba school in Rio de Janeiro, and *Dancing with Cuba*, a memoir of a year spent in Cuba.

ELIZABETH HARDWICK (1916–2007) was a literary critic and co-founder of *The New York Review of Books*. Among her works are *Sight-Readings*, *American Fictions*, *Bartleby in Manhattan and Other Essays*, *Seduction and Betrayal*, *Herman Melville*, and the novel *Sleepless Nights*.

NATALYA VIKTOROVNA HESSE was a longstanding friend of Elena Bonner and Andrei Sakharov. Before emigrating to the United States in 1984, she visited Bonner in Moscow and Sakharov under house arrest in Gorky.

TIM JUDAH is a British journalist. He reports on the Balkans for *The Economist*. Judah is the author of numerous books about the region, including *The Serbs: History, Myth and the Destruction of Yugoslavia* and *Kosovo: War and Revenge*.

RYSZARD KAPUŚCIŃSKI (1932–2007) was a Polish essayist, journalist, and poet. Among his translated works are *The Soccer War*, *The Emperor: Downfall of an Autocrat*, *Travels with Herodotus*, and *Shah of Shahs*.

AVISHAI MARGALIT is Professor Emeritus of Philosophy at the Hebrew University of Jerusalem. His books include *The Decent Society* and *On Compromise and Rotten Compromises*.

MARY MCCARTHY (1912–1989) was the author of the novels *The Group*, *The Groves of Academe*, and *Birds of America*; among her nonfiction books are *Venice Observed*, *The Stones of Florence*, *Vietnam*, and the autobiographies *Memories of a Catholic Girlhood* and *How I Grew*. *A Bolt from the Blue and Other Essays*, a collection of her literary, cultural, and political writings, was published in 2002 by New York Review Books.

V.S. NAIPAUL was born in Trinidad in 1932 and emigrated to England in 1950, after winning a scholarship to University College, Oxford. Among his novels are *A House for Mr. Biswas*, *A Bend in the River*, and *In a Free State*. Naipaul has also written several nonfiction works based on his travels, including *India: A Million Mutinies Now* and *Beyond Belief: Islamic Excursions Among the Converted Peoples*. He was knighted in 1990 and in 2001 received the Nobel Prize in Literature.

NICOLAS PELHAM has reported on the Arab world for twenty years and currently writes for *The Economist*. He has lived in, among other cities, Damascus, Cairo, Rabat, and Baghdad. He recently wrote a report about Sinai for the Royal Institute for International Affairs entitled "The Collapse of a Regional Buffer."

JERZY POPIEŁUSZKO (1947–1984) was a Roman Catholic priest and political activist. An outspoken champion of the Solidarity movement, he was murdered in 1984 by agents of the Polish Communist government. More than 250,000 people attended his funeral. Popiełuszko was beatified by Pope Benedict XVI in 2010.

YASMINE EL RASHIDI is an Egyptian journalist and editor. She is a contributing editor of *Bidoun*, a quarterly on Middle Eastern arts and culture. Her book *The Battle for Egypt: Dispatches from the Revolution* recounts her time in Cairo during the Arab Spring.

WILLIAM SHAWCROSS is a British writer and political essayist. His 1979 study *Sideshow: Kissinger, Nixon and the Destruction of Cambodia* was nominated for the Pulitzer Prize. Shawcross's other books include *The Quality of Mercy: Cambodia, Holocaust and Modern Conscience* and *The Shah's Last Ride: The Fate of an Ally.*

SUSAN SONTAG (1933–2004) was an American critic, essayist, novelist, film and theater director, and human rights activist. Her work addressed subjects ranging from camp, pornography, and fascist aesthetics to AIDS and photography. Her books include *Against Interpretation*, *On Photography*, *Illness as Metaphor*, *Regarding the Pain of Others*, and the novels *The Volcano Lover* and *In America.*

STEPHEN SPENDER (1909–1995) was an English poet and essayist. As a young man, he befriended W.H. Auden, Louis MacNeice, Cecil Day-Lewis, and Christopher Isherwood, a loose gathering often referred to as "the Auden Group" or "MacSpaunday." Spender published many collections of poetry, including *The Still Centre* and *Ruins and Visions*, in addition to volumes of literary criticism and autobiography.

VLADIMIR TOLZ is a Russian journalist and regular contributor to Radio Free Europe.

KANG ZHENGGUO is a Chinese scholar and poet. He is the author of *Confessions: An Innocent Life in Communist China.*